45637

Crewe

Station, Traffic and Footplate Working in the 1950s

46220

Crewe

Station, Traffic and Footplate Working in the 1950s

BILL REAR

Ian Allan PUBLISHING

Contents

Half title:
An unidentified Class 5 pilots 'Jubilee' class 4-6-0 No 45567 *South Australia* working the Down 'Red Rose' 12.30pm London Euston to Liverpool, seen here passing through Crewe about 3.30pm on the final leg of the nonstop journey. This train was a heavy one — on Saturdays it was made up to 14 vehicles, but possibly the limit had been exceeded, hence the need for a pilot engine working through. *Martin Welch*

Title page:
The Up 'Royal Scot' reporting number W96 was booked to pass through Crewe about 3.8pm. 'Princess Coronation' class Pacific No 46220 *Coronation* observes the 20mph speed limit as it passes through the station. The loco is immaculate in lined blue livery and the coaching stock appears to be all BR Standard Mark 1 vehicles. The loco was based at Glasgow Polmadie 66A shed but the traincrew from Carlisle were Upperby men. The fireman nonchalantly surveys the gathering on Platform 4 but, alas, despite the excess of steam, the exhaust injector is blowing back!
Tom Lewis — Manchester Locomotive Society

First published 1999

ISBN 0 7110 2657 2

Published by Ian Allan Publishing

an imprint of Ian Allan Publishing Ltd, Terminal House, Shepperton, Surrey TW17 8AS.
Printed by Ian Allan Printing Ltd, Riverdene Business Park, Hersham, Surrey KT12 4RG.

Code: 9909/B

Dedication

This book is dedicated to my grandson, Daniel Nicholas Davies, seen here shortly after his third birthday on the footplate of GWR 'Castle' class 4-6-0 No 5080 *Defiant*. This picture was taken on the day Llangollen Railway extended its operation to Carrog in February 1996.

This work is also dedicated to all Crewe footplatemen, but in particular to my late lamented good friend 'Piccolo' Pete Johnson and Tom Rigby, who gave free access to their personal diaries.

Introduction

There are several elements within this work that require explanation. It was necessary at an early stage to decide what to include and what to leave out of the text. Previous writings about Crewe seem to dwell on aspects and elements that explained about everyday life in the Works or the artisan staff at the sheds but little has appeared about the heart of the railway at Crewe, namely the station and train workings, apart from the occasional writings in the *Railway Magazine*, or *Trains Illustrated* in its 'Resorts for Railfans' series. Consequently, a section of the book deals with the traffic that called, passed through, started or terminated at the station. By its complexity it was necessary to limit what was included from available material, and to this end the choice was centred mainly on the summer of 1951 whilst the photographic content has been limited to views taken between 1949 and 1960.

Since most readers who recall the station in that period would now be over their half-century, they will remember a railway recovering from the excesses of World War 2, with traffic density probably at its peak. In all probability their observations were restricted to a Saturday, and therefore the analysis of the workings shown is concentrated on that day. The tabular information lists the starting and terminating points for the trains, the arrival, departure or passing time through Crewe, the train reporting number, train classification, platform number, or, in the case of freight traffic, the yard.

There then follows the engine and enginemen's diagrams into and out of the station. Of necessity, the link structure is abstracted from available records over a wider period of time, covering several years, as it has been impossible to obtain the details for one specific period.

The shed references are quoted giving the code that was applicable at the time, followed by the turn number. It will be seen that there are significant gaps in the information, which is unfortunate but unavoidable. It has been almost impossible to track down any diagrams for some sheds that worked into Crewe, let alone those for a specific period in time. Despite letters to newspapers and broadcast appeals over local radio, nothing has been forthcoming about Carlisle Upperby, Carnforth, Preston, Longsight Edge Hill or Rugby. It is highly likely that material which could fill the gaps is gathering dust and deteriorating in condition somewhere. Hopefully, this work will act as a catalyst and jog memories of long-forgotten memorabilia. Access to single scraps of paper can give valuable details that can add to the jigsaw of information. Whilst this study concentrates on drivers and firemen, the work and records of passenger and goods guards, shunters, signalmen, inspectors, foremen, porter signalmen, porter guards, platform porters and cleaners must not be overlooked or ignored. They were an integral part of railway life and the railway could not have functioned without them.

The photographs that support this work have been chosen to reflect the wide geographical route knowledge that Crewe footplatemen were required to know intimately. It would be impossible to limit the photographic coverage to views showing only Crewe-based work.

Acknowledgements

Grateful thanks are extended to many good friends for their assistance in the preparation of this book, which has extended over many years. Not the least, I must thank, belatedly, those good folk of Crewe who answered my appeal for information in the Crewe Chronicle nearly 10 years ago. Amongst former colleagues who responded were Jack Walker BEM, Cyril Harman and George Preece. Especial thanks are given to D. H. Smith; Blanche, widow of 'Piccolo' Pete Johnson and Tom Rigby. Without their help and collaboration this work would have been so much the poorer. Thanks too to Bill Lobb for his Control recollections.

For photographic contributions thanks are extended to Mike and Chris Bentley; Ben Brooksbank; Richard Casserley (for access to his father's collection); Gordon Coltas; Crewe Photographic Society (Tom Seaton and Harry Smith); Jim Davenport; G. I. Davies; Brian K. B. Green; Eddie Johnson; Norman Jones; Norman Kneale; Manchester Locomotive Society (for access to the negatives of Tom Lewis); Neville Stead; Terry Webb, Martin Welch and also Ron White of Colour-Rail.
Richard Strange of Steam Archive Services and Harry and Janet Wilson gave invaluable help in checking detail and proof reading. Ray Townsin helped in checking technical details.

Finally, thanks must be extended to my wife Kate for her patience, co-operation and support.

Bill Rear
1 May 1999

Right:
Crewe Station, Platform 5, c1957
This official photograph shows the modernised and cleaned up features familiar to so many travellers. Note the dated features such as the milk vending machine and, beyond, a weighing machine and a 'vibrator', the meaning of which has completely changed in recent years. *BR LM Region*

CROSS THE LINE
TO PLATFORMS
& FOR TRAINS TO LONDON, BIRM
SHREWSBURY, BRISTOL AND TH
SOUTH & CENTRAL WAL
GREAT WESTERN & NORTH STA
REFRESHMENT ROOM
SECOND CLASS
REFRESHMENT ROOM
FIRST CLASS
DINING AND TEA ROOM
GENTLEMEN
PLATFORM

PLATFORM 2
NORTH
GENTLEMEN
BOOKING HALL
REFRESHMENT ROOMS
LONDON CALLING
ASK FO

Historical Background

The original station at Crewe was opened in 1837, on the tracks of the Grand Junction Railway which ran between Birmingham and Newton Junction, where it connected with the tracks of the Liverpool & Manchester Railway. At that time, Crewe was just a very small hamlet set in typical flat Cheshire countryside. The station was located at a point where the Nantwich to Sandbach turnpike road crossed over the tracks which proved a convenient point for drawing local traffic. The original station consisted of one (some sources state two) small platform(s), one booking office, a waiting room and a lavatory located near to where the Crewe Arms Hotel now stands. There was also a small engine shed. The first train arrived there at 8.45am on 4 July 1837 and departed 11min later for Birmingham.

The decision to relocate the locomotive works from Edge Hill, Liverpool, to Crewe was taken by the railway directors in 1840. The move commenced in 1842 and established Crewe as a railway town. The company built houses, schools and a church and men were moved there from Liverpool. Later, a hospital and baths were provided.

The Chester & Crewe Railway Company made a physical connection with the Grand Junction on 1 October 1840, creating a junction of importance. The line from Manchester to Crewe was opened in 1842, followed in 1848 by the Kidsgrove to Crewe and finally, in 1858, the line to Shrewsbury and the west of England completed the pattern that still exists today. Over the years there have been alterations to the trackwork through the station. The first station proved inadequate very early on and a new station was built in 1845 and rebuilt in 1863. Between 1903 and 1906 the station was extended, adding another island platform, designated Platforms 1 and 2. At the same time the avoiding lines were laid under the North Junction enabling freight and some passenger trains from the new sidings at Basford Hall to bypass the station.

At its zenith, the station consisted of six main platform lines and 10 bay lines, covering some five acres of ground. The whole station site occupies some 26 acres. Until the 1986 remodelling, Down trains were dealt with on Platforms 1 and 2, whilst Up trains used Platforms 4, 5 and 6. Platform 3 was bi-directional.

The bay platforms designated 1 to 6 were at the south end of the station, whilst Bays 7 to 10 were at the north end. Local trains usually arrived at and departed from the bay platform lines, those for Stoke and Derby from Bays 5 and 6, whilst the former Great Western Railway used 3 or 4 Bay for its services to Wellington. Shrewsbury local trains also used these platforms. Normally Bays 1 and 2 were used for parcels traffic. Chester and North Wales trains starting from Crewe usually used No 7 Bay, opposite Platform 1 North. Liverpool trains used No 8 Bay whilst Northwich and Manchester locals worked from 9 and 10 Bays respectively. A prominent feature at the north end of the station up until the demolition of the old North Junction signalbox in 1939 was the 'Spider' bridge, which straddled the junction, passing through North Junction cabin in the process of climbing from the 'Old' Works to the station. This bridge carried the 15in gauge line, which provided direct communication from the works to the station. At one time loco stores and spares were taken from the various works departments to the station, to be loaded in 'road vans' which called at every motive power depot on the system on a regular schedule.

Above left:
Crewe Station, No 1 Platform, 24 June 1906
Although not in the timescale of the text of this work, this photograph has been included to complement the next photo. This view shows the first train to arrive at the new platform on opening day: the 8.45am Birmingham to Holyhead, standing at Platform 1 South.
Author's collection

Left:
Crewe Station, Platform 2, Late 1920s
Another photograph out of the timescale, but included to show Platform 2 with 'Royal Scot' class 4-6-0 arriving at the north end. The photograph has been slightly retouched to emphasise outlines.
Ian Allan Library

From 1906 few modifications were made to the station until 1960, when the overbridge carrying the Sandbach to Nantwich road was lifted for the electrification. The opportunity was taken to completely rebuild the front end forecourt. The stationmaster's office block was remodelled at the same time, and the administrative activities, together with the central signing-on point for the whole of the staff, were transferred to the block of offices on Platforms 1 and 2.

It was inevitable with a junction the size of Crewe that the signalling arrangements were complex and were continually remodelled. In the early years of this century, the old mechanical boxes were replaced with an electrical system devised and built at the London & North Western Railway's (LNWR) own works. On completion of the expansion and development programme for the station in 1907, there were nine signal cabins, containing over 1,000 levers, of which North and South Junction boxes had over 500.

Replacement signalboxes were provided at, and entitled, North and South Junctions respectively, after the outbreak of World War 2, in 1940. North Junction box was located in the fork between the Chester and the West Coast main lines, close to the site of its predecessor. South Junction box was located on the Up side. Both boxes were themselves superseded with the remodelling of the station in 1986 by a new electronic signalling centre on the site of the former North Shed. North Junction box survives as part of the Crewe Heritage Centre and displays a working exhibition of 1940s and 1950s signalling.

In 1951, over 400 regular passenger and parcels trains were dealt with at Crewe daily, and some 100,000 passengers joined or alighted from the trains each week. The GPO had a large sorting office nearby, and at one time 25,000 bags of parcel post was handled on the station weekly, amounting to about 250,000 parcels weekly. In addition, a considerable amount of letter post was handled. Until the late 1960s, there was a considerable quantity of newspaper traffic, some trains being 'dedicated' to news traffic in the Working Time Tables.

The work of the passenger station was administered by an area manager, who, in 1960, controlled some 1800 staff, working in many different sections including the:

- passenger station
- booking, enquiry and parcels office
- telegraph office and telephone exchange
- carriage sheds
- carriage sidings
- signalboxes
- motive power depot (North, South and Western)
- Carriage & Wagon Department
- administration

The operating responsibilities throughout the 24 hours of the day with regard to the working of Crewe station were covered by a movements assistant on each turn of duty. He was responsible for general efficiency and punctuality throughout the station area and he also dealt with mishaps or other unusual occurrences and was officer in charge in the absence of the area manager or his assistants.

The operational work of the passenger station was carried out by staff in various grades including the following:

• station inspectors	
• yard inspectors	} supervisors
• parcels inspectors	
• station and yard foremen	chargemen
• shunters	} supervisors
• ticket collectors	
• parcels handling staff	
• trainside porters	
• domestic porter	} supervisors
• carriage cleaners	
• ladies waiting room attendants	
• signalmen	
• guards	

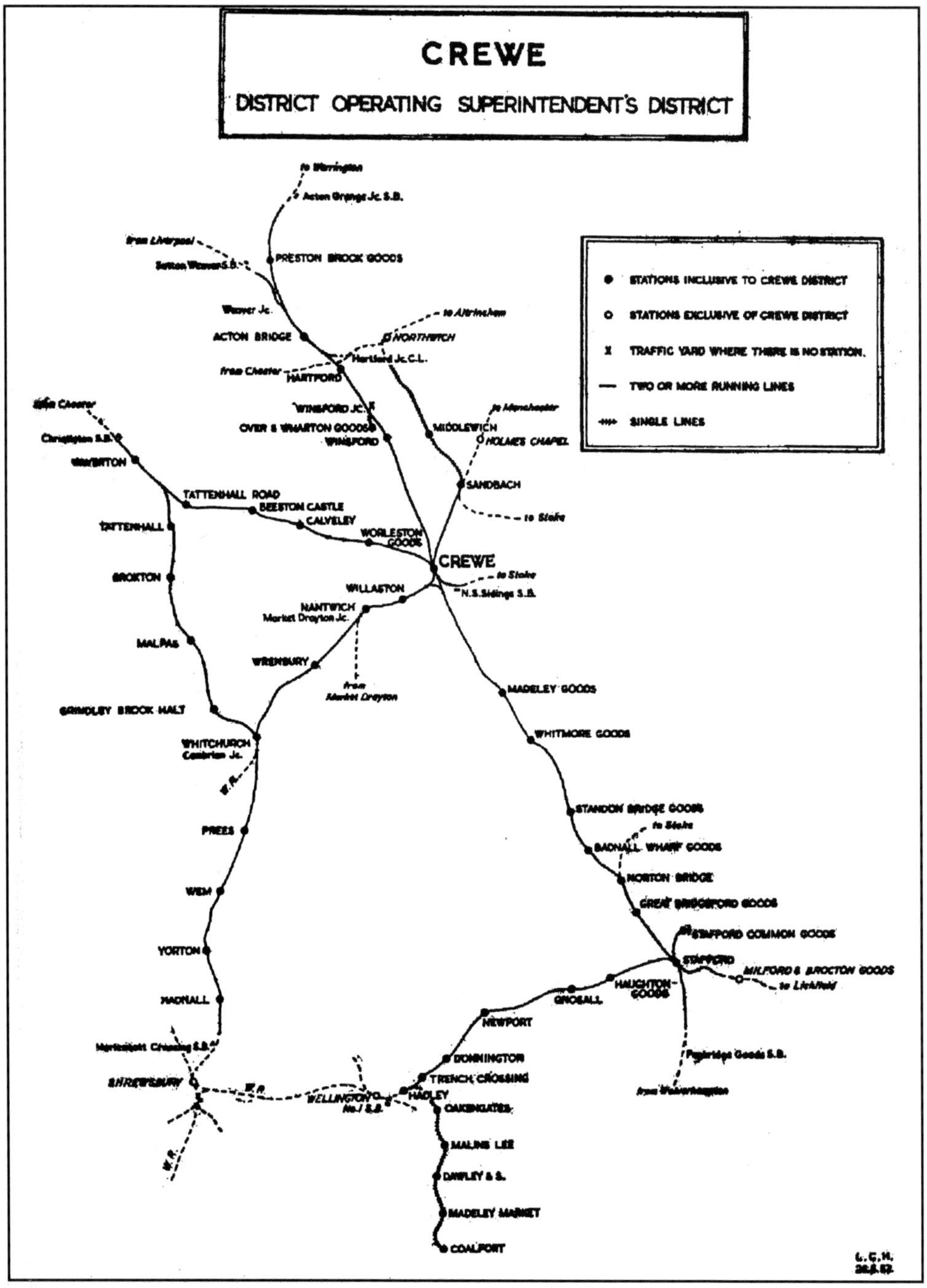

Above:
Crewe North Junction
'Royal Scot' class 4-6-0 No 46122 *Royal Ulster Rifleman* of Longsight 9A shed and sporting the 'Mancunian' headboard pulls into Crewe, heading south. This working did not stop at Crewe and the safety valves lift as the train coasts through the Up centre road ready for the climb up Whitmore. Departure from Manchester London Road was 9.45am and the reporting number was 58. The load was 12 vehicles, 285 tons. *Martin Welch*

Right:
Crewe Junction, 1910
A map taken from *Pre-Grouping Railway Junction Diagrams 1914*.
Ian Allan Publishing

Crewe District

A printed definition which outlines the parameters of the Crewe district is the publication entitled *Operating Control Organisation — Crewe District Operating Manager's District* issued by the Chief Operating Manager. In all probability this was the London, Midland & Scottish Railway (LMR) standard format used for this type of publication. Ultimately, as with all LMS stationery, it carried an ERO number which in this particular case was ERO 52457/2 for the Crewe book. (The adjoining Chester District was ERO 52457/33.) The earliest copy of this work held by the author dates from the first British Railways issue of January 1948. In all probability the first edition was produced with the introduction of the control operational structure throughout the LMS in 1929.

The edition was revised about five years later, taking account of various boundary changes. The title was modified to *London Midland Operating Area — Local Instructions in Connection with Train and Traffic Control Crewe District.*

In 1948 the Crewe District train and traffic control area extended from north of Milford & Brocton Goods/Penkridge to south of Acton Grange signalbox on the Anglo-Scottish West Coast main line. The boundary points defining the District were:

- The line from Shrewsbury to Stafford from Hadley, east of Wellington (on the Western Region) but including the former LNWR branch line from Coalport to Hadley. The former Great Northern Railway (GNR) line as far as Stafford Common Goods passed into LMR control upon Nationalisation.
- At Norton Bridge the station and junction were under Crewe control but beyond that point the line to Stoke was the responsibility of Stoke district, which also controlled the former North Staffs lines as far as North Staffs Sidings signalbox immediately southeast of Crewe.
- On the line from Shrewsbury to Crewe via Whitchurch, Crewe district extended as far as Harlescott Crossing signalbox. South of Whitchurch the Western Region line from Oswestry passed into Crewe control at Cambrian Junction, Whitchurch, as did the line from Whitchurch to Tattenhall Junction.
- On the Chester & Crewe line the district boundary was at Waverton. On the Manchester line, the district boundary was at Sandbach but Crewe district also controlled the single line to Middlewich and Northwich.

At Weaver Junction, responsibility for traffic to Liverpool passed to Liverpool Control.

The principles of district control were uniform throughout the former LMS territory, but there were one or two local differences. The objectives of control were set out in publication form issued by the operating superintendent at Euston for each of the relevant districts. The 1953 issue specific to Crewe was coded BR.30101/19.

- Train control designated points, usually signalboxes, who reported the movement of certain grades of traffic to the control office. Within the confines of Crewe itself this was a complex operation and 11 signalboxes fed information to Crewe control. This is defined on the next page!
- yard inspectors or shunters were designated as the responsible persons for reporting by telephone to control from their appointed yard, together with what they were required to report. The passenger station inspector reported the arrival, departure or passing of selected express freight trains, but no mention of the passenger traffic!

Other information required by control was the position at designated times of such diverse subjects as crippled wagons, brake vans, loco coal stock for North and South Sheds, the daily position of the works sidings and whether traffic could be accepted next morning prior to the first trip leaving the works for Basford Hall Sidings, the empty wagon stock inside the works as distinct from yard stock, the details of coal and coke traffic for shipment on hand not freed, of stock in transit, including the services by which despatched, and where applicable of the number of wagons, originating colliery, release, number, port, consignee and name of vessel.

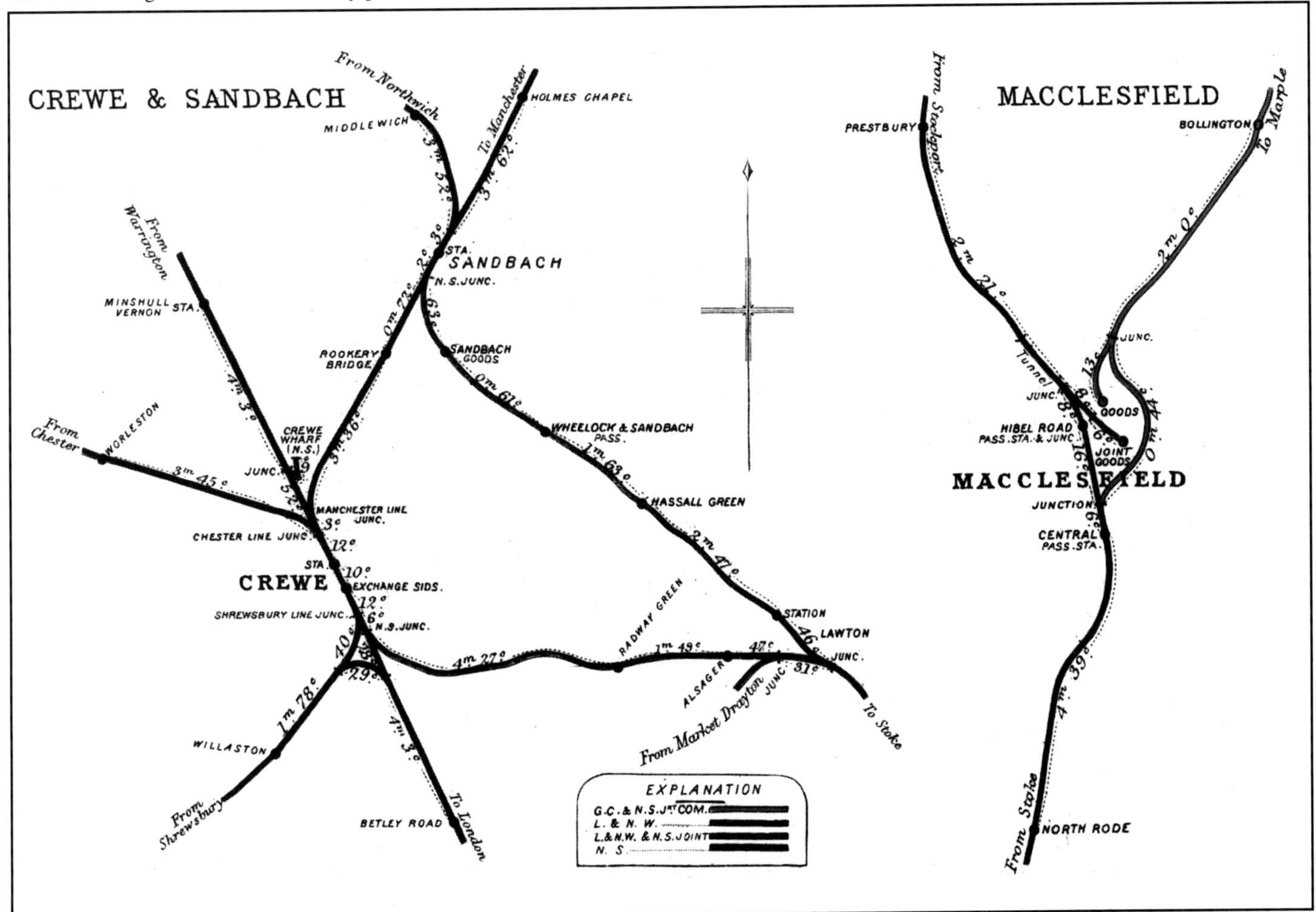

All stationmasters were required to telephone control at 5.30am or commencement of work with details and particulars of traffic or coaching stock stabled there each day, and also of any movement of special livestock, meat and fruit traffic for which no previous arrangements could be made. Control had the power to stop, or restrict temporarily, the flow of any particular traffic.

The local instructions had a specific section dealing with the use of motive power. The instructions about engine and/or crew release according to the diagrams were very specific and a further check comparing day by day and week by week ensured that any recurring delay was picked up and dealt with accordingly.

Comparison with the district local instructions for Crewe and other districts showed a uniformity in procedure, and apart from one or two specific local requirements could be interpreted for any district throughout the region.

Below:
Crewe North Junction
Rebuilt 'Royal Scot' class 4-6-0 No 46162 *Queen's Westminster Riflemen* pulls into No 3 Platform with an Up Class 1 train off the Chester line. The stock is still in LMS maroon and even the tender carries 'LMS' on the sides. The loco carries a Camden 1B shedplate. This was a Crewe North Turn, the loco first working out to Chester with a local train and then working through to Euston with the through coaches. In later years this would become a named train, the 'Welshman', with through carriages from Porthmadog, Pwllheli, Llandudno and Birkenhead. *Martin Welch*

Signalbox	To be reported
Crewe — Basford Hall Junction	Arrival, departure or passing of freight trains and light engines; also passenger and empty coach trains when travelling via the Crewe Independent lines.
Crewe — Coal Yard	Arrival and departure of freight trains and light engines. All trains when diverted from fast to slow lines and vice versa. Arrival, departure or passing of passenger and empty coach trains when travelling via the Up Independent lines.
Crewe — Coppenhall Junction	Arrival, departure or passing of freight and empty coach trains and light engines; also all trains when diverted from fast to slow lines and vice versa.
Crewe — North Junction	Arrival, departure or passing of freight trains to and from the Chester line and Crewe Works; also of freight trains passing through the passenger station.

Signalbox	To be reported
	Arrival, departure or passing of selected and special passenger trains and all milk, parcels and fish trains.
Crewe — North Staffs Sidings	*To Crewe Control* Arrival, departure or passing of freight trains, light engines, empty coach trains and selected and special passenger trains. Arrival of engines to work Up trains.Time of release of engines from freight work (Up sidings), from particulars supplied by yard inspector (shunter when no yard inspector in attendance).
Crewe — North Staffs Sidings	*To Stoke-on-Trent Control* Arrival, departure or passing of all trains and light engines to and from Stoke-on-Trent district.
Crewe — Salop Goods Junction	Arrival of engines for and departure of trains stabled on the Down fast independent line; also arrival and departure of

Above:
Crewe North End
A Liverpool to West of England express draws into Crewe hauled by 'Royal Scot' class 4-6-0 No *46132 The King's Regiment, Liverpool*. With immaculate timing, the Manchester London Road to West of England portion draws into the platform hauled by Class 5 Caprotti No 44748. The 'Scot' carries a Holyhead shedplate (6J) which suggests that the photograph was taken in the summer of 1954.
Martin Welch

Signalbox	**To be reported**
	Western Operating Area engines before and after turning, and trips to and from Crewe Works.
Crewe — Sorting Sidings Middle	Arrival and departure of all trains and light engines on the Up Slow and Up Arrival lines and departure of engines to Crewe South Motive Power Depot. Arrival and departure of Down freight trains and light engines on the Down Fast and Slow lines; also departure time of all engines off Down trains to Crewe South Motive Power Depot via the Down Engine line, stating train from which released. Time of release of engines from freight work from particulars supplied by the yard inspector (yard foreman when no yard inspector in attendance).
Crewe — Sorting Sidings North	Arrival, departure or passing of all trains . Arrival and Departure of engines on and off Crewe South Motive Power Depot.
Crewe — Sorting Sidings South	Arrival and departure of all trains on the Up Fast line and arrival of trains on Down Reception lines.Departure of engines for Crewe South Motive Power Depot via the Down Engine line. Arrival and departure of all trips to and from the North Staffs line.
Crewe — South Junction	Arrival, departure or passing of selected and special passenger trains and all parcels, milk and fish trains. Arrival, departure or passing of freight and empty coach trains on the Down loop. Arrival, departure or passing of Down freight trains (excluding those off the North Staffs line).
Crewe — Steelworks	Arrival, departure or passing of freight trains and light engines.

E.R.O. 53002/2

BRITISH RAILWAYS
LONDON MIDLAND REGION
(WESTERN DIVISION)

SHUNTING ENGINE AND LOCAL TRIP NOTICE

CREWE

OPERATING MANAGER'S DISTRICT

SEPTEMBER 27th 1948, until further notice

THE working of shunting engines and trips in the Crewe District will be as detailed, and each engine must carry a Target corresponding to the numbers shown in this book.

Lund Humphries, London & Bradford

Above:
Crewe, The Independent Lines, November 1951
An unidentified ex-LNWR 'G2' throws out plenty of smoke as it takes a Class G through freight train off the main line. Despite their age, these engines were strong and lasted until the early 1960s. They were not comfortable engines to fire and were prone to running 'hydraulic' if the boiler was over-full. *Bill Rear*

Below:
Crewe, Down Through No 1 Line, No Date
Crewe Works shunter No 58347 pulls past North Shed offices with the afternoon working to Basford Hall with supplies from the Works to various sheds. These old 17in goods engines were the mainstay of several works jobs but only those engaged on the W3 trip to Basford Hall emerged on to the main line. This engine was withdrawn in the week ending 14 March 1953. *Ben Brooksbank*

Freight Workings

Crewe was the nerve centre of the Western Division of the LMS and London Midland Region Western Division. It was also a focal point for remarshalling freight trains. The main concentration yard south of Crewe station, established by the LNWR for north-south traffic was known as Basford Hall Sidings, which ran parallel to the main line from Stafford. The southern connection with the main line was at Basford Hall Junction. A system of independent running lines, controlled by signalboxes, avoided Crewe passenger station and provided connections with the main lines to Chester, Liverpool, Carlisle and Manchester at the north end of the station. Whilst the passenger lines were worked through the station itself mainly by the absolute block system, the main freight lines were worked by the permissive block system, except between Salop Goods Junction or North Junction, Coal Yard and Sydney Bridge boxes where the absolute block regulations applied. The arrival, reception and departure lines and the lines between Sorting Sidings South and Crewe North Staffs Sidings were worked as a station yard.

Freight engine work was the province of Crewe South Shed, situated at the northern end of Basford Hall yard and adjoining the main line. Locomotives working through freight trains could access the sorting sidings at the start and finish of duty direct from the shed. The shunting of wagons necessary to remarshall the trains was undertaken by smaller engines which worked round the clock on a triple-manned rota, time being set aside for locomotive duties, usually on a replacement basis in order that shunting might not be delayed. In LNWR and early LMS days, this shunting was undertaken by tender and tank engines, downgraded passenger engines which were rather unsuited to this kind of work. With the advent of the LMS Standard Class 3F 0-6-0T, these replaced the superannuated designs and were generally better suited to shunting work. The first LMS-built diesel shunting engine was constructed in 1932 on the chassis of a Johnson-design Midland Railway Class 1F 0-6-0T steam locomotive, retaining its former number 1831. It worked the yard for many years and its remains could be seen about South Shed Yard as late as 1953. The LMS experimented with an assortment of contractor-built diesel shunters for this type of work before standardising on the English Electric design. By the outbreak of World War 2 there were several to be seen at work in Basford Hall Yard alongside the '3F' tanks.

Right:
Crewe Station Up Through Road, 23 June 1951
'Jubilee' class 4-6-0 No 45637 *Windward Islands* of Edge Hill 8A shed pulls through the Up Through road with a Class E express freight, 11.50am Edge Hill to Shrewsbury, which normally did not run on Saturdays but did on this particular day. This locomotive was destroyed in the Harrow & Wealdstone accident in October 1952 and was never rebuilt, becoming the first of its class to be withdrawn. *Tom Lewis — Manchester Locomotive Society*

Right:
Crewe, The Independent Lines, No Date
'Jubilee' class 4-6-0 No 45562 *Alberta*, believed to be a Leeds Holbeck engine, takes the avoiding line under North Junction with a Class F express freight bound for the West Coast main line. The use of passenger engines on express freight workings was commonplace. *Gordon Coltas*

In the summer 1951 period (18 June to 23 September) the Working Time Table gives the daily booked freight train movements (excluding Sundays) as follows:

	Mon	Tue	Wed	Thu	Fri	Sat
Down direction	136	160	163	162	160	129
Up direction	137	167	166	166	163	125

Analysis of the destinations and train paths in the WTT, either starting or passing through Crewe, is as follows:

Down direction	**No of**			**Trains per day**			
to	**paths**	**Mon**	**Tue**	**Wed**	**Thu**	**Fri**	**Sat**
Abergavenny Junction	2		1	1	1	1	1
Adswood Sidings	7	4	3	3	3	3	3
Aintree	3	2	2	2	2	2	
Bamfurlong	10	5	4	4	4	5	2
Birkenhead	10	4	7	7	7	7	4
Brewery Sidings	2	1	2	2	2	2	2
Broxton	1	1	1	1	1	1	1
Carlisle	15	7	10	10	10	10	7
Carnforth	3	1	2	2	2	2	2
Copley Hill	3	2	2	2	2	2	2
Crewe Coal Yard	2	1	1	1	1	1	1
Dallam	1					1	
Ditton Junction	1						1
Edge Hill	19	10	9	9	9	9	9
Ellesmere Port	1	1	1	1	1		1
Garstang	1						1
Glasgow Buchanan Street	1	1	1	1	1	1	
Grimesthorpe	1	1	1	1	1	1	
Guide Bridge	3	2	2	2	2	2	2
Haverton Hill	1		1	1	1	1	1
Healey Mills	1	1	1	1	1	1	1
Holyhead	1						1
Hooton	5	4	4	4	4	4	2
Longsight	1		1	1	1	1	1
Manchester London Rd	5	3	4	4	4	4	3
Middlewich	2		1	1	1	1	1
Mold Junction	12	4	7	7	7	6	7
Nantwich	1	1	1	1	1	1	1
Neville Hill	6	5	4	4	4	4	2
Northwich	2	2	2	2	2	2	2
Preston	3	1	2	2	2	1	2
Runcorn	3	2		1		1	
Sandbach	2	2	2	2	2	2	1
Shrewsbury	4	1	1	1	1	1	2
Speke Sidings	10	5	6	6	6	6	3
Stanley	1				1		
Stourbridge Junction	1	1	1	1	1	1	
Swansea	2	1	1	1	1	1	
Walton Old Junction	4	2	2	2	2	2	1
Warrington	7	3	5	5	5	5	2
Waverton	1	1	1	1	1	1	
Whitchurch Salop	3	2	2	3	2	2	1
Winsford Junction	2	2	2	2	2	2	1
Wrenbury	1				1		
Wyre Dock	4	1	2	2	2	2	1

Freight trains terminating at Crewe

Down direction	**No of**			**Trains per day**			
from	**paths**	**Mon**	**Tue**	**Wed**	**Thu**	**Fri**	**Sat**
Alsager	7	5	6	6	6	6	5
Badnall Wharf	1	1	1	1	1	1	
Basford Hall Tip	1	1	1	1	1	1	1
Bescot	5	2	2	2	2	2	2
Betley Road	1	1	1	1	1	1	
Broxton	1	1	1	1	1	1	
Burton Stretton Junction	1						1
Camden	5	2	3	3	3	3	2
Chaddesden	1		1				
Chatterley Sidings	1	1	1	1	1	1	1
Glebe Colliery	1	1	1	1	1	1	1
Grange Junction Sidings	4	3	3	3	3	3	1

Right:
Basford Hall Junction, 19 April 1952
A Stanier Standard Class 8F 2-8-0 No 48724 from 87K Swansea Paxton Street shed has pulled out of Basford Hall yard with a Class H freight onto the Up Slow line. An unidentified loco stands on the Down Fast, only the tender visible, whilst a freight passes under the roadbridge on the Down Slow, probably bound for Basford Hall yard. It is possible that this was the 3.50am Neville Hill to Bushbury which called at Basford Hall Sorting Sidings South for examination and change of train crew from 11.7am to 11.15am and was timed to pass Basford Hall Junction at 11.20am. *Tom Lewis — Manchester Locomotive Society*

Below right:
Stafford, No Date
Ex-LNWR Class 'G2A' 0-8-0 No 49119 of Warrington 8B shed passes through Stafford with a Class E freight from Bescot to Crewe Basford Hall. The loco is in a typically uncleaned condition but, that apart, they were very strong machines and could haul prodigious loads. They had one or two idiosyncrasies and were not designed for crew comfort but usually they would steam well. Their uneven exhaust beat made them easily identifiable to the spotter long before they appeared. *Brian Morrison*

from	No of paths	Mon	Tue	Trains per day Wed	Thu	Fri	Sat
Hadnall	1	1	1	1	1	1	
Harlescott Sidings	2	1		1	1	1	1
Heath's Junction	1	1	1	1	1	1	1
Kingswinford Junction	3	2	3	3	3	3	3
Longport Junction	1						1
Madeley	1	1	1	1	1	1	
Newcastle Junction	1	1					
Normacot	2	1	1	1	1	1	2
Northampton	2	1	1	1	1	1	
Nuneaton	3	1	1	1	1	1	2
Oswestry	1	1	1	1	1	1	
Oxley Sidings	10	8	7	7	7	7	8
Peterborough	1		1	1	1	1	
Pratt's Sidings	1	1					
Rugby	2		1	1	1	1	2
Sideway	1		1	1	1	1	1
Somers Town	1		1	1	1	1	1
Stafford	2	2	2	2	2	2	1
Stoke	5	2	4	4	4	4	4
Tamworth	1						1
Tutbury	1						1
Water Orton	1	1	1	1	1	1	
Whitchurch Salop	3	2	2	3	2	2	
Willesden	8	4	4	4	4	4	3
Worcester	2		2	2	2	2	2

Up direction to	No of paths	Mon	Tue	Trains per day Wed	Thu	Fri	Sat
Alsager Junction	10	6	9	9	9	9	5
Aston	2		1	1	1	1	2
Badnall Wharf	2	1	1	1	1	1	1
Banbury	3	2	3	3	3	3	1
Beeston	2		1	1	1	1	1
Bescot	1	1	1	1	1	1	1
Betley Road	2	2	2	2	2	2	1
Birmingham Curzon St	9	4	4	4	4	3	5
Botteslow Junction	1	1	1	1	1	1	1
Broad Street	4	2	3	3	3	2	1
Burton	2	1	1	1	1	1	1
Bushbury	11	7	6	6	6	6	4
Camden	4	3	3	3	3	3	1
Chaddesden	2	1	1	1	1	1	1
Coventry	1	1	1	1	1	1	1
Egginton Junction	2	1	1	1	1	1	
Etruria Junction	2	2	2	2	2	2	1
Grange Junction	3	1	3	3	3	3	1
Hadnall	1		1	1	1	1	1
Hockley	1		1	1	1	1	1
Hollinswood	1	1	1	1	1	1	1
Lawley Street	1			1			
Leicester	1		1	1	1	1	1
Little Eaton Junction	2	1	1			1	
Longport Junction	5	3	2	2	2	2	4
Madeley	1	1	1	1	1	1	
Maiden Lane	1			1	1	1	
Newcastle Junction	4	3	3	3	3	3	3
Normacot Junction	1	1	1	1	1	1	1
Northampton	2	1	2	2	2	2	1
Nottingham	2	1	1	1	1	1	1
Nuneaton	7	3	4	4	4	4	4
Oxley Sidings	11	9	10	10	10	10	8
Pratt's Sidings	1						1
Radway Green	1	1	1	1	1	1	1
Rugby	3	2	2	2	2	2	3
Shrewsbury	7	2	4	4	4	4	4
Stafford	1		1	1	1	1	1
Stoke	6	3	5	5	5	5	4
Sudbury Junction	6	3	3	3	3	3	3
Whitchurch Salop	3	3	3	3	3	3	1
Whitemoor Sidings	1	1	1	1	1	1	1
Wichnor	1	1					
Willesden HL	7	6	7	6	7	6	3
Worcester	1	1	1	1	1	1	1

Right:
Nuneaton, No Date
Stanier Class 8F 2-8-0 No 48111 of Nuneaton 2B shed shunts wagons in the Up sidings whilst 'Jubilee' class 4-6-0 No 45721 *Impregnable* stands at the Up Slow platform with a freight working to Rugby. Notice Nuneaton No 2 signal cabin behind the 'Jubilee'. Note too the very tall starting signal with repeating arm at lower level. *Horace H. Bleads*

Below right:
Stafford Up Side, No Date
Class 5 No 45278 of Willesden 1A Shed takes a Class C freight through Stafford. This was possibly the 8.33am Edge Hill to Nuneaton. The stock is either fully fitted or piped and permitted the train to run at a higher speed. Nuneaton men worked the train from Basford Hall Middle and were relieved by Rugby men at Nuneaton, who were in turn relieved by Willesden men for the final leg south from Rugby. *D. Sellman*

48111

45278

Freight trains terminating at Crewe

Up direction from	No of paths	Trains per day Mon	Tue	Wed	Thu	Fri	Sat
Bamfurlong	4	3	2	2	2	2	2
Blackpool	1	1	1	1	1	1	
Carlisle	10	5	6	6	6	6	6
Carnforth	3	1	2	2	2	2	1
Chester	1		1	1	1	1	1
Coal yard	3	1	1	1	1	1	2
Copley Hill	4	1	2	2	2	2	3
Crofton Hall/West Jnt	2	1	1	1	1	1	1
Edge Hill	8	4	7	7	7	7	3
Ellesmere Port	2		2	2	2	2	2
Folly Lane	1	1	1	1	1	1	
Garston Dam Bridge	7	7	7	7	7	7	
Harlescott Sidings	2	1	2	2	2	2	2
Heaton Norris	5	2	4	4	4	4	3
Low Gill	1						1
Middlewich	4	2	2	2	2	2	3
Mold Junction	7	3	3	3	3	3	3
Nantwich	2	2	2	2	2	2	2
Newton Heath	1		1	1	1	1	
Northwich	2	1	2	2	2	2	1
Port Sunlight	1	1	1	1	1	1	
Runcorn	1	1					
Sandbach	3	2	2	2	2	2	1
Shrewsbury	1	1					
Speke Sidings	3	1	1	1	1	1	2
Warrington	5	2	3	3	3	3	2
Waverton	1	1	1	1	1	1	
Whitchurch Salop	5	4	3	3	3	2	2
Widnes	1	1	1	1	1	1	1
Winsford Junction	2	1	1	1	1	1	1
Wyre Dock	2	1	1	1	1	1	1

Right:
Wigan Springs Branch, No Date
A somewhat grimy Class 5, No 45371, wearing a 12B Carlisle Upperby shedplate pulls out of the yard heading north. The loco carries Class F lamps signifying an unfitted express freight working. This engine was transferred to Upperby in the week commencing 9 January 1954 and remained there until 11 December 1966 when it moved to Kingmoor. *Tom Lewis — Manchester Locomotive Society*

Left:
Bletchley, April 1955
Stanier Class 8F No 48387 of Wellingborough 15A shed stands in Bletchley station awaiting the road, with the 9.35am mineral Class J from Gower's Siding to Bilton Siding. The train was booked to call at Bletchley from 10.34am to 10.36am for loco duties and to change crew. The station staff seem busy cleaning the gas lamps further down the platform. *W. Philip Conolly*

Fewer trains ran on Sundays; some trains ran only on specific weekdays. Others ran in different timings on certain days or had timing variations at intermediate points. On Saturdays, some trains which could not complete their journey before Sunday morning terminated short of the weekday destinations. Some workings into Crewe terminated in different yards on Saturdays compared to the rest of the week.

Basford Hall

Prior to 1927 the complex consisted of 30 double-ended Down and 14 dead-ended Up sidings, which were extended and supplemented by an additional six sidings in 1928 giving the yard a capacity of 2,858 wagons, all located on the Down side of the West Coast main line south of the station.

Traffic through Basford Hall Sorting Sidings was controlled from three signalboxes within the complex. Traffic entering or leaving the yard at the south end was the responsibility of Basford Hall Junction signalbox, located on the Up side of the main line. In the yard, Sorting Sidings South signalbox was located between the Down Slow goods line and the point where the Up reception lines merged.

Sorting Sidings Middle signalbox was strategically placed at the south end of the throat of the sorting sidings and Sorting Sidings North signalbox was at the convergence at the opposite end of the group of lines A to H.

The Up sidings consisted of Groups A to C with Group A closest to the main line south. The main Up arrival lines 1 and 2 divided the Up and Down groups. The siding allocation numbered lines outward. Up line No 1 was in Group C and Down line No 1 was in Group D.

The allocation was as follows:

Up Sidings

Group C

No	Wagon capacity	Allocation
-	-	Up Engine Line
1	78	NS Section Empties
2	83	NS Section Loads
3	78	Madeley Colliery
4	77	Stafford Line Locals, Sand Sidings and Permanent WayDepot and Wait Order Traffic

Group B

No	Wagon capacity	Allocation
5	77	Broad Street, Camden and Camden Exchange
6	76	Willesden Traffic for Express Freight
7	76	Willesden Mineral and Heavy Traffic for Fast Freight
8	63 }	Rugby and Exchange Traffic for Express Freight, including traffic for Northampton, Bletchley, Peterborough
9	62 }	

Group A

No	Wagon capacity	Allocation
10	68	Lichfield, Wichnor and Burton
11	68	Rugeley, Hednesford and Cannock
12	70	Coventry and District
13	73	Nuneaton and Exchange, excluding Leicester traffic
14	76	Stafford and Exchange
15	67	Bushbury Exchange
16	60	Bescot Exchange
17	52	LMS (Midland Section) via Birmingham
18	48	Curzon Street
19	46	LMS (North Staffs Section) Loads (1.25am to 6.20am), Leicester (6.20am to 1.25am)
20	52	Reservoir Siding

Down Sidings

Group D

No	Wagon capacity	Allocation
1	51	Crewe Warehouse
2	48	Mold Junction and beyond
3	49	Stations Chester to Birkenhead inclusive
4	50	Stations Crewe to Chester and for 'G' Group
5	46	GWR Exchange
6	48	Shrewsbury and South and Central Wales
7	50	Northwich Branch, Stations Crewe to Manchester, Whitchurch and Cambrian Line, Winsford and Exchange

Group E

No	Wagon capacity	Allocation
8	45	Nantwich
9	46	Stations Crewe to Wrenbury (excluding Nantwich), Crewe Coal Yard
10	46 }	
11	43 }	Marshalling
12	50 }	

Group F

No	Wagon capacity	Allocation
13	46	Traffic for 'D' Group
14	45	Northwich Exchange
15	45	Rookery Bridge, Sandbach and Middlewich Exchange
16	45	Runcorn, Ditton, Widnes and Garston
17	49	Winsford Jnt and Over and Wharton Branch, Winsford to Preston Brook and Sutton Weaver

Group G

No	Wagon capacity	Allocation
18	51	Crewe Warehouse
19	47	Springs Branch and Bamfurlong Exchange, including traffic for Wigan and Central Division via Wigan
20	51	Warrington Exchange
21	52	'Caledonian', 'Highland', LNE (GN of Scotland Section)
22	52	Upperby Exchange
23	51	Liverpool Stations
24	48	Earlestown, St Helens, including crippled wagons for Earlestown Works
25	49	Common Users

Group H

No	Wagon capacity	Allocation
26	51	Crewe Works
27	51	Yorkshire and all Manchester direction traffic
28	60	Cripples for Crewe Wagon Shops
29	68	Traffic for Cart Siding, Old Yard, Permanent Way Sidings, Gresty Lane, Cattle Market, Browns Mill and Theakstons Sidings
30	75	Preston Exchange, Lancaster Exchange and Carnforth Exchange

Gresty Lane

Difficulties in working traffic from the Shrewsbury line to Basford Hall caused the LMS to construct a new yard in 1928 at a point known as Gresty Lane, approximately one mile from Crewe station on the Down side of the Crewe to Shrewsbury line. The site was chosen for the reason that traffic sidings in this position immediately alongside the Crewe and Shrewsbury line were appropriately located for dealing with freight traffic coming from Shrewsbury and the west and consigned to points in the Northern and Eastern Divisions.

With the very considerable traffic arriving at Crewe from Whitchurch, Shrewsbury and beyond, and also from the Great Western Railway via Nantwich, Market Drayton Junction comprising both LMS and GW freight trains, considerable difficulties were at times occasioned in working the trains into Basford Hall yard, and as any scheme for enlarging the facilities at Basford would have little or no effect on improving the actual means of approach from the west, relief had to be found by creating new sidings which would permit the trains being dealt with at Crewe independently of the main sidings at Basford Hall.

Simultaneously with the new work at Gresty Lane, the Up group of sidings in Basford Hall were extended with the provision of six additional sidings and extension of the existing 14 sidings. Work started in September 1927 and was completed 12 months later, on target. The new yard comprised 19 traffic sidings with a capacity of 1,227 wagons and two arrival lines. A new signal cabin controlled access from the Shrewsbury line at the west end of the yard, known as Gresty Lane No 2 Box.

All trains from the GW line, also LMS trains from Whitchurch, Shrewsbury and beyond, terminated at Gresty Lane whereas formerly they had to be worked through to Basford Hall. Incoming trains were directed on to the No 1 or No 2 arrival roads, the engine coming to a stand at the water column situated near the entrance to the sidings at the far end. The train engine was then detached and sent on shed. A shunting engine picked up the wagons and sorted them into the various sidings. Through trains were made from Gresty Lane to Stockport, Manchester and beyond, and also to Garston, Liverpool, Warrington, Preston and Carlisle. Some traffic arrived at Gresty Lane Down sidings bound for the south, and this was tripped to Basford Hall Up sidings. Similarly, some traffic from the south to the north and east was tripped from Basford Hall sidings to Gresty Lane for the above-mentioned destinations. Some trains nevertheless worked from Basford Hall through to the same destinations and also on to the Shrewsbury line without calling at Gresty Lane sidings.

Trains from the Salop line could access the Independent lines and avoid working over passenger lines until they reached Sydney Bridge or the Coal Yard signalboxes, passing underneath North Junction.

Gresty Lane Sidings comprised Up and Down groups, although the former were some distance from the Down group and located within the triangle of lines between Basford Hall, the Independent lines and the main lines from Shrewsbury to the passenger station. Known as the Up Hill sidings, they consisted of two roads with a total capacity of 50 wagons.

Two signalboxes controlled traffic off the Shrewsbury line. Gresty Lane No 1 box was located at the junction of the lines from Basford Hall and the main line to the passenger station. Gresty Lane No 2 signalbox was built in 1928 at the time Gresty Lane Yard was built.

Left:
Lancaster, No Date
The 'WD' 2-8-0 engines were an integral part of the London Midland freight workings, being seen over most parts of the region. Here is No 90367 from Lostock Hall 24C shed on the Central Division, working a Class E express freight. This could have been the 3.10pm Heysham to Preston NU working which was a Lostock Hall job.
Eric Treacy

Right:
Rugby, No Date
Stanier Class 8F No 48037 of Toton 18A shed pulls away from Rugby with a Class J mineral train. In the background through the arch of the bridge can be seen the former Great Central line passing over the tracks. Note the style of the engine number on the smokebox plate, which went out of fashion early in British Railways days. Note too the length of train, all the wagon bodies being of wooden construction.
H. Weston

Up Hill Sidings

No	Wagon capacity	Allocation
1	25 }	These were for holding and sectionalising traffic, Crewe Warehouse, and traffic for Whitchurch, GW (Cambrian Section), Shrewsbury, South and Central Wales and GW Co, also traffic for Basford Hall put off through trains and cripple wagons for Crewe Wagon Shops handed over by GW Co.
2	25 }	

Down Sidings

No	Wagon capacity	Allocation
1	68	Crewe Warehouse
2	66	Basford Hall Down sidings
3	63	Common user empty wagons and vans
4	63	Basford Hall Up side and North Staffs traffic
5	59	Preston & PW line, including stations Preston to Lancaster & Heysham inclusive
6	59	Caledonian, GN of S, and Highland Section
7	64	Upperby Exchange
8	80	Liverpool
9	72	Warrington Exchange
10	72	Springs Branch, Bamfurlong Exchange, traffic for Wigan and Central Division via Wigan
11	69	Adswood Exchange, including stations Stockport to Diggle
12	69	Longsight Exchange
13	66	London Road
14	66	Huddersfield, Hillhouse and Heaton Lodge
15	62	Central Division via Phillips Park
16	62	LNE via Guide Bridge
17	58	Copley Hill Exchange, including Leeds proper
18	58	Huddersfield, Hillhouse & Heaton Lodge, Copley Hill Exchange (unsuitable traffic for express goods)
19	53	Crippled wagons for Crewe Wagon Shops

North Staffordshire Sidings

This was the smallest of the three freight yards. There were two groups of sidings on the Down side of the main line to Stoke, divided by the goods lines connecting Basford Hall and the NS main line, and which passed under the North Western main line. The smaller nest was located within the triangle and behind the site of the former North Staffs loco shed. The sidings in this group were not numbered. They were connected to the larger Down side sidings group numbered 1 to 8.

Down Sidings

No	Wagon capacity	Allocation
1	36	Backing-in road
2	37	Garston
3	39	Basford Hall
4	36	Mold Junction and beyond
5	30	Birkenhead Docks
6	24	Grange Lane
7	19	Hooton, including Ellesmere Port & Wirral Line
8	18	Chester and Exchange
Cripple	8 }	Private owners' wagons for repairs
Cripple	11 }	
Cripple Van	17	Stopped traffic and cripple wagons
Liverpool	18	Crewe Coal Wharf

Access to the Down and Up side sidings was controlled from Crewe North Staffs Sidings signalbox, located on the Down side close to the old engine shed. The Up side sidings consisted of four lines, as follows:

Up Sidings

No	Wagon capacity	Allocation
1	45	Alsager Exchange
2	46	Pratt's Sidings Exchange
3	56	Longport and Etruria Exchange
4	42	Stoke Yard and Cockshute Siding or Cliff Vale

Left:
Near Low Gill, No Date
The Lune Gorge was a lonely place at the best of times, and before the coming of the motorway, the sound of locomotives working hard echoed across the valley. In winter it was especially bleak and the railway seemed diminutive against the magnificent backdrop. Here 'Jubilee' class 4-6-0 No 45561 *Saskatchewan* heads north with a through freight, the driver intent and ever vigilant, whilst the smoke emerging from the chimney indicates that the fireman is hard at work.
Eric Treacy

Below:
Near Dillicar, 26 May 1952
Carlisle Upperby shed's 'Jubilee' No 45630 *Swaziland* in lined-out black livery with the wording 'BRITISH RAILWAYS' on the tender, heads south on its journey with a Class H through freight. This was the daily 10.10am Carlisle Upperby Yard to Winwick Quay. There appears to be a fine assortment of tank wagons in the consist. *E. D. Bruton*

Passenger Traffic and Station Workings

As might be expected, the station was a scene of continuous activity 24 hours a day, every day, including Sundays. The convergence of six routes called for extremely detailed planning, and at times platform space was at a premium. That it functioned so efficiently is a tribute to all concerned, for it must not be forgotten in this day and age when many trains no longer call at Crewe but pass through the remodelled junction, that until the end of steam very few Class A trains worked through without calling there. For most of those that did, particularly on the Anglo-Scottish workings, this required a change of train crew, guards and/or engine, with resultant light engine movements on and off shed. In the case of Up trains this required the replacement engine to be at the south end of the station ahead of the arrival time, conveniently close to enable a quick substitution to be made. As frequently happened, passenger stock had to be attached to/detached from the working at the same time, performed by one of the station shunt engines, a job for one of the standard LMS design Class 3F 0-6-0Ts. The author has fond memories of No 47523 which for a couple of years carried its BR number on the bunker and the 'ferret on the dartboard' logo on the tank sides, but still sported the LMS smokebox number 7523. Rumour has it that this was removed by one of the drivers prior to the loco visiting the works for overhaul, and the five-figure numberplate which adorned the smokebox was promptly removed upon its return! Pipework and fittings in the cab were scoured and burnished with a fanatical desire to dazzle, and woe betide the fireman who allowed them to become discoloured by not ensuring the blower was 'on' whenever the firehole door was opened. How many firemen spent five shillings on a tube of 'Solvo Autosol' paste, created for use on motorcycle chromed exhaust pipes, guaranteed to remove the 'bluing' effect of overheating, and now used here on the copper pipework, just to keep a certain driver happy! Normally this loco spent its days at the south end of the station, reposing at times in No 2 Bay, and at night keeping empty stock warm.

There were, inevitably, times when normal station working was plunged into disarray. Routes could be blocked because of engineering works, accident or mishap necessitating rerouteing of some services, or traffic could be delayed because of adverse conditions, causing trains to get out of sequence and throwing the platform working arrangements into chaos. At all hours of the day or night, Post Office traffic was heavy and barrowloads of mail were strategically placed opposite the point where the mail was to be loaded at the appointed time. Porters and GPO men would then be seen valiantly manoeuvring their charges out of the way as a late arrival at Platform 5 gave way to a working which arrived on time, requiring the staff to replace the barrows loaded to capacity with mailbags with others for a different destination. Who could ever forget the small petrol tractors towing six, eight, 10 or more trailers of mail, weaving around passengers and other obstacles which adorned the platform, as they headed for the north end of Platform 2? How many travel-weary passengers, with suitcases at their feet, and hands occupied with a cup of tea and a pork pie, expecting five minutes peace before their train was due, were suddenly told that due to late running, their train would now arrive at/depart from Platform 3 'over the bridge'.

I have long-standing memories of Platforms 1 & 2 (North) when Military Police RTOs were resident, at their busiest between 9pm and midnight on Sundays when servicemen were making their way back to their respective camps before the curfew. Inevitably there were those who had indulged at the bars on the platforms and had consumed more than was good for them. These RTOs were a breed apart, all about 7ft in height, usually with thick necks that disappeared under their distinctive red-banded caps. The glossy black peaks of their caps were at right angles to the flat tops, pressed against their noses and masking their eyes which peered out from under the rims. They had an unenviable job but some seemed to revel in their unpopularity, making arrogance an art form. They would stride up and down the platforms in pairs looking for miscreants who were improperly dressed, under the influence, making a nuisance of themselves, travelling without warrants, AWOL, on the run, etc. They had eagle-eyed vision and almost instinctively could spot a likely suspect hundreds of yards away.

An abiding memory is of a gloomy November night in 1951, as midnight and departure time approached for the Down Postal at the north end of Platform 2. Platform 1 opposite heaved with humanity awaiting a Holyhead train running late, the Swansea to York Mail stood in No 8 Bay, and chaos reigned supreme. Across the tracks there was a slight disturbance between two servicemen on the ramp of No 1, voices raised in slurred anger. Then, in the middle, heads and caps visible above the crowd, could be seen two 'redcaps', a path opening up in front of them as they steamed majestically towards their clients. We could not fully hear what was said, but evidently the disturbance demanded quick action, and in unison the two redcaps picked one 5ft 4in dishevelled cap-less, tie-less airman and, with one continuous movement, wheeled-about and marched off south in formation, their victim facing north, feet about 18in off the platform, kicking furiously, his voice rising in crescendo screaming 'Lemmi go, you strawberry-headed bastards, I'll...' Even as they receded, you could sense the shaven heads of the redcaps bristling with the insults, which doubtless they would record word for word on the charge sheet.

On another occasion the same two (who were nicknamed Claude and Clarence for some unknown reason) demanded entry to the footplate seeking another victim, whom they suspected was hiding in the tender. They were refused admission and were obliged to back off, to the amusement of the massed ranks, but nevertheless stood on the platform peering into the cab until the train moved off. Their 'client' was a National Serviceman who had either lost or never had a travel warrant, was probably AWOL and certainly improperly dressed, to boot. He was, nevertheless, a fireman from Stafford doing his national service, returning to camp at Preston. He was known to the driver who had taken pity on him and provided an escape route from a confrontation. He climbed into the cab on the driver's side, out of the fireman's door and crouched on the bottom step. Once the train was on the move and clear of the platform he climbed back in and travelled in the cab to Preston, where he dropped off in to the six-foot as the train approached the platform.

A final memory of the' redcaps' at Crewe suffices. Travelling back from Euston 'on the cushions' on another Sunday evening with servicemen and women packed throughout the length of the train, a Crewe travelling ticket collector came in to our compartment as we approached Watford and quietly informed us that he believed the toilet next to ours contained more than its normal complement of one person, asking us to keep an eye on what happened until we reached Crewe. Outside the door, an RAF serviceman stood twiddling a WAAF cap and holding two tickets. 'My wife is inside' was the bland assurance and, if that was so, she was having a helluva time with some ghosts judging by the noises that filtered through the partition. Nothing happened at Rugby nor at Stafford — and at Crewe the massed ranks of redcaps were assembled at the north end of Platform 2, facing every door and window of the leading coaches, or so it seemed, assisted by civilian ticket checkers and platform inspectors, as humanity tried to evacuate the train. As the service personnel got off, their warrants were checked by all and sundry. The moment of truth eventually arrived and out of the toilet came 11 servicemen, puce from the shortage of oxygen, almost asphyxiated by the pall of cigarette smoke that preceded their departure. All were led gently away by the caring and sympathetic redcaps, to recover in their own private rest room, for onward destination and presumably the inevitable jankers.

Requests were occasionally made by redcaps to search the footplate, looking for clients, but invariably they were refused, usually in a civil manner. On the odd occasion, however, they were told to 'f... off' by one who in the past had obviously less than happy memories of the Military Police.

Platform work was very smartly performed, of necessity. Extracts from the Arrivals & Departures book will show just how tight some of the timings were. In the case of the aforementioned midnight Down Postal, Crewe North men and engines worked the train from Euston (8.30pm departure, Reporting Number 157). The locomotive was Crewe North Turn 4 (Class 8P) which had worked to Euston the same morning with the Up Postal. The train crew comprised No 1 Link men, working Turn 275 to Euston, lodging at Camden and returning with the 8.30pm (Turn 279). Arrival time at Crewe Platform 2 was scheduled for 11.44pm, with immediate release for the locomotive, due on shed at 11.49pm. Meanwhile, the train was worked forward by Crewe North loco. Turn 5 (Class 8P) gonged off North Shed at 11.30pm, ready for immediate hook-on and the midnight departure. Train crew were again

Above left:
Crewe Station, Platform 2, No Date
An unidentifiable 'Jubilee' class 4-6-0 pulls into Platform 2 with the 1.5pm Saturdays Only Euston to Glasgow Central. This train ran only for 10 weeks in the high summer. This is not the sharpest of photographs but is included to show Crewe station 'B' signalbox. *Ben Brooksbank*

Centre left:
Crewe Station, South End, No Date
Stanier Pacific, 'Princess Coronation' No 46238 *City of Carlisle* based at Camden 1B shed. It is shown here working the W36 — the 8.20am Liverpool to Euston, but which was booked to call at Crewe, which begs the question what was it doing on the Up Through road, which has no platform, if it was booked to stop? It is possible that the reporting number was incorrect and also the shadows suggest that the time was nearer midday than 9.18am. *N. E. Stead Collection*

Below left:
Crewe Station, Platform 5
Stanier Class 4 2-6-4T No 42590 on station shunting duties propels two coaches from Glasgow on to the back of the Manchester to Plymouth working. This photograph has been reproduced before but has been included to show typical station work at Crewe in the steam era, when attaching and detaching of coaches was a normal operation. *Tom Lewis — Manchester Locomotive Society*

Right:
Madeley, 16 August 1959
Engineering works on the Up Fast line meant that all southbound traffic had to use the Slow line. Here unrebuilt 'Patriot' No 45533 *Lord Rathmore* eases a Class A working past the site of work. Apart from a crane lifting parcels off wagons, most of the settling is done with manpower. *Martin Welch*

5A men, this time Turn 139 in Link 3, which they worked through to Glasgow Central. Departure time was critical. The moment the departing Glasgow cleared the platform, its place was taken by the 8.52pm Euston to Holyhead, which was booked to call at 12 midnight, departing 12.11am.

Considerable interchange of postal traffic took place throughout the day, both through working of vanloads, transfer of bagged sorted mail and from the Royal Mail sorting office on the station. Barrowloads of sacks of mail are synonymous with Crewe station. Night-time, however, saw the peak of this activity, and although some impression of the amount of traffic handled may be gleaned from the film *Night Mail*, shown at regular intervals on TV, what was portrayed was insignificant in comparison to the actual amount handled in a normal working 24 hours period. Even these amounts paled in to insignificance when the Christmas rush was at its peak, with dozens of extra trains converging on Crewe (and doubtless at other centres) in the small hours.

Despite the avoiding lines that carried through freight (and some passenger trains) under North Junction and around the station, bypassing the platform roads, there was nevertheless some freight traffic that passed through the station. These were generally at the quieter times of the day, but nevertheless more frequently than most realised. For many years there was regular traffic in fish from Scotland and the west Lancashire ports to the south. Crewe North had a job in No 1 Link working the 2.50pm Wyre Dock to Broad Street Fish which paused in the Up Through line for 20min or so to effect a loco and train crew change. In 1952 Willesden men worked the train forward with Crewe North loco Turn 33, which was nominally for a Class 5, but in fact usually produced one of 5A's unrebuilt 'Patriot' locos. These were just as effective on the Class C working, which ran through from Wyre Dock without a booked stop en route to Crewe. The 1951 schedules show the loco that worked from Wyre Dock to Crewe then worked to Shrewsbury, a Willesden loco taking over the fish at Crewe station on the Up Through road.

The summer months saw increased passenger traffic and freight work was kept down to the minimum from Friday night. Several through passenger workings avoided the platform roads, and engines and/or train crew were changed in Basford Hall Yard. Workings off the Chester line not booked to call included the 'Welshman' from Portmadoc and Pwllheli, which used the Up Through line, and memories of passing through the station at the statutory restricted speed of 20mph, watching the seething mass of people who in turn watched us enviously, while everyone from train crew, guard and 500 or so passengers casually regarded the less fortunate mortals with smug expressions on their faces, before the necessity of getting back to work for the climb up Whitmore.

Many trains started and terminated at Crewe, and empty stock movements were generally in the hands of the '3F' 0-6-0T shunters that resided at South Shed. These usually spent 22 hours on continuous duty, being remanned every 8 hours or so, before making for South Shed to clean the fire and refuel before returning to the station. Coaching stock was disposed to the south end of the station, where extensive coach sidings were located on either side of the main line. There was always a substantial reserve of stock at the disposal of the Carriage Department which would provide vehicles for any additional trains that were required. It was part of the training for young firemen and drivers to spend some time on these duties, but generally the jobs were the perks of those senior drivers who had opted out of their rightful place on the main passenger links, irregular hours and lodging turns for the more mundane, lower paid but predictable flat 8hr shifts. Meals could be prepared at home, safe in the knowledge that practically nothing could disrupt the booking-off time before the lord and master returned, unless, of course, he was in the habit of pausing for liquid refreshment on the way! Twenty-two turns made up the passenger shunting duties, the drivers of which were attached to North Shed, the locomotives being the responsibility of South Shed. There were also two bank engine jobs, uphill and downhill, a relic from the days when trains heading north or south would routinely require assistance for a variety of reasons. The North Shed drivers working these turns had to have good route knowledge, and could expect to be called upon to assist frequently. With the advent of Stanier engines on to most main line jobs, their usefulness diminished but nevertheless the work survived until the late 1950s.

The bank engine link comprised three sets of North Shed men. For many years after World War 2, two LMS Standard Class 2P 4-4-0 engines (Nos 658 and 659) were attached to these diagrams. These loafed about the station, sometimes removing a coach or moving stock from one platform to another, but rarely moving outside the station limits. Just occasionally it was necessary for one or the other to venture out on the main line, and the uphill bank engine was seen at Euston from

time to time. Inevitably there was no booked work for the engine and men, Camden having little or no use for a Class 2P anyway, so under the slightest pretext, the loco was attached to the front of the first train heading north after being coaled and having its fire cleaned at 1B. 'Piccolo' Pete Johnson recalled such a trip, and was less than complimentary about the engine's riding qualities whilst acting as pilot to the train engine. It was unusual but not unknown for the uphill bank engine and crew to work a round trip to Euston and back in a single shift. The rewards were to be found in the wage packet the following week, when mileage payments were one hour's pay for every 15 miles over the statutory 150-mile agreement, a round trip earning an extra 10 hours pay (roughly a quarter of the flat weekly wage, at this time). Towards the end of the 1950s the '2P' locomotives were replaced by spare engines from North Shed, usually Class 5s, although 2-6-4Ts and 'Jubilees' were also regular performers.

Another memory of the north end of the station was the footbridge connecting North Shed with the platforms, and which at one time was connected to the old 'Spider Bridge' demolished in 1939 or thereabouts. This was supposed to be private but it provided a fantastic viewpoint across North Junction and was almost permanently occupied by the spotting fraternity. During school hours it was usually free of observers, but outside these hours there was a collection of youngsters (and not so young people) who observed and recorded the passage of trains until darkness fell. At weekends the numbers swelled considerably and in school holidays and on summer weekends in particular there would be hundreds of people on the bridge, causing problems to train crew who had to squeeze past the gathered ranks. The Railway Police did their best to clear the footbridge, but it was a hopeless task. Occasionally a small group of youngsters would survey the landscape and, lusting after the collection of locomotives in North Shed, would take a chance and make a run for the shed. Usually their progress was spotted from the Loco Superintendent's office and they would be headed off and escorted back to the footbridge. Some made it through the 'tunnel' that led in to the shed and a few managed to get between the locos in the shed road to record their catch. In the gloom of the shed confines they were usually able to get by unseen, but the moment they ventured out in to the shed yard they were seen by Joe Stockton, the Foreman Cleaner, and rounded up, to be escorted off the premises. Almost without exception, the culprits were polite and mostly well behaved and made no attempt to evade capture, accepting that they had trespassed, and were let off with a stern warning. One or two would attempt to bluff their way out of a telling off, but there was no animosity on either side.

These youngsters were not all local to Crewe; indeed most had come to 'Mecca' from far-off places. The refreshment rooms and bookstalls did a roaring trade in crisps and soft drinks although buying foodstuffs was considered by many to be an unnecessary luxury as they had brought their own refreshments with them. The bookstalls kept vast stocks of Ian Allan *ABCs*. The manager of the Wymans bookstall on Platform 2 once told me that LMR Region books were usually sold out, some several hundred as soon as the new additions arrived, closely followed by the LMR Shed Allocations book, with the Western Region edition a poor third. He kept only nominal stocks of the Eastern and Southern Region *ABCs*, but rarely were any left by the end of the season. *Trains Illustrated* sold in considerable numbers, these sales outstripping almost every other publication, although a 'naughty' French magazine, *Paris-Hollywood*, available only under the counter, was also sold in large numbers, mainly to lusty cleaners, apprentice fitters from the Works and others that might come under the category of the 'dirty mac' brigade.

One abiding memory of the spotters stands out. In the summer of 1952, on, I think, the August Bank Holiday Saturday about 1pm, there were upwards of 200 youngsters gathered on the footbridge and many more at the ramps of Platforms 1 and 2 trying to get on the bridge, which was swaying with the unaccustomed weight of gathered humanity. On North Shed there was considerable activity, engines moving about the yard, others wending their way through the station to take up or coming off workings, a constant flow of train crews making their way between the station and the shed. Such was the congestion on the footbridge at these times that most crews disregarded the safety order and crossed over the tracks to get to the station rather than squeeze their way through the crowd. On this occasion, for some unknown reason, there seemed to be an unusual buzz of noise between the ranks of spotters, as if something was afoot. At the platform ramps, the Railway Police were doing their usual best to clear the bridge without success. All of a sudden, the massed ranks of loco spotters erupted, and with one unstoppable charge, ran down the ramp into the North Shed forecourt, down the tunnel and into the shed. There was no way that anyone could have predicted this invasion, but once inside the shed they came to a halt, as if uncertain what to do next. Reinforcements to authority appeared from every direction in an instant, and those who had joined the charge from the ramps and climbed the steps were halted before they made the top landing. The rebellion subsided and the massed ranks turned tail and made their way back to the footbridge under supervision. The footbridge was somehow cleared and access to all but authorised personnel was subsequently barred at the steps on the platform by large men, some in

police uniforms, others in rubber macs and bowler hats, who politely but firmly refused all pleadings. It must be said that even under such extreme circumstances, the youngsters were well behaved and polite. No one admitted knowing who had instigated such a spontaneous reaction, and as far as I am aware, it never happened again. Had the invasion *not* stopped in front of the Arrangements Board and carried on into the depths of the shed, the implications for a mishap or accident to a young trespasser would have been too horrific to contemplate.

There were inevitably one or two who infiltrated the spotters who were more intent on mischief than on observing, but they were usually warned off by the majority who saw their activities as a threat to their privileged position. Their activities were usually confined to such misdemeanours as filching Weekly Speed Restrictions, Special Traffic Notices or the occasional Working Timetables from the pockets of passing train crews, although quite often these would be given away upon request by the less conscientious crewman. Others resorted to the temptation of dropping missiles down the chimney if the loco was strategically placed, although a driver might deliberately place the loco with the chimney directly under the footbridge, which had the effect of smoking out those directly above, to thwart such practices. Other less attractive habits indulged in by some youngsters included the spate of distance and target spitting that was considered amusing by some, although frowned upon by others. One suffered the misfortune of misjudging his accuracy and his effort landed on the black jacket of a burly fireman from Walsall, who promptly collared the youth and having wiped the expectorant off his jacket with the lad's hair, gave him the benefits of a full bronchial 50-a-day smoker's lungs square in the forehead. The now slightly green-looking youth promptly emptied the contents of his stomach in to the four-foot, and was later seen desperately washing his hair in the commodious toilet hand basins, with a somewhat tearful expression on his face.

At one time there was an obsession to touch nameplates, harmless enough when a 'Scot', 'Patriot' or 'Jubilee' was involved and the nameplate could be reached from the platform, but drivers drew the line at attempts to touch the high nameplate of a 'Duchess'. The presence of oil on the foot-framing did not seem to deter some, and the blackened knees of the short-trousered members bore testimony that some had made the attempt. More usual was the plea to 'cab the loco', ie get on the footplate, and some drivers were content to allow this provided the 'hard hats' were not immediately obvious. Trouble was that once one youngster got on board, then a tidal wave followed and it became a matter of urgent necessity to get them all off before authority arrived. Most drivers refused the plea, politely but firmly. Approaches via the fireman were inevitably referred to the driver for permission, for the driver was in charge, and woe betide any fireman who usurped his master's authority.

Mention has been made of the 'hard-hatted' brigade, for the mark of authority on the station was not so much the uniformed station staff but those who sported the black bowler hat, and even more so the black rubberised overcoat. For many years such a figure gravitated between the north ends of Platforms 1 and 2, rubber mac and black bowler worn whatever the weather, with black waistcoat, dark trousers, flannel shirt, black tie and highly polished black shoes. In his pocket were visible the current Special Traffic Notices, Speed Restrictions and the Station Working Books. He was a thin, melancholic figure, about 6ft in height, who never smiled. He always appeared about 9pm and was visible until 1am or thereabouts — no one can be certain what time he came on or went off duty. He had a small official ERO 449 notebook and made the occasional entry in it with the regulation-issue indelible purple pencil, and acknowledged train crews if spoken to first. No one seemed to know his name, but he was always referred to as 'The North End Platform Inspector'. He was rarely away from his post and was a landmark figure for many years. Everyone assumed he was a member of staff and it came as a considerable shock to all and sundry to discover he was not a railwayman at all but worked for a local firm of undertakers! No one knew where he lived or anything about his private life whatsoever.

It must not be forgotten that Crewe was 'invaded' by the GWR and the Western Region, which ran a service from Wellington via Market Drayton under a running agreement from Nantwich. Passenger trains worked in to Nos 3 or 4 Bays at the south end of the station, but the main traffic handled by the Western men was freight, which worked out of Gresty Lane Yard. The passenger workings were handled by 0-6-0 pannier tanks, or the larger 2-6-2 engines off Wellington shed. The freight was handled by the usual variety of Western locomotives, such as 'Granges' or 'Halls', and the ubiquitous '43xx' class 2-6-0s. Occasionally, when a special through passenger working off the Western to points north arrived at the station, the Western locomotive went onto North Shed to turn and for loco duties before returning to Gresty Lane. Ordinarily, Western Region engines turned on the triangle at South Shed and never ventured up to the north end of the station. In pre-Grouping days, both the Cambrian and North Staffordshire companies' trains regularly worked in to the station, and certain practices hung over well in to the 1950s.

Traffic flow through the station fluctuated throughout the day. Sometimes it was heavier in the Up direction and at other times Down line traffic was busier.

Left:
Norton Bridge Looking South, June 1957
This is another Saturdays Only working that should have commenced from Crewe but was extended to start from Euston. W111 is shown in the Working Time Tables as the 4.25pm Crewe to Bangor but traffic demands were so heavy that several trains on this day were extended. Here rebuilt 'Patriot' No 45545 *Planet* hauls 14 coaches through Norton Bridge on the Down Fast line. *C. M. and J. M. Bentley Collection*

Right:
Shilton, August 1953
Shilton station closed in September 1957 but the signalbox remained open until October 1963. Here 'Jubilee' class loco No 45584 *North West Frontier* is working the 12.20pm Saturdays Only Blackpool Central to Euston (W396). This was a long-time member of Blackpool North shed. On the platform a small boy watches the train passing. Two people stand in the window of the station office that straddles the tracks, whilst the home signal arm is just visible over the building roof. *John P. Delaney*

Mondays

	12am	1am	2am	3am	4am	5am	6am	7am	8am	9am	10am	11am
Up	11	13	8	14	13	17	17	15	13	17	16	18
Down	13	9	17	10	15	18	12	20	13	20	17	18
Total	24	22	25	24	28	35	29	35	26	37	33	36

	12pm	1pm	2pm	3pm	4pm	5pm	6pm	7pm	8pm	9pm	10pm	11pm
Up	25	17	18	23	19	22	16	16	21	16	18	16
Down	8	14	13	22	19	19	18	20	15	18	23	17
Total	33	31	31	45	38	41	34	36	36	34	41	33

Tuesdays to Fridays (with some daily variations)

	12am	1am	2am	3am	4am	5am	6am	7am	8am	9am	10am	11am
Up	19	24	17	19	18	21	23	19	15	16	19	19
Down	18	16	23	16	18	21	17	25	17	20	14	24
Total	37	40	40	35	36	42	40	44	32	36	33	43

	12pm	1pm	2pm	3pm	4pm	5pm	6pm	7pm	8pm	9pm	10pm	11pm
Up	17	18	25	26	25	24	18	19	26	16	22	17
Down	13	24	13	22	21	22	19	23	16	17	28	20
Total	30	42	38	48	46	46	37	42	42	33	50	37

Saturdays

	12am	1am	2am	3am	4am	5am	6am	7am	8am	9am	10am	11am
Up	21	22	15	22	17	16	16	15	12	16	20	21
Down	17	15	18	19	16	14	11	15	19	18	22	22
Total	38	37	33	41	33	30	27	30	31	34	42	43

	12pm	1pm	2pm	3pm	4pm	5pm	6pm	7pm	8pm	9pm	10pm	11pm
Up	26	17	20	23	24	24	19	20	26	17	14	14
Down	17	22	18	26	27	22	18	19	12	17	18	13
Total	43	39	38	49	51	46	37	39	38	34	32	27

The above table shows the flow pattern in late June 1951 after the introduction of the summer schedules. It should be noted that arrivals and departures are calculated separately, although the train was a through working, pausing en route. Those trains that passed through the station without stopping are included in the departures section. Included in these figures are the freight trains, most of which used the avoiding lines around the station or under the North Junction. It should be remembered that a few freight trains paused in the station itself, usually at quiet periods when there was no likelihood of disruption to passenger traffic. It will be noted that Sunday traffic has been excluded, except for the late trains that passed through or called at Crewe early on Monday mornings. Likewise, late Saturday evening trains that reached Crewe on Sundays have been omitted.

Traffic fell in to three distinct patterns. Monday saw many freight trains and some passenger workings running at different times to the rest of the week. There were some additional Friday Only evening trains. Saturdays, particularly in the summer months, saw the exclusion of freight work except for unavoidable workings which, in many cases, were retimed to run through the junction in the less busy times. The traditional holiday period saw regular Saturday workings to the popular seaside resorts, in particular to Rhyl and Llandudno on the North Wales coast, and also to Blackpool. Outside the scope of this work, but having a direct bearing on traffic flow nevertheless, were the Saturday Only 'Holiday Camp' workings to Butlin's Camps, particularly to Penychain on the Cambrian Coast, via Chester, Llandudno Junction, Bangor and Afonwen.

Sifting through the mass of detail, perhaps it is worth confining observations to blocks of timings when the spotting fraternity would be out in force. Consequently what follows below covers only the most intensive periods on a summer Saturday, between 3pm and 5pm, disregarding the night-time period after 9pm which was even more intensive, particularly on weekdays.

Dealing with the Down direction first. Whilst it would not have been seen from the platform, the 12.18pm Class F freight from Bescot to Crewe pulled in to Basford Hall Sorting Sidings North, due 3pm. This was hauled by a Crewe South Class 5 (Turn 1032) and worked by Bescot men (Turn 185).

At the same time a Class K freight worked out of Basford Hall Sorting Sidings North to Middlewich, hauled by one of Crewe South Class 4F 0-6-0, and manned by 5B men Turn 1364.

About the same time, the 10.25am Swansea to Manchester Mayfield was due in Platform 2 North. (Reporting No 245.) This was the 2.10pm from Shrewsbury, and the working was double-headed as far as Crewe, where a Blackpool Class 5, with North Shed men (Turn 728) detached and went on shed. The train engine is unknown, but is believed to be from Shrewsbury as was its crew. The train worked forward at 3.9pm.

At 3.4pm the 11.58am Euston to Workington drew in to Platform 1. This was a Camden locomotive turn which worked on to Preston. The Camden men (Turn 245) were relieved on the platform by Preston Turn 203. Departure was at 3.12pm.

At 3.5pm the 12.5pm Euston to Liverpool Lime Street pulled in to Platform 2 South. This was a Bletchley engine and men's working but details are unknown. Departure was at 3.10pm.

At 3.7pm the 1.30pm Birmingham to Blackpool North (Reporting No 335) passed through the station in Platform 1 through line, worked by a Blackpool engine and men.

At 3.16pm the 1.30pm from Derby pulled in to No 5 Bay Platform. This was booked to a Class 4P 4-4-0 Compound, Turn 99.

Also at 3.16pm the 1.45pm Birmingham to Manchester London Road drew in to Platform 2, hauled by Edge Hill loco Turn 15. North Shed men (Turn 556) were relieved by Turn 610 for onward working, which departed at 3.20pm. This was followed almost immediately by the 1.55pm Birmingham to Crewe working, due Platform 2 at 3.22pm. Engine details are not known, but the crew were Stafford men. Locomotive and stock then formed the 3.35pm to Liverpool Lime Street. The train crew changed and Warrington men worked forward.

At 3.35pm the Calveley Milk departed behind North Shed Class 2P 4-4-0 Turn 55 and men, Turn 909.

The 11am Aberystwyth to Manchester London Road pulled in to Platform 1 North at 3.36pm behind a Longsight Class 5 with Shrewsbury men at the controls. This departed at 3.45pm. Meanwhile at 3.42pm the Paignton to Manchester Victoria (Reporting Number 379) overtook it on No 1 Through road without stopping. This was worked by a Shrewsbury engine and men.

An empty stock working from Stoke to Crewe ran through No 2 avoiding road at 3.38pm. The unspecified Stafford engine was worked by Uttoxeter men.

At 3.45pm a Class D freight departed Gresty Lane at 3.45pm bound for Neville Hill, behind South Shed Class 5 Turn 1034 and men, Turn 1341. Another Class J freight departed from Sorting Sidings North at 3.48pm bound for Birkenhead. Abergavenny Turn 42 provided the power, with Crewe South men Turn 1467.

The 9.25am Bournemouth to Liverpool Lime Street ran in to Platform 2 North at 3.47pm. Camden Turn 233 provided the power from New

Above:
Rugby, No 5 Signalbox, 2 September 1950
Unrebuilt 'Patriot' No 45504 *Royal Signals* pulls away from Rugby with a special working. This was a Crewe North 5A shed engine with Crewe North men at the controls. The train was a relief from Euston to Llandudno and was booked to pass Crewe at 2.33pm. This job was covered by men who were working as a control set, ie not attached to any specific link. The gantry outside No 5 box is an LNWR lower quadrant pattern. *H. Weston*

Street, with Edge Hill men working Turn 233 departed for Liverpool at 3.53pm.

The 10.55am Class D freight from Camden to Basford Hall ran in to the North group of sidings at 3.51pm behind Willesden Turn 590 and men Turn 66.

At 4pm a Class A passenger to Manchester London Road departed from Platform 2 South. Stockport provided the power, and possibly the train crew. A Western Region local passenger working from Wellington ran in to No 2 Bay on the hour and 2min later the 3.30pm empty stock from Pratt's Sidings clanked through No 2 Through road behind a Holyhead 'Scot' with North Shed Turn 640 in charge.

At 4.4pm the 12.5pm from Euston arrived at Platform 1 South hauled by a Crewe North 'Scot' Turn 22 and Camden men on Turn 213.

Three minutes later the 1.5pm from Euston to Glasgow Central, Reporting No 143, arrived at Platform 2 at 4.7pm. Carlisle Upperby provided the men and power and the train continued at 4.14pm. As soon as the platform road was clear, its place was taken by the 1.15pm Euston to Glasgow at 4.17pm. A Camden Pacific was the power for the entire journey, but Crewe North men on Turn 330 were replaced by Polmadie men working Turn 17.

Meanwhile at 4.12pm the 8.55am Paignton to Manchester London Road ran in to Platform 1. It is unknown whether Shrewsbury or Longsight provided power and traincrew. The train moved forward at 4.20pm.

The 4.25pm for Bangor (Reporting No 111) departed from No 7 Bay behind North Shed Turn 41 with Llandudno Junction men on Turn 161 in charge. At the same time the 4pm ECS from Stoke passed through on No 2 avoiding line. Stoke provided power and men.

The 11.15am Swansea High Street to Manchester London Road pulled in to Platform 1 at 4.26. This was hauled from Shrewsbury by North Shed Turn 1, a 'Duchess' Pacific that would work the 11.12pm to Perth on the same evening. No 6 Link North Shed men took the engine onto North shed on arrival, and were replaced by a Rugby Class 5 4-6-0 with North Shed men on Turn 612 in charge.

A Class D freight departed from Basford Hall at 4.30pm bound for Carlisle Kingmoor Yard. South Shed Class 5 Turn 1030 was the power, with Upperby men on Turn 103 in charge.

The 4.32pm local to Northwich departed from No 9 Bay. This was a North Shed engine and men, using an Ivatt Class 2MT 2-6-2T for the push-pull service.

At 4.33pm a Crewe to Blackpool Central working departed from Platform 2 North, behind a Blackpool Class 5 and men. At the south end of the platform, the 1.30pm from Euston to Blackpool arrived left at the same time, behind Camden Turn 12 loco, which worked through to destination. Blackpool North provided the train crew throughout on Turn 68, which departed at 4.35pm.

Meanwhile at the same time a Class H freight departed Basford Hall North bound for Warrington. A Crewe South Class 5 and men were in charge.

At 4.36pm the 10.5am from Exeter to Manchester London Road was scheduled to call at Platform 1. Again, details of the power and men are unknown, but are believed to be from Shrewsbury shed.

Another freight passed behind the platform roads at 4.43pm on its way from Nuneaton to Hooton. Power was provided by South Shed. The Nuneaton men were replaced by Chester LM Turn 270 in Basford Hall.

A local stopping train departed from No 8 Bay at 4.47pm bound for Manchester London Road. It is believed that this was a Longsight turn.

At 4.50pm the 8.45am from Plymouth to Liverpool Lime Street pulled in to Platform 2 North. A Bushbury Class 5 was the power, Turn 151, and the loco worked through to destination. North Shed men on Turn 596 replaced Shrewsbury Turn 76 on the platform, which departed at 5pm.

At 4.59pm the 10.45am Class C Parcels from Euston moved up No 1 Through road hauled by an Edge Hill Class 5 with North Shed men on Turn 325 in charge. The loco was detached from the stock and went on North Shed for disposal, whilst the stock was disposed of by one of the station shunt engines.

There were slightly fewer trains in the Up direction for the same period, possibly because holidaymakers took advantage of the Bank Holiday weekend and extended their stays to include the Monday.

The 9.30am from Glasgow Central to Birmingham New Street (Reporting No 98) pulled in to Platform 4 at 2.55pm. This was worked by a North Shed Pacific (Turn 4), manned by Polmadie men. Engine and men detached and went on North Shed, replaced by a North Shed 'Royal Scot' class 4-6-0 on Turn 10, and men, Turn 550. Departure was at 3.15pm.

At 3.1pm the 1.25pm Class J freight from Heaton Norris ran under North Junction and terminated at Basford Hall Middle. A Crewe South 2-8-0 on Turn 1001 was worked by Stockport men, Turn 279.

The 10am Glasgow Central to Euston passed through the station at 3.8pm hauled by Polmadie Pacific Turn 1. Upperby men, Turn 60, worked it through to Euston.

Another Class H freight, the 1pm from Edge Hill to Basford Hall Middle, negotiated the independent lines, due 3.13pm. No details of engine or train crew are known, but it is likely that these were provided by Edge Hill or Warrington.

The Western Region local to Wellington pulled out of No 3 Bay at 3.15pm. As usual, Wellington shed provided the power but Crewe Western shed supplied the train crew, on Turn 2.

At 3.20pm the 10.12am Edinburgh to Birmingham New Street pulled in to Platform 5. Another loco and crew change took place, and a North Shed Class 6, Turn 19, driven by Upperby men, Turn 124, was replaced by an Aston locomotive and men (Turn 157). Departure south was at 3.28pm.

The 1.5pm Llandudno to Euston (Reporting No 270) drew in to Platform 3 at 3.21pm behind a Longsight Turn 12 engine. North Shed Turn 680 were replaced by compatriots on Turn 310.

A Class B local passenger for Shrewsbury pulled out of No 4 Bay at 3.28pm. Rugby loco Turn 9 was worked by North Shed men, Turn 727.

Another Class K freight from Heaton Norris, the 8.26am, used the avoiding lines to arrive at Basford Hall Middle at 3.30pm behind South Shed ex-LNWR 0-8-0 on Turn 1020 with Turn 1333 at the helm.

Another Class A off the North Wales coast, Reporting No 116, ran in to Platform 6 at 3.32pm. This was the 1.20pm Llandudno to Derby, which worked forward at 3.40pm. Locomotive and crew details are not known. It may have been a Derby engine, with Alsager, Stoke or

Left:
Leighton Buzzard, July 1960
'Princess Coronation' class Pacific No 46243 *City of Lancaster* from Crewe North 5A shed storms through Leighton Buzzard with a Down working. The train comprises a mixed bag of stock with what appears to be Eastern Region stock after the first coach. The chimney exhaust is light grey which shows the fireman has just put a round into the box. The man himself can be seen sitting on his seat, seemingly oblivious that the exhaust injector is blowing back! *John C. Baker*

Left:
Euston, 16 August 1958
The reporting number W74 indicates that this train is the 8.30am SO Carlisle to Euston. Upperby shed Pacific No 46243 *City of Lancaster* stands at the buffers at Euston at the completion of the journey. The booked arrival time was 4.15pm. Alongside is another arrival, the reporting number W56 indicating that this was the 9.5am from Llandudno. The latter was worked by North Shed men, the former was the responsibility of a Carlisle train crew. *Michael J. Axcell*

Right:
Birmingham New Street, 4 April 1953
'Royal Scot' class 4-6-0 No 46143 *The South Staffordshire Regiment* stands at New Street awaiting departure with the 11.15am to Glasgow Central. This was a Longsight 9A shed engine and would be detached at Crewe, its place for the trip north taken by a Polmadie Pacific. The loco looks in ex-works condition. Behind is an ex-LNWR 0-6-2T on station pilot duties. Crewe North men were at the controls.
J. R. Anstey

Uttoxeter men working through but it was definitely not Llandudno Junction, Chester or Crewe men in charge.

The 10.6am Glasgow Central to Euston also pulled in to Platform 4 at 3.32pm. Camden Pacific Turn 4 worked through but North Shed men, Turn 182, were relieved by Camden men, Turn 236 who departed at 3.49pm.

A Class J freight departed off North Staffs Sidings bound for Alsager Junction. Alsager provided the power and men.

This was followed by the 1.55pm from Blackpool North to Stoke, Reporting No 388, which pulled in to Platform 5 behind a Rugby Class 5. The loco worked through, North Shed men Turn 241 being relieved on the platform by Turn 641. Departure was at 3.48pm.

Yet another working on the North Staffs line followed. This was the 1.40pm Llandudno to Derby, which drew in to Platform 6 at 3.51pm and stood for 11min. Inward power and crew are unknown but were possibly supplied by Chester. A North Shed Class 5, Turn 43, and men, Turn 635, took over for the outward leg.

There followed the 3.5pm from Manchester London Road to Birmingham New Street, which pulled in to Platform 5 at 3.54pm. Rugby loco Turn 4 worked through, North Shed Turn 607 were relieved by compatriots on Turn 908 and departure was at 4.7pm.

At 3.55pm a Class H freight left Gresty Lane sidings for Oxley. The locomotive was not known but the train crew were Oxley men on a return working.

The 3pm from Liverpool Lime Street to Cardiff (Reporting No 234) drew in to Platform 3 at 3.55pm and stood for 14min before working forward. Engine and crew are unknown, but were from either Edge Hill or Shrewsbury.

The 2.50pm from Rhyl to Birmingham New Street ran through the station to Sorting Sidings South, behind Aston loco Turn 8. North Shed Turn 682 were relieved by the same shed Turn 514.

A path was available at 4pm for a Class J working to Madeley (Reporting No 39) from Middle Sidings, but this was shown as 'suspended'. No engine or men were specified and it is possible that on the occasions on which this train ran, a control set was used.

The 8.55am Perth to Euston was booked to Platform 4 at 4.6pm behind Camden Turn 1 which had taken over the train at Carlisle. Upperby men Turn 122 were relieved by Willesden men Turn 65 for the remainder of this duty which departed Crewe at 4.15pm.

Next came the 3.15pm from Manchester London Road to Plymouth, due Platform 5 at 4.10pm and hauled by a Longsight Class 6, Turn 7, with Longsight men Turn 314 in charge. They were relieved by North Shed men Turn 706 who worked the train as far as Shrewsbury. Departure was at 4.20pm.

Platform 4 next saw the arrival of the 1.55pm Holyhead to Euston at 4.18pm behind Camden loco Turn 20. Holyhead men, Turn 82, were relieved by Willesden men Turn 72, who departed at 4.26pm.

The 4.20pm Crewe to Leek local passenger pulled out of No 6 Bay at 4.20pm behind Stoke Turn 34 for engine and men.

At 4.24pm (4.26pm actual), the 10.50am Workington to Euston (Reporting No 254) followed the Holyhead train in to Platform 4, behind a Preston loco which worked through, departing 10min later. It is not known who provided the train crew, but it is likely to have been Preston men.

Yet another working off the North Wales Coast passed through the Up Through road at 4.28pm. This was the 2.25pm from Llandudno to Birmingham New Street, hauled by Aston loco Turn 7. North Shed men Turn 684 were relieved at Basford Hall Middle where they handed over to Aston men Turn 158 for the remainder of the journey. At 4.30pm a Class G engine and brake (Reporting No 93) departed North Staffs Sidings for Radway Green. It was probably an Alsager engine and men, but details are not known for certain.

At 4.39pm a local passenger, the 3.20pm from Manchester Mayfield to Crewe, pulled in to Platform 6 behind Longsight loco Turn 420 and men Turn 252. One minute later, at 4.40pm, Class H through freight departed North Staffs Sidings bound for Stoke. Stoke probably provided the power and crew.

At 4.50pm the 2.30pm Holyhead to Birmingham New Street drew in to Platform 3 and departed 8min later. It is not certain who provided power and train crew, possibly Aston or Stafford. At 4.51pm the 1.30pm Barrow-in-Furness to Crewe (Reporting No 266) terminated at Platform 5. This was North Shed loco Turn 11 (a 'Jubilee') and Turn 207 train crew.

At 4.56pm the 4.10pm from Liverpool Lime Street to Euston arrived at Platform 4, due 4.56pm and timed to depart at 5.8pm. Edge Hill provided the power and men who worked through to destination.

As well as the regular scheduled trains, there was considerable additional traffic in the form of extra excursion trains mainly to the popular seaside destinations. The weekly Special Traffic Notices throw some light on the extent of these workings, exemplified by a summary of the additional traffic for Saturday, 4 August abstracted from the *W1 Programme of Special Trains* issue No 31 (ERO 19101) as follows:

Down direction — Crewe to North

Rep No		Train	pass	arr	vehicle/load
W731	Relief	Coventry to Glasgow Central	-	12.10am	12/300 tons
W689	Relief	Glasgow Central	-	12.20	9/270 tons
W692	Relief	Euston to Glasgow Central	-	1.35	15/450 tons
W951	Relief	Crewe to Llandudno	-	1.53	7/210 tons
W698	Relief	Euston to Glasgow	3.5	-	9/280 tons
W660	Relief	Bristol to Manchester London Rd	-	3.30	8/240 tons
W691	Relief	Euston to Liverpool	-	3.53	8/270 tons
W693	Relief	Crewe to Manchester London Rd	-	4.00	7/255 tons
M977	Relief	Leicester to Blackpool North	-	4.03	not given
W639	Relief	Cardiff to Manchester London Rd	-	4.11	9/270 tons
M980	Relief	Leicester to Morecambe and Barrow	-	5.25	11/330 tons
M981	Relief	Leicester to Holyhead	-	5.48	11/330 tons
W575	Relief	Leek to Liverpool Lime St	6.20	-	10/300 tons
W563	Relief	Uttoxeter to Liverpool Lime St	6.28	-	10/300 tons
W587	Relief	Meir to Llandudno	6.35	-	11/330 tons
W583	Relief	Normacot to Blackpool North	6.47	-	11/330 tons
W577	Relief	Tunstall to Llandudno	7.00	-	11/330 tons
W711	Relief	Stafford to Blackpool Central	-	7.12	10/300 tons
W721	Relief	Birmingham to Llandudno	-	7.24	10/300 tons
W585	Relief	Stoke to Morecambe	7.34	-	10/300 tons
W565	Relief	Cheadle to Blackpool North	7.40	-	11/330 tons
W687	Relief	Stafford to Llandudno	-	7.45	10/300 tons
M985	Relief	Leicester to Llandudno	8.08	-	11/330 tons
W582	Relief	Creswell to Morecambe	-	8.11	10/300 tons
W592	Relief	Stoke to Bangor	8.20	-	12/360 tons
W810	Relief	Creswell to Llandudno	8.25	-	11/330 tons
W574	Relief	Longport to Blackpool Central	8.33	-	11/330 tons
W576	Relief	Stoke to Liverpool Lime St	-	8.43	10/300 tons
W727	Relief	Walsall to Blackpool Central	-	9.10	10/300 tons
W815	Relief	Stoke to Llandudno	9.12	-	11/330 tons
W816	Relief	Etruria to Llandudno	9.25	-	11/330 tons
M798	Relief	Leicester to Llandudno	-	9.47	11/330 tons
W351	Relief	Stoke to Blackpool North	9.50	-	11/330 tons
W569	Relief	Stoke to Penychain	9.58	-	10/300 tons
W695	Relief	Crewe to Manchester London Rd	-	10.38	8/240 tons
W811	Relief	Stoke to Llandudno	10.57	-	11/330 tons
W681	Special	Euston to Liverpool Riverside	11.55	-	8/240 tons
W570	Relief	Leek to Llandudno	12.6pm	-	11/330 tons
W729	Relief	Birmingham to Glasgow Central	-	12.24	10/300 tons
W615	Relief	Stoke to Blackpool Central	1.08	-	11/330 tons
W639	Special	Towyn to Sunderland	1.25	-	9+5 vans/370 tons
W701	Relief	Euston to Holyhead	-	2.20	10/330 tons
W667	Relief	Paignton to Rose Grove	3.33	-	10/300 tons
W683	Relief	Euston to Glasgow Central	-	4.15	10/300 tons
W668	Relief	Cardiff to Manchester Mayfield	-	4.26	9/270 tons
W640	Relief	Taunton to Manchester London Rd	-	4.44	10/300 tons
M975	Relief	Bournemouth to Rose Grove	-	8.37	10/300 tons
W723	Relief	Euston to Manchester London Rd	-	9.15	10/300 tons

48 extra trains

Right:
Carnforth, No Date
'Patriot' class 4-6-0 No 45500 *Patriot*, the first of the class and a rebuild from a 'Claughton', pulls away from Carnforth with the Up 'Lakes Express', the 11.10am Windermere to Euston, reporting number W86. This train also carried a portion from Workington that traversed the Cockermouth, Keswick & Penrith line and which combined with the Windermere portion at Carnforth. This loco was transferred to Carlisle in the week commencing 6 November 1954 and remained there until 26 July 1958 when it moved to Blackpool. This photograph was probably taken in the summer of 1955.
Eric Treacy

Up direction — North to Crewe

Rep No		Train		arr	pass	vehicle/load
W596	Relief	11.25pm	Manchester London Rd to Euston	-	12.17am	not given
S642	Emcar	11.40	Manchester Mayfield to Crewe	12.34	-	10/300 tons
S216	Emcar	12.1am	Edge Hill to Stoke	12.58	-	10/300 tons
W603	Relief	12.20	Liverpool Lime St to Euston	1.24	-	10/300 tons
W542	Relief		Johnstone to Euston	2.18	-	10/300 tons
W706	Special	2.30	Crewe to Midland Division	2.30	-	8 vans/205 tons
W543	Relief		Glasgow Central to Euston	-	2.32	14/480 tons
W525	Special	12.10	Preston to Western Region	-	-	22/535 tons (Pigeons)
W544	Relief		Glasgow Central to Euston	4.28	-	12/360 tons
W632	Relief	3.45	Holyhead to Euston	6.09	-	10/300 tons
W600	Relief	8.10	Liverpool Lime St to Euston	-	9.07	10/300 tons
W642	Relief	8.45	Rhyl to Coventry via avoiding line	-	10.03	10/300 tons
W581	Emcar	10.30	Crewe to Stoke	-	-	6/180 tons
W663	Special		Towyn to Nottingham	10.49	-	10/300 tons Move 4N7
W514	Relief	9.25	Morecambe to Birmingham	11.28	-	10/300 tons
W513	Relief		Workington to Birmingham	12.16pm	-	10/300 tons
W636	Regular	8.10	Afonwen to Crewe extended to Nott'h'm, via av	-	12/22	11/330 tons
W650	Relief	10.22	Llandudno to Coventry	-	12.29	10/300 tons
W601	Relief	11.30	Liverpool Lime St to Birmingham	12.35	-	12/360 tons
W520	Regular	9.20	Windermere to Crewe extended to Euston	12.40	-	not given

Rep No		Train		arr	pass	vehicle/load
W523	Relief	11.00	Blackpool North to Birmingham via Coal Yd	-	1.10	11/330 tons
W519	Relief	11.20	Morecambe to Birmingham	1.19	-	10/300 tons
W521	Relief	10.40	Windermere to Birmingham	1.43	-	10/300 tons
W668	Relief	11.53	Llandudno Junction to Coventry via avoiding line	-	1.50	10/300 tons
W526	Relief	12.00pm	Blackpool Central to Coventry via Coal Yard	-	2.00	not given
W524	Relief	12.45	Blackpool North to Leamington via Coal Yard	-	2.33	11/330 tons
W648	Regular	12.30	Llandudno to Llan Jn extended to Nottingham	-	2.33	11/330 tons
W602	Relief	1.50	Liverpool Lime St to Euston	-	2.42	10/300 tons
W318	Regular	11.25	Penychain to Warrington diverted to Coventry	3.11	-	not given
W669	Relief	1.00	Llandudno to Birmingham	3.38	-	10/300 tons
W529	Relief	2.10	Blackpool Central to Walsall	4.00	-	11/330 tons
W234.2	Relief	3.05	Liverpool Lime St to Birmingham	4.11	-	11/330 tons 2nd portion
W528	Relief	2.45	Blackpool Central to Coventry	4.35	-	11/330 tons
W610	Relief	3.55	Liverpool Lime St to Euston	-	4.43	10/300 tons
W527	Relief	3.10	Blackpool North to Birmingham	5.02	-	not given
W548	Relief		Glasgow Central to Euston	5.28	-	12/360 tons
W530	Relief	3.56	Blackpool Central to Birmingham and Derby	5.48	-	10/300 tons
S703	Emcar		Llandudno to Stoke	6.07	-	20/600 tons
W644	Regular	4.15	Llandudno to Crewe extended to Birmingham	6.15	-	not given
W531	Relief	4.25	Blackpool Central to Birmingham	6.17	-	11/330 tons
W664	Relief	4.00	Holyhead to Euston	6.43	-	10/300 tons
W656	Relief	6.00	Holyhead to Euston	8.23	-	15/450 tons
S977	Emcar	7.40	Llandudno to Crewe	9.53	-	20/600 tons

43 extra trains

It will be seen that 22 Down and 14 Up direction trains bypassed Crewe, either through the station or via the avoiding lines. Some passenger workings off the Stafford lines were routed in to Basford Hall yard and those destined for Liverpool, Manchester and the West Coast main line sometimes used the 'Muck Hole' Independent lines which passed underneath North Junction. Workings to the Chester line passed behind No 1 Platform, whilst those from the North Wales coast and workings destined for the North Staffs lines passed through the station on the through lines. Frequently crew changes were necessary and for those workings timed at Basford Hall, relieving and relieved crews walked to and from South Shed. Trains off or for the North Staffs line changed crews at North Staffordshire Sidings and usually passed through the station without stopping.

These extra trains resulted in many regular trains being retimed, the revised timings being listed in the relevant programme. For space reasons these have not been included here.

This was the August Bank Holiday weekend, which possibly explains the slight imbalance between Down and Up extras on the Saturday. It is noticeable too that in the Down direction on this day there were no Adex, Halfex or Garex trains running through Crewe, although there were several excursions running off the Central Division to Blackpool. Possibly this was due to the extreme demands on power and stock, there being simply nothing available. Only two workings classified as Specials worked north. W681 was a 'boat train' to Liverpool Riverside to connect with RMS *Parthia*. The train make-up consisted of BTK, 2-TO, RK, 2-FO and BTK. The second Down Special, W639, was a

Left:
Low Gill, No Date
Polmadie Pacific No 46221 *Queen Mary* coasts through Low Gill station with the Up 'Mid-Day Scot' working. This was the 1.30pm Glasgow Central to Euston, reporting number W126. The Polmadie loco would come off at Crewe and be replaced by a North Shed Class 7P. Note the neat platforms with flower beds and white-painted posts. In the background is the signalbox. Probably this photograph dates from 1959, for Low Gill station closed to all traffic on 7 March 1960. *Eric Treacy*

Below left:
Near Dillicar, 5 June 1952
Against the backdrop of Fell Head, BR Standard Class 6MT 4-6-2 No 72001 *Clan Cameron* forges towards the water troughs with the 2pm Manchester Victoria and 2.15pm Liverpool Exchange to Glasgow Central working, the two portions combining at Preston. The Polmadie-based locomotive would have worked through from Manchester and the work was shared between Polmadie and Newton Heath men. *E. D. Bruton*

Military Movement (Move 4M1) conveying 14 officers, 406 other ranks and 30 tons of baggage in nine corridor coaches and five vans. Military specials were commonplace, and the same day saw another departure from Towyn (Move 4W5) to Montrose and Aberdeen and a Cadet special from Dereham to Penrith, although both avoided Crewe. All the other trains in the Down direction were 'Relief' to regular workings, and in 1951 I cannot remember ever seeing any Relief trains running empty. Every train on a summer Saturday was packed; every platform seemed to be choked with humanity from early morning until late evening. In the Up direction on the Saturday in question, the extra trains consisted of several regular workings that were extended to distant points. W706, the 2.30am from Crewe to the Midland Division (destination unspecified), was a Pigeon Special, as was W525 from Preston to the Western Region and both trains were of considerable weight. The other Special was yet another Military Movement from Towyn (4N7), which came off the Western Region at Chester, bound for Nottingham.

On the following Bank Holiday Monday there were 28 additional train movements in the Down direction and 41 heading south through the station. Included amongst these workings were several Excursion trains to and from popular destinations.

Although many Class A trains worked through, a substantial number commenced or terminated at Crewe, and with platform space at a premium, it was essential that stock was moved out as quickly as possible. Most carriage stock was stored south of the station and movements were in the hands of Class 3F 0-6-0T engines. The locomotives were strategically placed and their allotted duties were covered in the local trip working notices. They were triple-manned and visited the sheds daily at quiet periods of time. Despite their relatively small size, these were powerful locomotives capable of moving very heavy loads, which they frequently did. Sometimes, due to unforeseen circumstances, it became necessary to act with great haste, requiring expertise on the part of the enginemen. As previously stated, the shunting

Right:
Shap, 19 May 1949
Stanier 'Princess Coronation' Pacific No 46227 *Duchess of Devonshire*, in lined-out black livery with the wording 'BRITISH RAILWAYS' on the tender, climbs Shap with the Down 'Royal Scot', the 10am Euston to Glasgow Central. The second to 12th coaches appear to be a set painted in one of the experimental liveries. The locomotive carries the old LMS shedcode for Polmadie — 27A. The remains of a platelayer's hut can be seen in the foreground, minus roof. *Eric Treacy*

Centre right:
Penrith, 5 June 1950
Class 5 4-6-0 No 45139 of Carlisle Upperby 12B shed working a Class H through freight trundles through the station with an Up working. This was possibly the 10.10am Carlisle Viaduct Yard to Winwick Quay. The first booked stop was at Carnforth, for examination and change of train crew. Fowler Class 4F No 44121 with tender cab waits outside the Penrith No 1 Signalbox. This engine was also attached to Upperby shed. The Upperby shed code changed from 12B to 12A on 19 June 1950, when Carlisle Canal shed became 12B. *E. D. Bruton*

Below right:
Carlisle Citadel, No Date
A fine display of power lined up at the south end of the station. Class 5 No 45227 from Bank Hall 27A shed stands alongside No 46130 *The West Yorkshire Regiment* from Crewe North. Fellow stablemate No 46150 *The Life Guardsman* stands at the head of the 'Mid-Day Scot', reporting number W126, which puts the time of the photograph at about 3.40pm. A couple of spotters adorn the station platform watching the proceedings. *A. Leather*

driving duties were mainly the preserve of senior enginemen who had opted out of main line work for one reason or another; equally it was the training ground for the newly qualified passed fireman or registered but unplaced driver on the block who was marked up to cover. Passed firemen awaiting their move up the promotional ladder and the next mark-up when they might reasonably expect to become registered were allocated to the shunting jobs as firemen, convenient for the shed foremen who might need a driver in a hurry. At the other end of the scale a recently qualified passed cleaner could, like as not, serve some time on the shunting jobs. At one time or another, everyone served on the station shunters and, although it was not as glamorous as main line work, learned their craft on these jobs.

So it was with 'Piccolo' Pete Johnson. On one occasion he was on the Down side Carriage Shunt, and was required to deal with two trains in quick succession, moving them from the Up side to the Down sidings across South Junction. The foreman shunter pointed out that unfortunately the earlier working was running late, and there was very little time to move one set and return for the second unless the two sets could be dealt with in one move. The challenge was irresistible, and some side bets were placed on Pete's ability to complete the move successfully or block South Junction completely and cause chaos, which in turn would demand scalps. The combined load totalled 25 vehicles (about 700 tons), and word of the attempt got around the complex instantaneously, more money being pledged. The only condition Pete demanded was a clear run with the massive load which the signalmen in South Junction box guaranteed. In the intervening 10min available, Pete ensured that his fireman had the fire white hot in readiness and after setting the first load back onto the second train, awaited the peg. Now a 'Jinty' in full forward gear and regulator was something to be heard let alone seen, and progress from a standing start even for this massive train was quite spectacular. Needless to say, the task was performed satisfactorily, money changed hands and the station reverted to its normal casual business, and although one or two discreet questions were asked, there were no 'official' enquiries.

Empty stock movements of up to 20 vehicles were not uncommon, but usually these were the province of the regular workings such as the Horse & Carriage from Holyhead to Crewe and not of local trip workings.

Less spectacular, but equally demanding, were some of the freight turns at South Shed, where loads of several hundred tons were routinely conveyed.

Royal Mail traffic was quite considerable, concentrating as it did in the small hours where trains were timed to connect and exchange in the minimum time. In the 3 hours from 10pm to 1am, over 100 trains passed through Crewe, many workings conveying mainly mail traffic with provision for the odd passenger. The co-operation required between station and Royal Mail staff was absolute and the amount of bagged traffic exchanged bears witness to the efficiency of the operation. In addition, it must be remembered that the railway also conveyed considerable quantities of newspaper traffic, which was loaded into designated dedicated vehicles. Parcels were loaded into specific areas within each van, the station being ready at prearranged positions to off load and transfer bundles of the still-warm papers, their wet ink rubbing off on to uniforms, which accounted for some porters' uniforms looking in less than pristine condition. In both mail and newspaper traffic, there was the need to shunt vans. These were placed in a set order, so that a shunting locomotive might follow them up the platform and immediately couple up and draw off the stock or attach to the rear of another working. Newspaper traffic was constant all the year round but mail peaked at Christmas time. The 10 days up to Christmas Day saw extra trains running to cope with the demands of the Post Office, and of course all connections had to be maintained irrespective of the increased demand. Whilst the postmen got credit for delivering the mail on time, it would have been impossible without an equal effort by railwaymen of all grades, none more so than at Crewe.

Carlisle Citadel, No Date
Under the roof of Citadel station, Stanier Pacific No 46240 *City of Coventry* stands at the head of the 9am Perth to Euston, reporting number W110. Meanwhile, 'Jubilee' class 4-6-0 No 45642 *Boscawen* stands at the head of another Class A working, ready for departure. This engine was attached to Manchester Newton Heath 26A Shed. It is not clear what its train working was. On the extreme right of the picture, ex-LNER stock stands in the Newcastle bay platform.
Eric Treacy

Motive Power

Passenger and freight motive power provision was concentrated at North and South Sheds respectively. Overall locomotive and train crew provision outside the designed schedules came under the watchful eye of Crewe Traffic Control, who were able to abstract drivers and firemen from the Control sets to cover the day-to-day requirements. The former Great Western shed at Gresty Lane was brought into this equation upon Nationalisation in 1948, and it has been recorded that 'spare' Western Region men from Gresty Lane would be required to work on North or South shed diagrams at the discretion of the Controller. On the London Midland Region proper, although the sheds had separate entities, seniority and promotion for train crew encompassed both sheds. The Western Shed nevertheless remained under Western Region control and was a sub-shed to Wellington.

Passenger work was regarded as technically superior to freight work, mainly on account of the need to adhere precisely to the running times. Firemen and drivers were required to work through the links and frequently a driver who might have 30 years of railway service had still not gained a place in the top passenger links. However, other factors were involved. A man with the same length of service under his belt might forgo seniority in the prestige links working to Perth, Glasgow, Carlisle and Euston (which consisted mostly of night work and lodging turns) for a more mundane but less stressful life in the lower links. The single-manned diesel shunting links working in Basford Hall Sorting Sidings were especially popular amongst the elderly drivers who might have medical reasons for forgoing life on the main line.

A driver based at Crewe from the mid-1920s until the end of steam would have the widest route card of all men working on Britain's railways and, until the practice of lodging turns was abolished, shared the record for working the longest regular single journey with Camden and Carlisle Upperby men over a distance of 299 miles. Crewe men worked to Perth — and most of the North Shed turns were overnight turns. It is perhaps significant that Perth drivers declined to share these workings when they were introduced. Polmadie drivers held no such inhibitions and worked to Crewe, Liverpool, Manchester and Leeds on turn and turn about work. It was not every driver's ultimate ambition, or, in some cases, within their capabilities, to work on such demanding schedules. Consequently the duties that constituted the Perth and Glasgow links were regarded by both the Drivers' LDC and Management as voluntary and a man could forgo his place in those links without penalty. Nor must it be forgotten that the driver was only one member of the team, and his fireman must be equally up to the task of firing intelligently for sustained periods. The fireman was probably both physically at his fittest, and psychologically at his peak performance level. Examination of the schedules within this book will reveal the intensity of the work expected of train crews.

Crewe in its heyday employed several hundred drivers and a similar number of firemen, with many passed cleaners who were available on call for firing duties. Men would report for duty at all hours of the day and night, working in conditions which, 30 years on, might seem glamorous, but in reality were harsh, difficult and often dangerous. A newly registered passed fireman was usually inducted to the driving procedure on preparation turns. In time-honoured fashion and according to Crewe practice, the fireman was expected to 'go beneath', but this was not usually the practice elsewhere. The delights of oiling the inside motion of 'Princess Royal' No 46201 *Princess Elizabeth* on a freezing winter night by the light of a flickering oil lamp, groping for that elusive little end cork whilst melting snow trickled down the boiler and dripped on to one's neck, tend to make one view the present preservation scene with some cynicism.

Nor must the part played by the maintenance staff in the sheds be forgotten. For every set of train crew there were the men who maintained the locomotives, ranging from examining fitter to shed labourer. Life for the artisan staff at Crewe has been dealt with by Alan Baker in his excellent work *Crewe Sheds*, and it would be pointless to try to emulate what he has so graphically described. Likewise, the office staff needed to know every detail about engines and men, and woe betide the list clerk who overlooked seniority when allocating work to a passed fireman, or, for that matter, assumed a passed man's route knowledge.

It will be appreciated that Crewe, being the hub of the Western Division of the LMS and London Midland Region, had a substantial number of locomotives of various classes based at the depot. The usual procedure was to have the engine rosters compiled with the motive power allocated according to the minimum number of engines required to cover each roster, with a reserve to cover additional workings for the district. Thus there might be 10 Class 8 locomotives allocated for eight diagrams, and an analysis of the total picture reveals the extent of the working. It is worth comparing the daily locomotive requirements with the allocation lists, remembering that frequently Crewe was required to provide power for emergencies as well as the additional traffic that was always materialising. A study of the Special Traffic Notices will give some idea of the sort of additional traffic that was generated on a daily basis.

Perhaps the popular image of the life of a Crewe driver and his mate has receded somewhat since steam all but disappeared off the main line, for working conditions have changed beyond recognition at most depots that survive. Today, a Crewe driver works mostly alone, on an HST, a

Right:
Crewe North End
The two LMS-design main line diesel locomotives, Nos 10000 and 10001, draw into Crewe on a murky day hauling the Up 'Royal Scot'. These units were based at Camden and worked through to Glasgow Central, working turn and turn about with Class 8 Pacifics. Normally Camden men shared the work south of the border with Carlisle Upperby men. *Ben Brooksbank*

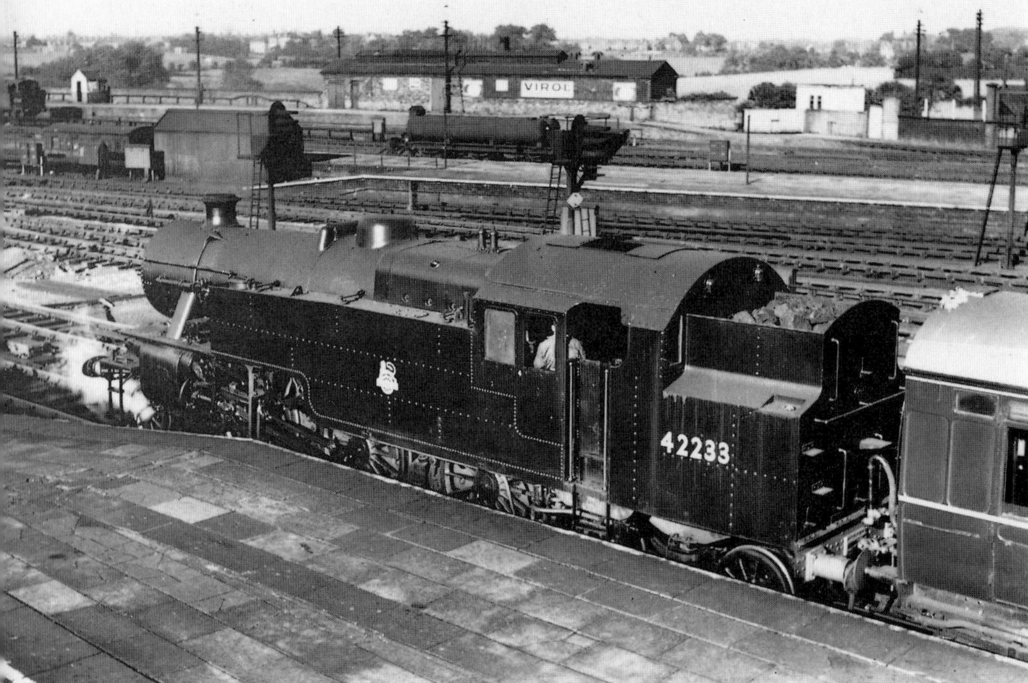

Left:
Crewe, Down Through Road
'Royal Scot' class 4-6-0 No 46140 *The King's Royal Rifle Corps* sets back on to the Horse Landing line, sporting Class C headlamps. The loco is in ex-works condition. Note the footbridge that spanned the station and connected all platforms with foot access to North Shed. This was the favourite location for spotters as they had an uninterrupted view across North Junction and tantalising glimpses of locos on shed. *R. Gee, E. M. Johnson Collection*

Centre left:
Crewe, No 7 Bay, 10 September 1950
Fairburn 2-6-4T No 42233 stands at the head of a Chester stopping train, paintwork gleaming after receiving an Intermediate overhaul in Crewe Works. Note that the engine has been returned to traffic with the minimum of ornamentation. Probably this was the 4.25pm Chester which was diagrammed to this type of engine. On arrival Crewe men were relieved by Chester men, Turn 270, who took the train on to Bangor. They then worked back light engine to Chester where the crew were relieved and the engine turned. After servicing, the engine shunted at Chester from 3.30am until 6.20am. It then worked the 6.36am to Crewe with Whitchurch men who also worked a local to Shrewsbury at 8.37am, then worked the 10.30am to Wellington and return. Finally the loco and men returned to Crewe with the 12.5pm local and went on North Shed after shunting the stock. Having completed its running-in turn, this Stoke engine would be returned to its home shed in due course. *B. K. B. Green*

Below left:
Crewe, Down Through No 1 Line, Summer 1955
'Princess Royal' class 4-6-2 No 46212 *Duchess of Kent* of 5A shed sets back on the Down Through No 1 line with two extra coaches to add to the W239 Saturdays Only 7.30am Cheadle (Staffs) to Llandudno. To find a Pacific on the North Wales Coast was somewhat unusual but not unknown, and doubtless the strengthening of the train justified the Class 8 power. In such cases, locomotives were changed south of the station as this train was not booked to call and would use the Down Through No 1 road to access the Chester line. An unidentified 'Royal Scot' stands on the Horse Landing line. *Martin Welch*

Right:
Crewe Station, South End, 26 September 1953
Two Class 5 4-6-0s — No 44904 of Carnforth 11A Shed and an unidentified colleague — head through the station en route for South Shed. A third member of the class, No 44938, pollutes the atmosphere in Platform 4 Bay. *B. K. B. Green*

Class 90 electric, Classes 37 and 47 diesel locomotives or various 'Sprinter' units, Classes 153, 156 or 158, etc and much of the main line work has been lost. Crewe men no longer work north of Carlisle, their route knowledge is confined between Euston and Carlisle via Nuneaton and Birmingham, Crewe to Holyhead and Derby, and from Liverpool and Manchester to Cardiff. Indeed, at the time of writing, most of the daily work at Crewe is now centred around EWS freight traffic, although First North Western Trains has a presence and still 'buys in' drivers' services. There is very little extra occasional traffic.

So how was it in the 1950s? The object of this book is to outline the traffic and footplate work as it was in the years following Nationalisation, as a tribute to the thousands of men of Crewe and their families, and as a reference point for future historians who may have difficulty in understanding the importance of Crewe as a railway town.

The LMS method of specifying the time was for 12.1 to represent 1min past midnight, whereas 12/01 was one minute past midday.

For example: the 7.35pm Camden to Edge Hill Parcels was a Class C train, arriving at Crewe Basford Hall Sorting Sidings North at 11.26pm, and departing at 12.5am. It was worked by Edge Hill (8A) locomotive diagram 12 and Edge Hill men on Turn 766. It should also be noted that Camden departure was on Friday evening.

In some cases a locomotive was worked through to the train's destination but was remanned at Crewe, as in the above example. The change would have been shown in the Men diagram column. Frequently there was more than one engine on the diagram, which could cover two, three or more days' workings, but it was not the practice to show the differences on the Rostered Turns.

In some cases, the information is unknown, and where there is an element of doubt, these columns are left empty. In cases where the shed providing the motive power is known, but the engine diagram number is not, the details are shown as follows: 2A/-. In a few cases, the locomotives and men were off the Western Region shed at Wellington, of which Crewe (Gresty Lane) was sub to the sub-shed. These are shown as Crewe/—, although the diagrammed work was listed with Crewe South, as was the work at Whitchurch and Middlewich.

It was the practice on the London Midland & Scottish Railway, and subsequently in the London Midland and Scottish Regions of British Railways to arrange the schedules in the following order:

Passenger Engine Turns
Passenger Engine and Men's Turns
Passenger Enginemen's Turns
Freight Engine Turns
Freight Engine and Men's Turns
Freight Enginemen's Turns

The Engine Turns were cross-referenced with the Enginemen's Turns, irrespective of whether the enginemen were from the same depot as the locomotive or not. Where the men were from another depot, the coding for their shed would prefix their turn number. Usually gaps were provided between the various sectors to allow for changes or modifications to a duty. It must be stressed that the format used was different on the other regions.

Depending on the size and importance of the shed concerned, usually a low turn number would indicate an Engine Turn. In some cases, however, where the number of engines allocated was small, as in the case of Holyhead (7C), the number of diagrams involved would likewise be small.

In the case of Crewe, where passenger and freight work was allocated to North or South Shed, the Passenger Turns were listed from Turn 1 to Turn 999. South Shed Turns commenced from 1000 upwards. Grouped with the South Shed sheets were Crewe (Gresty Lane), Whitchurch, Middlewich and Crewe Works.

Footplate Work at Crewe

A feature at Crewe was the large number of Control Turns (often called 'the block'), ie sets of men with no booked work, but who, nevertheless, signed on at scheduled times and waited for a job to turn up — in current train crew parlance, 'spare'. During the period under scrutiny (July 1951) it was virtually unknown for a crew 'on the block' to escape without having some work, even if it only meant relieving a set of enginemen on

the station and taking their engine to the designated shed, or acting as caretaker on the engine until the scheduled crew turned up. It was the normal practice for both passed cleaners and passed firemen to spend up to two years 'on the block' until promotion caused by a retirement came, and a driver or fireman was allocated his place according to seniority in one of the links.

As with most sheds, the work was allocated to links of men which could vary in size from three to 20 sets of men. The Local Departmental Committee (LDC) negotiated with management as to what work went into the various links. The LDC also agreed with management whether promotion to a specific link was designated 'volunteer' work, as senior men might not wish to work the strenuous night turns in links two or three and opt to stop in a lower link, so forgoing the prestige of working to Glasgow or Perth. Equally, some firemen might decline to work in these links without penalty. Equally, the management might consider that some firemen were not capable of work in these links for a variety of reasons and decline to place them, despite seniority or the fireman's own preference.

After a passed cleaner had 'done his time' on the block, there followed a spell on South Shed in the shunting links. He would next spend several years at North Shed on passenger work, gaining experience on the variety of engines and routes, before graduating to South Shed for a spell in the freight links.

Having 'escaped' from the block, there followed an extended period of time at South Shed firing on shunting, trip and freight jobs, followed by a couple of seasons in the lower passenger links. Subject to ability, aptitude (and availability), a fireman could reasonably expect to be placed in No 4 or No 1 Link (mainly work to Carlisle and Euston), possibly a spell in No 2 (Perth) and No 3 (Glasgow) Links, before working back down the lower passenger links of the structure. The promotion progression was set down in local agreements between the LDC and the Management and is reproduced elsewhere.

It will be noted that the dates quoted below for the link work are not consistent, and whilst this is to be regretted, it is unavoidable. Details have been abstracted from the personal diaries of several men, and taken over a range of years.

An undated document — believed to be 1960 — details Crewe Link Progression as follows:

Below:
Crewe, Platform 2 North, 25 June 1949
'Princess Coronation' Pacific No 46225 *Duchess of Gloucester* in LMS livery of black lined with straw and maroon stands at the head of W97 'Mid-Day Scot' from Euston to Glasgow. This was a Saturday and members of the spotting fraternity are visible on the footbridge and platform end. Notice the smokebox front, cut down to accommodate the streamlined casing and the 'BRITISH RAILWAYS' lettering on the tender. The loco sports a Camden 1B shedplate, but in the week ending 1 October 1949 the engine was transferred to Crewe North. *R. W. Hinton, T. J. Webb Collection*

Bottom left:
Crewe, Down Through No 2 Line, No Date
'Princess Royal' class 4-6-2 No 46211 *Queen Maud* sets back on its way to North Shed, probably having been detached from an Up train from the north. In 1951 the distribution of the complete class was as follows: from week ending 30 September 1950 until week ending 23 June 1951 the allocation was Camden (1), Crewe North (7) and Edge Hill (5); then until week ending 7 July 1951 it was 2, 6, 5; until week ending 21 July 1951 it was 2, 7, 4; until week ending 15 June 1951 it was 1, 8, 4; on 16 September 1951 it was 1, 7, 3 and 2 at Polmadie; from week ending 22 September 1951 it was 1, 5, 5, 2; and from week ending 10 November 1951 it was 1, 6, 4, 2. Thus, Crewe had variously 7, 6, 7, 8, 7, 5, 6. Nominally the 'Turbomotive' (No 46202) was based at Camden but for all of this time the loco was out of service and in store in Crewe Works pending a decision on its future. *Martin Welch*

Right:
Crewe Station, No 3 Bay, 6 April 1952
Fairburn-designed Standard Class 4MT 2-6-4T No 42174 of Derby 17A shed stands at the head of a local working to Stoke and Derby. Notice that the loco is in the lined-out livery but with the wording 'BRITISH RAILWAYS' on the tank sides. Note too the style of numbering on the smokebox door. The station roof looks in need of immediate attention. *B. K. B. Green*

Appendix 'A'
(Minute 3553)
Crewe Link Progression — Drivers
P — Permanent, filled by application to advertisement
L — Light duty, filled by LDC

New Link Number	Depot	No of Sets	Remarks
1	North	12	
2	North	8	
3	North	6	
4	North	12	
5	North	12	
6	North	12	
7	North	12	
8	North	12	
P9 (a)	North	10	P12 Derby MU Diesels
P9 A	North	12	Derby EMU Diesels
P10 (b)	North	12	P13 Diesels EMU
P12	North	3	Northwich
P13	North	3	Station bank Up Side
14	South	12	
15	South	12	
P16	South	12	
17	South	12	
18	South	10	
18A	South	8	
P19	South	12	Yorkshire
P20	South	12	Whipsnade
P21	South	3	EMC & Triangle Shunt Ballast
22	North	84	Special
L23	South	1	Trial Engine
P24	South	36	Diesel Shunt
P24A	South	14	
25	South	24	South Shunt & Warehouse Trips
L26(c)	South	18	Diesel Shunt & Prep to be Diesel trained for coverage for 24 and 24A.
L26A	South	8	Shunt
P27	South	3	Coal Shunt & Warehouse Trips
L27A	South	1	Wagon Shop
L28	South	3	
L28A	South	2	Works Shunt turn only (eyesight)
P30	North	3	Station Shunt
P31	North	4	Station Shunt
P32	North	3	Coal Shunt & Rag Mail
P33	South	3	Setting Engines
P34	South	3	Shed Shunt
L35	South	2	Engine to Shop
P36	South	6	Ashpit Turners & ETE Shunts
P37	South	3	Tank Fillers
L38	North	3	Shed Shunt
P39	North	3	Ashpit Turners
L40	North	3	
L41	North	3	Setting Engines
L42	North	7	

Total: 459 drivers

Notes:
(a) Men rostered to steam work in these links may be utilised to cover diesel turns in the links in the event of there being no special link DMU-trained drivers available.
(b) Entry into No 10 link will be by application, but applicants must be prepared to undertake diesel and electric MU work, and accept the conditions laid down for entry into Permanent Links. The conditions applicable to applicants for vacancies in links below 22 Link will still apply so far as No 10 is concerned.
(c) not stated.

Appendix 'B'
(Minute 3553)
Crewe Link Progression — Firemen

New Link Number	Depot	No of Sets	Remarks
21	South	3	Ballast
20	South	12	Whipsnade
19	South	12	Yorkshire
18	South	10	
17	South	12	
16	South	12	
15	South	12	
14	South	12	
18A	South	8	
13	North	3	Station Bank Engine
12	North	3	Northwich
1	North	18	
2	North	12	
3	North	12	
4	North	12	
5	North	8	
6	North	6	
7	North	12	
8	North	12	
10A	North	12	
22	North	84	Special
23	South	1	Trial Engine
39	North	3	Ashpit Turner
35	South	4	Engines to Shops
38	North	3	Shed Shunt
34	South	3	Shed Shunt
36	South	3	Ashpit Turner
37	South	3	Tank Filler
40	North	3	Tank Filler
28	South	3	Preparation
28A	South	2	Works Preparation
27	South	3	Coal Shunt and Warehouse Trip
26	South	18	Diesel Shunt and Preparation & Shunt
26A	South	8	
25	South	24	Station Shunt, Warehouse Trips and Preparation
30 Rag	North	3	Station Shunt, Coal Shunt and Mail
31	North	4	
32	North	3	
42	North	9	CME Works
P27A	South	1	Wagon Shop

Total: 388 firemen

A final point. The working week was deemed to start on Monday at 12.1am, which is reflected in the layout of the tables.

Left:
Crewe Down Through No 1 Line, 7 May 1949
In the heady days following Nationalisation the various regions painted a selection of engines in different liveries and permutations of lining and lettering. Likewise, until a renumbering scheme had been finalised, for a short while engines emerging from the workshops were given the regional prefix, in the ex-LMS case, 'M'. One such engine so treated was LMS Standard Class 5 4-6-0 No M4763, seen here heading tender-first towards North Shed. The livery in this case was LNER green with orange and black lining. The wording 'BRITISH RAILWAYS' adorned the tender. All too soon the engines re-entered the works and reappeared in the final version of livery. *H. C. Casserley*

Centre left:
Crewe Station, South End, No Date
An Ivatt Class 2MT 2-6-2T No 41212 stands off No 3 Bay whilst running round stock in the platform. This engine was attached to Warrington shed 8B and the reason for its appearance at Crewe is unclear. *Martin Welch*

Below left:
Crewe Station. No 3 Bay Platform, 1 June 1954
The station provided connection facilities with the GWR which usually operated from Bays 3 or 4 at the south end of the station. Here 2-6-2T No 4158 of Wellington 84H shed stands at the head of a local working to Wellington. Most Western Region passenger trains running in to Crewe were worked by Gresty Lane men although Wellington men signed for the road and worked into the station.
D. Murdoch, N. E. Stead Collection

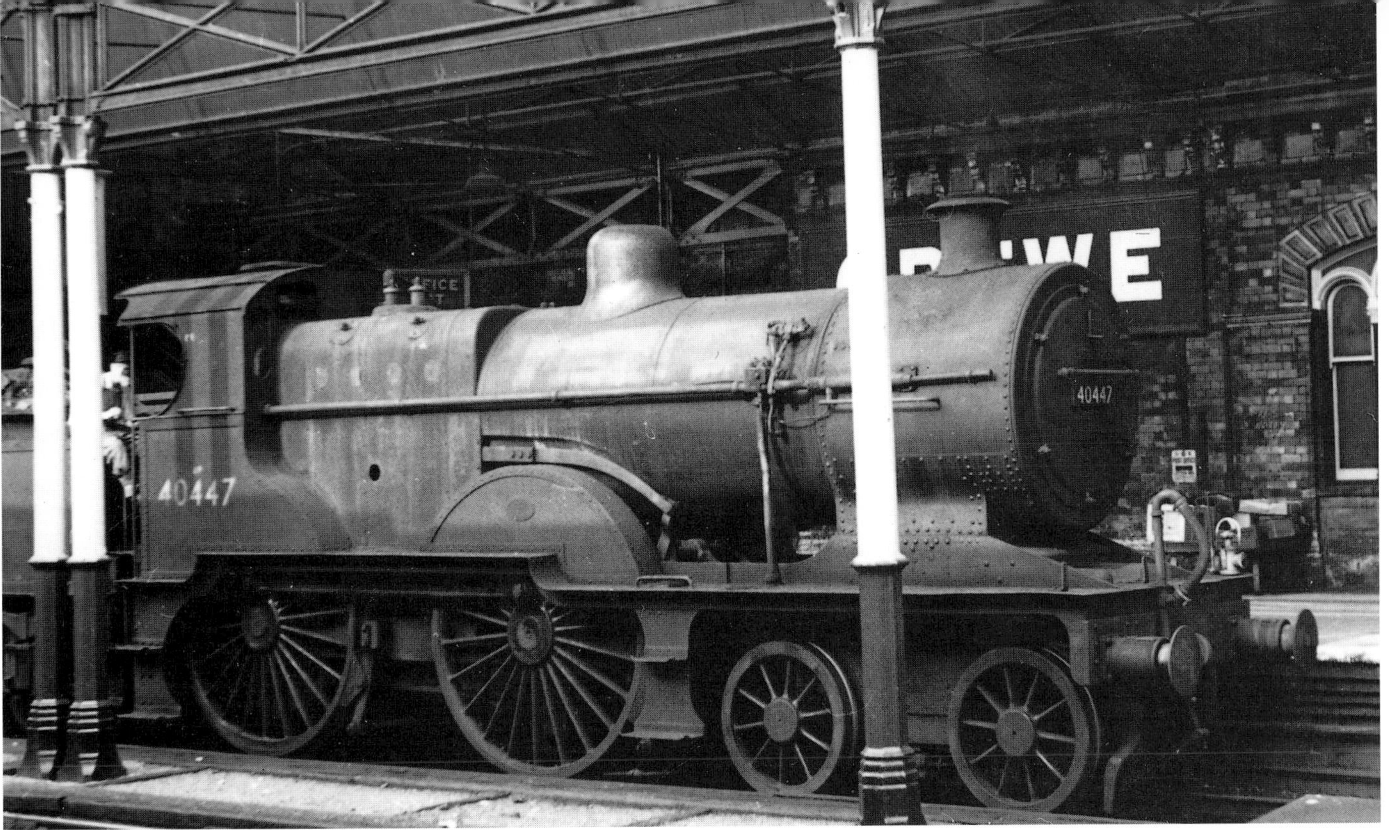

Above:
Crewe Station, 8 August 1953
This ex-Midland Railway Class 2P 4-4-0 No 40447 was received from Nuneaton in September 1952 and spent a lot of time outstationed at Whitchurch. It is not certain what work it was performing when this photograph was taken, for the engine is carrying Class K lamps, which signified a freight, mineral or ballast train or, alternatively, an officers' special train. Perhaps the District Engineer is pausing at Platform 5 to have his billycan topped up in the station buffet!
H. C. Casserley

Below:
Crewe Station, No 3 Platform, No Date
'Britannia' class Pacific No 70048, as yet unnamed, stands in No 3 platform with the Up 'Irish Mail', Holyhead to Euston. Five engines, Nos 70045-9, were allocated to Holyhead in June and July 1954 for the 'Irish Mail' workings, replacing 'Royal Scot' locomotives which were transferred away. Holyhead men preferred the 'Scots' and eventually the 'Britannias' were transferred to Crewe North on 2 November 1959. This engine remained unnamed until 1958 when it received the name *The Territorial Army 1908-1958*. The 'Day Mail' ran during the summer months only and on weekdays consisted of eight vehicles, 266 tons from Holyhead; four vehicles were attached at Llandudno and a further two vehicles at Chester giving a train of 14 vehicles, 452 tons. On Saturdays the load was slightly less. The reporting number was W48. Only 4min were booked for the stop at Crewe. The train ran nonstop to Watford, then Euston, due at 1.18pm.
Gordon Coltas

North Shed

North Shed

The only known complete set of Crewe diagrams for engines and men dates from 19 June 1951 and is in the possession of the author. Nevertheless it has been possible to draw on the personal diaries of several railway people, which give a broader insight into the way the duties changed over the years. It will be noted that some work moved between the links and appears twice! Turns 1 to 78 were Engine Turns. Nos 91 to 122 were designated 'Engines and Men's Turns'. Enginemen's Turns commenced with Turn 130.

Engine Turns

The number of North Shed engines booked daily was as follows:

Monday	Tuesday	Wednesday	Thursday	Friday	Saturday	Sunday
50	55	52	52	56	60	40

Turns 1 to 5 were for Class 8 Pacific locomotives, which required 11 engines to cover the booked work. There were eight turns for Class 7, 19 turns for Class 6, 19 turns for Class 5, three turns for Class 4 and four turns for Class 2 engines. It should be noted that whilst the majority of the turns worked every day, some did not. For example, Turn 78 was shown booked to a two-cylinder Class 4 2-6-4T engine which worked only on Sunday! Because engines were stopped for routine maintenance on a regular basis, there were additional engines allocated to cover for stoppages.

Engine and Enginemen's Turns

These consist of 17 men's turns working with five North Shed engines. Six men's turns worked to Derby, three to Manchester London Road, one to Liverpool Lime Street, three to Rhyl, one to Shrewsbury and Wellington and three on the Northwich motor train. As with the engine workings, some worked on only one day, others worked throughout the week. The three trips to Rhyl, in fact, worked the same train (4.25pm), with differences in timing or work — Turn 102 worked Mondays Only, Turn 104 worked Tuesdays to Thursdays and Turn 105 worked Fridays Only.

Enginemen's Workings

It should be noted that lodging turns had separate turn numbers for the outward and return working, which were not necessarily consecutive. The LM Region practice at this time was to put the outward workings first, followed by the return working turns, and where there were differences in the work, each variant might be given a different turn number. A variation for one day in the period of operation was given a different turn number, although the difference might only be a timing change at one point or modification to the route taken. Taking Turn 159 as an example, this consisted of working the 1.20pm Crewe to Carlisle on Tuesdays to Saturdays. The men lodged at Upperby. Turn 160 was the return working on Wednesday to Friday (4.28am Fish), and Turn 161 on Saturday, which was the 4.25am Fish!

The summer of 1951 shows a breakdown of the daily booked turns at North Shed as follows:

Monday	Tuesday	Wednesday	Thursday	Friday	Saturday	Sunday
142	134	131	133	146	170	62

The work was 'blocked' as follows:

Turns 130 to 135 and 145 to 146 worked to Perth and return. This work was exclusive to No 2 Link.
Turns 137 to 144 worked to Glasgow and return. This was exclusive to No 3 Link.
Turns 159 to 186 worked between Crewe and Carlisle.
Turns 200 to 245 worked between Crewe and Warrington, Preston, Morecambe, Blackpool and Windermere.
Turns 250 to 361 worked between Crewe and Euston.
Turns 382 to 395 worked to Stafford, Coventry or Rugby.
Turns 500 to 565 worked to Birmingham New Street.
Turns 576 to 599 worked between Crewe and Liverpool.
Turns 600 to 622 worked to Stockport, Manchester London Road or Mayfield.
Turns 623 to 641 worked to Stoke, Creswell or Derby.
Turns 650 to 699 worked to Chester, Llandudno or Holyhead.
Turns 701 to 732 worked to Shrewsbury or Hereford.

There is then a gap, the remainder of the work that followed consisting of Banking (Turns 900 to 905) or station shunting turns (Turns 907 to 974). There was a preparation turn (977) and Turn 999 designated as '6.35am Trials to Whitchurch'.

As mentioned elsewhere, the work was blocked to reflect the seniority of the men, with most of the West Coast main line work contained in Links 1 to 5. Links 2 and 3 were specialist volunteer links, and a driver could forgo promotion to these without forfeit. It will be noted that the Perth and Glasgow links consisted of an eight-week cycle, whereas Nos 1, 4 and 5 Links consisted of 12 sets of men. At one time the Glasgow link was expanded to 12 sets of men, but this did not find favour with the regular drivers and after only a few weeks it reverted to its eight-week structure. There was a period of stability between 1949 and 1960, when, apart from variations in certain train times and some realignment of work in No 1 Link, the duties remained pretty much the same throughout, even to the extent of keeping the same turn numbers.

It must be pointed out at this stage that with each amendment to traffic, which could occur several times during the validity of the overall timetable, changes to duties meant that work was moved between links. It will be seen that, for example, the 7.2pm Crewe to Euston on Thursdays moved from No 1 Link to No 2 Link with the introduction of the new schedules in June 1952. The change, however, took place on 16 June ahead of the commencement of the summer schedules on 30 June. Sadly, no reliable records have emerged to show what work replaced it.

No 1 Link

No 1 Link consisted of work to Euston and Carlisle, but from 1948 to 1952 most of the work was southbound. The advent of additional traffic working north presented an opportunity to restructure the West Coast diagramming and, as a result, the number of jobs to Carlisle increased, although there were still more jobs working south than north.

This link was regarded as the 'cream' of the North Shed work, although some may disagree. Some jobs were exclusive to North Shed, not always to No 1 Link, whilst other work was shared on a turn and turn about basis with other sheds.

No 2 Link

This was an eight-week link. It was probably the most arduous set of duties on the London Midland Region, consisting of work between Crewe and Perth, with a trip to Glasgow Central and Euston included to retain route knowledge. All the duties were lodging turns and night workings and, although prestigious, permanent night working did not appeal to everyone. Many a fireman was pressurised into relinquishing his place in the link by the demands of romance, although for some, the thought of firing 300 miles at one go with some of the hardest 'hitters' on North Shed also acted as a deterrent!

No 3 Link

This was also an eight-week link, although for a very brief while in 1952 it was extended to 12 weeks as an experiment which was unsuccessful. The duties in this link were almost as demanding as the Perth jobs, working between Crewe and Glasgow Central, with a couple of trips to Euston thrown in. Most work was night-time, all work involved lodging but there were some daylight hour duties included, namely the 4.19pm Glasgow on Mondays, Wednesdays and Fridays, and the 12.54pm on Sundays.

No 4 Link

Probably this link and No 5 were more subject to changes than any other, reflecting the shifting nature of the work covered. A 12-week link, it contained work to Euston and Carlisle, but consisted mostly of out and home duties to Liverpool, Preston and Rugby, with trips to Birmingham and Manchester to retain route knowledge.

No 5 Link

This work was similar to No 4 Link, with occasional lodging turn jobs to Euston and Carlisle, work to Morecambe and Rhyl, and more work to Birmingham. No 6 Link was similarly structured and generally the point of commencement for a now-experienced fireman coming off the block to be weaned onto the demands and rigours of passenger train work. Some of the turns in both 5 and 6 Links worked passenger one way and freight the other. At one time a fireman in No 5 Link would work 13 trips to Birmingham in succession, which certainly reinforced his route knowledge!

No 9 Link

At this time was the preserve of work to Derby, and firemen in this link were usually preparing to take their driving examination. When one got marked up into this link it was a signal to get out the rule book and start swotting up in earnest. One had three attempts at the test, but failure on the first attempt was considered ominous.

The remainder of North Shed work consisted of permutations of routes and times. Whilst not wishing to diminish the importance of the work done, from an outsider's point of view the work was more mundane and considerably less glamorous than life on the West Coast main line.

Below:
Crewe North Shed, No Date
A foreigner in the camp! Western Region 'Hall' class 4-6-0 No 4986 *Aston Hall* heads towards North Shed, probably to turn before taking up a return working. Behind are the North Shed offices and loco stores. Just visible is the white-painted arch over the 'tunnel' that led into the shed. *Ben Brooksbank*

Bottom:
Crewe Up Through Road, 23 June 1951
'Royal Scot' No 46101 *Royal Scots Grey* of Crewe North 5A shed coasts through the station with a Liverpool to Euston working. This was possibly the 2pm from Lime Street, which was booked to pass through Crewe at 2.45pm.
Tom Lewis — Manchester Locomotive Society

North Shed Allocations

15 July 1951

MR '2P' 4-4-0 Total: 4
40332
40402
40425
40527

LMS '2P' 4-4-0 Total: 2
40659
40660

LMS '4P' 4-4-0 Total: 2
40933
41076

Ivatt '2MT' 2-6-2T Total: 3
41229
41288
41289

Fowler '4P' 2-6-4T Total: 1
42318

Fairburn '4P' 2-6-4T Total: 1
42677

Stanier '5MT' 4-6-0 Total: 19
44678
44679
44680
44681
44682
44683
44684
44685
44758
44759
44761
44762
44764
44765
44766
44770
44771
45033
45434

'Patriot' '6P' 4-6-0 Total: 13
45502
45503
45504
45506
45507
45509
45510
45511
45513
45529
45543
45547
45548

'Jubilee' '6P' 4-6-0 Total: 11
45586
45587
45592
45634
45666
45674
45678
45684
45686
45689
45724

'Royal Scot' '6P' 4-6-0 Total: 9
46101
46118
46125
46128
46130
46134
46140
46148
46166

'Princess Royal' class '8P' 4-6-2 Total: 7
46205
46207
46208
46209
46210
46211
46212

'Princess Coronation' class '8P' 4-6-2 Total: 9
46225
46229
46233
46234
46235
46243
46246
46248
46252

LNWR '1P' 2-4-2T Total: 1
46680

Total: 82

Left:
Crewe South End, Platform 2
'Princess Coronation' Pacific No 46246 *City of Manchester* draws into Platform 2 with the 1.30pm Euston to Glasgow Central — the 'Mid-Day Scot', reporting number W97. This train halted at Crewe from 4.11pm until 4.20pm. Crewe men worked the train out of Euston and were relieved on the platform by another set of Crewe men who worked the train through to destination. In the mid-1950s the North Shed engine was replaced at Carlisle by another North Shed engine off Upperby shed and worked forward to Glasgow. *S. D. Wainwright*

Crewe North (5A) Engine Turns

15 July 1951

Mon	Tue	Wed	Thu	Fri	Sat	Sun	Loco Type	Time	First Outward Trip	Days	Time	Last Inward Trip	Days
1A	1A	1A	1A	1A	1A	1A	Class 8P 4-6-2	11.10pm	Crewe to Perth	SX & Sun	9.48pm	Perth to Crewe	S
1B	1B	1B	1B	1B	1B	1B	Class 8P 4-6-2	11.10pm	Crewe to Perth	SO	8.25pm	Perth to Crewe	Sun
2A	2A	2A	2A	2A		2A	Class 8P 4-6-2	10.29pm	Crewe to Perth	SX & Sun	8.15pm	Perth to Crewe	D
2B	2B	2B	2B	2B	2B	2B	Class 8P 4-6-2	1.5am	Crewe to Glasgow Central	Sun	5.45pm	Glasgow Central to Crewe	Sun
3A	3A	3A	3A	3A	3A	3A	Class 8P 4-6-2	1.5am	Crewe to Glasgow Central	D	5.40pm	Glasgow Central to Crewe	D
3B	3B	3B	3B	3B	3B	3B	Class 8P 4-6-2	7.50am	Crewe to Euston	MSX	7.20pm	Euston to Crewe	MSX
4A	4A	4A	4A	4A	4A	4A	Class 8P 4-6-2	12.37am	Crewe to Euston	D & Sun	8.30pm	Euston to Crewe	D & Sun
4B	4B	4B	4B	4B	4B	4B	Class 8P 4-6-2	1pm	Crewe to Glasgow Central	D	9.30am	Glasgow Central to Crewe	D
4C	4C	4C	4C	4C	4C	4C	Class 8P 4-6-2	12.54pm	Crewe to Glasgow Central	Sun	9.30am	Glasgow Central to Crewe	Sun
5A	5A	5A	5A	5A	5A	5A	Class 8P 4-6-2	12mn	Crewe to Glasgow Central	SX & Sun	6.25pm	Glasgow Central to Crewe	D & Sun
5B	5B	5B	5B	5B	5B	5B	Class 8P 4-6-2	11.58pm	Crewe to Glasgow Central	SO	5.20pm	Euston to Crewe	D
	8				8		Class 7P 4-6-0 'Royal Scot'	11.25am	Crewe to Holyhead	SO	12.2am	Euston to Crewe	TO
10	10	10	10	10	10	10	Class 7P 4-6-0 'Royal Scot'	5.14am	Crewe to Birmingham New St	D	11.15pm	Birmingham New St to Crewe	D
11A	11A	11A	11A	11A	11A	11A	Class 7P 4-6-0 Rebuilt 'Jubilee'	2.18am	Crewe to Windermere	MX	3.55pm	Manchester Exchange to Barrow	D
11B	11B	11B	11B	11B	11B	11B	Class 7P 4-6-0 Rebuilt 'Jubilee'	6.55am	Barrow to Workington	D	1.30pm	Barrow to Crewe	D
12	12		12	12	12		Class 7P 4-6-0 'Royal Scot'	4am	Crewe to Euston	MthO	8.52pm	Euston to Crewe	MThO
19A	19A	19A	19A	19A	19A	19A	Class 6P 4-6-0	3.16am	Crewe to Carlisle	MSX			
19B	19B	19B	19B	19B	19B		Class 6P 4-6-0	2.37am	Carlisle to Stranraer	SX	10pm	Stranraer to Carlisle	SX
19C	19C	19C	19C	19C	19C		Class 6P 4-6-0				8.35am	Carlisle to Crewe	SX
21	21	21	21	21	21	21	Class 6P 4-6-0	11.52pm	Crewe to Broad Street	FSX	3.30pm	Broad Street to Crewe	SX
22A	22A	22A	22A	22A	22A	22A	Class 6P 4-6-0	2.30am	Crewe to Birmingham New St	MSX	9.38am	Grange Junction to Crewe N [LE] SX	
22B	22B	22B	22B	22B		22B	Class 6P 4-6-0	7.55am	Crewe to Euston	MSX			
22C	22C	22C	22C	22C	22C	22C	Class 6P 4-6-0				10.45am	Euston to Crewe	FSX
23A	23A	23A	23A	23A	23A	23A	Class 6P 4-6-0	11.27pm	Crewe to Euston	SX	7.5pm	Euston to Birmingham New St	SX
23B	23B	23B	23B	23B	23B		Class 6P 4-6-0	2.50am	Birmingham N St to Leamington	SX	4.17pm	Liverpool Lime St to Crewe	SX
24A	24A	24A	24A	24A	24A		Class 6P 4-6-0	8.50pm	Crewe to Euston	D			
24B	24B	24B	24B	24B	24B	24B	Class 6P 4-6-0	7.35am	Euston to Rugby	D	7.10am	Preston to Crewe	MX
27A	27A	27A	27A	27A	27A	27A	Class 6P 4-6-0	5.10pm	Crewe to Manchester L Rd	SX	2.58am	Heaton Norris JS to Aston GoodsMX	
	27B	27B	27B	27B	27B	27B	Class 6P 4-6-0	2.15am	Bescot to Carlisle Kingmoor	MSX			
	27C	27C	27C		27C	27C	Class 6P 4-6-0				*as req'd*	Carlisle to Crewe	WThO
28	28	28	28	28	28		Class 6P 4-6-0	6pm	Crewe to Carlisle	SX	4.28am	Carlisle to Crewe	MX
29	29	29			29	29	Class 6P 4-6-0	10.40am	Crewe to Carlisle Viaduct Yd	MO	12.40am	Euston to Crewe	Sun
	30			30	30	30	Class 6P 4-6-0	11.44pm	Crewe to Shrewsbury	FO	4.45am	Euston to Crewe	O
33A	33A	33A	33A	33A	33A	33A	Class 5 STD 4-6-0	12.10pm	Crewe to Shrewsbury	SX	9.58pm	Shrewsbury to Crewe	SX
33B	33B	33B	33B	33B	33B	33B	Class 5 STD 4-6-0	2.25am	Crewe to Blackpool North	SX	10.35pm	Shrewsbury to Crewe	SX
33C	33C	33C	33C	33C	33C	33C	Class 5 STD 4-6-0	6.50am	Crewe to Birmingham New St	SX	as req'd	Preston Ribble Sdgs to Crewe	TWThO
36	36	36	36	36	36		Class 5 STD 4-6-0	2pm	Crewe to Liverpool Lime St	SX	as req'd	Stoke to Crewe North Shed	MSX
39A	39A	39A	39A	39A			Class 6P 4-6-0	10.55am	Crewe to Chester	SX	11.18pm	Chester to Willesden	SX
39B	39B	39B	39B	39B	39B		Class 6P 4-6-0	4.10pm	Willesden to St Pancras	SX	9.32pm	Camden to Crewe Basford Hall	SX
40A	40A	40A	40A	40A	40A		Class 5 STD 4-6-0	4.10am	Crewe to Stoke	D	2.10pm	Edge Hill to Nuneaton	SX
40B	40B	40B	40B	40B	40B	40B	Class 5 STD 4-6-0	3.50am	Blaby Sdgs to Crewe BH	MSX	8.52pm	Stoke to Crewe	MSX
41	41	41	41	41	41	41	Class 5 STD 4-6-0	1.35pm	Crewe to Derby	SX	2am	Garston Speke Sdgs to Crewe BH	MX
42A	42A	42A	42A	42A			Class 5 STD 4-6-0	11.20am	Crewe BH to Warrington	SX	9.45pm	Warrington ES to Crewe N Staffs	SX
	42B	42B	42B	42B	42B		Class 5 STD 4-6-0	5am	Crewe to Liverpool Lime St	MX	3.00am	Nuneaton to Crewe BH	MSX
43	43	43	43	43	43	43	Class 5 STD 4-6-0	8.27pm	Crewe to Preston	SX	as req'd	Patricroft to Crewe	MX
44	44	44	44	44	44	44	Class 5 STD 4-6-0	5.5pm	Crewe to Liverpool Lime St	SX	6.30am	Birmingham New St to Crewe	D
45				45	45	45	Class 5 STD 4-6-0	9.40am	Crewe to Blackpool North	FO	8.30pm	Blackpool North to Crewe	MO
53	53	53	53	53	53	53	Class 2P STD 4-4-0	8.30am	No 1 Up Side Bank	D & Sun			
54	54	54	54	54	54	54	Class 2P STD 4-4-0	6.5am	No 4 Down Side Bank	D & Sun			

Mon	Tue	Wed	Thu	Fri	Sat	Sun	Loco Type	Time	First Outward Trip	Days	Time	Last Inward Trip	Days
55	55	55	55	55	55		Class 2P STD 4-4-0	2am	No 11 South End Shunt	SX	4.50pm	Calveley to Crewe	SX
57	57	57	57	57	57	57	Class 2P STD 4-4-0	as req'd	District Engineers Special Engine	D & Sun			
				60	60		Class 7P 4-6-0 'Royal Scot'	10.50pm	Crewe to Perth	FO	8.55pm	Perth to Crewe	SO
					61	61	Class 7P 4-6-0 'Royal Scot'	7.50am	Crewe to Euston	SO	10.50am	Euston to Crewe	SunO
	62	62	62				Class 7P 4-6-0 'Royal Scot'	4am	Crewe to Euston Cpld	TWO	8.52pm	Euston to Holyhead	WO
				66	66		Class 5 STD 4-6-0	4.25pm	Crewe to Bangor	FO	*as req'd*	Walsall to Crewe	SO
					67		Class 5 STD 4-6-0	5.30am	Crewe to Chester	SO	4pm	Bangor to Crewe	SO
				68	68		Class 5 STD 4-6-0	11.36pm	Crewe to Leeds City South	FO	*as req'd*	Preston to Crewe	SO
					69		Class 5 STD 4-6-0	9.53am	Crewe to Shrewsbury	SO	*as req'd*	Shrewsbury to Crewe	SO
				70	70		Class 5 STD 4-6-0	10.30pm	Crewe to Willesden	FO	11.22am	Euston to Crewe	SO
					71		Class 5 STD 4-6-0	5.20am	Crewe to Liverpool Lime St	SO	7.20pm	Liverpool Lime St to Crewe	SO
						78	Class 4 STD 2-6-4T 2 cyl	1.45am	Crewe to Stoke	SunO	6.50am	Stoke to Crewe	SunO
91	91/2	91/2	91/2	91/2	93		Class 5 STD 4-6-0	4.2pm	Crewe to Derby	SX	8.15pm	Derby to Crewe	SX
97/8	97/8	97/8	97/8	97/8	99/100l	101	Class 4P 4-4-0 Compound	8.10am	Crewe to Derby	SX	11.30pm	Manchester London Rd to Crewe	SX
102/3	106/4	106/4	106/4	106/5	107		Class 4 STD 2-6-4T 2-cyl	4.25pm	Crewe to Chester	SX	12.5pm	Shrewsbury to Crewe	SX
					112/3		Class 4P 4-4-0 Compound	8.10am	Crewe to Derby	SO	9.20pm	Alderley Edge to Crewe North Shed	SO
120/1	120/1	120/1	120/1	120/1	120/2		Class 2P STD 2-6-2T VC	6.15am	Crewe to Northwich	D	6.50pm	Northwich to Crewe	D
50	55	52	52	56	60	40		**Total Daily Engine Rostered Turns**					

Left:
Basford Hall Junction, 19 April 1952
'Royal Scot' class 4-6-0 No 46161 *King's Own* storms past Basford Hall Junction signalbox on the Up Fast line. There is no indication what the working was, but the locomotive was shedded at Crewe North 5A at the time and possibly was working a train to Birmingham New Street. Notice the freight train in Basford Hall Yard. *Tom Lewis — Manchester Locomotive Society*

Class 8 Engine Workings
Full Details for 15 July 1951

Turn 1

Engine Workings Only
Two Class 8P (4-6-2)

'A'				(7.30pm from Euston)		
SX & Sun	Pass	11.10pm	Crewe	Perth	6.1am	(130)(131)
				Crewe depart 11.15pm Sun		
				(7.30pm from Euston)		
SO	Pass	11.10pm	Crewe	Perth	6.15am	(132)
'B'						
D				(5.15pm from Inverness)		
D	Pass	9.48pm	Perth	Crewe	4.52am	(133)
Sun	Pass	8.25pm	Perth	Crewe	3.40am	(134)
SX	Pass	10.20am	Crewe	Shrewsbury	11.3am	(702)
SX	Pass	4pm	Shrewsbury	Crewe	4.50pm	
SO	Pass	10.40am	Crewe	Shrewsbury	11.36am	(703)
SO	Pass	3.38pm	Shrewsbury	Crewe	4.23pm	

Turn 2

Two Class 8P (4-6-2)

'A'				(7.20pm from Euston)		
SX & Sun	Pass	10.29pm	Crewe	Perth	4.48am	(135)
'B'						
D	Pass	8.15pm	Perth	Crewe	3.40am	(136)
				(11.15pm [Sat] from Birmingham)		
Sun	Pass	1.5am	Crewe	Glasgow	6.50am	(12A/93)(Sc R)
Sun	Pass	5.45pm	Glasgow	Crewe	12.48am	(66A/10)

Turn 3

Two Class 8P (4-6-2)

'A'				(11.15pm [SX] 11.10pm [Sun] from Birmingham)		
D	Pass	1.5am	Crewe	Glasgow	6.48am	(143)
D	Pass	5.40pm	Glasgow	Crewe	12.41am	(140)
				(5.35pm from Inverness)		
Sun	Pass	5.2am	Crewe	Euston	8.25am	(390)(2A/64)
Sun	Pass	7.20pm	Euston	Crewe	10.16pm	(1B/230)
'B'				(8.25pm from Perth)		
MO	Pass	4am	Crewe	Euston	7.10am	(281)
MO	Pass	7.20pm	Euston	Crewe	10.16pm	(1B/230)
MSX	Pass	7.50am	Crewe	Euston	11.17am	(299)
MSX	Pass	7.20pm	Euston	Crewe	10.16am	(1B/230)
				(11.25pm ex-Birmingham)		
SO	Pass	1.15pm	Crewe	Glasgow C	6.35pm	(12A/108)(Sc R)
Sun	Pass	10.15am	Glasgow C	Crewe	4.17pm	(Sc R)(12A/64)

Turn 4

Three Class 8P (4-6-2)

'A'				(6.25pm from Glasgow)		
D & Sun	Postal	12.37am	Crewe	Euston	4am	(266)(267)
D & Sun	Postal	8.30pm	Euston	Crewe	11.44pm	(277)(279)(284)
'B'				(11.15am ex-Birmingham)		
D	Pass	1pm	Crewe	Glasgow C	6.20pm	(66A/11, 13, 16)
				(11.15am ex-Birmingham)		
D	Pass	1pm	Crewe	Glasgow C	6.20pm	(137)
				(11.15am ex-Birmingham)		
Sun	Pass	12.54pm	Crewe	Glasgow C	7pm	(137)

'C'						
D	Pass	9.30am	Glasgow C	Crewe	2.55pm	(138)(Sc R)(12A/94)
Sun	Pass	9.30am	Glasgow C	Crewe	3.34pm	(Sc R)(173)

Turn 5				**Two Class 8P (4-6-2)**		
'A'				(8.30pm from Euston)		
SX & Sun	Postal	12am	Crewe	Glasgow C	5.25am	(139)
SO	Postal	11.58pm	Crewe	Glasgow C	5.30am	(164)(Sc R)
'B'						
D & Sun	Postal	6.25pm	Glasgow C	Crewe	12.25am	(66A/14)(179)
MO	Pass	7.50am	Crewe	Euston	11.17am	(299)
				(5.35pm from Inverness)		
MX	Pass	5.2am	Crewe	Euston	8.20am	(291)
D	Pass	5.20pm	Euston	Crewe	8.28pm	(268)(251)

Left:
Crewe North Junction
'Jubilee' class 4-6-0 No 45680 *Camperdown* of Longsight 9A shed coasts into Platform 3 with a Manchester to West of England express. Judging by the fresh ballast, some track renovation has taken place. Note the North Junction signal cabin gleaming white. In the background locomotives move slowly near the North Shed outlet. *Martin Welch*

Crewe North (5A) Enginemen's Turns

July 1951

Outward Trip											Inward Trip				
Mon	Tue	Wed	Thu	Fri	Sat	Sun	Time		Work	Loco	Time		Work	Loco	Date/Notes
91	91	91	91	91			4.2pm	Crewe-Derby	Pass	5A/91	8.15pm	Derby-Crewe	Pass	5A/91	
92	92	92	92	92			12.40am	Crewe-Manchester London Rd	Pass	5A/91	4.15am	Heaton Norris JS-Crewe Gresty Lane	TF	5A/91	
					93		1.35pm	Crewe-Derby	Pass	5A/91	5.54pm	Derby-Crewe	Pass	5A/91	
97	97	97	97	97			8.10am	Crewe-Derby	Pass	5A/97	1.30pm	Derby-Crewe	Pass	5A/97	
98	98	98	98	98			7.53pm	Crewe-Manchester London Rd	Pass	5A/97	11.30pm	Manchester London Rd-Crewe	Pcls	5A/97	
					99		9.8am	Crewe-Derby	Pass	5A/97	1.30pm	Derby-Crewe	Pass	5A/97	
					100		5.5pm	Crewe-Liverpool Lime St	Pass	5A/97	10.10pm	Liverpool Lime St-Crewe	Pass	5A/97	
						101	9.35am	Crewe-Derby	Pass	5A/97	2.10pm	Derby-Crewe	Pass	5A/97	
102							4.25pm	Chester-Rhyl	Pass	5A/102	11.6pm	Chester-Crewe	Pass	6A/13	
	104	104	104				4.25pm	Chester-Rhyl	Pass	5A/102	11.6pm	Chester-Crewe	Pass	7C/11	
				105			4.25pm	Chester-Rhyl	Pass	5A/102	11.6pm	Chester-Crewe	Pass	7C/11	
					107		8.37am	Crewe-Shrewsbury-Wellington	Pass	5A/102	11.25am	Shrewsbury-Crewe	Pass	5A/107	
					112		8.10am	Crewe-Derby	Pass	5A/112	12.32pm	Derby-Crewe	Pass	5A/112	
					113		6.10pm	Crewe-Manchester L Rd-Wilmslow	Pass	5A/112	8.57pm	Wilmslow-Alderley Edge-Crewe	ECS LE	5A/112	
120	120	120	120	120	120		6.15am	Crewe-Northwich-Crewe	Motor	5A/120	7.32am	Crewe-Northwich-Crewe	Motor	5A/120	
121	121	121	121	121			4.32pm	Crewe-Northwich-Crewe	Pcls	5A/120	5.55pm	Crewe-Northwich-Crewe	Motor	5A/120	
					122		12.38pm	Crewe-Northwich-Crewe	Motor	5A/120	4.32pm	Crewe-Northwich-Crewe	Motor	5A/120	
						130	11.15pm	Crewe-Perth	Pass	5A/1		*Book off Perth*			*Lodge*
131	131	131	131	131			11.10pm	Crewe-Perth	Pass	5A/1		*Book off Perth*			*Lodge*
					132		11.10pm	Crewe-Perth	Pass	5A/1		*Book off Perth*			*Lodge*
133	133	133	133	133	133			*Lodge*			9.48pm	Perth-Crewe	Pass	5A/1	
						134		*Lodge*			8.25pm	Perth-Crewe	Pass	5A/1	
135	135	135	135	135		135	10.29pm	Crewe-Perth	Pass	5A/2		*Book off Perth*			*Lodge*
136	136	136	136	136	136			*Lodge*			8.15pm	Perth-Crewe	Pass	5A/2	
						137	12.54pm	Crewe-Glasgow Central	Pass	5A/4		*Book off Glasgow Polmadie*			*Lodge*
138								*Lodge*			9.30am	Glasgow-Crewe	Pass	5A/4	
139	139	139	139	139		139	12mn	Crewe-Glasgow Central	Postal	5A/5		*Book off Glasgow Polmadie*			*Lodge*
140	140	140	140	140	140			*Lodge*			5.40pm	Glasgow-Crewe	Pass	5A/3	
141		141		141			4.19pm	Crewe-Glasgow Central	Pass	1B/2+3		*Book off Glasgow Polmadie*			*Lodge*
	142		142		142			*Lodge*			1.30pm	Glasgow-Crewe	Pass	1B/2	
143	143	143	143	143	143		1.5am	Crewe-Glasgow Central	Pass	5A/3		*Book off Glasgow Polmadie*			*Lodg*
144	144	144	144	144	144			*Lodge*			11.15pm	Glasgow-Crewe	Pass	66A/2	
				145			10.50pm	Crewe-Perth	Pass	5A/60		*Book off Perth*			*Lodge*
					146			*Lodge*			8.55pm	Perth-Crewe	Pass	5A/60	
150							1.25am	Crewe-Carlisle	Pass	12A/5		*Book off Carlisle Upperby*			*Lodge*
151								*Lodge*			6.30pm	Carlisle-Crewe	Ety Van	8A/32	
	159	159	159	159	159		1.20pm	Crewe-Carlisle	Pass	66A/1		*Book off Carlisle Upperby*			*Lodge*
		160	160	160	160			*Lodge*			4.28am	Carlisle-Crewe	Fish	5A/28	
						161		*Lodge*			4.25am	Carlisle-Crewe	Fish	8A 6	
					164		11.58pm	Crewe-Carlisle	Postal	5A/5		*Book off Carlisle Upperby*			*Lodge*
						165		*Lodge*			2.50pm	Carlisle-Crewe	Pcls	5A/27	
					172		6.37pm	Crewe-Carlisle	Pcls	12A/22		*Book off Carlisle Upperby*			*Lodge*
						173		*Lodge*			12.15pm	Carlisle-Crewe	Pass	5A/4	
				174			1.54pm	Crewe-Carlisle	Pass	1B/2		*Book off Carlisle Upperby*			*Lodge*
					175			*Lodge*			8.5am	Carlisle-Crewe	Pass	1B/34	

Outward Trip Mon	Tue	Wed	Thu	Fri	Sat	Sun	Time		Work	Loco	Inward Trip Time		Work	Loco	Date/Notes
					178		12.50am	Crewe-Carlisle	Pass	5A/22		*Book off Carlisle Upperby*			Lodge
					179			*Lodge*			9pm	Carlisle-Crewe	Postal	5A/5	
				181			10.36pm	Crewe-Carlisle	Pass	1B/34		*Book off Carlisle Upperby*			Lodge
					182			*Lodge*			12.28pm	Carlisle-Crewe	Pass	1B/4	
183							2.5am	Crewe-Carlisle	Pass	5A/19		*Book off Carlisle Upperby*			*Lodge*
184								*Lodge*			9.30pm	Carlisle-Crewe	Fish	12A/6	
				185			11.20pm	Crewe-Carlisle	Pass	1B/2		*Book off Carlisle Upperby*			*Lodge*
					186			*Lodge*			3.52pm	Carlisle-Crewe	Pass	5A/22	
200							6am	Crewe-Warrington-Preston	Pass	10B/20	9.51am	Preston-Crewe	Pass	12A/13	
	201	201	201	201	201		6am	Crewe-Warrington-Preston	Pass	10B/20	9.51am	Preston-Crewe	Pass	12A/13	
						202	7.50am	Crewe-Preston	Pass	28A/65	11.50am	Preston-Crewe	Pcls	11A/1	
	204	204	204	204	204		2.25am	Crewe-Preston	Pass	5A/33	6.12am	Preston-Crewe	Pcls	5B/1034	
205							3.5am	Crewe-Preston	Pcls	5A/28	7.10am	Preston-Crewe	Cpld	5A/28	
206	206	206	206	206			9.25am	Crewe-Preston	Pass	66A/2	2.15pm	Wyre Dock-Crewe	EF [C]	5A/33	
					207		9.25am	Crewe-Carnforth	Pass	66A/2	2.42pm	Carnforth-Crewe	Pass	5A/11	
208	208	208	208	208			12.30pm	Crewe-Warrington	Pcls	12A/18	5.20pm	Warrington-Crewe	Pass	5B/1039	
209							2.5am	Crewe-Preston	Cpld	66A/2	5.30am	Preston-Crewe	Pass	10B/4	
	216						3.16am	Crewe-Preston	Pcls	5A/19	6.34am	Preston-Crewe	Fish	5A/28	
217							2.5am	Crewe-Preston	Pass	5A/19		*return as required*			
	218	218	218	218			5.45am	Crewe-Morecambe	Pcls	11A/6		*return as required*			
	219	219	219				1.54pm	Crewe-Preston	Pass	1B/2		*return as required*			
						220	2.57am	Crewe-Preston	Pass	8A/15		*return as required*			
	221	221	221	221	221		3.28am	Crewe-Preston	Pcls.	5A/24	7.10am	Preston-Crewe	Cpld	5A/24	
222				222			3.2pm	Crewe-Preston	Pass	1B/18		*return as required*			
223							9.27pm	Crewe-Preston	Pass	1B/12		*return as required*			
224							3.12pm	Crewe-Preston	Pass	10B/4		*return as required*			22/29 June only**
225							3.12pm	Crewe-Preston	Pass	10B/4	8.30pm	Blackpool North-Crewe	Pass		
	226	226	226				3.12pm	Crewe-Preston	Pass	10B/4		*return as required*			
				227			3.12pm	Crewe-Preston	Pass	2A/—	8.30pm	Blackpool North-Crewe	Pass	28A/64	commence 6 July
				228			3.12pm	Crewe-Preston	Pass	2A/—		*return as required*			22/29 June only **
					229		1.35pm	Crewe-Preston	Pass	10B/4		*return as required*			23/30 June **
					230		1.35pm	Crewe-Windermere	Pass	10B/4		*return as required*			22/29 only **
					231		2.12pm	Crewe-Blackpool Central	Pass	1A/1		*return as required*			to July 20 only
					232		2.12pm	Crewe-Blackpool Central	Pass	1A/1		*return as required*			8/15 Sept only **
					233		10.39am	Crewe-Morecambe	Pass	2C/3		*return as required*			
					234		3.16am	Crewe-Preston	Pcls.	12A/17		*return as required*			15/22 Sept only **
					237		10.31am	Crewe-Blackpool North	Pass	3E/8	3.40pm	Blackpool North-Crewe	Pass	3E/8	
238				238			9.40am	Crewe-Blackpool North	Pass	5A/45		*return as required*			
					239		8.6am	Crewe-Blackpool North	Pass	3D/—	12.15pm	Blackpool North-Crewe	Pass	3D/—	
					240		11.7am	Crewe-Blackpool North	Pass	4A/2		*return as required*			
					241		8.58am	Crewe-Blackpool North	Pass	2A/—	1.55pm	Blackpool North-Crewe	Pass	2A/—	
					242		10.23am	Crewe-Blackpool North	Pass	5A/36		*return as required*			
					243		6am	Crewe-Warrington-Preston	Cpld	12B/16		*return as required*			to 9 Sept only
					244		11.35am	Crewe Gresty Lane-Blackpool North	Pass	5A/30		*return as required*			
245							2.25pm	Crewe-Blackpool Central	Pass	1B/12		*return as required*			10/17 Sept only**
250	250	250	250	250			11.27pm	Crewe-Euston	Pcls	5A/23		*Book off Camden*			*Lodge*
	251	251	251	251	251			*Lodge*			5.20pm	Euston-Crewe	Pass	5A/5	
266	266	266	266	266	266		12.37am	Crewe-Euston	Postal	5A/4		*Book off Camden*			*Lodge*
						267	12.37am	Crewe-Euston	Postal	5A/4		*Book off Camden*			*Lodge*
268								*Lodge*			5.20pm	Euston-Crewe	Pass	5A/5	
	269	269	269	269				*Lodge*			7.30pm	Euston-Crewe	Pass	1B/7	
					270						7.20pm	Euston-Wigan	News	7C/2	
						271					7.30pm	Euston-Crewe	Pass	8A/—	
274	274	274	274	274	274		1.10am	Crewe-Euston	Pass	1B/13		*Book off Camden*			*Lodge*

Outward Trip											Inward Trip				
Mon	Tue	Wed	Thu	Fri	Sat	Sun	Time		Work	Loco	Time		Work	Loco	Date/Notes
						271					7.30pm	Euston-Crewe	Pass	8/A—	
274	274	274	274	274	274		1.10am	Crewe-Euston	Pass	1B/13		*Book off Camden*			*Lodge*
						275	1.10am	Crewe-Euston	Pass	1B/13		*Book off Camden*			*Lodge*
276								*Lodge*			6.20pm	Euston-Crewe	Pass	1B/12	
	277	277	277	277				*Lodge*			8.30pm	Euston-Crewe	Postal	5A/4	
					278			*Lodge*			7.50pm	Willesden-Crewe	Pcls	2A/4	
						279		*Lodge*			8.30pm	Euston-Crewe	Postal	5A/4	
281	281	281	281	281	281		4am	Crewe-Euston	Pass	1B/11		*Book off Camden*			*Lodge*
						282	4am	Crewe-Euston	Pass	12A/—		*Book off Camden*			*Lodge*
	283	283	283	283				*Lodge*			9.25pm	Euston-Crewe	Pass	12/A—	
284					284			*Lodge*			8.30pm	Euston-Crewe	Postal	5A/4	
						285		*Lodge*			9.25pm	Euston-Crewe	Pass	12/A—	
286							3am	Crewe-Willesden	Pcls	1B/17		*Book off Willesden*			*Lodge*
287								*Lodge*			9.25pm	Euston-Crewe	Pass	12/A—	
290							4.27am	Crewe-Euston	Pass	1B/11		*Book off Camden*			*Lodge*
	291	291	291	291	291		5.2am	Crewe-Euston	Pass	5A/5		*Book off Camden*			*Lodge*
292								*Lodge*			7.35pm	Camden-Crewe Basford Hall	EF [C]	8A/—	
	293	293	293	293				*Lodge*			11.5pm	Euston-Crewe	Pass	1B/17	
					294			*Lodge*			10.30pm	Willesden-Crewe	Pcls	7C/7	
						297	8.35am	Crewe-Euston	Pass	5A/22		*Book off Camden*			*Lodge*
						298	5.2am	Crewe-Euston	Pass	5A/3		*Book off Camden*			*Lodge* 23 Sept**
299	299	299	299	299			7.50am	Crewe-Euston	Pass	5A/3		*Book off Camden*			*Lodge*
					300		9am	Crewe-Euston	Pass	7C/7		*Book off Camden*			*Lodge*
301								*Lodge*			11.5pm	Euston-Crewe	Pass	1B/17	
	302	302	302	302	302	302		*Lodge*			12.2am	Euston-Crewe	Pass	1B/17	
303							9am	Crewe-Euston	Pass	4B/1		*Book off Camden*			*Lodge*
	304							*Lodge*			1.37am	Euston-Wolverhampton-Crewe	News	9A/—	
305							8.42am	Crewe-Euston	Pass	1B/11		*Book off Camden*			*Lodge*
	306							*Lodge*			12.2am	Euston-Crewe	Pass	5A/8	
308		308		308			11.28am	Crewe-Euston	Pass	1B/19		*Book off Camden*			*Lodge*
	309		309				1pm	Crewe-Euston	Pass	1B/1		*Book off Camden*			*Lodge*
					310		3.31pm	Crewe-Euston	Pass	9A/—		*Book off Camden*			*Lodge*
	311	311	311	311				*Lodge*			4.45am	Euston-Crewe	Pcls	5A/30	
					312			*Lodge*			9.20am	Euston-Crewe	Pass	1B/31	
						313		*Lodge*			6.30am	Euston-Crewe	Pass	5A/19	
						317	12.50pm	Crewe-Euston	Pass	5A/22		*Book off Camden*			*Lodge*
318	318	318	318	318			1.35pm	Crewe-Chester-Euston	Pass	1B/17		*Book off Camden*			*Lodge*
319		319		319				*Lodge*			10.40am	Euston-Crewe	Pass	1B/2	
	320		320					*Lodge*			12.40pm	Euston-Wolverhampton-Crewe	Pass	1B/13	
					321			*Lodge*			11.58am	Euston-Crewe	Pass	1B/18	23/30 June only **
					322			*Lodge*			11.22am	Euston-Chester	Pass	5A/70	
323		323		323			1pm	Crewe-Euston	Pass	1B/1		*Book off Camden*			*Lodge*
	324		324					*Lodge*			10.40am	Euston-Crewe	Pass	1B/2	
					325			*Lodge*			10.45am	Euston-Crewe	Pass	8A/—	
						326	2.30pm	Crewe-Euston	Pass	1B/31		*Book off Camden*			*Lodge*
327								*Lodge*			11.50am	Euston-Crewe	Pass	1B/18	
329	329	329	329	329	329		7.3pm	Crewe-Euston	Pass	1B/2		*Book off Camden*			*Lodge*
	330	330	330	330	330			*Lodge*			1.15pm	Euston-Crewe	Pass	1B/3	
						331		*Lodge*			3pm	Euston-Crewe	Pcls	9A/—	24 June-8 July only **
						332		*Lodge*			4.40pm	Euston-Crewe	Pass	1B/20	
						350	8.35pm	Crewe-Euston	Pcls	9A/—		*Book off Camden*			*Lodge*
351								*Lodge*			4.55pm	Euston-Crewe	Pass	1B/11	

Outward Trip Mon	Tue	Wed	Thu	Fri	Sat	Sun	Time		Work	Loco	Inward Trip Time		Work	Loco	Date/Notes
				352			5pm	Crewe-Euston	Pass	1B/31		*Book off Camden*			*Lodge*
					353			*Lodge*			11.30am	Euston-Wolverhampton-Crewe	Pass	1B/13	
					354		5.26pm	Crewe-Euston	Pass	7C/1		*Book off Camden*			*Lodge*
						355		*Lodge*			3pm	Euston-Crewe	Pcls	9A/—	
				356			11.50pm	Crewe-Euston	Pass	28A/61		*Book off Camden*			*Lodge*
					357			*Lodge*			7.30pm	Euston-Crewe	Pass	9A/—	25 Aug-15 Sept**
358			358				4am	Crewe-Euston	Cpld	5A/12		*Book off Camden*			*Lodge*
359			359					*Lodge*			8.52pm	Euston-Crewe	Pass	5A/12	
	360	360					4am	Crewe-Euston	Cpld	5A/62		*Book off Camden*			*Lodge*
	361	361						*Lodge*			8.52pm	Euston-Crewe	Pass	5A/62	
382	382	382	382	382			5.55pm	Crewe-Stafford	Pass	2A/—	8.15pm	Stafford-Crewe Basford Hall	TF	17B/25	
	383	383	383	383	383		7.55am	Crewe-Rugby	Pcls	5A/22		*return as required*			
					384		8.50pm	Crewe-Rugby	Pcls	5A/24	11.30pm	Rugby-Crewe BH	TF	2A/515	
385	385	385	385	385			8.50pm	Crewe-Rugby	Pcls	5A/24	1.06am	Rugby-Crewe B/H.	EF [D]	8B/1	
					386		11.28am	Crewe-Rugby	Pass	1B/19	3.0pm	Nuneaton-Crewe BH	TF	5B/1054	
				387			11.50pm	Crewe-Rugby	Pass	28A/61	5.59am	Rugby-Crewe	Pcls	2A/—	22 June-17 Aug
					388		1.52pm	Crewe-Coventry	Pass	28A/65		*return as required*			
					389		10.55am	Crewe-Rugby	Pass	5B/1031		*return as required*			30 June-7 July**
						390	5.2am	Crewe-Rugby	Pass	5A/3		*return as required*			
391				391			10.30pm	Crewe-Rugby	Vans	5A/22	2.37am	Rugby-Crewe BH	TF	2A/9	
394	394	394	394	394			1.55pm	Crewe-Rugby	Pcls	2A/—		*return as required*			
					395		6.5pm	Crewe Brook Sidings-Rugby	Pcls	2A/—		*return as required*			
						500	3.20pm	Crewe-Stafford	Pcls	9A/—		*return as required*			
						501	9.31am	Crewe-Birmingham New St	Pass	8A/—	12.10pm	Birmingham Vauxhall-Crewe North	LE	8A/—	
						502	11.20am	Crewe-Birmingham New St	Pass	5A/11	3.55pm	Birmingham New St-Crewe	Pcls	5A/11	
						503	6.42pm	Crewe-Birmingham New St	Pass	5A/10	11.10pm	Birmingham New St-Crewe	Pass	5A/10	
						504	6.45pm	Stafford-Birmingham New St	Pass	5B/1050	10.10pm	Birmingham New St-Crewe	Pass	5B/1050	
						507	4pm	Crewe-Birmingham New St	Pass	3D/7		*return as required*			
					508		2.45am	Crewe-Birmingham New St	Fish	12A/—	5.55am	Birmingham New St-Walsall-Crewe	Pass		
					509		2.27pm	Crewe-Birmingham New St	Pass	3D/13	6.24pm	Birmingham New St-Stafford-Crewe	Pass	3D/13	
					510		5.11pm	Crewe-Birmingham New St	Pass	2A/—		Birmingham Fordhouses-Stafford	LE		
						511	4.47pm	Crewe-Birmingham New St	Pass	3C/4		*return as required*			
					512		5.30am	Crewe-Birmingham New St	Pass	12A/—		*return as required*			
					513		4.55pm	Crewe-Birmingham New St	Pass	1B/20		*return as required*			
					514		4.14pm	Crewe Basford Hall-B'ham New St	Pass	17A/—		*return as required*			
540	540	540	540	540			12.45am	Crewe-Birmingham New St	Pass	5A/44	6.30am	Birmingham New St-Crewe	Pass	5A/44	
					541		12.45am	Crewe-Birmingham New St	Pass	5A/44	6.30am	Birmingham New St-Crewe	Pass	5A/44	
549	549	549	549	549	549		5.14am	Crewe-Birmingham New St	Pass	5A/10	11.15am	Birmingham New St-Crewe	Pass	5A/10	
550	550	550	550	550	550		3.15pm	Crewe-Birmingham New St	Pass	5A/10	8.20pm	Birmingham New St-Crewe	Pass	3D/5	
551							5.40am	Crewe-Birmingham New St	Pass	2A/—		*return as required*			
					552		9.35pm	Crewe-Birmingham New St	Pcls	3D/10		*return as required*			
553	553	553	553	553			6.50am	Crewe-Birmingham New St	Pass	5A/33	9.45am	Birmingham New St-Stafford	Pass	5A/33	
					554		6.50am	Crewe-Birmingham New St	Pass	8A/32		*return as required*			
555	555	555	555	555			9.10am	Crewe-Birmingham New St	Pass	8A/15	1.45pm	Birmingham New St-Crewe	Pass	8A/15	
					556		9.10am	Crewe-Coventry	Pass	8A/15	12.45pm	Coventry-Birmingham New St-Crewe	Pass	8A/15	
					557		7.10pm	Crewe-Stafford	Pass	9A/101	10.30pm	Stafford-Crewe Basford Hall	TF	17B/25	
	559	559	559	559			2.30am	Crewe-Birmingham New St	Fish	5A/22	7.15am	Bescot-GrangeJunction-Crewe	Eties LE	5A/22	
561	561	561	561	561			4.7pm	Crewe-Birmingham New St	Pass	2A/—	10.10pm	Birmingham New St-Crewe	Pass	2A/—	
562	562	562	562	562			8.15pm	Crewe-Birmingham New St	Pass	8A/—	1.45am	Birmingham New St-Crewe	Pcls	8A/—	
564	564	564	564	564	564		*11.20am	Crewe-Birmingham New St	Pass	9A/—	3.50pm	Birmingham New St-Crewe	Pass	9A/—	[*11.12am SO]
565	565	565	565	565	565		1.8pm	Crewe-Stafford-Birmingham New St	Pass	8A/13	6.5pm	Birmingham New St-Crewe	Pass	8A/13	
					576		6.30pm	Crewe-Liverpool Lime St	Pass	9A/10	11.45pm	Liverpool Lime St-Crewe	Pass	9A/10	
577	577	577	577	577			7.48pm	Crewe-Liverpool Lime St	Pass	8A/13	12.40am	Edge Hill-Crewe Station	EF [F]	5A/36	

Outward Trip Mon	Tue	Wed	Thu	Fri	Sat	Sun	Time		Work	Loco	Inward Trip Time		Work	Loco	Date/Notes
				578			3.48pm	Crewe-Liverpool Lime St	Pass	8A/32	7.31pm	Wavertree-Crewe	Pass	8A/27	
579	579	579	579	579			5pm	Crewe-Liverpool Lime St	Pass	2A/3	7.20pm	Liverpool Lime St-Crewe	Pass	8A/27	
					580		7.58am	Crewe-Liverpool Lime St	Pass	3D/—	10.30am	Liverpool Lime St-Crewe	Cpld	3D/—	to 8 Sept
581	581	581	581	581			3.35pm	Crewe-Liverpool Lime St	Pass	8A/15	6.25pm	Edge Hill-Crewe Gresty Lane	EF [F]	8A/15	
582	582	582	582	582			9.10am	Crewe-Liverpool Lime St	Pass	8A/26	11.50am	Edge Hill-Crewe Gresty Lane	EF [F]	3C/1	
					582		9.10am	Crewe-Liverpool Lime St	Pass	8A/26	1.5pm	Liverpool Lime St-Crewe	Pass	5A/23	
	583	583	583	583			5am	Crewe-Liverpool Lime St	Pcls	5A/42	8.20am	Edge Hill-Crewe Basford Hall	EF [F]	5A/42	
					583		5am	Crewe-Liverpool Lime St	Pcls	5A/42	10.30am	Liverpool Lime St-Crewe	Pass	5A/42	
	584	584	584	584			5.20am	Crewe-Liverpool Lime St	Pass	84G/5	9.20am	Edge Hill-Crewe Gresty Lane	EF [E]	84G/5	
585	585	585	585	585			8.48am	Crewe-Liverpool Lime St	Pass	5A/40	2pm	Edge Hill-Crewe Basford Hall	EF [F]	5A/40	
					586		8.48am	Crewe-Liverpool Lime St	Pass	5A/40	1.15pm	Edge Hill-Crewe Basford Hall	EF [F]	12A/320	
					587		10.50am	Crewe-Liverpool Lime St	Pass	3D/10	4.17pm	Liverpool Lime St-Crewe	Pass	3D/10	
						588	5.20am	Crewe-Liverpool Lime St #	Pass	84G/5	10.40am	Liverpool Lime St-Crewe	Pass	84G/5	# via Warrington
						589	7.17pm	Crewe-Liverpool Lime St	Pass	9A/—	10.10pm	Liverpool Lime St-Crewe	Pass	5A/44	
	590	590	590	590	590		12.30am	Crewe-Liverpool Lime St	Pass	1A/1	5.15am	Edge Hill-Crewe Station	EF [E]	1A/1	
						591	12.30am	Crewe-Liverpool Lime St	Pass	5A/43	5am	Edge Hill-Crewe Basford Hall	TF	5A/43	
592	592	592	592	592			12.18pm	Crewe-Liverpool Lime St	Pass	12A/17	4.20pm	Edge Hill-Crewe North Staffs Sidings	TF	12A/17	
593							7.42am	Crewe-Liverpool Lime St	Pass	3B/151	12.10pm	Edge Hill-Crewe Basford Hall	EF [F]	8A/13	
	593	593	593	593			7.42am	Crewe-Liverpool Lime St	Pass	2A/8	10.55am •	Edge Hill-Crewe North Staffs Sidings	TF	8A/13	
					593		7.42am	Crewe-Liverpool Lime St	Pass	2A/8	11.40am	Liverpool Lime St-Crewe	Pass	2A/8	
594							5.20am	Crewe-Liverpool Lime St	Pass	84G/5	9.5am	Liverpool Lime St-Crewe	Pass	84G/5	
595							2.35am	Crewe-Liverpool Lime St	News	8A/32	8am	Liverpool Lime St-Crewe	Cpld	8A/32	
					596		5pm	Crewe-Liverpool Lime St	Pass	3B/151	9.5pm	Edge Hill-Crewe Gresty Lane	EF [E]	3B/151	
597	597	597	597	597			9.40pm	Crewe-Liverpool Lime St	Pass	5A/41	2am	Garston-Crewe Basford Hall	TF	5A/41	
598	598	598	598	598			5.5pm	Crewe-Liverpool Lime St	Pass	5A/44	10.10pm	Liverpool Lime St-Crewe	Pass	5A/44	
					599		5.20am	Crewe-Liverpool Lime St	Pass	5A/71	8.50am	Liverpool Lime St-Shrewsbury-Crewe	Pass	5A/71	
600	600	600	600	600			3.22pm	Crewe-Manchester London Rd	Pass	12B/—	6.25pm	Manchester Mayfield-Crewe	Pass	12B/—	
601	601	601	601	601			6.10pm	Crewe-Manchester London Rd	Pass	84G/2	9.30pm	Manchester London Rd-Crewe	EF [F]	84G/2	
602	602	602	602	602			9pm	Crewe-Manchester London Rd	Pass	84G/4	2.00am	Stockport-Crewe	Pcls	84G/4	
603	603	603	603	603			12.45pm	Crewe-Manchester London Rd	Pass	84G/2	5.11pm	Manchester London Rd-Crewe	Pass	84G/2	
604	604	604	604	604			4.47pm	Crewe-Manchester Mayfield	Pass	2A/4	8.50pm	Manchester London Rd-Crewe Gresty Lane	EF [D]	2A/4	
605	605	605	605	605	605		6.45am	Crewe-Manchester London Rd	Pass	9A/9	9.15am	Manchester London Rd-Shrewsbury-Crewe	Pass	9A/9	
					606		3.45pm	Crewe-Manchester London Rd	Pass	84G/—		*return as required*			
607	607	607	607	607	607		7.50am	Crewe-Manchester London Rd	Pass	2A/—	3.5pm	Manchester London Rd-Crewe	Pass	2A/—	
608							5.10pm	Crewe-Manchester London Rd	Pass	5A/27		*return as required*			
					609		10.55am	Crewe-Manchester London Rd	Pass	2A/—	3.5pm	Manchester London Rd-Crewe	Cpld	2A/—	
					610		3.22pm	Crewe-Manchester London Rd	Pass	8A/15	8.15pm	Manchester London Rd-Crewe	Pass	8A/15	
					611		2.28pm	Crewe-Manchester Mayfield	Pass	3D/2	6.15pm	Manchester Longsight-Crewe Basford Hall	TF	3D/2	
					612		4.30pm	Crewe-Manchester London Rd	Pass	2A/—	8.30pm	Manchester London Rd-Crewe Gresty L	EF [E]	2A/—	
					613		8.10pm	Crewe-Manchester London Rd	Pass	9A/—	11.55pm	Manchester London Rd-Crewe	Pass	9A/—	
					614		5.10pm	Crewe-Manchester London Rd	Pass	5A/44	9.37pm	Manchester London Rd-Crewe	Pass	5A/44	
				615			11.36pm	Crewe-Stockport	Pass	@	12.17am	Stockport-Crewe	Pass	25G/—	@ not shown
					616		7.53pm	Crewe-Manchester London Rd	Pass	9A/3	1.33am	Stockport-Crewe	Pcls	9A/3	
						617	4.8am	Crewe-Manchester London Rd	Pass	5A/11	8.42am	Manchester London Rd-Crewe	Pass	5A/11	
						618	10.50am	Crewe-Manchester London Rd	Pass	5A/22	2.30pm	Manchester London Rd-Crewe	Pass	5A/22	
						619	4pm	Crewe-Manchester London Rd	Pcls	3D/5	7.5pm	Manchester London Rd-Crewe	Pass	3D/5	
						620	8.18pm	Crewe-Manchester London Rd	Pass	9A/9	11.30pm	Manchester London Rd-Crewe	News	9A/9	
	621	621	621	621	621		2.42am	Crewe-Manchester London Rd	Pass	9A/11	9.25am	Manchester London Rd-Crewe	Pass	9A/10	
						622	12.5am	Crewe-Stockport	Pass	5A/27		*return as required*			
623	623	623	623	623	623		11.20am	Crewe-Derby	Pass	9A/14	5.8pm	Derby-Crewe	Pass	9A/14	
624	624	624	624	624	624		5.10pm	Crewe-Stafford-Wolverhampton	Pass	84G/5	7.37pm	Wolverhampton-Stafford-Crewe	LE Pass	84G/5	
625	625	625	625	625			5.52pm	Crewe Carriage Works-Creswell	Pass	5A/40	7.25pm	Creswell-Stoke-Crewe	LE Pass	5A/40	

Outward Trip Mon	Tue	Wed	Thu	Fri	Sat	Sun	Time		Work	Loco	Inward Trip Time		Work	Loco	Date/Notes
626	626	626	626	626	626		4.10am	Crewe-Stoke-Stone	Pass	5A/40	7.48am	Stone-Stoke-Crewe	Pass	5A/40	
627	627	627	627	627	627		5.7am	Crewe-Derby	Pass	9A/14	9.15am	Derby-Crewe	Pass	9A/14	
628	628	628	628	628			6.45am	Crewe-Derby	Pass	84G/2	11.17am	Derby-Crewe	Pass	84G/2	
					628		6.45am	Crewe-Derby	Pass	84G/2	10.50am	Derby-Crewe	Pass	84G/2	
						629	6.50am	Crewe-Derby	Pass	84G/5	10.50am	Derby-Crewe	Pass	84G/5	
						630	5.35pm	Crewe-Derby	Pass	84G/5	8.40pm	Derby-Crewe	Pass	84G/5	
	631	631	631	631	631		1am	Crewe North Staffs Sidings-Stoke	EF [E]	8A/505	4.30am	Stoke-Crewe North Staffs Sidings	Cpld	9A/12	
632							2.50am	as passenger to Stoke			6.15am	Stoke-Crewe	LE	9A/12	
					635		4.2pm	Crewe-Derby	Pass	2A/9	8.15pm	Derby-Crewe	Pass	2A/9	
						636	1.45am	Crewe-Stoke-Crewe	Pass LE	5A/78	4.10am	Crewe-Blythe Bridge-Crewe	News	5A/78	
637	637	637	637	637			1.35pm	Crewe-Derby	Pass	5A/41	5.54pm	Derby-Crewe	Pass	5A/41	
					638		2.26am	Crewe-Stoke	EF [F]	5A/36	9.45am	Stoke-Crewe	Pass	5A/36	
					639		12.12pm	Crewe-Derby	Pass	7A/6	5.8pm	Derby-Crewe	Pass	7A/6	
					640		12.55pm	Crewe-Stoke	Pass	7A/3	3.30pm	Pratts Sidings-Crewe	ECS	7A/3	
					641		3.40pm	Crewe-Stoke-Crewe	Pass LE	2A/—	7.45pm	Crewe-Stoke-Crewe	Pass LE	9A/14	
650	650	650	650	650			7.48am	Crewe-Chester	Pass	7C/2	12.52pm	Chester-Crewe	Pcls	9A/12	
					651		7.48am	Crewe-Chester	Pass	1B/17	1.53pm	Chester-Crewe Basford Hall S Sdgs South	Pass	1B/32	
					652		10.26pm	Crewe-Chester	Pass	3D/5	11.40pm	Chester-Crewe Basford Hall	TF	3D/5	
						653	9.20am	Crewe-Chester	Pass	6B/4	11.45am	Chester-Crewe	Pass	1B/17	
						654	11.5am	Crewe-Llandudno	Pass	5A/10	4.5pm	Llandudno-Crewe	Pass	5A/10	
655	655	655	655	655			5.3pm	Crewe-Chester	Pass	7C/12	11.5pm	Mold Junction-Chester-Crewe	Frt TF	9A/400	
656							9.20am	Crewe-Chester	Pass	9A/12	11.35am	Chester-Crewe	Pass	7C/12	
					657		8.15am	Crewe-Llandudno	Pass	3C/5	12.55pm	Llandudno-Crewe	Cpld	3C/5	to 1 Sept
					658		8.15am	Crewe-Llandudno	Pass	3C/5	11.45am	Llandudno-Warrington Arpley-Crewe	Pass LE	3C/5	8 Sept only **
					659		8.15am	Crewe-Llandudno	Pass	3C/5	12.55pm	Llandudno-Crewe	Pass	3C/5	15 Sept only **
660							4.10am	Crewe Basford Hall -Whitchurch-Chester	EF Pass	5B/1055		*return as required*			
						664	2.55pm	Crewe-Llandudno	Pass	4B/1	7.40pm	Llan.Junction-Chester-Crewe	Cpld Pass	5A/41	
						667	6.57pm	Crewe-Chester	Pass	7A/6	8.15pm	Chester-Crewe	Pcls	7C/11	
668							7.35am	Crewe-Chester	Pass	Whit 1	10.20am	Mold Junction-Crewe North Staffs Sidings	Frt	5B/1041	
	669	669	669	669			7.35am	Crewe-Chester	Pass	Whit 1	10.55am	Birkenhead-Crewe North Staffs Sidings	TF	5B/1041	
	670						10.55am	Crewe-Chester	Pass	5A/39		*return as required*			
671							1.15pm	Crewe-Chester	Pass	7C/7	5.40pm	Dundas Sidings-Crewe North Staffs Sdgs	Eties	5B/1052	
					672		10.23am	Crewe-Llandudno	Pass	3E/10	2.25pm	Llandudno-Crewe	Cpld	3E/10	
					673		11am	Crewe-Llandudno Junction	Pass	7C/2	3.29pm	Llandudno Junction-Crewe	Pass	1B/20	
					674		2.36am	Crewe-Holyhead	Pass	1A/8		*return as required*			
				675			8.35pm	as passenger to Holyhead			1.10am	Holyhead-Crewe	Pass	7C/5	
				676			4.25pm	Crewe-Bangor-Llandudno Junction	Pass LE	5A/66	11.18pm	Chester-Crewe Basford Hall	EF	5A/39	
					677		10.47am	Chester-Coventry	Pass	2A/—		*return as required*			
				678			5.3pm	Crewe-Llandudno Junction	Cpld	1B/21		*return as required*			
					679		10.5am	Chester-Birmingham New St	Pass	5A/66		Walsall-Crewe North	LE	5A/66	
					680		9.5am	Crewe-Llandudno Junction	Pass	9A/12	1.5pm	Llandudno-Crewe	Pass	9A/12	
					681		9.30am	Crewe-Llandudno Junction	Pass	3D/8		*return as required*			to 7 July only **
					682		9.30am	Crewe-Llandudno	Pass	3D/8	2.10pm	Llandudno-Rhyl-Crewe	ECS Pass	3D/8	from 14 July
						683	10.26pm	as passenger to Holyhead			3.45am	Holyhead-Crewe	Pass	1A/8	
					684		9.40am	Crewe Basford Hall-Llandudno	Pass	3E/7	2.25pm	Llandudno-Crewe	Pass	3E/8	
					685		10.47am	Crewe Basford Hall-Llandudno	Pass	2B/—	2.57pm	Llandudno Junction-Chester	Pcls	2B/—	
					686		10.35am	Crewe-Llandudno	Pass	17A/—	2.50pm	Llandudno-Crewe	Cpld	17A/—	
					687		10.23am	Crewe-Llandudno	Pass	2A/35	2.50pm	Llandudno-Crewe	Pass	2A/35	23/30.June only **
					688		10.11am	Crewe Basford Hall-Llandudno	Pass	2A/35	2.50pm	Llandudno-Crewe	Pass	2A/35	
					689		10.11am	Crewe Basford Hall-Llandudno	Pass	2A/35	2.50pm	Llandudno-Crewe	Pass	2A/35	8 Sept only **
					690		10.23am	Crewe Basford Hall-Llandudno	Pass	2A/35	2.50pm	Llandudno-Crewe	Pass	2A/35	15 Sept only**
					691		11.16am	Crewe-Llandudno	Pass	9A/14	5.15pm	Llandudno-Crewe	Pass	9A/14	

Outward Trip Mon	Tue	Wed	Thu	Fri	Sat	Sun	Time		Work	Loco	Inward Trip Time		Work	Loco	Date/Notes
					692		11.25am	Crewe-Holyhead	Pass	5A/8	3.5pm	Holyhead-Crewe	Pass	7C/1	to 1 Sept
					693		9.20am	as passenger to Holyhead			3.5pm	Holyhead-Crewe	Pass	7C/1	15 Aug/22 Sept only **
					694		12.32pm	Crewe-Llandudno	Pass	1B/31		*return as required*			23 June only **
					695		1.58pm	Crewe-Llandudno	Pass	1A/1	7.20pm	Llandudno-Crewe	Pass	1A/1	
					696		1.58pm	Crewe-Llandudno	Pass	1A/1		*return as required*			15 Sept only **
					697		7.50pm	Crewe-Chester	Pass	7A/3	1.00am	Chester-Crewe	Pcls	5A/28	
						698	10.32pm	Crewe-Llandudno	Pass	3D/7	2.0pm	Llandudno-Crewe	Pass	3D/7	
					699		9.42am	Crewe-Llandudno	Pass	2A/31	1.20pm	Llandudno-Crewe	Cpld	2A/31	
701	701	701	701	701			5.25pm	Crewe-Shrewsbury	Pass	8A/5	7.56pm	Shrewsbury-Crewe	Pass	8A/5	
					701		5.25pm	Crewe-Shrewsbury	Pass	1B/22	7.20pm	Shrewsbury-Crewe	Pass	1B/22	
702	702	702	702	702			10.20am	Crewe-Shrewsbury	Pass	5A/1	4.0pm	Shrewsbury-Crewe	Pass	5A/1	
					703		10.40am	Crewe-Shrewsbury	Pass	5A/1	3.38pm	Shrewsbury-Crewe	Pass	5A/1	
705	705	705	705	705			8.16pm	Crewe-Shrewsbury	Pass	5B/1039	11.30pm	Shrewsbury Harlescott-Crewe Gresty Lane	TF	84G/108	
					706		4.17pm	Crewe-Shrewsbury	Pass	9A/7	7.56pm	Shrewsbury-Crewe	Pass	9A/7	
					707		8.16pm	Crewe-Shrewsbury	Pass	84G/2	11.30pm	Shrewsbury Harlescott-Crewe Gresty Lane	TF	9A/412	
					708		8.16pm	as passenger to Hereford			1.23am	Hereford-Crewe	Pcls	9A/4	
709	709	709	709	709			12.10pm	Crewe-Shrewsbury	Pass	5A/33	4.35pm	Shrewsbury Harlescott-Crewe Basford Hall	TF	84G/103	
710	710	710	710	710			6.10pm	Crewe-Shrewsbury	Pass	12A/13	9.45pm	Shrewsbury-Crewe	Pass	2A/3	
					710		6.10pm	Crewe-Shrewsbury	Pass	12A/13	9.58pm	Shrewsbury-Crewe	Pcls	9A/9	
					711		11.20am	Crewe-Whitchurch-Crewe	ES Pass	8A/26	2.0pm	Crewe-Liverpool Lime St-EdgeHill-Crewe	Pass EF	8A/26	
712	712	712	712	712			6.40pm	Crewe-Shrewsbury	Fish	5A/33	10.35pm	Shrewsbury-Crewe	Pass	5A/33	
					713		12.10pm	Crewe-Shrewsbury	Pass	9A/14	4.35pm	Shrewsbury Harlescott-Crewe Basford Hall	TF	84G/103	
	714	714	714	714			2.35pm	Crewe Up Sidings-Shrewsbury	Pcls	2B/5	5.45pm	Shrewsbury-Crewe	Pass	84G/4	
715							2.15am	Crewe-Shrewsbury	Pass	84G/1	8.40am	Shrewsbury-Crewe	Pass	84G/22	
						716	3.35pm	Crewe-Calveley-Crewe	ES Milk	5A/33	6.45pm	Crewe-Salop-Crewe	Pass	5A/33	
	717	717	717	717	717		4.3am	Crewe-Shrewsbury	Pcls	84G/4	8.40am	Shrewsbury-Crewe	Pass	2B/5	
718	718	718	718	718	718		10.30am	Crewe-Shrewsbury	Pass	9A/10	5.30pm	Shrewsbury-Crewe	Pass	9A/10	
					719		10.7am	Crewe-Shrewsbury	Pass	9A/9		Shrewsbury-Crewe	LE	9A/9	
						721	12.10pm	Crewe-Shrewsbury	Pass	84G/4	4.25pm	Shrewsbury-Crewe	Pass	84G/4	
				722			4.17pm	Crewe-Shrewsbury	Pass	9A/37	8.35pm	Shrewsbury Harlescott-Crewe Gresty Lane	EF [H]	84G/107	
723	723	723	723	723			9.18pm	Crewe-Shrewsbury	Pass	5B/1032	3.24am	Shrewsbury-Crewe	Pass	84G/5	
724							3.28pm	Crewe-Shrewsbury	Pass	84G/22	5.45pm	Shrewsbury-Crewe	Pass	84G/4	
					725		2.37pm	Crewe-Shrewsbury-Stafford	Pcls	2B/5	7.44pm	Stafford-Crewe	Pass	5B/1030	
	726						3.28pm	Crewe-Shrewsbury	Pass	2A/9	6.5pm	Crewe Bank-Crewe Basford Hall	TF	2A/9	
		726	726	726			3.28pm	Crewe-Shrewsbury	Pass	2A/9	6.20pm	Shrewsbury Harlescott-Crewe Gresty Lane	TF	2A/9	
					727		3.28pm	Crewe-Shrewsbury	Pass	2A/9	6.20pm	Shrewsbury Harlescott-Crewe Gresty Lane	TF	84G/102	
					728		11.15am	Crewe-Shrewsbury	Pass	28A/59	2.10pm	Shrewsbury-Crewe	Cpld	28A/59	
					729		9.53am	Crewe-Shrewsbury	Pass	5A/69		*return as required*		5A/69	
					730		9.53am	Crewe-Shrewsbury	Pass	5A/69	12.5pm	Crewe-Whitchurch-Crewe	Cpld Pass	5A/69	8 Sept only **
				731			11.44pm	Crewe-Shrewsbury	Pass	5A/30		*return as required*			22 June/7 Sept only**
				732			11.44pm	Crewe-Shrewsbury	Pass	5A/30		*return as required*			
900	900	900	900	900	900		8.30am	Up Side Bank		5A/53					
901	901	901	901	901	901		3.20pm	Up Side Bank		5A/53					
902	902	902	902	902	902		10.40pm	Up Side Bank		5A/53					
						903	9.5pm	Up Side Bank		5A/53					
904	904	904	904	904	904		6.5am	Down Side Bank		5A/54					
905	905	905	905	905	905		12.55pm	Down Side Bank		5A/54					
	907	907	907	907	907		2am	South End Station Shunt		5A/55					
	908	908	908	908	908		8.50am	South End Station Shunt		5A/55					
909	909	909	909	909			3.35pm	Crewe-Calveley	ECS	5A/55	4.50pm	Calveley-Crewe	Milk	5A/55	
					909		3.35pm	Crewe-Calveley	Pcls	5A/55	5.13pm	Calveley-Crewe	Milk	5A/55	

Outward Trip										Inward Trip			
Mon	Tue	Wed	Thu	Fri	Sat	Sun	Time	Work	Loco	Time	Work	Loco	Date/Notes
913	913	913	913	913	913		8am	No 2. Up Side Shunt	5B/1071				
914	914	914	914	914	914		3.20pm	No 2. Up Side Shunt	5B/1071				
915	915	915	915	915			10.40pm	No 2. Up Side Shunt	5B/1071				
					916		10.40pm	No 2. Up Side Shunt	5B/1071				
						917	8.5am	No 2. Up Side Shunt	5B/1071				
						918	3.10pm	No 2. Up Side Shunt	5B/1071				
						922	8.30am	No 3. Down Bays Shunt	5B/1072				
923							12.25am	No 3. Down Bays Shunt	5B/1072				
924	924	924	924	924	924		6.25am	No 3. Down Bays Shunt	5B/1072				
925	925	925	925	925	925		1.45pm	No 3. Down Bays Shunt	5B/1072				
926	926	926	926	926			11.5pm	No 3. Down Bays Shunt	5B/1072				
					927		9.5pm	No 3. Down Bays Shunt	5B/1072				
						928	4.40am	No 3. Down Bays Shunt	5B/1072				
930	930	930	930	930	930		1pm	No 5. Down Carriage Sdgs S End Shunt	5B/1073				
931	931	931	931	931	931		7.45pm	No 5. Down Carriage Sdgs S End Shunt	5B/1073				
938	938	938	938	938			12.30pm	No 6. Down Bays North End Shunt	5B/1074				
939	939	939	939	939			7.5pm	No 6. Down Bays North End Shunt	5B/1074				
	940	940	940	940	940		2.25am	No 6. Down Bays North End Shunt	5B/1074				
					941		1pm	No 6. Down Bays North End Shunt	5B/1074				
					942		6.45pm	No 6. Down Bays North End Shunt	5B/1074				
						945	6pm	No 7. Down Bays Shunt	5B/1075				
946							12.45am	No 7. Down Bays Shunt	5B/1075				
947							8.5am	No 7. Down Bays Shunt	5B/1075				
948	948	948	948	948			10.30pm	No 7. Down Bays Shunt	5B/1075				
	949	949	949	949	949		5am	No 7. Down Bays Shunt	5B/1075				
953							6am	No 8. Down Carriage Sdgs S End Shunt	5B/1076				
954	954	954	954	954			10pm	No 8. Down Carriage Sdgs S End Shunt	5B/1076				
	955	955	955	955	955		5.50am	No 8. Down Carriage Sdgs S End Shunt	5B/1076				
					956		10pm	No 8. Down Carriage Sdgs S End Shunt	5B/1076				
						957	2am	No 8. Down Carriage Sdgs S End Shunt	5B/1076				
960	960	960	960	960	960		9am	No 9. Down Carriage Sdgs N End Shunt	5B/1070				
						961	9am	No 9. Down Carriage Sdgs N End Shunt	5B/1070				
						962	3.45pm	No 9. Down Carriage Sdgs N End Shunt	5B/1070				
970							4am	No 2. Up Side Shunt	5B/1071				
	971	971	971	971	971		2.35am	Relieving Turns 8A/257; 954; 915					
972	972	972	972	972			11.34am	Relieving Turns 561; 140; 931					
973							3.40pm	Preparation & Relieving Duties					
	974	974	974	974	974		12.20pm	Relieving Turns 949; 960, 623.					
						976	10.40am	Down Side Bank	5A/54				
977							12.15am	Preparation Turns 715; 549; 628; 607; 97					
	977	977	977	977			12.15am	Preparation Turns 559; 549; 650; 607; 97					
					977		1am	Preparation Turns 621;549;628;112;607;99					
980	980	980	980	980			9.30pm	Passenger Station Shunt	8A/27				
					981		11.50pm	Passenger Station Shunt	8A/—				
999	999	999	999	999	999		6.35am	Trials to Whitchurch					
142	**134**	**131**	**133**	**146**	**170**	**62**		**Total Daily Rostered Turns**					

[Note ** Indicates Turn *not* included in totals]

Crewe North (5A) Enginemen's Workings July 1951

Shunt Shed and for fitters as required

Turn	Days	Set	Hours
Turn 2000	D	One Set	6am to 2pm
Turn 2001	D	One Set	2pm to 10pm
Turn 2002	D	One Set	10pm to 6am
Turn 2003	MO	One Set	12.1am to 6am
Turn 2004	SX	One Set	10pm to 6am
Turn 2005	SuO	One Set	10am to 4pm
Turn 2006	SuO	One Set	4pm to 12am

Ashpit Turners

Turn	Days	Set	Hours
Turn 2008	D	One Set	6am to 2pm
Turn 2009	D	One Set	2pm to 10pm
Turn 2010	D	One Set	10pm to 6am
Turn 2011	SuO	One Set	6am to 6pm
Turn 2012	SuO	One Set	6pm to 2am
Turn 2013	MO	One Set	2am to 6am

Assisting at Coaling Plant

Turn	Days	Set	Hours
Turn 2014	D	One Set	2pm to 10pm
Turn 2015	D	One Set	6am to 2pm

Shunt and Drop Loco Coal Trips to Basford Hall

Turn	Days	Set	Hours	From	To	Arr	Notes
Turn 2016	D	One Set	6am to 2pm				
	To also work:						
	D	Trip	8.30am	North Shed	South Shed	8.45am	No 20 Trip
	D	LE	9.30am	South Shed	Sorting Sidings North	9.35am	
	D	Trip	9.45am	Sorting Sidings North	North Shed	10am	
	D	Trip	10.30am	North Shed	Sorting Sidings North	10.45am	
	D	LE	11.30am	Sorting Sidings North	North Shed	11.45am	
Turn 2017	SuO	One Set	8am to 4pm				

Loco Coal Shunt and Feeding Tippler

Turn	Days	Set	Hours
Turn 2018	D	One Set	8am to 4pm
Turn 2019		Not Used	

Store Van to Station and South Shed
Then to Old Yard Rep No 45

Turn	Days	Set	Hours	
Turn 2020	D	One Set	5.30am to 1.30pm	5B/1090
Turn 2021	D	One Set	1pm to 9pm	5B/1090

Engine Arrangers

Turn	Days	Set	Hours
Turn 2022	D	One Driver	6am to 2pm
Turn 2023	D	One Driver	2pm to10pm
Turn 2024	D	One Driver	10pm to 6am
Turn 2025	SuO	One Driver	6am to 6pm
	SuO	One Driver	6pm to 6am

Above:
Crewe, Down Through No 2 Road, 3 June 1952
Class 5 No 44687, with outside Caprotti valve gear, double chimney and Skefko roller bearings trundles through the complex on its way to North Shed. This engine was built in 1951 and was very free running. It was based at Longsight at the time. It is a great pity that this fine engine was not preserved. *B. K. B. Green*

Right:
Crewe, Down Through No 2 Line, 28 April 1951
Midland Railway-design Class 3F 0-6-0 No 43226 wearing a Derby 17A shedplate passes through the Down Through No 2 road with a train of empties from Sideway (Stoke) to Speke sidings. The train, believed to have departed at 9.30am, was booked to call for inspection at North Staffs Sidings south of the station. The locomotive was normally provided by Speke Junction and why a Derby engine should be on the working is a mystery.
H. C. Casserley

Setting Engines for Fire Droppers

Turn 2026	D	One Driver	6am to 2pm
Turn 2027	D	One Driver	2pm to 10pm
Turn 2028	D	One Driver	10pm to 6am

Filling Tanks and Arranging Engines in Coal Hole

Turn 2029	D	One Driver	6am to 2pm
Turn 2030	D	One Set	2pm to 10pm
Turn 2031	D	One Set	10pm to 6am
Turn 2032	MO	One Driver	12mn to 6am
Turn 2033	SuO	One Driver	6am to 2pm

Shed and Station Sets

Turn 2034	D		One Set	6am to 2pm			
			Prepare Engine For:	**Turn No**	**Leaves Shed.**		
			9.25am Carlisle	206	8.45am 'L'		
			Take out, relief in Station at 9.20am by Turns 206 and 207				
Turn 2035	D		One Set	2pm to 10pm			
	SO		Relieve 1.30pm	from Barrow (Turn 207) at 4.51pm		} 30 June and	
SO			4.55pm	Shunt (Pass) Crewe	5.30pm	} 15/22 Sept	5A/11
SO		LE	-	CreweNorth Shed	5.35pm	only	
Turn 2036	D		One Set	10pm to 6am			
Turn 2037	SX		One Set	6am to 2pm			
Turn 2038	SX		One Set	2pm to 10pm			
Turn 2039	SX		One Set	10pm to 6am			

Engines Crewe Works to Crewe North Shed

Turn 2040	D	One Set	8am to 4pm

Taking Engines from Front Road

Turn 2041		One Set	10pm to 6am

Control Sets

Note: Subject to two hours variation before or after booking-on times shown:

Turn 2100

Days	No of Sets	Booking-on time
D	1	1am
D	1	2am
D	2	4am
D	2	5am
D	2	6am
D	3	7am
D	2	8am
D	1	9am
D	2	10am
D	2	12pm
D	1	1pm
D	1	2pm
D	1	5pm
D	1	7pm
D	1	9pm
D	1	10pm
D	1	11pm
Sun	1	12.5am
Sun	1	2am
Sun	1	3am
Sun	2	4am
Sun	5	5am
Sun	2	6am
Sun	1	7am
Sun	1	9am
Sun	2	10am
Sun	4	12pm
Sun	1	2pm
Sun	1	3pm
Sun	1	4pm
Sun	1	6pm
Sun	1	8pm
Sun	1	10pm

Above

Crewe, Down Through No 2 Road, Sunday 9 August 1953

A stranger in the camp! Colwick (38A) shed 'B1' No 61186 coasts through the Down Through line working the E330 Halfex, Pleasley to Llandudno. The load was 10 vehicles, 300 tons. The train came on to Western Division metals at Egginton Junction at 10.55am where the crew were changed. It then stopped for water at Uttoxeter and Stoke-on-Trent and halted to change train crew again at Crewe station, as seen here. Departure was 12.12pm and stops were made at Chester, Rhyl and Colwyn Bay, arriving at Llandudno at 2pm. Return departure was at 7pm and after the Chester stop the train proceeded to Kidsgrove Central for water and crew change. Next stop for water was at Uttoxeter, and LM men came off at Egginton Junction at 10.10pm when the train continued to its destination. This information was abstracted from the W2 STN No 32 dated Saturday 8 August to Friday 14 August 1953. *B. K. B. Green*

North Shed Links 1 to 5

No 1 Link — 12 sets
Crewe North. March to June 1952
Source: 'Piccolo' Pete Johnson

MONDAY		TUESDAY		WEDNESDAY		THURSDAY		FRIDAY		SATURDAY		SUNDAY	
Time & Destination	Turn	Time & Destination	Turn	Time & Destination	Turn	Time & Destination	Turn	Time & Destination	Turn	Time & Destination	Turn	Time & Destination	Turn
7.50am Euston	299	12.2am Crewe	301	7.50am Euston	299	12.2am Crewe	302	4.5am Euston	281			4.5am Euston	282
								9.25pm Crewe	283			8.30pm Crewe	285
		1.20pm Carlisle	159	4.28am Crewe	160	1.20pm Carlisle	159	4.28am Crewe	160	Rest Day			
7.2pm Euston	329	1.15pm Crewe	330			7.2pm Euston	329	1.15pm Crewe	330	6.37pm Carlisle	172	12.15pm Crewe	173
Rest Day		7.50am Euston	299	12.2am Crewe	302	7.50am Euston	299	12.2am Crewe	302				
4.27am Euston	290			5.2am Euston	291			5.2am Euston	291				
7.35pm Crewe	292			11.5pm Crewe	293			11.5pm Crewe	293				
1.15am Carlisle	150					4.28 Crewe	160			4.28am Crewe	160	Rest Day	
6.30pm Crewe	151			1.20pm Carlisle	159			1.20pm Crewe	159				
9.25am Preston	206	9.25am Preston	206	9.25am Preston	206	Rest Day		9.25am Preston	206	9.25am Preston	207		
2.50pm Crewe		2.50pm Crewe		2.50pm Crewe				2.50pm Crewe		2.30pm Crewe@			
		5.2am Euston	291			5.2am Euston	291						
		11.5pm Crewe	293			11.5pm Crewe	293			7.2pm Euston	329	3pm Crewe	331
1.15pm Chester	318			1.15pm Chester	318			Rest Day		10am	Spare		
2.40pm Euston		12.40pm Crewe	320	2.40pm Euston		12.40pm Crewe	320						
2.5am Carlisle	183			4.5am Euston	281					4.5am Euston	281		
9.30pm Crewe	184			9.25pm Crewe	283					8.30pm Crewe	284		
		4.5am Euston	281			4.5am Euston	281					12.37am Euston	267
		9.25pm Crewe	283			9.25pm Crewe	283					7.15pm Crewe	271
		12.37am Euston	266			Rest Day				6.5am Crewe	175		
		7.15pm Crewe	274					1.54pm Carlisle	174				

Note: @ = 2.30pm Morecambe to Crewe SO

Below:
Crewe North Junction
Stafford shed (5C) Standard Class 2P 4-4-0 No 40678 pulls into the station off the Chester line, with the 5.52pm evening working from Crewe carriage works to Stoke and Creswell. There was a corresponding morning train that called all stations from Creswell and after setting down ordinary passengers, proceeded to the old carriage works where the stock remained during the day. This working was commenced when Stoke locomotive works closed and staff transferred to Crewe. The carriage works buildings were demolished to make way for the electric traction depot. *Martin Welch*

No 2 Link — 8 sets
Crewe North. 30 June-14 September 1952
Source: Author's Records

MONDAY		TUESDAY		WEDNESDAY		THURSDAY		FRIDAY		SATURDAY		SUNDAY	
Time & Destination	Turn	Time & Destination	Turn	Time & Destination	Turn	Time & Destination	Turn	Time & Destination	Turn	Time & Destination	Turn	Time & Destination	Turn
10.29pm Perth	135	8.15pm Crewe	136					10.29pm Perth	135	8.15pm Crewe	136		
11.10pm Perth	131	9.48pm Crewe	133			11.10pm Perth	131	9.48pm Crewe	133			10.29pm Perth	135
8.15pm Crewe	136					10.29pm Perth	135	8.15pm Crewe	136				
		11.10pm Perth	131	9.48pm Crewe	133			11.10pm Perth	133	9.48pm Crewe	133		
		10.29pm Perth	135	8.15pm Crewe	136			10.50pm Perth	145	8.55pm Crewe	146		
				10.29pm Perth	135	8.15pm Crewe	136			11.10pm Perth	132	8.25pm Crewe	134
				12am Glasgow	139								
				5.40pm Crewe	140			7.3pm Euston	329	1.15pm Crewe	330	11.10pm Perth	130
9.48pm Crewe	133			11.10pm Perth	131	9.48pm Crewe	133						

Left:
'Jubilee' class 4-6-0 No 45686 *St Vincent* pulls into Crewe off the Manchester line with a forces special from the Central Division , hence the reporting number C868. The loco carries a Camden 1B shedplate. Its ultimate destinaiton is not known. An unrebuilt 'Patriot' heads a train of vans in the distance. *S.D.Wainwright*

Left:
Crewe North Junction
Pacific No 46238 *City of Carlisle* coasts into Platform 3 off the West Coast main line with an Up Class 1 for Euston. The loco was allocated to Camden at this time and judging by the short length of the train (six vehicles) would be strengthened at Crewe. Leading coach is a six-wheel restaurant car still in LMS maroon. In the distance a Class 5 4-6-0 pulls across the junction, possibly heading for Liverpool. *Martin Welch*

No 3 Link — 8 sets
Crewe North. March to June 1951
Source: D. H. Smith

MONDAY		TUESDAY		WEDNESDAY		THURSDAY		FRIDAY		SATURDAY		SUNDAY	
Time & Destination	Turn	Time & Destination	Turn	Time & Destination	Turn	Time & Destination	Turn	Time & Destination	Turn	Time & Destination	Turn	Time & Destination	Turn
				1.5am Glasgow 11.15pm Crewe	143 144			1.5am Glasgow 11.15pm Crewe	143 144				
		1.5am Glasgow 11.15pm Crewe	143 144							1.5am Glasgow 11.15pm Crewe	143 144		
				12.37am Euston 7.30pm Crewe	266 269			12am Glasgow 5.40pm Crewe	139 140				
12am Glasgow 5.40pm Crewe	139 140			1.10am Euston 8.30am Crewe	274 277			4.19pm Glasgow	141	1.30pm Crewe	142		
1.5am Glasgow 11.15pm Crewe	143 144					1.5am Glasgow 11.15pm Crewe	143 144						
4.19pm Glasgow	141	1.30pm Crewe	142	4.19pm Glasgow	141	1.30pm Crewe	142					12am Glasgow 5.40pm Crewe	139 140
						12am Glasgow 5.40pm Crewe	139 140	7.3pm Euston	329	1.15pm Crewe	330	12.54pm Glasgow	137
9.30am Crewe	138			12am Glasgow 5.40am Crewe	139 140			5.2am Euston 10.30pm Crewe#	291 294				

Note: # = 10.30pm off Willesden

Above:
Crewe North End
'Princess Coronation' Pacific No 46236 *City of Bradford* pulls into the station off the West Coast main line. This was possibly the 8.20am off Carlisle which was diagrammed to a Camden Pacific. The train crew consisted of Crewe North men who worked south from Carlisle and were relieved by another set of North Shed men for the journey to Euston. Note the gas cylinder wagon used for recharging the restaurant cars. *Ben Brooksbank*

No 4 Link — 12 sets
Crewe North. March to June 1954
Source — author's records

MONDAY	TUESDAY	WEDNESDAY	THURSDAY	FRIDAY	SATURDAY	SUNDAY
Time/Destination	**Time/Destination**	**Time/Destination**	**Time/Destination**	**Time/Destination**	**Time/Destination**	**Time/Destination**
3.54pm Liverpool 10.10pm Crewe	5.5pm Liverpool 11.53pm W'ton-Crewe	5.5pm Liverpool 11.53pm W'ton-Crewe	5.5pm Liverpool 11.53pm W'ton-Crewe	5.5pm Liverpool 11.53pm W'ton-Crewe	6pm Carlisle (L)	12.44pm Crewe
10.42am Liverpool 4.17am Crewe	10.42am Liverpool 4.17am Crewe	10am Spare	11.27am Northampton 3.6pm Rugby-Crewe	Rest Day	11.27am Northampton 3.6pm Rugby-Crewe	
7.42am Liverpool 10.15am Crewe	5.45am Preston 11.16am Crewe	7.50am Euston (L) 11.50pm Crewe		8.48am Liverpool 11.40am Crewe	8.48am Liverpool 11.40am Crewe	
12.51am Euston (L) 6.20pm Crewe		1.10am Euston (L) 5.35pm Crewe	6.15pm Euston (L)	4.30pm Crewe	Rest Day	
7.48pm Liverpool 11.45pm Crewe	7.48pm Liverpool 11.45pm Crewe	7.48pm Liverpool 11.45pm Crewe	7.48pm Liverpool 11.45pm Crewe	7.48pm Liverpool 11.45pm Crewe	7.35pm Manchester	2.50am Crewe
Rest Day	7.42am Liverpool 10.15am Crewe	5.45am Preston 11.16am Crewe	5.45am Preston 11.16am Crewe	5.45am Preston 11.16am Crewe	5.45am Preston 11.16am Crewe	10.55am Manchester 2.30pm Crewe
1.54pm Carnforth 6.6pm Crewe	4.40pm Preston 8.39pm Crewe	4.40pm Preston 8.39pm Crewe	4.40pm Preston 8.39pm Crewe	3.54pm Liverpool 10.10pm Crewe	5.30pm Birmingham 10.10pm Crewe	
4.40pm Preston 8.39pm Crewe	Rest Day	9.40am Rugby Parcels 1.30pm Crewe BHSS	9.7am Euston (L)	5.40am Crewe		
10.46pm Rugby Parcels 1.27am Crewe Parcels	10.46pm Rugby Parcels 1.27am Crewe Parcels	10.46pm Rugby Parcels 1.27am Crewe Parcels	10.46pm Rugby Parcels 1.27am Crewe Parcels	10.46pm Rugby Parcels 1.27am Crewe Parcels	7.48pm Liverpool	12.10am Crewe
8am Spare	9.45am Liverpool 11.50am Crewe	Rest Day	9.45am Liverpool 11.50am Crewe	9.45am Liverpool 11.50am Crewe	9.45am Liverpool 11.50am Crewe	
8.48am Liverpool 11.40am Crewe	8.48am Liverpool 11.40am Crewe	8.48am Liverpool 11.40am Crewe	12.51am Euston (L) 6.20pm Crewe		10am Spare	10.50am Liverpool 2.10pm Crewe
8am Spare	7.48am Euston (L) 11.50pm Crewe		Rest Day	9.40am Rugby Parcels 1.30pm Crewe BHSS	12.18pm Liverpool 5.40pm Crewe	

Note: (L) denotes Lodging Turn

Below:
Crewe North End
Stanier Class 5 No 45254 drifts into Crewe with a working off the Chester line. The stock livery is mainly 'blood and custard' although the third and fifth coaches are still in LMS maroon. The reporting number W638 suggests that this was an 'extra', but from where and to where is anybody's guess. The loco was attached to Crewe North Shed. *Martin Welch*

Right:
Crewe North Junction
An unidentified 'Jubilee' pilots fellow classmate No 45592 *Indore*, seen here pulling away from Platform 1 at the north end of the station. Details of the working are not known but it is possible this was the 12 noon Euston to Workington which was a heavy train — 14 vehicles and which might have been strengthened, hence the pilot loco. The train will take the Down Fast line once outside the station limits, as indicated by the 'F' on the signal indicator. The North Shed buildings have the usual assortment of goods wagons alongside. Note the seven-plank wagon with loco wheels and the line of loco coal wagons. *Ben Brooksbank*

No 5 Link — 12 sets
Crewe North. December to May 1956
Source — Tom Rigby

MONDAY	TUESDAY	WEDNESDAY	THURSDAY	FRIDAY	SATURDAY	SUNDAY
Time/Destination	**Time/Destination**	**Time/Destination**	**Time/Destination**	**Time/Destination**	**Time/Destination**	**Time/Destination**
7.48am Euston (L)	12.2am Crewe	8.58am Euston (L)	12.2am Crewe	8.58am Euston	12.2am Crewe	7.29pm Manchester 10.10pm Crewe
3.37pm Manchester 6.20pm Crewe Parcels	3.37pm Manchester 6.20pm Crewe Parcels	3.37pm Manchester 6.20pm Crewe Parcels	3.37pm Manchester 6.20pm Crewe Parcels	3.37pm Manchester 6.20pm Crewe Parcels	Rest Day	
4.22pm Euston (L)	12.pm Crewe Parcels	4.22pm Euston (L)	12. Crewe Parcels	1.9pm Birmingham 6.pm Crewe	2.28pm Birmingham 6.25pm Crewe	
Rest Day	5.17am Birmingham 11.25am Crewe	5.45am Morecambe *as required*	5.45am Morecambe *as required*	5.45am Morecambe *as required*	9.20am Rhyl 12.35pm Chester	
8.17pm Birmingham 1.45am Crewe	8.17pm Birmingham 1.45am Crewe	8.17pm Birmingham 1.45am Crewe	8.17pm Birmingham 1.45am Crewe	8.17pm Birmingham 1.45am Crewe		12.5pm Birmingham as passenger
5.10am Manchester 9.45am Crewe	Rest Day	7.43am Liverpool 10.55am Crewe BHSS	7.43am Liverpool 10.55am Crewe BHSS	7.43am Liverpool 10.55am Crewe BHSS	7.43am Liverpool 10.55am Crewe BHSS	
2.7am Carlisle (L) 6.30pm Crewe	5.13pm Liverpool 11.45pm Crewe	5.13pm Liverpool 11.45pm Crewe	5.13pm Liverpool 11.45pm Crewe	5.13pm Liverpool 11.45pm Crewe		2.3am Liverpool 6.am Crewe LE
12.5pm Liverpool 3.10pm Crewe NSS	12.5pm Liverpool 3.10pm Crewe NSS	Rest Day	12.5pm Liverpool 3.10pm Crewe NSS	12.5pm Liverpool 3.10pm Crewe NSS	12.5pm Liverpool 3.10 Crewe NSS	9.35am Euston (L) 11.57pm Crewe
	9.40am Rugby 1.30pm Crewe BHSS	8.48am Liverpool *as required*	7.48am Euston (L)	12.2am Crewe	8.58am Euston (L)	12.2am Crewe
3.33pm Birmingham 8.20pm Crewe	3.33pm Birmingham 8.20pm Crewe	3.33pm Birmingham 8.20pm Crewe	Rest Day	3.33pm Birmingham 8.20pm Crewe	3.33pm Birmingham 8.20pm Crewe	
12.45am Birmingham 6.30am Crewe	3.48am Birmingham 9.20am Crewe	3.48am Birmingham 9.20am Crewe	3.48am Birmingham 9.20am Crewe	3.48am Birmingham 9.20am Crewe	3.48am Birmingham 9.20 Crewe	
1.9pm Birmingham 6.pm Crewe	1.9pm Birmingham 6.pm Crewe	1.54pm Carlisle (L)	8.20am Crewe		1.9pm Birmingham 6.pm Crewe	

Note: (L) denotes Lodging Turn

South Shed (5B)

July 1951

For operational purposes both sheds were treated as one and Crewe South duties commenced at Turn 1000 following on from the North Shed sequence. It must be remembered that some duties required North Shed men to book off at Crewe South and vice versa. However, it will be noted that whilst North Shed had dozens of lodging turns, South Shed had very few. Additionally, Crewe South diagrams included the Locomotive Works diagrams. Conversely, many Crewe South engines working station shunting duties were listed under and manned by North Shed men. As was usual, there were many shed turns involving train crew that were confined to shed limits and these were to be found after the duties that operated outside shed limits. North Shed duties under this category were listed after the South Shed running turns, commencing at Turn 2000.

Engine Turns

The number of South Shed engines booked daily for July 1951 was as follows:

Mon	Tue	Wed	Thu	Fri	Sat	Sun
50	55	52	52	56	60	40

Where engine turns were shown as booked to four engines, these were four-day workings, although in some cases, usually on a Sunday, an engine was stood down when not required. A breakdown of the South Shed Engine duties gives Turns 1001 to 1018 allocated to 18 Stanier Class 8F 2-8-0 locomotives but only six duties, using the 18 engines, were active. Turns 1001 and 1004 were four-day workings, each requiring four engines; Turns 1005 and 1017 required three. Turns 1003 and 1018 required two locomotives. Turns 1002 and 1006-16 were not used. As with standard LMS and BR LMR (Western Division) procedure, there were 23 Class 8F engines for the six working duties.

Turns 1019 and 1020 were the preserve of ex-LNWR Class 7F 0-8-0s, the latter being a two-day working. There were four engines of classes 'G1', 'G2' and 'G2A' to cover the diagrammed work and Turns 1110-2 which were booked to Engine & Men's Workings and which required one engine. Turns 1021 to 1029 were not used.

Thirty-eight Class 5 4-6-0 engines were available to cover 29 booked jobs. Turns 1030 and 1032 each required four engines for the rota. Turns 1034, 1036, 1037 and 1038 needed three engines each duty. Turns 1033 and 1039 needed two engines and Turns 1031, 1035, 1040, 1041 and 1050 were booked to single engines. Turns 1042 to 1049 were not used.

Of the 17 2-6-0s allocated, Turns 1051 and 1055 required three engines each. Turns 1052 and 1054 required four, whilst Turns 1053 and 1056 were booked to one engine each. There is no indication as to which duties were covered by the eight Fowler engines or the nine Stanier versions. Engine & Men's Turn Nos 1118-22 required one engine of this class.

There were five Fowler Class 4F 0-6-0 engines for Turn 1062, which was booked to Middlewich men, Turn 1063 and Engine and Men's Turns 1126/7, and Turn 1129 which was designated Ballast Trips as required.

Enginemen's Workings

As with North Shed duties, the work was blocked into links, with the distance jobs blocked into 12 sets of men. Some links had semi-official names that lasted into the 1960s, hence 'Whipsnade' and 'Yorkshire' links. The origins of the former are unknown, but in LNWR and early LMS days the 'Yorkshire' link men had worked freight traffic through to Leeds. Trips to that city were cut back shortly after the Grouping, South Shed men only working to Stalybridge or Adswood Sidings, although the locomotives continued to work through. For example, 5B Turn 1001 worked from Harlescott (Shrewsbury) to Neville Hill. Equally, South Shed men would use engines from other sheds on their regular element of the diagram. For example, Longsight men, Turn 254, worked the 7.10pm Class A passenger from Manchester London Road to Cardiff as far as Crewe, due in Crewe station at 7.58pm. The Longsight loco (9A Turn 11) detached, drew forward and stood off the platform. At 9pm Crewe South men working Turn 1134 relieved the Longsight men and on arrival of the 7pm Class C Freight (Fish) Wyre Dock to Broad Street at 9.32pm, attached to the stock and worked forward departing at 10pm to Willesden No 6, due there 2.12am. There they were in turn relieved by Willesden men, Turn 1120, who worked the train to its destination. Crewe South men meanwhile lodged and return worked the 7.35pm Willesden Brent to Crewe Basford Hall, Turn 5B/1135 with 5B Class 5 2-6-0, Turn 1051.

Lodging turns worked to Willesden with a Class C freight as mentioned above. Turn 1233, which took over the 2.40pm from Camden to Glasgow Buchanan Street as far as Carlisle Dentonholme at Basford Hall Middle at 6.56pm with a Carlisle Upperby Class 5, 12A Turn 300, was also a Class C working. This train had the nickname 'Doodlebug' but the reason for this choice of name is lost in the mists of time. This returned with another Class C working, colloquially known as 'The Sleepers', the 4.42pm Carlisle Upperby to Willesden, as far as Crewe station with a 5B Class 5. 5A men relieved the South Shed crew and took the loco to South Shed. The train worked forward at 9.20pm hauled by another South Shed Class 5 (Turn 1033) worked by Willesden Turn 809. Most of the lodging turns were in No 1 Link.

The non-Lodging Turn work consisted of out and home working to a variety of destinations, and it would be pointless duplicating what can be found in the full details of Enginemen's Workings elsewhere after this section. There was a lot of yard and trip work as would be expected, details also to be found elsewhere.

Attached to the South Shed list were the firemen's turns on Crewe Works. Of the 19 weekday turns six duties were booked 'Firemen Only', the driver being attached to the CME Workshop Staff, those worthies signing on in the works at the 'Deviation' entrance. They were a race apart, mostly at the end of their footplate careers, and their shifts seemed to be 'office hours'. Whilst some firemen enjoyed being in the works, most preferred to be out on the main line. Raising steam on the vacuum pits, testing engines fresh off the erecting shop and not moving more than a few yards tended to become monotonous. Perhaps the most exciting works job was the twice-daily trip to Basford Hall and return, Target W1, which departed at 7.30am and 1.45pm. W2 Trip shunted the Old Works.

Twenty-five control sets were designated Turn 2100 and that in 1951 booked on daily. These duties were subject to a 2hr variation before or after their designated times with a concentration at 7am and midday. On Sundays there were 26 sets, with no less than five sets booked for 5am and four sets at 12 noon. These were to cover engineering duty requirements and relief. In addition, there were spare sets of men with no booked work who signed on at all hours of the day and night. 'The block', as it was commonly known, varied from summer to winter. In July 1951 there were 106 sets, which decreased to 85 sets in September with the commencement of the winter timetables.

Right:
Crewe South Shed, No Date
An evocative view of South Shed with locomotives standing on most roads awaiting their next turn of duty. The coal stage stands gaunt, towering above and dwarfing the locomotives. The walkway glistens in the hazy atmosphere. *E. N. Kneale*

South Shed (5B) Engine Allocations

Monday 15 July 1951

Fowler '5F' 2-6-0 Total: 8
42785
42810
42811
42815
42856
42920
42926
42939

Stanier '5F' 2-6-0 Total: 9
42950
42952
42955
42956
42968
42972
42980
42983
42984

MR '3F' 0-6-0 Total: 1
43189

S&DJ '3F' 0-6-0 Total: 1
43207

LMS '4F' 0-6-0 Total: 5
44079
44125
44301
44341
44344

Stanier '5MT' 4-6-0 Total: 37
44708
44807
44827
44832
44834
44911
45006
45013
45028
45030
45038
45041
45044
45048
45060
45067
45073
45074
45093
45108
45128
45131
45134
45148
45185
45189
45195
45198
45239
45240
45254
45270
45271
45294
45300
45301
45369

LMS '3F' 0-6-0T Total: 18
47266
47280
47330
47344
47384
47414
47431
47450
47523
47524
47526
47595
47598
47608
47633
47661
47670
47680

Stanier '8F' 2-8-0 Total: 23
48251
48252
48253
48255
48256
48257
48258
48259
48260
48261
48262
48263
48286
48287
48288
48289
48290
48291
48292
48294
49295
48296
48297

'G1' and 'G2A' 0-8-0 Total: 3
49210
49230
49271

'G2' 0-8-0 Total: 1
49407

L&Y '0F' 0-4-0ST Total: 3
51204
51218
51221

LNWR '2F' 0-6-0 Total: 2
58426
58429

Total: 111

Above:
Crewe North Shed, June 1953
By this date the new coal and ash plants had been completed and were in regular use. The old steel-frame structure had been demolished and the shed yard tidied up generally. North Shed's reputedly best 'Princess Royal' Pacific, No 46210 *Lady Patricia*, is seen here at rest on No 48 road, standing in the evening sun, blue paint a little faded but in excellent mechanical order. In six hours time this loco will be at the head of the 10.29pm to Perth. *Bill Rear*

Left:
Crewe North Shed, 7 May 1949
LMS Standard Class 5 4-6-0 No 44717 was the last engine of batch Nos 44698-717 from Lot No 192, completed at Horwich in 1948. It entered traffic at Crewe North on 2 December 1948 and remained at the shed until July 1950 when it transferred to Saltley. It is seen here in the condition it entered traffic with the lined-out black livery, but sporting the wording 'BRITISH RAILWAYS' on the tender. Behind the engine is the old steel-frame coaling tower that was built in 1909 and was replaced by the ferro-concrete version in 1951. *H. C. Casserley*

Above:
Crewe North Shed, 23 June 1956
A view of North Shed taken from Edleston Road bridge looking towards the station. An unidentified Pacific stands on one of the shed roads. The coaling plant and ashpit hoppers dominate the skyline, with only yard lamps visible. No overhead power lines. Note the sleepers in the six-foot.
C. M. and J. M. Bentley Collection

Centre right:
Crewe North Shed, July 1949
Stanier 'Princess Coronation' class Pacific No 46252 *City of Leicester* stands in the shed yard with a collection of cleaners in the cab, surveying the photographer. Behind the tender is the old steel-frame coaling plant whilst just visible behind the firebox can be seen the scaffolding for the replacement ferro-concrete coaling plant. This loco was attached to North Shed until June 1950 when it was transferred to Camden, only to return to 5A at the end of September of the same year. It received its black lined-out livery and lettering in April 1949 and according to Jenkinson, was repainted in lined-out green in February 1952. *R. K. Blencowe, T. J. Webb Collection*

Below right:
Crewe North Shed (Abba), July 1950
The first of the class, No 46220 *Coronation*, stands outside Abba shed looking immaculate after a visit to Crewe Works. The blue livery gleams in the hazy light and the engine looks every inch a picture. An examining fitter stands close by. Once running-in trials had been completed the engine would return to its home shed, Polmadie, 66A.
Bill Rear

Crewe South 5B Engine Turns

July 1951

Mon	Tue	Wed	Thu	Fri	Sat	Sun	Loco Type.		Time	First Outward Trip	Days	Time	Last Inward Trip	Days
1001A	1001A	1001A	1001A	1001A			Class 8F STD	2-8-0	2.22am	Crewe BH to Shrewsbury	MSX	9.5am	Harlescott to Neville Hill	SX
1001B	1001B	1001B	1001B	1001B	1001B		Class 8F STD	2-8-0	2.35am	Copley Hill to Hillhouse	MX	6.55pm	Guide Bridge to Heaton Norris	SX
1001C	1001C	1001C	1001C	1001C	1001C		Class 8F STD	2-8-0	8.50am	Guide Bridge to Birkenhead	SX			
1001D	1001D	1001D	1001D	1001D	1001D		Class 8F STD	2-8-0	5.15am	Hooton to Alsager Jnt	MX	8.20am	Alsager Jnt To Crewe NSS	D
1003A	1003A	1003A	1003A	1003A	1003A		Class 8F STD	2-8-0	10.29am	Gresty Lane to Healey Mills	SX		Healey Mills to Wakefield Shed	SX
1003B	1003B	1003B	1003B	1003B	1003B	1003B	Class 8F STD	2-8-0	3.35am	Crofton Hall to Crewe BH	MX	5am	Warrington to Crewe BH	MSX
1004A	1004A	1004A	1004A	1004A	1004A		Class 8F STD	2-8-0	4.18pm	Crewe BH to Bushbury	SX	2.20am	Oldbury to Bescot	MX
1004B	1004B	1004B	1004B	1004B	1004B		Class 8F STD	2-8-0	9.27am	Bescot to Witton	SX	5.53pm	Bescot to Shrewsbury	SX
1004C	1004C	1004C	1004C	1004C	1004C		Class 8F STD	2-8-0	7.40am	Harlescott to Whitchurch	SX	11.30am	Whitchurch to Shrewsbury	SX
1004D	1004D	1004D	1004D	1004D	1004D		Class 8F STD	2-8-0	1.5am	Harlescott to Hooton	SX	2.20pm	Port Sunlight to Crewe NS	SX
1005A	1005A	1005A	1005A	1005A	1005A	1005A	Class 8F STD	2-8-0	6.5am	Crewe GL to Neville Hill	SX		Neville Hill to Mirfield Shed	SX
1005B	1005B	1005B	1005B	1005B	1005B	1005B	Class 8F STD	2-8-0	1.40am	Mirfield to Birkenhead	MX	10.15pm	Birkenhead to Liverpool Rd	MX
1005C	1005C	1005C	1005C	1005C	1005C		Class 8F STD	2-8-0	11.20am	Patricroft to Jacksons Sdgs	SX	5am	Eccles SL to Crewe BH	D
1017A	1017A	1017A	1017A	1017A	1017A		Class 8F STD	2-8-0	5.27am	Crewe BH to Northwich	D	7.25pm	Crewe BH to Nuneaton	D
1017B	1017B	1017B	1017B	1017B	1017B	1017B	Class 8F STD	2-8-0	7.20am	Nuneaton Shed to Tamworth	SX	7.32pm	Tamworth to Harlescott	SX
1017C	1017C	1017C	1017C	1017C	1017C		Class 8F STD	2-8-0					as required — Shrewsbury to Crewe	D
1018A	1018A	1018A	1018A	1018A	1018A		Class 8F STD	2-8-0	6.35am	Crewe to Willesden Sudbury	MX			
1018B	1018B	1018B	1018B	1018B	1018B	1018B	Class 8F STD	2-8-0				4.20am	Willesden to Crewe BH	MX
1019	1019	1019	1019	1019	1019	1019	Class 7F LNW	0-8-0	6.15am	Crewe BH to Edge Hill	D		Chaddesden to South Shed	SX
1020A	1020A	1020A	1020A	1020A	1020A		Class 7F LNW	0-8-0	7.45am	Crewe BH to Adswood	D	12.18am	Moston to Heaton Norris JS	MX
1020B	1020B	1020B	1020B	1020B	1020B	1020B	Class 7F LNW	0-8-0	8.26am	Heaton Norris JS to Crewe BH	D		Winsford Station to South Shed	MX
1030A	1030A	1030A	1030A	1030A	1030A		Class 5 STD	4-6-0	4.30pm	Crewe BH to Carlisle K	D			
1030B	1030B	1030B	1030B	1030B	1030B	1030B	Class 5 STD	4-6-0	10.10am	Carlisle to Winwick Quay	SX			
1030C	1030C	1030C	1030C	1030C	1030C	1030C	Class 5 STD	4-6-0	5.45am	Walton Old Jnt to Carnforth	SX			
	1030D	1030D	1030D	1030D	1030D	1030D	Class 5 STD	4-6-0				4.15am	Carnforth to Crewe GL	MSX
1031	1031	1031	1031	1031	1031	1031	Class 5 STD	4-6-0	2.50am	Crewe BH to Willesden HLS			as required Nuneaton shed to Crewe South	
1032A	1032A	1032A	1032A	1032A	1032A	1032A	Class 5 STD	4-6-0	9.18pm	Crewe to Shrewsbury	FSX	6.35am	Harlescott to Bamfurlong Jnt	MSX
1032B	1032B	1032B	1032B	1032B		1032B	Class 5 STD	4-6-0	4.15am	Springs Branch to Carnforth	MX	12.5pm	Carnforth to Sellafield (return to 11A as required)	MSX
1032C	1032C	1032C	1032C	1032C	1032C		Class 5 STD	4-6-0	3.22am	Carnforth to Bushbury	SX			
1032D	1032D	1032D	1032D	1032D	1032D		Class 5 STD	4-6-0				8am	Bescot to Crewe BH	MSX
1033A	1033A	1033A	1033A	1033A	1033A	1033A	Class 5 STD	4-6-0	9.20pm	Crewe to Willesden HLS	SX	7am	Euston to Willesden SS ECS Rep No 6	MX
1033B	1033B	1033B	1033B	1033B	1033B	1033B	Class 5 STD	4-6-0				10.25pm	Camden to London Road	SX
1034A	1034A	1034A	1034A	1034A	1034A	1034A	Class 5 STD	4-6-0	7.40am	Crewe BH to Carlisle L Rd	SX			
1034B	1034B	1034B	1034B	1034B	1034B		Class 5 STD	4-6-0	4.5am	Carlisle to Crewe	MX	3.45pm	Crewe GL to Neville Hill	D
1034C	1034C	1034C	1034C	1034C	1034C		Class 5 STD	4-6-0				10.45am	Copley Hill to Crewe GL	SX
1035	1035	1035	1035	1035	1035	1035	Class 5 STD	4-6-0	4.5am	Crewe to Whitchurch	MX	8.25pm	Shrewsbury to Crewe (Pass)	SX
1036A	1036A	1036A	1036A	1036A	1036A	1036A	Class 5 STD	4-6-0	4.20am	Crewe GL to Copley Hill	D	8.50pm	Copley Hill to Aston Goods	SX
1036B	1036B	1036B	1036B	1036B	1036B	1036B	Class 5 STD	4-6-0	9.25am	Aston Goods Trip	SX	11.14pm	Curzon Street to Preston ES	SX
1036C	1036C	1036C	1036C	1036C	1036C		Class 5 STD	4-6-0	12.30pm	Farington Jnt To Coppull Hall Siding	SX	8.25pm	Preston to Crewe BH	SX
1037A	1037A	1037A	1037A	1037A	1037A		Class 5 STD	4-6-0	5am	Crewe BH to Willesden HLS	SX	10.5pm	Willesden to Crewe	SX
1037B	1037B	1037B	1037B	1037B			Class 5 STD	4-6-0	9.40am	Crewe to Waverton	SX	2.25pm	Waverton to Crewe BH	SX
1037C	1037C	1037C	1037C	1037C	1037C		Class 5 STD	4-6-0	12.35am	Crewe GL to Carlisle Viaduct	MX	4.42pm	Carlisle Upperby to Crewe GL	SX
1038A	1038A	1038A	1038A	1038A	1038A		Class 5 STD	4-6-0	8.10am	Crewe BH to Peterboro	D	11.50pm	Welham to M Harboro	SX
1038B	1038B	1038B	1038B	1038B	1038B		Class 5 STD	4-6-0	10.5am	Welham to Bescot	D			
1038C	1038C	1038C	1038C	1038C	1038C		Class 5 STD	4-6-0	3.15am	Bescot to Carlisle London Rd	SX			
1038D	1038D	1038D	1038D	1038D	1038D		Class 5 STD	4-6-0				3.10am	Carlisle Upperby to Crewe GL	SX

Mon	Tue	Wed	Thu	Fri	Sat	Sun	Loco Type.		Time	First Outward Trip	Days	Time	Last Inward Trip	Days
1039A	1039A	1039A	1039A	1039A			Class 5 STD	4-6-0	6.7am	Crewe BH to Walton Old Jnt	SX	8.16pm	Crewe to Shrewsbury	SX
1039B	1039B	1039B	1039B	1039B	1039B		Class 5 STD	4-6-0	5.20am	Harlescott to Bamfurlong	SX	8.35pm	Wigan to Crewe	SX
1040	1040		1040	1040	1040	1040	Class 5 STD	4-6-0	3.40am	Crewe BH to Wyre Dock	MSX		Wyre Dock to Crewe S Shed LE	SX
1041	1041	1041	1041	1041	1041		Class 5 STD	4-6-0	10.35pm	Crewe NS to Hooton	SX	10.55pm	Birkenhead to Crewe NS	SX
1050	1050	1050	1050	1050	1050	1050	Class 5 STD	4-6-0	6.15pm	Crewe BH to Birkenhead	SX	4.55am	Ellesmere Port to Crewe BH	SX
1051A	1051A	1051A	1051A	1051A	1051A		Class 5 STD	2-6-0	10.5am	Crewe to Willesden Sud	SX			
1051B	1051B	1051B	1051B	1051B	1051B	1051B	Class 5 STD	2-6-0	10.45am	Willesden No 58 Trip	D			
1051C	1051C	1051C	1051C	1051C			Class 5 STD	2-6-0	3.55am	Willesden to Crewe BH		12.55pm	Warrington to Crewe GL	MSX
1052A	1052A	1052A	1052A	1052A	1052A	1052A	Class 5 STD	2-6-0	6.42am	Crewe BH to Mold Junction	SX	1.15am	Chatterley's Sdgs. To Alsager Shed	
1052B	1052B	1052B	1052B	1052B	1052B	1052B	Class 5 STD	2-6-0	7.42am	Alsager to Beeston	MX		Beeston to Crewe as required	MX
1053	1053	1053	1053	1053	1053		Class 5 STD	2-6-0	6.20am	Crewe SS North. to Sandbach	MX	11.45pm	Northwich to Crewe BH	D
1054A	1054A	1054A	1054A	1054A	1054A	1054A	Class 5 STD	2-6-0	1am	Crewe BH to Leicester	D	8.15am	Leicester to Nuneaton DS	MX
	1054B	1054B	1054B	1054B	1054B		Class 5 STD	2-6-0	4.15am	Three Spires Jnt to Middlewich	MSX		Middlewich to Crewe S Shed as required	
1055A	1055A	1055A	1055A	1055A	1055A		Class 5 STD	2-6-0	1.42am	Crewe to Coventry Goods	D	2.25pm	Nuneaton to Hooton to Mold Jnt	D
1055B	1055B	1055B	1055B	1055B	1055B		Class 5 STD	2-6-0	12.50pm	Saltney to Walton Old Jnt	SX	5.5pm	Warrington to Saltney	SX
1055C	1055C	1055C	1055C	1055C	1055C		Class 5 STD	2-6-0	1am	Mold Junction to Bushbury	D	12.18pm	Bescot to Crewe BH	MX
1056	1056	1056	1056	1056		1056	Class 5 STD	2-6-0	9am	Crewe BH to Whitchurch	SX	12.14pm	Broxton to Crewe GL	SX
1062	1062	1062	1062	1062	1062		Class 4F STD	0-6-0	4.56am	Crewe Station to Northwich	D	10pm	Middlewich to South Shed	D
1063	1063	1063	1063	1063	1063		Class 4F STD	0-6-0	2.50am	Crewe to Stoke (Pass)	MX	8pm	Middlewich to Crewe BH	SX
1064	1064	1064	1064	1064	1064		Class 3F Mid	0-6-0		P. Way Triangle Yard Shunt				
1070	1070	1070	1070	1070	1070	1070	Class 3F STD	0-6-0T	9am	No 9.Down Carriage Sidings N End	D			
1071	1071	1071	1071	1071	1071	1071	Class 3F STD	0-6-0T	4am	No 2 Up Side Shunt	D+Sun			
1072	1072	1072	1072	1072	1072	1072	Class 3F STD	0-6-0T	8.30pm	No 3 Down Bays Shunt	D+Sun			
1073	1073	1073	1073	1073	1073	1073	Class 3F STD	0-6-0T	1pm	No 5 Down Carr. Sdgs S End	D+Sun	1.00pm until 6am — D; 1pm until 3am		Sun
1074	1074	1074	1074	1074	1074	1074	Class 3F STD	0-6-0T	12.30pm	No 6 Down Bays & Dn Carriage Sidings		12.30pm SX to 9am MX; 1pm SO to 6am		Sun
1075	1075	1075	1075	1075	1075	1075	Class 3F STD	0-6-0T	6pm	No 7 Down Bays Shunt		6pm Sun to 1pm MO; 10.30pm SX to 1pm		MX
1076	1076	1076	1076	1076	1076	1076	Class 3F STD	0-6-0T	4pm	No 8 Down Carriage Sdgs S End		4pm MO to 1pm MO; 10pm SX to 1pm		MX
1079	1079	1079	1079	1079	1079		Class 3F STD	0-6-0T	6am	Gresty Green Shunt		6am to 10pm		D
1080A	1080A	1080A	1080A	1080A	1080A		Class 3F STD	0-6-0T	6am	No 12 Trip		6am SX to 5.15am MX; 6am to 8pm		SO
1080B	1080B	1080B	1080B	1080B	1080B	1080B	Class 3F STD	0-6-0T	8am	RSD Shunt		8am to 3.30pm D; 8am to 2.30pm		Sun
1080C	1080C	1080C	1080C	1080C	1080C	1080C	Class 3F STD	0-6-0T	6am	No 18 Trip		6.00am MO to 10.00pm MO; 10.00pm MX to 10pm MX; 10pm SO to 2pm		Sun
1080D	1080D	1080D	1080D	1080D	1080D	1080D	Class 3F STD	0-6-0T	7.30am	No 10 Trip		7.30am to 2.25pm (D); 4.30pm to 12.30am (MX); 11am to 7pm		Sun
					1080		Class 3F STD	0-6-0T	8am	RSD Shunt		8.00am to 4pm		SO
1081	1081	1081	1081	1081	1081		Class 3F STD	0-6-0T	8am	Basford Hall SSN to Gresty Lane	D	1.00pm	Gresty Lane to Basford Hall SSN	
1082	1082	1082	1082	1082	1082	1082	Class 3F STD	0-6-0T	6am	Crewe Warehouse NE Shunt	D+Sun	No 13 Trip 6am Mon to 5pm Sats; 8.30am to 4.30pm Sundays		
1083	1083	1083	1083	1083	1083		Class 3F Mid	0-6-0	6.45am	P Way Shops Shunt	D		No 44 Trip	
1084A	1084A	1084A	1084A	1084A	1084A	1084A	Class 2F LNW	0-6-0		Wheeldrop Shunt				
1084B	1084B	1084B	1084B	1084B	1084B	1084B	Class 2F LNW	0-6-0		Breakdown North Shed				
1085	1085	1085	1085	1085	1085	1085	Engine Fresh Off Works		12.1am	Loco Shed Shunt	D+Sun	12.1am Mondays to 9.45pm Sundays		
1086	1086	1086	1086	1086	1086		Class 6F LNW	0-8-0		Crewe Works				
1087	1087	1087	1087	1087	1087		Class 3F STD	0-6-0T		Crewe Works				
1088A	1088A	1088A	1088A	1088A	1088A		Class 2F LNW	0-6-0		Crewe Works				
1088B	1088B	1088B	1088B	1088B	1088B		Class 2F LNW	0-6-0		Crewe Works				
1088C	1088C	1088C	1088C	1088C	1088C		Class 2F LNW	0-6-0		Crewe Works				
1088D	1088D	1088D	1088D	1088D	1088D		Class 2F LNW	0-6-0		Crewe Works				
1088E	1088E	1088E	1088E	1088E	1088E		Class 2F LNW	0-6-0		Crewe Works				
1088F	1088F	1088F	1088F	1088F	1088F		Class 2F LNW	0-6-0		Crewe Works				
1088G	1088G	1088G	1088G	1088G	1088G		Class 2F LNW	0-6-0		Crewe Works				
1088H	1088H	1088H	1088H	1088H	1088H		Class 2F LNW	0-6-0		Crewe Works				
1089A	1089A	1089A	1089A	1089A	1089A		Class 2F L&Y	0-6-0ST		Crewe Works				
1089B	1089B	1089B	1089B	1089B	1089B		Class 2F L&Y	0-6-0ST		Crewe Works				
1089C	1089C	1089C	1089C	1089C	1089C		Class 2F L&Y	0-6-0ST		Crewe Works				

Mon	Tue	Wed	Thu	Fri	Sat	Sun	Loco Type.		Time	First Outward Trip	Days	Time	Last Inward Trip	Days
1090	1090	1090	1090	1090	1090		Class 1P LNW	2-4-2T		Crewe Works		5.30am	Loco Stores Vans No 45 Trip	
1091A	1091A	1091A	1091A	1091A	1091A		Class 1F LNW	0-4-2T		Crewe Works				
1091B	1091B	1091B	1091B	1091B	1091B		Class 1F LNW	0-4-2T		Crewe Works				
1092	1092	1092	1092	1092	1092		Class 0F Cal	0-4-0ST		Crewe Works				
1095	1095	1095	1095	1095	1095	1095	Diesel Shunter	0-6-0	6am Monday to 2pm		Sunday		No 1 Trip. 'D' Group Shunt	
1096	1096	1096	1096	1096	1096	1096	Diesel Shunter	0-6-0	6am Monday to 4pm		Sunday		No 2 Trip. 'E' Group Shunt	
1097	1097	1097	1097	1097	1097	1097	Diesel Shunter	0-6-0	10pm Sunday to 6pm		Sunday		No 3 Trip. 'F', 'G' & 'H' Group Shunt	
1098	1098	1098	1098	1098	1098	1098	Diesel Shunter	0-6-0	10pm Sunday to 4pm		Sunday		No 4 Trip. Gresty Lane Down Side Shunt	
1099	1099	1099	1099	1099	1099	1099	Diesel Shunter	0-6-0	6am Monday to 6am		Sunday		No 4A Trip. Gresty Lane Shunt	
1100	1100	1100	1100	1100	1100	1100	Diesel Shunter	0-6-0	6am Monday to 6am		Sunday		No 5 Trip. North Staffs. Sidings Up Side Shunt	
1101	1101	1101	1101	1101	1101	1101	Diesel Shunter	0-6-0	6am Monday to 2pm		Sunday		No 6 Trip. Sorting Sidings South Shunt	
1102	1102	1102	1102	1102	1102	1102	Diesel Shunter	0-6-0	6am Monday to 2pm		Sunday		No 7 Trip. Sorting Sidings North Shunt	
1103	1103	1103	1103	1103	1103	1103	Diesel Shunter	0-6-0	10pm Sunday to 2pm		Sunday		No 8 Trip. Basford Hall Up Side Shunt	
1104	1104	1104	1104	1104	1104	1104	Diesel Shunter	0-6-0	6am Monday to 6am		Sunday		No 9 Trip. North Staffs. Sidings Down Side Shunt	
1105	1105	1105	1105	1105	1105	1105	Diesel Shunter	0-6-0	6am Mondays to 5pm		Saturday		No 11 Trip. Crewe Warehouse SE Shunt.+ 8.30am-4.30pm Sun	
1106	1106	1106	1106	1106	1106	1106	Diesel Shunter	0-6-0	6am Monday to 6am		Sunday		No 14 Trip. Up Side Shunt	
1107	1107	1107	1107	1107	1107	1107	Diesel Shunter	0-6-0	6am Monday to 6am		Sunday		No 16 Trip. No rth Staffs. Sidings and Sorting Sidings South	
1108	1108	1108	1108	1108	1108	1108	Diesel Shunter	0-6-0	6am Monday to 6pm		Sunday		No 25 Trip. Gresty Lane Shunt	
1110/1	1110/1	1110/1	1110/1	1110/1		1112	Class 7F LNW	0-8-0	9.15am	Crewe BH to Badnall Wharf	SX	1.30am	Sideway to Crewe North Staffs Sdgs	MX
1118/20	1119/20	1119/20	1119/20	1119/20	1121	1122	Class 5	2-6-0	6.15am	Crewe S Sdgs N to Coal Yard	SX	7pm	Sandbach to Crewe Basford Hall	SX
1126/7	1126/7	1126/7	1126/7	1126/7	1126/7		Class 4F	0-6-0	6.35am	Basford Hall to Nantwich	SX	7.57pm	Winsford Junction To Basford Hall	SX
1129	1129	1129	1129	1129	1129		Class 4F	0-6-0	7.30am	Ballast Trips as required	MSX	6am	Ballast Trips as required, Mondays & Saturdays only	
1131/2	1131/2	1131/2	1131/2	1131/2	1131/2		Class 3F	0-6-0T	5.30am	Basford Hall to Betley Road	D	5.5pm	Betley Road to Basford Hall (empties)	D
118	**120**	**119**	**120**	**120**	**114**	**56**			**Total Daily Rostered Engine Turns**					

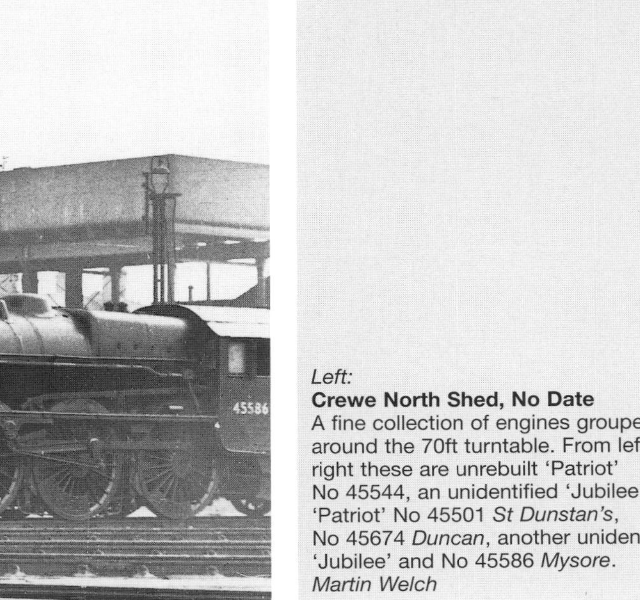

Left:
Crewe North Shed, No Date
A fine collection of engines grouped around the 70ft turntable. From left to right these are unrebuilt 'Patriot' No 45544, an unidentified 'Jubilee', 'Patriot' No 45501 *St Dunstan's*, No 45674 *Duncan*, another unidentified 'Jubilee' and No 45586 *Mysore*.
Martin Welch

Crewe South 5B Enginemen's Turns

Mon	Tue	Wed	Thu	Fri	Sat	Sun	Time	Outward Trip	Work	Loco	Time	Inward Trip	Work	Loco
1110	1110	1110	1110	1110			9.15am	Basford Hall-Badnall Wharf	Frt	5B/1110	2pm	Badnall Wharf-Basford Hall	Frt	5B/1110
1111	1111	1111	1111	1111			8.55pm	North Staffords Sdgs-Newcastle Jnt	TF	5B/1110	1.30am	Sideway-Crewe North Staffs Sdgs	EF (F)	5B/1110
						1112	9am	Basford Hall-Middlewich	TF	5B/1110	1.30pm	Middlewich-Crewe Basford Hall	TF	5B/1110
1118							6.15am	Sorting Sidings North-Coal Yard	Trip	5B/1118	11.40am	Coal Yard-Basford Hall Up Sdgs	Trip	5B/1118
	1119	1119	1119	1119	1119		5am	Sorting Sidings North-Coal yard	Trip	5B/1118	11.40am	Coal Yard-Basford Hall Up Sdgs	Trip	5B/1118
1120	1120	1120	1120	1120			2.35pm	Basford Hall SSN-Sandbach	Frt	5B/1118	5pm	Sandbach-Basford Hall	Frt	5B/1118
					1121		2.33pm	Basford Hall-Ditton Junction	TF	5B/1118		*return as required*	LE	5B/1118
						1122	4am	Sorting Sdgs North-Coal Yard	Trip	5B/1118	8.43am	Winsford-Sorting Sidings North	EBV	5B/1118
1126	1126	1126	1126	1126	1126		6.35am	Basford Hall-Nantwich	Frt	5B/1126	9.45am	Nantwich-Basford Hall	Frt	5B/1126
1127	1127	1127	1127	1127	1127		1.55pm	Gresty Lane-Winsford Junction	Min	5B/1126	7.57pm	Winsford Junction-Basford Hall	Min	5B/1126
1129	1129	1129	1129	1129	1129		7.30am	Ballast Trips		5B/1129				
1131	1131	1131	1131	1131	1131		5.50am	Basford Hall-Betley Road	Ballast	5B/1131	11.40am	Betley Road-Basford Hall	Ballast	5B/1131
1132	1132	1132	1132	1132			1.5pm	Basford Hall-Betley Road	Ballast	5B/1131	5.5pm	Betley Road-Basford Hall	Ety	5B/1131
1134	1134	1134	1134	1134			10pm	Crewe-Willesden	EF(C)	9A/11		*Lodge*		
	1135	1135	1135	1135				*Lodge*			7.35pm	Willesden-Crewe Basford Hall	EF(D)	5B/1051
					1136			*Lodge*			3.25pm	Willesden-Crewe Basford Hall	EF (E)	8B/3
1159							4.8am	Basford Hall South-Rugby	EF (E)	2A/515		*return as required*		
1160							10.50am	Basford Hall-Rugby	EF(D)	5B/1051		*return as required*		
1161							9.20pm	Crewe Station-Rugby	EF(C)	5B/1033	12.35am	Rugby-Basford Hall	EF(D)	5A/39
1164							6.5am	Basford Hall-Rugby	TF	5B/1018		*return as required*		
	1165	1165	1165	1165	1165		6.35am	Basford Hall-Rugby	TF	5B/1018		*return as required*		
1166							5am	Basford Hall-Rugby	EF(E)	5B/1037		*return as required*		
	1167		1167				2.50am	Basford Hall South-Rugby	EF(F)	5B/1031		*return as required*		
						1168	5.45pm	Crewe-Rugby	EF(E)	5B/1054		*return as required*		
	1169	1169	1169	1169			6.53am	Crewe Station-Rugby	EF(E)	1A/1		*return as required*		
1172	1172	1172	1172	1172	1172		8.10am	Basford Hall-Rugby	EF (E)	5B/1038		*return as required*		
1173							5.15pm	Basford Hall-Rugby	EF (E)	1A/525	10.55pm	Rugby-Basford Hall	EF (D)	5B/1051
1174	1174	1174	1174	1174	1174		6.35pm	Basford Hall-Rugby	TF	2A/8		*return as required*		
	1175	1175	1175	1175	1175		1.39am	Basford Hall South-Nuneaton	EF (F)	8A/27	6.51am	Nuneaton-Basford Hall	EF (E)	2A/515
				1176	1176		2.46pm	Basford Hall South-Rugby	EF (D)	12A/320		*return as required*		
1177							12.40am	Basford Hall-Rugby	EF (F)	1A/7		*return as required*		
						1178	1.22am	as pass to Rugby			4.18am	Rugby-Basford Hall	TF	2A/9
					1179		10.35pm	Basford Hall-Rugby	EF (D)	5B/1051	2.10am	Rugby-Basford Hall	EF (E)	26A/—
					1180		12.28am	Basford Hall-Rugby	EF (D)	5A/39		*return as required*		
					1184		11pm	Basford Hall South-Nuneaton	EF (F)	8A/508	3.25am	Nuneaton-Rugby	EF (F)	8A/27
1185	1185	1185	1185	1185	1185		1.42am	Basford Hall-Coventry	EF (F)	5B/1055		*return as required*		
1186	1186	1186	1186	1186			3.45pm	Basford Hall South-Nuneaton	EF (E)	5A/40		*return as required*		
1187							3.10am	Ball Hall Middle-Nuneaton	EF (F)	8A/27		*return as required*		
		1188	1188	1188	1188		12.40am	Basford Hall Middle-Rugby	EF (E)	2A/3	5am	Rugby-Basford Hall	EF (D)	26A/—
	1189	1189	1189	1189			10.5am	Basford Hall South-Nuneaton	EF (E)	5A/42		*return as required*		
					1191		10.40pm	Basford Hall-Nuneaton	TF	5B/1018		Nuneaton-Crewe South	LE	5B/1018
	1192	1192	1192	1192	1192		1am	Basford Hall-Nuneaton	EF (E)	5B/1054	4.55am	Nuneaton-Basford Hall	EF (E)	2B/116
1194	1194	1194	1194	1194			5.22pm	Basford Hall-Madeley	Eties	17B/25	6.30pm	Madeley-Basford Hall	Min	17B/25
	1196	1196	1196	1196	1196		2.10am	Basford Hall-Stafford	TF	17B/25	7am	Stafford-Basford Hall	TF	17B/25
1197							5.5am	Basford Hall-Stafford	TF	1A/590	8.35am	Stafford-Grange Junction	Eties	5A/22
1200							4.45am	Crewe Station-Bushbury	EF (E)	5B/1032		Bushbury-Crewe South	LE	5B/1032
					1201		10.5pm	Basford Hall Middle-Bushbury	TF	3D/3	1.8am	Bushbury-Basford Hall	TF	3D/3
	1202	1202	1202	1202	1202		1.30am	Basford Hall South-Bushbury	EF (F)	3D/205	5.50am	Bushbury-Basford Hall North	TF	9A/4

Mon	Tue	Wed	Thu	Fri	Sat	Sun	Time	Outward Trip	Work	Loco	Time	Inward Trip	Work	Loco
					1203		8.49pm	Basford Hall South-Bushbury	TF	3D/2	1.40am	Bushbury-Basford Hall	TF	3D/2
		1204					6.30am	Basford Hall South-Lawley Street	EF (F)	6C/205A		Lawley St-Crewe	LE	6C/205A
1205							10.22pm	Basford Hall South-Curzon Street	EF (D)	3D/2		*return as required*		
1206	1296	1296	1296	1206			4.18pm	Basford Hall-Bushbury	TF	5B/1004		*return as required*		
	1207	1207	1207	1207	1207		2.55am	Basford Hall Middle-Bushbury	TF	5B/1055	8am	Bescot-Basford Hall	EF (F)	5B/1032
1208	1208	1208	1208	1208			11.15am	Basford Hall South-Bushbury	TF	9B/101		*return as required*	LE	9B/101
					1209		6.1pm	Basford Hall-Bushbury	TF	5B/1004	11.10pm	Bushbury-Basford Hall	EF (F)	10C/13
1210							2pm	Basford Hall South-Bushbury	EF (F)	3B/151		*return as required*		
1211							2.55am	Basford Hall Middle-Bushbury	TF	5B/1055		Bushbury-North Shed	LE	5B/1055
1212							11.38am	Basford Hall South-Wichnor	Eties	5B/1040		Wichnor-South Shed	LE	5B/1040
1213							7.55am	Basford Hall South-Bushbury	TF	5B/1032		*return as required*		
1214	1214	1214	1214	1214			2.55pm	Basford Hall South-Bushbury	TF	25G/337		*return as required*		
					1215		12.23am	Basford Hall Middle-Bushbury	EF (F)	5B/1034	3.10am	Bushbury-Basford Hall North	TF	5A/33
	1216	1216	1216	1216			1.50pm	Basford Hall South-Bushbury	EF (E)	84G/102		Bushbury-Stafford	LE	84G/102
1217							1.45am	Basford Hall South-Bushbury	EF (E)	84G/102		Bushbury-Stafford	LE	84G/102
1218							7.45am	Basford Hall-Bescot	TF	5B/1058		Bescot-South Shed	LE	5B/1058
						1219	11.15pm	Basford Hall-Bushbury	EF (E)	8A/33	4.25am	Bushbury-Basford Hall North	TF	3D/205
						1220	12.50am	Basford Hall South-Bushbury	EF (E)	84G/102		Bushbury-Shrewsbury	LE	84G/102
1221							3.37am	Basford Hall South-Bushbury	EF (F)	5A/40	7.58am	Bushbury-Basford Hall North	TF	9A/4
					1222		6.15am	Crewe Station-Bushbury	TF	10C/13		*return as required*		
1233	1233	1233	1233	1233			6.56pm	Basford Hall-Carlisle Dentenholme	EF (C)	12A/300		*Lodge*		
	1234	1234	1234	1234				*Lodge*			4.42pm	Carlisle Upperby-Crewe	EF (C)	5B/1037
					1235			*Lodge*			4.34pm	Carlisle Upperby-Basford Hall	EF (D)	12A/17
1238							3.30am	Basford Hall-Bamfurlong Junction	Frt	1A/525	6.35am	Bamfurlong NE-Gresty Lane	TF	1A/525
1239							2.20am	Gresty Lane-Springs Branch	EF (E)	12A/320	5.16am	Springs Branch-Basford Hall South	TF	5B/1032
	1240	1240	1240	1240	1240		2.45am	Basford Hall-Preston Ribble Sidings	EF (E)	5B/1036		*return as required*		
1241	1241	1241	1241	1241			6.30am	Gresty Lane-Bamfurlong Junction	EF (E)	84G/102	11.55am	Bamfurlong NE-Basford Hall	EF (F)	10A/306
		1242		1242			5.15am	Basford Hall North-Warrington	EF (D)	12A/322		*return as required*		
					1243		5.15am	Basford Hall North-Bamfurlong	EF (D)	12A/322		*return as required*		
						1244	10.35am	Basford Hall-Springs Branch	EF (F)	5B/1032	12/12pm	Springs Branch-Gresty Lane	TF	5B/1040
1245	1245	1245	1245	1245	1245		7.25pm	Basford Hall-Bamfurlong	EF (E)	12A/321	11pm	Bamfurlong-Gresty Lane	EF (D)	12A/17
1246							3.55am	Gresty Lane-Bamfurlong	TF	5B/1032	7.15am	Bamfurlong-Gresty Lane	EF (D)	5B/1038
				1247			10.1pm	Gresty Lane-Bamfurlong	TF	5B/1032		*return as required*		
						1248	5.10am	Basford Hall-Springs Branch	TF	5A/33		*return as required*		
					1267		2.30am	Basford Hall-Preston Ribble Sidings	EF (F)	5B/1039		*return as required*		
	1268	1268	1268	1268			3.40am	Basford Hall-Preston Ribble Sidings	EF (F)	28B/103		*return as required*		
					1269		9.15pm	Basford Hall-Preston Ribble Sidings	EF (E)	28B/103		*return as required*		
1270	1270	1270	1270	1270			9.35pm	Basford Hall-Bamfurlong Junction	EF (E)	12A/319	12.18am	Bamfurlong Sdgs-Gresty Lane	EF (F)	12A/321
						1271	1.45am	Basford Hall-Warrington	TF	5B/1020	4.25am	Warrington ES-Basford Hall	TF	5B/1020
						1272	7.50pm	Gresty Lane-Preston Ribble Sidings	TF	11A/1	12.10am	Preston NU-Basford Hall	TF	12A/331
	1273	1273	1273	1273			8am	Basford Hall-Warrington	TF	5B/1051	12.55pm	Warrington ES-Gresty Lane	TF	5B/1051
1274							11.20am	Basford Hall -Warrington	TF	5A/42		*return as required*		
1275							6.42am	Basford Hall-Bamfurlong	TF	5B/1039	11.37am	Bamfurlong-Basford Hall	TF	12A/322
	1276	1276	1276	1276	1276		10.45pm	Basford Hall-Preston Ribble Sidings	EF (F)	5A/33		*return as required*		
	1277	1277	1277	1277	1277		4.50am	Basford Hall-Bamfurlong Sidings	EF (D)	12A/320	6.38am	Bamfurlong Sidings-Gresty Lane	TF	5B/1030
					1278		8.17pm	Gresty Lane-Bamfurlong	EF (E)	84G/—	10.48pm	Bamfurlong-Basford Hall South	EF (E)	84G/—
1279	1279	1279	1279	1279			9.50pm	Basford Hall-Bamfurlong	TF	10A/306	3.5am	Bamfurlong-Basford Hall	EF (E)	12A/319
1280							12.55am	Basford Hall-Walton Old Junction	TF	11A/250	5am	Warrington ES-North Staffs Sdg	TF	11A/250
1282	1282	1282	1282	1282			11.15pm	Basford Hall-Winsford Junction	TF	5B/1020		Winsford Junction-South Shed	LE	5B/1020
					1283		4.35pm	Basford Hall-Warrington	TF	5B/1034	10.45pm	Warrington-Basford Hall South	EF (F)	5B/1034
	1284	1284	1284	1284			12.50pm	Basford Hall-Warrington	EF (F)	3D/205		*return as required*		
						1290	5.30am	Basford Hall North-Warrington	TF	8B/3		*return as required*		

Mon	Tue	Wed	Thu	Fri	Sat	Sun	Time	Outward Trip	Work	Loco	Time	Inward Trip	Work	Loco
1291	1291	1291	1291	1291			10.25pm	Basford Hall-Warrington	TF	5B/1003	5am	Warrington ES-Basford Hall	TF	5B/1003
	1292	1292	1292	1292	1292		12.35am	Gresty Lane-Bamfurlong Junction	EF (F)	5B/1037	3.35am	Bamfurlong-Basford Hall	TF	11A/250
1293	1293	1293	1293	1293			7.40am	Basford Hall North-Bamfurlong	TF	5B/1034	12.38pm	Bamfurlong-Gresty Lane	TF	12A/23
	1294	1294	1294	1294			8.35am	Gresty Lane-Bamfurlong Sidings	TF	5B/1032	12.38pm	Bamfurlong-Gresty Lane	TF	12A/23
	1295	1295	1295	1295			5.27am	Crewe Station-Bamfurlong	EF (E)	5B/1038	11.37am	Bamfurlong-Basford Hall	TF	12A/322
	1296	1296	1296	1296	1296		4.5am	Crewe Station-Bamfurlong	EF (D)	5A/27	7.15am	Bamfurlong-Gresty Lane	EF (D)	5B/1038
1297	1297	1297	1297	1297			7.23am	Basford Hall-Aintree	EF (F)	21A/—		Aintree-Crewe	LE	21A/—
1298							6.50am	Basford Hall-Warrington	TF	3D/205		*return as required*		
						1299	5.30pm	Basford Hall-Carnforth	EF (D)	12A/300	9.40pm	Carnforth-Crewe Station	EF (E)	84G/102
1300	1300	1300	1300	1300			9.15pm	Basford Hall-Preston Ribble Sidings	EF (F)	11A/250		*return as required*		
						1301	5pm	Basford Hall-Carnforth	EF (E)	12A/23	8.20pm	Carnforth-Gresty Lane	EF (D)	5B/1056
1327	1327	1327	1327	1327			7.15am	Gresty Lane-Edgeley Junction	EF (F)	5B/1005	11.26am	Edgeley Junction-Basford Hall	Min	26A/633
1328	1328	1328	1328	1328			10.40pm	Gresty Lane-Edgeley Junction	TF	26A/624		*return as required*		
						1329	10.25pm	Gresty Lane-Adswood Sidings	EF (F)	5B/1035	3.40am	Heaton Norris JS-Gresty Lane	TF	5B/1035
1330							1.5am	Gresty Lane-London Road	EF (F)	84G/5		*return as required*		
1331							1.15am	Gresty Lane-Adswood Sidings	TF	26A/633	4.21am	Edgeley Junction-Basford Hall	TF	25G/301
1332							10.5am	Basford Hall-Adswood Sidings	TF	9A/4		*return as required*		
1333	1333	1333	1333	1333	1333		7.45am	Basford Hall-Chelford	Frt	5B/1020	12/52pm	Chelford-Basford Hall	Frt	5B/1020
1334							10.29am	Gresty Lane-Stalybridge	TF	5B/1003		*return as required*		
	1335	1335	1335	1335	1335		4.20am	Gresty Lane-Edgeley Junction	TF	5B/1036	7.25am	Heaton Norris-Basford Hall	Min	5B/1003
						1336	5.15am	as passenger to Stockport			7.22am	Heaton Norris-Basford Hall	Min	84G/103
					1341		3.45pm	Gresty Lane-Edgeley Junction	EF (D)	5B/1134	6pm	Heaton Norris-Gresty Lane	TF	5B/1034
1342	1342	1342	1342	1342			10.30pm	Gresty Lane-Edgeley Junction	TF	26A/633	2.58am	Heaton Norris-Basford Hall South	TF	5A/27
	1343	1343	1343	1343			10.29am	Gresty Lane-Adswood	TF	5B/1003	1.13pm	Edgeley Jnt-Basford Hall South	TF	3D/200
					1344		10.10am	Gresty Lane-Adswood	TF	84G/103		*return as required*		
1345							3.35am	Gresty Lane-Edgeley Junction	TF	25G/302	6.55am	Heaton Norris-Basford Hall	Min	5B/1033
						1346	11.15pm	Gresty Lane-Edgeley Junction	TF	84G/103		*return as required*		
	1347	1347	1347	1347			8.2am	Basford Hall-Adswood	EF (F)	9A/4	1.29pm	Heaton Norris-Gresty Lane	TF	5B/1033
1348	1348	1348	1348	1348	1348		1.20am	Gresty Lane-Adswood Sidings	TF	25D/124	5.20am	Heaton Norris-Basford Hall	TF	25G/301
1351							2am	Gresty Lane-Hillhouse	TF	35G/301		*return as required*		
1352							6.58am	Basford Hall-Adswood Sidings	EF (E)	9A/415	1.13pm	Edgeley Jnt-Basford Hall South	TF	25G/337
1353	1353	1353	1353	1353			8pm	Gresty Lane-Stalybridge	TF	25G/301		*return as required*		
					1354		9.5pm	Gresty Lane-Edgeley Junction	EF (F)	5B/1005		*return as required*		
	1361	1361	1361	1361			7.8am	Basford Hall North-Middlewich	Eties	5B/1054		Middlewich-South Shed	LE	5B/1054
1362							4.56am	Crewe-Northwich	Pcls	5B/1062		*return as required*		
1363	1363	1363	1363	1363	1363		8.30am	Basford Hall-Northwich	Min	5B/1053	11.43am	Northwich-Basford Hall	Min	5B/1053
1364	1364	1364	1364	1364	1364		3pm	Basford Hall North-Middlewich	Frt	5B/1063	7.40pm	Middlewich-Basford Hall	Min	5B/1063
1365	1365	1365	1365	1365	1365		8am	Basford Hall North-Gresty Lane	Frt	5B/1081	1pm	Gresty Lane-Basford Hall North	Frt	5B/1081
1367	1367	1367	1367	1367	1367		6.20am	Basford Hall Sorting S North-Sandbach	Frt	12A/319	12pm	Sandbach-Basford Hall	Frt	12A/319
1368	1368	1368	1368	1368	1368		5.27am	Basford Hall-Northwich	Frt	5B/1017	9.35am	Northwich-Basford Hall	Frt	5B/1017
	1375	1375	1375	1375	1375		2.50am	Crewe-Stoke	Pass	5B/1063	4.30am	Stoke-North Staffs Sidings	Min	5B/1063
1376							7.10am	North Staffordshire Sidings-Longport	Eties	25D/124	11.26am	Alsager Jnt-North Staffs Sidings	Cpld	25D/124
					1377		5.15pm	Crewe Station-Longport Junction.	Eties	6C/201	12.35am	Longport Jnt-North Staffs Sidings	TF	6C/201
1378							4.32am	North Staffords Sdgs-Newcastle Jnt	Eties	86K/42	6.55am	Newcastle Jnt-South Shed	LE	86K/42
	1380	1380	1380				2.55pm	North Staffords Sdgs-Egginton Jnt	EF (F)	6C/205		Egginton Junction-South Shed	LE	6C/205
	1381	1381	1381	1381			2.26am	Crewe Station-Stoke	EF (F)	5A/36		Stoke-North Shed	LE	5A/36
1392	1392	1392	1392	1392			11.10pm	Basford Hall-Edge Hill	EF (D)	8A/33	4.20am	Edge Hill-Basford Hall	TF	8A/33
1393							1.35am	Basford Hall-Garston Speke Sidings	TF	6C/201	4.15am	Garston Speke Sidings-Basford Hall	TF	6C/201
	1394						1.45am	Basford Hall-Edge Hill	EF (D)	8A/27		*return as required*		
1395							5.30am	Gresty Lane-Runcorn	TF	5B/1040	10am	Runcorn-Basford Hall South	Eties	5B/1040
	1396	1396	1396	1396			11.39am	North Staffordshire Sidings-Runcorn	Min	17A/317		*return as required*		
	1398	1398	1398	1398	1398		5.35am	Basford Hall North-Garston Speke Sdgs	TF	12A/17		*return as required*		

Mon	Tue	Wed	Thu	Fri	Sat	Sun	Time	Outward Trip	Work	Loco	Time	Inward Trip	Work	Locol
1399							4.30am	Gresty Lane-Edge Hill	EF (F)	5B/1019		*return as required*		
	1400	1400	1400	1400	1400		6.15am	Basford Hall-Edge Hill	TF	5B/1019		*return as required*		
1401							4.43am	South Shed-Winsford Junction	LE	12A/321	5.58am	Winsford Jnt-Runcorn	TF	12A/321
1402							9.10am	Basford Hall-Over & Wharton	TF	5B/1001	11.15am	Over & Wharton-Runcorn	Frt	5B/1001
					1448		1.27pm	Basford Hall-Edge Hill	TF	8A/33	6.25pm	Edge Hill-Gresty Lane	EF (F)	8A/33
1449							1pm	South Shed-Cattle Market	LE	11A/250	2.30pm	Cattle Market-South Shed	LE	11A/250
					1456		3pm	as passenger to Chester			5.40pm	Dundas Sidings-Normacot	Eties	5B/1037
	1457	1457	1457	1457			4.10am	North Staffordshire Sidings-Birkenhead	EF (F)	8A/—		*return as required*		
					1458		4.10am	North Staffordshire Sidings-Birkenhead	EF (F)	6C/201		*return as required*		
					1459		10.26pm	as passenger to Birkenhead			2.50am	Ellesmere Port-Basford Hall	TF	6C/204
1460	1460	1460	1460	1460			9am	Basford Hall-Broxton	Frt	5B/1056	12.14pm	Broxton-Crewe Gresty Lane	Frt	5B/1056
1461							1am	Basford Hall -Mold Junction	TF	5B/1053	3.55am	Mold Jnt South Yd-Basford Hall	TF	5B/1053
1462	1462	1462	1462	1462			9.40am	Basford Hall-Waverton	Frt	5B/1037	2.25pm	Waverton-Basford Hall	Frt	5B/1037
						1463	3.40am	Basford Hall-Birkenhead	TF	3D/3		*return as required*		
	1464	1464	1464	1464			1.35pm	North Staffordshire Sidings-Chester	Min	6C/201	5.40pm	Dundas Sdgs-North Staffs Sdgs	Eties	5B/1052
	1465	1465	1465	1465			4.56am	Basford Hall-Birkenhead	EF (E)	3D/3		*return as required*		
1466							1.30pm	Basford Hall-Mold Junction	TF	5B/1032		Mold Jnt-Crewe South	LE	5B/1032
					1467		3.48pm	Basford Hall-Birkenhead	TF	86K/42		*return as required*		
					1468		12.50am	North Staffs Sdgs-Mold Junction	EF (F)	5D/345	5.10am	Mold Junction-North Staffs Sdgs	TF	5D/345
					1469		4.25pm	as passenger to Llandudno Junction			7.1pm	Llandudno Junction-Basford Hall	EF (E)	6B/4
1475	1475	1475	1475				10/58pm	Basford Hall-Shrewsbury	EF (F)	84G/104	4.40am	Harlescott-Gresty Lane	EF (E)	84G/102
1476	1476	1476	1476				9/42pm	Basford Hall-Shrewsbury	EF (E)	86K/42		Harlescott-South Shed	LE	86K/42
					1477		6.30pm	Basford Hall-Coleham	TF	5B/1001	11.50pm	Harlescott-Gresty Lane	TF	8B/4
	1478	1478	1478	1478			2.22am	Basford Hall-Abbey Foregate	TF	5B/1001	6.35am	Harlescott-Gresty Lane	TF	5B/1032
				1479			8.35pm	Basford Hall-Shrewsbury Station	EF (E)	86K/42		*return as required*		
						1484	9.45pm	Basford Hall-Coleham	TF	84G/104	2.5am	Harlescott-Gresty Lane	TF	5B/1032
		1485					6.50pm	Gresty Lane-Whitchurch	EBV	5B/1056	7.55pm	Whitchurch-Gresty Lane	EF (F)	5B/1056
1499	1499	1499	1499	1499			9pm	P Way Shops Shunt		5B/1083				
1500	1500	1500	1500	1500	1500		6am	Sorting Sidings South Shunt	Diesel	5B/1101				
1501	1501	1501	1501	1501	1501		2pm	Sorting Sidings South Shunt	Diesel	5B/1101				
1502	1502	1502	1502	1502	1502		10pm	Sorting Sidings South Shunt	Diesel	5B/1101				
						1503	6am	Sorting Sidings South Shunt	Diesel	5B/1101				
1506	1506	1506	1506	1506	1506		6am	Up Side Shunt	Diesel	5B/1106				
1507	1507	1507	1507	1507	1507		2pm	Up Side Shunt	Diesel	5B/1106				
1508	1508	1508	1508	1508			10pm	Up Side Shunt	Diesel	5B/1106				
					1509		10pm	Up Side Shunt	Diesel	5B/1106				
1512	1512	1512	1512	1512			6am	No 12 Trip Shunt		5B/1080				
1513	1513	1513	1513	1513			1.30pm	No 12 Trip Shunt		5B/1080				
1514	1514	1514	1514	1514			9.25pm	No 12 Trip Shunt		5B/1080				
					1515		6am	No 12 Trip Shunt		5B/1080				
					1516		1.5pm	No 12 Trip Shunt		5B/1080				
1518							6am	No 18 Trip Shunt		5B/1080				
1519	1519	1519	1519	1519	1519		2.5pm	No 18 Trip Shunt		5B/1080				
1520	1520	1520	1520	1520	1520		10pm	No 18 Trip Shunt		5B/1080				
	1521	1521	1521	1521	1521		6am	No 18 Trip Shunt		5B/1080				
						1522	6.10am	No 18 Trip Shunt		5B/1080				
1525	1525	1525	1525	1525	1525		7.55am	SS North-Gresty Lane-Wagon Shop	Trip	5B/1080		Wagon Shop Shunt		
1526	1526	1526	1526	1526			4.55pm	SS North-Gresty Lane -Wagon Shop	Trip	5B/1080		Wagon Shop Shunt		
						1531	11.25am	SS North-Gresty Lane-Wagon Shop	Trip	5B/1080		Wagon Shop Shunt		
						1532	3.10pm	Warehouse Shed Shunt		5B/1080	5.45pm	Wagon Shop Shunt		
1537							6am	Gresty Lane Shunt	Diesel	5B/1099				
	1538	1538	1538	1538	1538		6am	Gresty Lane Shunt	Diesel	5B/1099				

Mon	Tue	Wed	Thu	Fri	Sat	Sun	Time	Outward Trip	Work	Loco	Time	Inward Trip	Work	Loco
1539	1539	1539	1539	1539	1539		2pm	Gresty Lane Shunt	Diesel	5B/1099				
1540	1540	1540	1540	1540	1540		10.5pm	Gresty Lane Shunt	Diesel	5B/1099				
1541	1541	1541	1541	1541	1541		8am	RSD Shunt		5B/1080				from 8 Sept
			1542	1542			8am	RSD Shunt		5B/1080				to 7 Sept
			1543				2.45pm	RSD Shunt		5B/1080				to 6 Sept
				1544			2.45pm	RSD Shunt		5B/1080				to 7 Sept
						1545	8am	RSD Shunt		5B/1080				
					1546		8am	RSD Shunt		5B/1080A				to 8 Sept
1604	1604	1604	1604	1604	1604		6am	Sorting Sidings Middle Shunt	Diesel	5B/1095				
1605	1605	1605	1605	1605	1605		2pm	Sorting Sidings Middle Shunt	Diesel	5B/1095				
1606	1606	1606	1606	1606	1606		10pm	Sorting Sidings Middle Shunt	Diesel	5B/1095				
						1607	6am	Sorting Sidings Middle Shunt	Diesel	5B/1095				
1610	1610	1610	1610	1610	1610		6am	Basford Hall 'E' Group Shunt	Diesel	5B/1096				
1611	1611	1611	1611	1611	1611		2pm	Basford Hall 'E' Group Shunt	Diesel	5B/1096				
1612	1612	1612	1612	1612	1612		10pm	Basford Hall 'E' Group Shunt	Diesel	5B/1096				
						1613	5.5am	Basford Hall 'E' Group Shunt	Diesel	5B/1096				
						1614	12.10pm	Basford Hall 'E' Group Shunt	Diesel	5B/1096				
						1615	10pm	No 3 Trip Shunt	Diesel	5B/1097				
1616	1616	1616	1616	1616	1616		6am	No 3 Trip Shunt	Diesel	5B/1097				
1617	1617	1617	1617	1617	1617		2pm	No 3 Trip Shunt	Diesel	5B/1097				
1618	1618	1618	1618	1618	1618		10pm	No 3 Trip Shunt	Diesel	5B/1097				
						1619	5.5am	No 3 Trip Shunt	Diesel	5B/1097				
						1620	12.10pm	No 3 Trip Shunt	Diesel	5B/1097				
						1621	10pm	Gresty Lane Down Side Shunt	Diesel	5B/1098				
1622	1622	1622	1622	1622	1622		6am	Gresty Lane Down Side Shunt	Diesel	5B/1098				
1623	1623	1623	1623	1623	1623		2pm	Gresty Lane Down Side Shunt	Diesel	5B/1098				
1624	1624	1624	1624	1624	1624		10pm	Gresty Lane Down Side Shunt	Diesel	5B/1098				
						1625	5.5am	Gresty Lane Down Side Shunt	Diesel	5B/1098				
						1626	11.35am	Gresty Lane Down Side Shunt	Diesel	5B/1098				
1628	1628	1628	1628	1628	1628		6am	North Staffs Sidings Up Side Shunt	Diesel	5B/1100				
1629	1629	1629	1629	1629	1629		2pm	North Staffs Sidings Up Side Shunt	Diesel	5B/1100				
1630	1630	1630	1630	1630			10pm	North.Staffs Sidings Up Side Shunt	Diesel	5B/1100				
					1631		10pm	North Staffs Sidings Up Side Shunt	Diesel	5B/1100				
1634	1634	1634	1634	1634	1634		6am	Sorting Sidings North Shunt	Diesel	5B/1102				
1635	1635	1635	1635	1635	1635		2pm	Sorting Sidings North Shunt	Diesel	5B/1102				
1636	1636	1636	1636	1636	1636		10pm	Sorting Sidings North Shunt	Diesel	5B/1102				
						1637	6am	Sorting Sidings North Shunt	Diesel	5B/1102				
						1639	10pm	Basford Hall Up Shunt	Diesel	5B/1103				
1640	1640	1640	1640	1640	1640		6am	Basford Hall Up Shunt	Diesel	5B/1103				
1641	1641	1641	1641	1641	1641		2pm	Basford Hall Up Shunt	Diesel	5B/1103				
1642	1642	1642	1642	1642	1642		10pm	Basford Hall Up Shunt	Diesel	5B/1103				
						1643	6am	Basford Hall Up Shunt	Diesel	5B/1103				
1646	1646	1646	1646	1646	1646		6am	North Staffs Sidings Down Side Shunt	Diesel	5B/1104				
1647	1647	1647	1647	1647	1647		2pm	North Staffs Sidings Down Side Shunt	Diesel	5B/1104				
1648	1648	1648	1648	1648			10pm	North Staffs Sidings Down Side Shunt	Diesel	5B/1104				
					1649		10pm	North.Staffs.Sidings Down Side Shunt	Diesel	5B/1104				
1650							6am	Sorting Sidings South Shunt	Diesel	5B/1107				
	1651	1651	1651	1651	1651		6am	Sorting Sidings South Shunt	Diesel	5B/1107				
1652	1652	1652	1652	1652	1652		2pm	Sorting Sidings South Shunt	Diesel	5B/1107				
1653	1653	1653	1653	1653	1653		10pm	Sorting Sidings South Shunt	Diesel	5B/1107				
1660	1660	1660	1660	1660	1660		6am	Warehouse North End Shunt		5B/1082				
1661	1661	1661	1661	1661			2pm	Warehouse North End Shunt		5B/1082				

Mon	Tue	Wed	Thu	Fri	Sat	Sun	Time	Outward Trip	Work	Loco	Time	Inward Trip	Work	Loco
1662	1662	1662	1662	1662			10pm	Warehouse North End Shunt		5B/1082				
					1663		5.10am	Warehouse North End Shunt		5B/1082				
					1664		10.40am	Warehouse North End Shunt		5B/1082				
						1665	8.20am	Warehouse North End Shunt		5B/1082				
1668	1668	1668	1668	1668			6am	Warehouse South End Shunt	Diesel	5B/1105				
1669	1669	1669	1669	1669			2pm	Warehouse South End Shunt	Diesel	5B/1105				
1670	1670	1670	1670	1670			10pm	Warehouse South End Shunt	Diesel	5B/1105				
					1671		5.10am	Warehouse South End Shunt	Diesel	5B/1105				
					1672		12.20pm	Warehouse South End Shunt	Diesel	5B/1105				
						1673	8.30am	Warehouse South End Shunt	Diesel	5B/1107				
	1699	1699	1699	1699	1699		10.30am	Preparation Shift						
1700							1.30am	Preparation Shift						
1701	1701	1701	1701	1701	1701		9am	Preparation Shift						
1702							2pm	Preparation Shift						
1703							3.40pm	Preparation Shift						
	1704	1704	1704	1704			2.50pm	Preparation Shift						
					1705		2.55pm	Preparation Shift						
	1706	1706	1706	1706			2am	Preparation Shift						
1707							12.5am	Preparation Shift				Diesel Driver only		
1708							12.15am	Preparation Shift				Diesel Driver only		
1753	1753	1753	1753	1753			7.30am	Triangle Yard Shunt		5B/1064				
					1754		6.15am	Triangle Yard Shunt		5B/1064				
1755	1755	1755	1755	1755	1755		6.15am	P Way Shops Shunt		5B/1083				
1756	1756	1756	1756	1756			1.20pm	P Way Shops Shunt		5B/1083				
148	**140**	**143**	**142**	**142**	**116**	**37**		**Total Daily Rostered Turns**						

Right:
Crewe South End, 9 May 1954
Unrebuilt 'Patriot' class 4-6-0 No 45503 *The Royal Leicestershire Regiment*, a Crewe North engine, draws away from the station with a Class A train comprising some non-corridor stock, bound for Shrewsbury. The train was actually calling at most stations but was given express headlamps for timing purposes. *B. K. B. Green*

Crewe South 5B Enginemen's Turns

July 1951

Turn	Days	Staff	Hours	Duties
Turn 2047	D	One Set	6am to 2pm	
Turn 2048	D	One Set	2pm to 10pm	
Turn 2049	D	One Set	10pm to 6am	shunting shed
Turn 2050	Sun	One Set	6am to 2pm	and drop
Turn 2051	Sun	One Set	10pm to 6am	(Turn 1055)
Turn 2051a	MO	One Set	12.1am to 6am	
Turn 2052	Sun	One Set	2pm to 9.45pm	
Turn 2053	D	One Set	6am to 2pm	
Turn 2054	D	One Set	2pm to 10pm	turning engines
Turn 2055	D	One Set	10pm to 6am	on ashpit
Turn 2056	Sun	One Set	6am to 2pm	
Turn 2057	Sun	One Set	2pm to 10pm	
Turn 2058	Sun	One Set	10pm to 6am	turning engines on ashpit
				setting engines
				and filling tanks
Turn 2058a	D	One Set	1.30pm to 9.30pm	moving engines on old ashpit
Turn 2059	SX	One Set	8.30am to 4.30pm	loco coal trips South Shed
Turn 2060	SO	One Set	7am to 3pm	to Basford Hall etc (Turn 2063)

D Trip 10.15am South Shed to Basford Hall South 10.20am also 10.45am Trip SS South to NS Sidings when required and when engine of 8.54am from Chatterley is required for washing out etc, to work to NS Sidings, and Change Footplates with 5E Turn 64 enginemen on latter train and work LE to South Shed. (CPE 3353).

Turn	Days	Staff	Hours	Duties
Turn 2061	D	One Driver	6am to 2pm	
Turn 2062	D	One Driver	2pm to 10pm	setting engines for
Turn 2063	D	One Driver	10pm to 6am	firedroppers
Turn 2064	Sun	One Driver	6am to 2pm	
Turn 2065	D	One Set	6am to 2pm	
Turn 2066	D	One Set	2pm to 10pm	filling tanks and arranging
Turn 2067	D	One Set	10pm to 6am	engines on coal hole
Turn 2068	Sun	One Set	6am to 2pm	
Turn 2069 / Turn 2070	MO	Two Firemen	12.1am to 6am	shop shunters

Left:
Crewe Station, South End, Platform 2, 9 May 1954
Rebuilt 'Patriot' No 45530 *Sir Frank Ree* of Longsight 9A shed negotiates the pointwork off the Down Fast line and coasts into Platform 2 with a Euston to Manchester London Road working.
B. K. B. Green

Below left:
Crewe South Junction, 4 September 1950
Rebuilt 'Royal Scot' class 4-6-0 No 46125 *3rd Carabinier* pulls away from Crewe on the Up Slow line with the 9.30am Glasgow Central to Birmingham New Street working. This was a regular North Shed working, the men placed in No 6 link. Note that the steam sanders are in action, to assist in getting the heavy train on the move. The loading on Mondays and Saturdays was 14 vehicles, 430 tons. The reporting number was W98. *Eric Treacy*

Above right:
Crewe South End, Platform 2, August 1949
Rebuilt 'Royal Scot' No 46115 *Scots Guardsman* pulls into Platform 2 with a Euston to Liverpool Lime Street working. This was probably the 8.30am off Euston, Reporting Number W39, at one time the preserve of the 'Turbomotive'. Load was usually 12 vehicles, 382 tons, well within the capabilities of a 'Scot'. The loco was on loan to Carlisle Upperby in the week ending 5 March 1949, then transferred to Longsight in the week ending 1 October 1949. It is possible that it sported a 5A plate as a result of being on loan as opposed to a permanent allocation at this time.
Derek Cross

Centre right:
Crewe South End, 1950
By 1950 the number of unrebuilt 'Royal Scot' class engines was getting fewer and fewer. One of the last to remain in this condition was No 46137 *The Prince of Wales's Volunteers (South Lancashire)* seen here in the hybrid livery of 1946-style LMS livery and lining with 'BRITISH RAILWAYS' lettering on the tender and the post-Nationalisation number on cab sides and smokebox. The train is bound for Shrewsbury and carries Class 2 lamps. Note too the three six-wheel milk tankers.
Ian Allan Library

Below right:
Crewe Station South End, Platform 3, September 1950
Unrebuilt 'Patriot' class 4-6-0 No 45504 *Royal Signals* shunts stock into Platform 3, attaching to the 11.40am working from Liverpool to Rugby. The photographer does not give details of the time of the working, but it is likely to be around 1pm. The Passenger Train Marshalling book shows the transfer of some stock off and onto the working, which would account for the fact that the locomotive is carrying a single headlamp (probably with red shade) on the buffer beam. *Derek Cross*

Crewe Works Engineman's Turns

(Based at Crewe South Shed)

Note:

Where 'Firemen Only' Turns indicated, Driver is attached to the CME Workshop staff.

Mon	Tue	Wed	Thu	Fri	Sat	Sun		Work	Type	
2076	2076	2076	2076	2076	2076		7.30am	Works-Basford Hall	Frt	10am Basford Hall-Works
2077	2077	2077	2077	2077	2077		1.45pm	Works-Basford Hall	Frt	4pm Basford Hall-Works
2079	2079	2079	2079	2079	2079		6.45am	Old Works Shunt		
2080	2080	2080	2080	2080	2080		2pm	Old Works Shunt		
2082	2082	2082	2082	2082	2082		8am	Deviation Shunt		
2083	2083	2083	2083	2083	2083		7.30am	Deviation Shunt		W4 Trip
						2083	8am	Deviation Shunt		W4 Trip
2084	2084	2084	2084	2084	2084		7.30am	Work as required (Fireman only)		W5 Trip
						2084	8am	Work as required (Fireman only)		W.5. Trip
2085	2085	2085	2085	2085			6.00am	Work as required (Fireman only)		W6 Trip
					2085		7.30am	Work as required (Fireman only)		W6 Trip
						2085	8.00am	Work as required (Fireman only)		W6 Trip
2086	2086	2086	2086	2086	2086		7.30am	Work as required (Fireman only)		W8 Trip
						2086	8.00am	Work as required (Fireman only)		W8 Trip
2087	2087	2087	2087	2087			6am	Work as required (Fireman only)		W11 Trip
					2087		7.30am	Work as required (Fireman only)		W11 Trip
2088	2088	2088	2088	2088	2088		7.30am	Work as required		W12 Trip
2088a	2088a	2088a	2088a	2088a	2088a		7.30am	Work as required		W7 Trip
						2088a	8am	Work as required		W7 Trip
2089	2089	2089	2089		2089	2089	8am	Work as required (Fireman only)		W10 Trip
				2089			7am	Work as required (Fireman only)		W10 Trip
2090	2090	2090	2090	2090	2090	2090	8am	Work as required		W3 Trip
2091	2091	2091	2091	2091	2091		7.30am	Work as required		W9 Trip
2092	2092	2092	2092	2092	2092		8am	Work as required (Fireman only)		W14 Trip
2093	2093	2093	2093	2093	2093		8am	Work as required		Vacuum Pits
2094	2094	2094	2094	2094	2094		10am	Work as required		Vacuum Pits
2095	2095	2095	2095	2095	2095		7.30am	Moving Engines		W13 Trip Erecting Shop to Vacuum Pits
19	**19**	**19**	**19**	**19**	**19**	**7**		**Total Daily Rostered Turns**		

Above:
Crewe Works, General Offices, 1949
The original Crewe to Chester line was used as the access to the workshops at an early date. This view shows Stanier Class 8F No 48133 allocated to Toton shed working on works duty W1 and running light engine towards the vacuum pits. The setting is positively rural although the general offices are behind the hedge. The line was properly controlled from boxes, one of which was located between the millwright's shop and the steelworks. It was the normal practice to 'commandeer' suitable engines off works before they were returned to traffic and these were used to work 'dead' engines about the works, to the weighbridge and to South Shed. *Ben Brooksbank*

Crewe Gresty Lane (Western Region)

Gresty Lane shed work became listed under the LM Region Control shortly after Nationalisation, but this was for administration purposes. In July 1951 ex-GWR men kept to their own work as before, although the Engine and Men's diagrams were issued from the LM office. One change was that the Gresty Lane shunt locomotive turn was handed over to a South Shed diesel shunter. This locomotive came off South Shed at 5.45am Monday morning and then worked continuously until 6pm Sunday when it returned to South Shed for servicing. The firemen for these five duties (Turns 26 to 30) became surplus to requirements and in some cases were absorbed into the LM sheds' rosters, retaining their seniority. As vacancies occurred, they were transferred back to Western Region sheds, although frequently they forfeited their right to transfer, finding LM shed work more lucrative! Freight work dominated the duties and enginemen worked round the block. In times of locomotive shortage LM Control authorised the loan of a 5B engine with strict instructions for its immediate return from its destination, if necessary working light engine so that the WR did not use it for its own work.

Gresty Lane Turns 1 to 5 were Passenger Enginemen's work, and consisted of work between Crewe and Wellington or Wolverhampton. Locomotives were attached to Wellington shed and usually consisted of 0-6-0 pannier or 2-6-2T tank engines.

Freight Enginemen's Turns used a variety of Western Region engines from several depots and men worked to Wellington and Oxley Sidings. The work fluctuated considerably during the 1950s, and it is understood that until Nationalisation Gresty Lane men worked to Banbury and Oxford.

Crewe (Western) Shed

Enginemen's Workings
July 1951

Mon	Tue	Wed	Thu	Fri	Sat	Sun	Time	Outward Trip	Work	Loco	Time	Inward Trip	Work	Loco
1	1	1	1	1	1		6.5am	Crewe to Wellington	Pass	Wellington	11.22am	Wolverhampton to Crewe	Pass	Wellington
		2			2		3.15pm	Crewe to Wellington	Pass	Wellington	9.25pm	Wellington to Crewe	Pass	Wellington
3	3		3	3			5.10pm	Crewe to Wellington	Pass	Wellington	9.25pm	Wellington to Crewe	Pass	Wellington
						4	6.40am	Crewe to Wellington	Pass	Wellington	9.15am	Wellington to Crewe	Pass	Wellington
						5	8.35pm	Crewe to Wellington	Pass	Wellington	10.55pm	Wellington to Crewe	Pass	Wellington
10	10	10	10	10	10		7.05am	Gresty L to Wellington	Frt	84B/—	12.15pm	return as passenger		
11	11	11	11	11	11		11am	Gresty L to Oxley Sdgs	T Frt	85A/—		return as required		
12	12	12	12	12	12		12pm	Gresty L to Oxley Sdgs	Frt	84B/—	3.58pm	Oxley Bch Jnt To Crewe	T Frt	81F/—
13	13	13	13	13	13		12.52pm	*as pass to Wellington*			2.31pm	Wellington to Crewe	Frt	84B/—
14	14	14	14	14	14		8.05pm	Gresty Green-Oxley Sdgs	T Frt	84F/—	1.6am	Oxley Bch Jnt To Crewe	T Frt	82C/—
15	15	15	15	15	15		8.50pm	*as pass to W'hampton*			1.40am	Oxley Sidings to Crewe	EF(F)	85A/—
16	16	16	16	16			10.24pm	Gresty L to Oxley Sdgs	EF(D)	2A/4	2.37am	Oxley Bch Jnt To Crewe	T Frt	84B/—
					16		10.35pm	Gresty L. to Oxley Sdgs	EF(F)	2A/4	2.37am	Oxley Bch Jnt To Crewe	T Frt	84B/—
						17	9.30am	Gresty Green-Oxley Sdgs	TF	85A/—	1.30pm	Oxley Sidings to Crewe	TF	85A/—
26	26	26	26	26	26		6am	Gresty Lane Shunt (Driver only)		5B/1108				
27	27	27	27	27	27		2pm	Gresty Lane Shunt (Driver only)		5B/1108				
28	28	28	28	28	28		10pm	Gresty Lane Shunt (Driver Only)		5B/1108				
						29	6am	Gresty Lane Shunt (Driver Only)		5B/1108				
						30	1.25pm	Gresty Lane Shunt (Driver Only)		5B/1108	6pm	Gresty Lane to South Shed		5B/1108
32	32	32	32	32	32		7.15am	Gresty Green Shunt		5B/1079				
33	33	33	33	33	33		2.25pm	Gresty Green Shunt		5B/1079				
40	40	40	40	40	40		8.30am	Preparation Set						
41	41	41	41	41	41		4.10pm	Preparation Set						
42	42	42	42	42			9.57am	Relieving and Preparation Set						
43							12.1am	Preparation Set						
	44	44	44	44	44	44	11.39pm	Preparation Set						
45a	45a	45a	45a	45a	45a		7.00am	Control Set						
45b							2pm	Control Set						
	45b	45b	45b	45b	45b		3pm	Control Set						
45c	45c	45c	45c	45c	45c		11pm	Control Set						
21	**21**	**21**	**21**	**21**	**20**	**6**		**Total Daily Rostered Turns**						

Wellington (WR) Engines

July 1951

'1600' class 0-6-0PT Total: 1
1619

'2021' class 0-6-0PT Total: 1
2030

'5700' class 0-6-0PT Total: 11
3613
3687
3732
3749
3760
5758
7754
9624
9630
9639
9742

'5101' class 2-6-2T Total: 6
4154
5109
5125
5138
5139
5178

'4400' class 2-6-2T Total: 3
4401
4605
4606

Total: 22

Above:
Crewe Steelworks Box, 1957
The approach to Crewe off the Chester line ran alongside Crewe Works, with the boiler shop level with the Steelworks box. Bridge No 7 seen here gave access to the works without the need to travel the mile into the town to gain the deviation entrance. In the far distance can be seen the higher building known as the Steelworks, which was used for scrapping engines. Beyond that can just be made out the 'Eagle Bridge' so named because the bridge pillars were adorned by cast metal eagles which, it is reputed, F. W. Webb rescued from a load of scrap metal destined for the furnaces. One of the eagles survives on the preserved 1940 North Junction box in Crewe Heritage Centre. *BR LM Region*

Middlewich Sub-Shed

July 1951

Middlewich was a very small shed and had no locomotives sub-shedded in the town, but utilised a Crewe South Shed Class 4F 0-6-0, 5B Turn 1062.

There were three Enginemen's Turns daily, Monday to Saturday, but no booked Sunday work. These duties consisted mainly of freight shunting at Middlewich, with a light engine working to South Shed at 10pm Monday to Friday, returning with the 4.56am Crewe to Northwich Parcels next day. On Saturday evening departure time for South Shed was 9pm, the crew returned as passengers on the Sundays Only 1.28am North Staffs Sidings to Winsford (8.40pm Nottingham to Edge Hill). This was due at Winsford station at 1.49am. The duty card had the cryptic note added that they had to walk from Winsford to Middlewich to sign off, which, by road, was 4.2 miles! The loco was worked out to Middlewich on Monday morning by 5B Turn 1362 who were relieved by Middlewich men on arrival.

Mon	Tue	Wed	Thu	Fri	Sat	Sun	Time	First Outward Trip	Work	Loco	Time	Last Inward Trip	Work	Loco	
1							7am	Middlewich Freight Shunt		5B/1062					
	2	2	2	2			5.39am	Middlewich to Northwich	Pcls	5B/1062	6.10am	Northwich to Middlewich	LE	5B/1062	#
3	3	3	3	3			2.00pm	Middlewich Freight Shunt		5B/1062					
4	4	4	4	4			10pm	Middlewich to South Shed	LE	5B/1062	4.56am	Crewe to Middlewich	Pcls	5B/1062	
					5		5.39am	Middlewich to Northwich	Pcls	5B/1062	6.10am	Northwich to Middlewich	LE	5B/1062	@
					6		1pm	Middlewich Freight Shunt		5B/1062					
					7		9pm	Middlewich to South Shed	LE	5B/1062	1.28am	return as passenger			
3	3	3	3	3	3			**Total Daily Rostered Turns**							

— then Freight Shunt until 2pm
@ — then Freight Shunt until 1pm

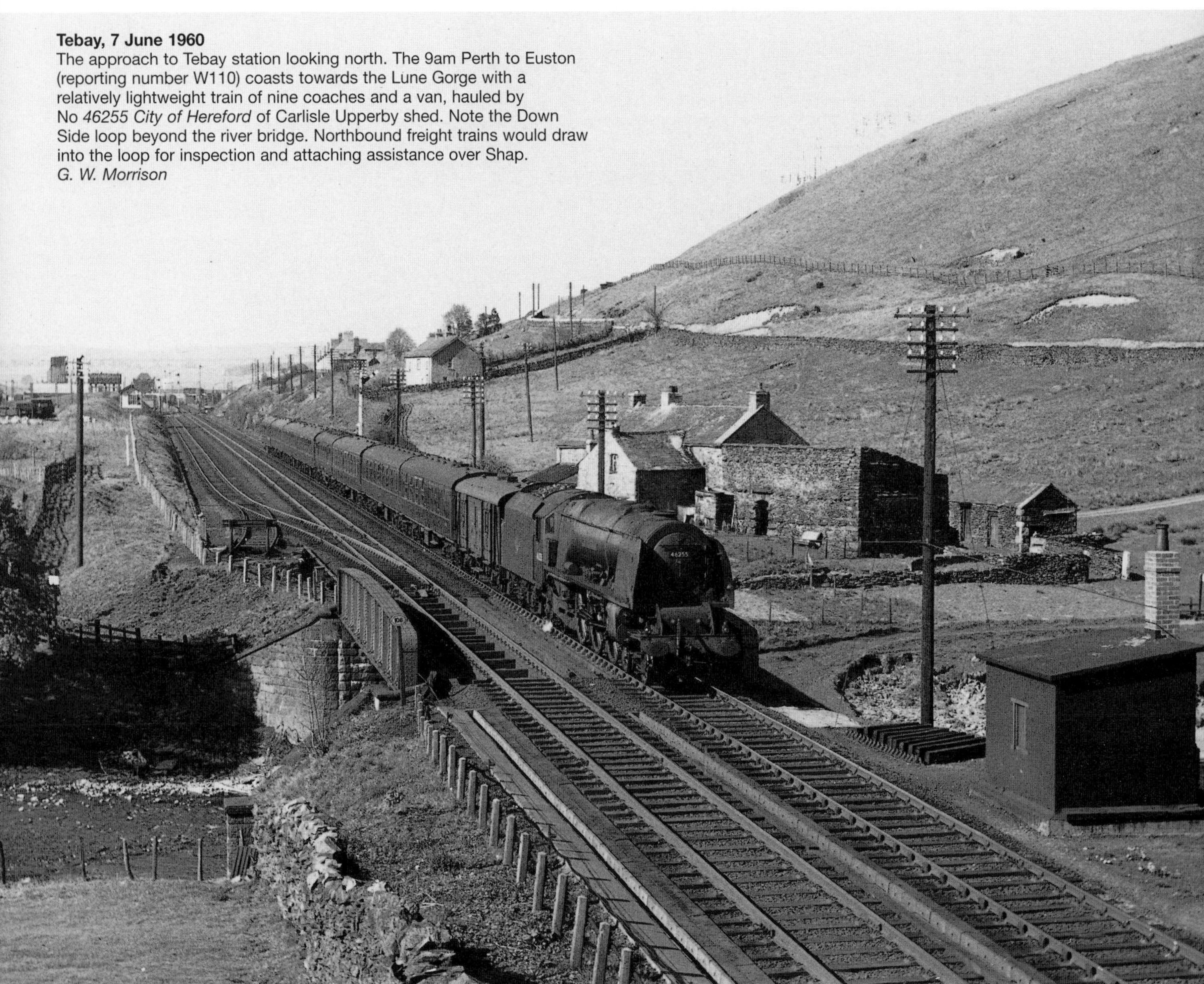

Tebay, 7 June 1960
The approach to Tebay station looking north. The 9am Perth to Euston (reporting number W110) coasts towards the Lune Gorge with a relatively lightweight train of nine coaches and a van, hauled by No *46255 City of Hereford* of Carlisle Upperby shed. Note the Down Side loop beyond the river bridge. Northbound freight trains would draw into the loop for inspection and attaching assistance over Shap.
G. W. Morrison

Whitchurch Sub-Shed

July 1951

In 1951 this small sub-shed to Crewe had an allocation of only three Class 2P 4-4-0 engines which were engaged solely on passenger and local shunt work. Locos used at Whitchurch were included in the Crewe North allocation. On 29 July 1951 Nos 40332, 40402 and 40425 were observed on Whitchurch shed.

There were seven Enginemen's Turns Monday to Friday, with eight turns on Saturdays. There was no regular Sunday work. Whitchurch men signed for the road to Crewe, Crewe to Chester via Beeston Castle, Whitchurch to Chester via Broxton and Malpas, Oswestry via Ellesmere (shown in the Western Region Service Timetables, Section 16); Shrewsbury via Wem, and Shrewsbury to Wellington via Upton Magna. The trip to Shrewsbury thence to Wellington utilised Crewe North 2-6-4T on Turn 106.

Most of the work was local passenger but Turn 4 worked the 12.30am Class F freight from Basford Hall to Whitchurch on Sunday morning. In LNWR days Whitchurch men worked through trains via Crewe to Birkenhead and Stafford but these workings ceased shortly after Grouping.

Turn 1

One Class 2P (STD)

SX	Pass	6.45am	Whitchurch	Crewe	7.16am	(6)
SX	Pass	7.35am	Crewe	Chester	8.8am	(5A/668 and 669)
SX			COAL			
SX	Pass	4.10pm	Chester	Whitchurch	4.56pm	(7)
SX		5pm	**Shunt (Pass and Frt)**	Whitchurch	10pm	(9) (10)
SO		6.30am	**Shunt (Pass and Frt)**	Whitchurch	1pm	(5)
SO	Pass	1.35pm	Whitchurch	Chester	2.17pm	
SO	Pass	5.20pm	Chester	Whitchurch	6.8pm	
SO	Pass	6.45pm	Whitchurch	Chester	7.27pm	(4)
SO	Pass	10.5pm	Chester	Whitchurch	10.53pm	
SO	LE	11.15pm	Whitchurch	Crewe Basford Hall	11.59pm	(Tender first)
Sun	EF	12.30am	Crewe Basford Hall	Whitchurch	1.10am	

Turn 8

One Class 2P (STD)

(As Enginemen's Turns 8-12).

Turn 15

One Class 2P (STD)

(As Enginemen's Turns 15-18)

Whitchurch Enginemen's Workings July 1951

Mon	Tue	Wed	Thu	Fri	Sat	Sun	Time	Outward Trip	Work	Loco	Time	Inward Trip	Work	Loco
					3		1.35pm	Whitchurch to Chester	Pass	Whitchurch 1	5.20pm	Chester to Whitchurch	Pass	Whitchurch 1
					4		6.45pm	Whitchurch to Chester	Pass	Whitchurch 1	12.30am	Basford Hall to Whitchurch	EF	Whitchurch 1
					5		6.30am	Passenger and Freight Shunt		Whitchurch 1				
6	6	6	6	6			6.45am	Whitchurch to Crewe	Pass	Whitchurch 1	12.05pm	Shrewsbury to Whitchurch	Pass	5A/106
7	7	7	7	7			12.49pm	Whitchurch to Crewe	Pass	5A/44	4.10pm	Chester to Whitchurch	Pass	Whitchurch 1
8	8		8	8			8.11am	Whitchurch to Chester	Pass	Whitchurch 8	11.42am	Chester to Whitchurch	Pass	Whitchurch 8
		8					8.11am	Whitchurch to Chester	Pass	Whitchurch 8	3.10pm	Shrewsbury to Whitchurch	Pass	Whitchurch 8
9	9		9	9			4.20pm	Whitchurch to Chester	Pass	Whitchurch 8	6.10pm	Chester to Whitchurch	Pass	Whitchurch 8
		10					4.20pm	Whitchurch to Chester	Pass	Whitchurch 8	6.10pm	Chester to Whitchurch	Pass	Whitchurch 8
					11		6.45am	Whitchurch to Crewe	Pass	Whitchurch 8	12.40pm	Chester to Whitchurch	Pass	Whitchurch 8
					12		1.25pm	Passenger and Freight Shunt		Whitchurch 8				
15	15	15	15	15			6.30am	Passenger and Freight Shunt		Whitchurch 15				
16	16	16	16	16			4.38pm	Whitchurch to Crewe	Pass	Whitchurch 15	7.50pm	Crewe to Whitchurch	Pass	Whitchurch 15
					17		8.11am	Whitchurch to Chester	Pass	Whitchurch 15	2.12pm	Chester to Whitchurch	Pass	Whitchurch 15
					18		4.38pm	Whitchurch to Crewe	Pass	Whitchurch 15	7.50pm	Crewe to Whitchurch	Pass	Whitchurch 15
20	20	20	20	20	20		8.17am	Whitchurch to Oswestry	Pass	Whitchurch	11.20am	*return as passenger*		
7	7	7	7	7	8			**Total Daily Rostered Turns**						

— shunt until 10pm

Above:
Tebay, October 1956
Stanier Class 5MT 4-6-0 No 44953 from Carstairs shed coasts down the bank into Tebay station with the 1.55pm Carlisle Upperby Yard to Edge Hill, a Class E express freight working. On the right is the North Eastern yard and the line over Stainmore to Kirkby Stephen.
B. A. Butt

Below:
Scout Green Signalbox, May 1957
A Crewe South 5B shed working, Stanier 2-6-0 No 42959 draws past Scout Green signalbox with a fully fitted Class C freight. This was probably the 12.33pm Garston to Carlisle Viaduct Yard, a train which ran 'as required' but usually ran. The train was booked to run without stopping from Garston to Tebay where it was examined and a banking engine positioned for the ascent of Shap. *W. J. V. Anderson*

Appendices (Weekly Traffic Flows)

Down Direction — Monday Only

Commence 18 June 1951
Note: Italics under departure time denote passing time

Time Dep	From	Destination	Rep No	Train Class	Days Run	Crewe Arr	Crewe Dep	Platform or Yard	To Crewe from South Men Diag	To Crewe from South Loco Diag	From Crewe to North Men Diag	From Crewe to North Loco Diag
8.30pm	Euston	Glasgow Central	157	A	D	11.44pm	12am	2 South	5A/4	5A/279	5A/5	5A/139
12.5am	Crewe	York	201	A	MO	11.27pm	12.1am	8 Bay	-	-	9B/	9B/
8.52pm	Euston	Holyhead	163	A	MO	12am	12.11am	2	5A/12	5A/359	7C/	7C/
9.10pm	Euston	Glasgow Central	169	A	D	*pass 12.15am*		2 Through	12A/	12A/	12A/	12A/
9.17pm	Euston	Glasgow St Enoch	175	A	MO-Q	*pass 12.23am*		2 Through	12A/	12A/	12A/	12A/
10.55pm	Wellington	Crewe		B	MO	12.26am	-	2 Bay	Wellington	Crewe/5	-	-
10.50pm	Birmingham	Glasgow Central	291	A	MO-Q	12.27am	12.50am	2				
12.41am	Crewe	Manchester L Rd	293	A	D	-	12.41am	1 North	-	-	5A/91	5A/92
12.45am	Crewe	Liverpool Lime St	267	A	MO	-	12.45am	1 South	-	-		
11.10pm	Birmingham	Glasgow Central	299	A	D	12.53am	1.5am	1	5A/10	5A/503	5A/3	5A/143
12.55am	Crewe	Walton Old Junction		H	MO	-	12.55am	BHSS North	-	-	11A/250	5B/1280
1am	Crewe	Mold Junction		H	MO	-	1.00am	BHSS North	-	-	5B/1053	5B/1461
1.5am	Crewe	Manchester L Rd		F	MO	-	1.5am	Gresty Lane	-	-	84G/5	5B/1330
1.15am	Crewe	Adswood Sidings		H	MO	-	1.15am	Gresty Lane	-	-	26A/633	5B/1331
9.25pm	Euston	Glasgow Central	171	A	D	1.13am	1.25am	2	12A/5	5A/285	12A/5	5A/150
1.35am	Crewe	Garston Speke Sdgs		H	MO	-	1.35am	BHSS North	-	-	6C/201	5B/1393
12.30am	Harlescott Sidings	Carlisle		F	MO	1.48am	2.50am	Gresty Lane				
10.50pm	Euston	Perth	195	A	MO	1.55am	2.5am	2	7C/—	1B/235	5A/19	5A/183
2am	Crewe	Neville Hill		H	MO	-	2am	Gresty Lane	-	-	25G/301	5B/1351
11.5pm	Euston	Blackpool North	183	A	MO	2.2am	2.25am	1			5A/33	28A/69
2.10am	Crewe	Holyhead	1	A	MO	-	2.10am	7 Bay	-	-	7A/157	6A/41
1.5am	Harlescott Sidings	Carlisle		E	MO	2.10am	2.20am	Gresty Lane	5B/1001	84G/194	-	-
11.15pm	Euston	Crewe	183	A	MO-Q	2.11am	-	2			-	-
2.16am	Crewe	Windermere	193	A	MO	-	2.16am	1	-	-		
2.20am	Crewe	Springs Branch		E	MO	-	2.20am	Gresty Lane	-	-	12/320	5B/1239
2.25am	Crewe	Birkenhead		H	MO	-	2.25am	BHSS North	-	-		
11.40pm	Euston	Carlisle	21	A	SX	*pass 2.35am*		2 Through	1B/1	1B/100	1B/1	1B/100
2.35am	Crewe	Liverpool Lime St	231	A	MO	-	2.35am	2 South	-	-	8A/32	5A/595
2.42am	Crewe	Manchester L Rd	207	A	D	-	2.42am	8 Bay	-	-	9A/—	1B/185
9.32pm	Camden	Crewe		D	SX	2.41am	-	BHSS North	5A/39	5B/1161	-	-
11.40pm	Euston	Glasgow Central	21	A	MO	*pass 2.50am*		2 Through				
10pm	Euston	Preston	3	C	SX	2.51am	3.2am	-	5A/24	2B/93	5A/24	2B/93
3.5am	Crewe	Preston	167	C	MO	-	3.05am	Down Sidings	-	-	5A/28	5A/205
12.20am	Euston	Manchester L Rd	9	A	D	*pass 3.25am*		2 Through	9A/—	1B/160	9A/—	1B/160
2.5am	Harlescott Sidings	Bamfurlong		H	MO	3.25am	3.55am	Gresty Lane	5B/1032	5B/1484	5B/1032	5B/1246
3.30am	Crewe	Bamfurlong		H	MO	-	3.30am	BHSS North	-	-	1A/525	5B/1238
1.30am	Oxley	Crewe		H	MO	3.34am	-	Gresty Lane			-	-
12.30am	Euston	Liverpool Lime St	213	A	D	*pass 3.35am*		2 Through	8A/—	1B/142	8A/—	1B/142
3.35am	Crewe	Copley Hill		H	MO	-	3.35am	Gresty Lane	-	-	25G/302	5B/1345
3.10am	Stafford	Crewe		C	MO	3.49am	-		5A/24	2A/107	-	-
2.43am	Harlescott Sidings	Edge Hill		H	MO	4.3am	5.8am	Gresty Lane				
4.10am	Crewe	Birkenhead		F	MO	-	4.10am	North Staffs Sdgs	-	-		
4.10am	Crewe	Whitchurch		H	MO	-	4.10am	BHSS Middle	-	-	5B/1055	5A/660
12.5am	Cardiff	Liverpool Lime St	215	A	D	4.10am	5.20am	2 South	84G/5	84G/63	84G/5	5A/594
3.20am	Pratt's Sidings	Crewe	3	J	MO	4.15am	-	Gresty Lane			-	-
4.20am	Crewe	Edge Hill		F	MO	-	4.20am	BHSS North	-	-		
4.45pm	Penzance	Manchester L Rd	217	A	D	4.28am	5.10am	2				
4.30am	Crewe	Edge Hill		F	MO	-	4.30am	Gresty Lane	-	-	5B/1019	5B/1399
2.48am	Amington Sidings	Edge Hill		E	MO	4.38am	4.55am	BHSS North				
4.43am	Crewe South Shed	Winsford Junction		G	MO	-	4.43am	South Shed	-	-	12A/321	5B/1401
4.45am	Crewe	Runcorn		H	MO	-	4.45am	BHSS North	-	-		
4.45am	Crewe	Birkenhead		J	MO	-	4.45am	North Staffs Sdgs	-	-		
4.56am	Crewe	Northwich		C	D	-	4.56am	7 Bay	-	-	5B/1062	5B/1362
12.30am	Camden	Crewe		D	SX	4.57am	5.15am	BHSS North		1A/816	-	-
5am	Crewe	Copley Hill		H	MO	-	5am	Gresty Lane	-	-	5B/1036	9B/69
5.3am	Crewe	Chester		B	SX	-	5.3am	-	-	-	7C/12	5A/655
12.2am	Euston	Crewe	189	A	D	5.4am	-	3	1B/17	5A/302	-	-
5am	Alsager Junction	Crewe	84	K	D	5.18am	-	North Staffs Sdgs			-	-
7.25pm	Fratton	Crewe		C	MO	5.21am	-	1 Through			-	-
3.15am	Bescot	Carlisle London Rd		E	SX	5.22am	5.27am	Station	5B/1038	3A/192	5B/1038	10A/654
12.46am	Northampton	Crewe		H	MO	5.26am	-	BHSS North		5A/391	-	-

Time Dep	From	Destination	Rep No	Train Class	Days Run	Crewe Arr	Crewe Dep	Platform or Yard	To Crewe from South Men Diag	To Crewe from South Loco Diag	From Crewe to North Men Diag	From Crewe to North Loco Diag
5.27am	Crewe	Northwich	25	K	D	-	5.27am	BHSS North	-	-	5B/1017	5B/1368
5.30am	Crewe	Runcorn		H	MO	-	5.30am	Gresty Lane	-	-	5B/1040	5B/1395
4am	Oxley Sidings	Crewe		E	MSO	5.45am	-	Gresty Lane			-	-
5.55am	Crewe	Walton Old Junction		H	MO	-	5.55am	BHSS North	-	-	5B/1039	8B/570
4.40am	Harlescott Sidings	Carlisle		E	SX	5.55am	6.30am	Gresty Lane	84G/102	5B/1475	84G/102	5B/1241
3.30am	Bescot	Warrington		H	MO	5.57am	6.50am	BHSS North	3D/205	5B/1219	3D/205	5B/1298
6am	Crewe	Warrington		B	D	-	6am	1 North	-		10B/20	5A/200
3.47am	Bescot	Crewe		H	MO	6.11am	-	BHSS North	5B/1034	3A/183	-	-
6.15am	Crewe	Northwich		B	D	-	6.15am	9 Bay	-	-	5A/120	5A/120
6.15am	Crewe	Crewe Coal Yard	17	K	MO	-	6.15am	BHSS North	-	-	5B/1118	5B/1118
6.20am	Crewe	Sandbach	23	K	D	-	6.20am	BHSS North	-	-	12A/319	5B/1367
6.42am	Crewe	Bamfurlong		H	MO	-	6.42am	BHSS North	-	-	5B/1039	5B/1275
6.45am	Crewe	Manchester L Rd		B	D	-	6.45am	8 Bay	-	-	9A/9	5A/605
12.15am	Willesden	Adswood Sidings		E	MO	6.54am	6.58am	BHSS North	9A/415	1A/815	91/415	5B/1352
6.15am	Stoke	Crewe		G	MO	6.55am	-	-		5A/632	-	-
2.20am	Northampton	Walton Old Junction		H	MO	7.5am	8.00am	BHSS North				
7.15am	Crewe	Neville Hill		F	SX	-	7.15am	Gresty Lane	-	-	5B/1005	5B/1327
6.45am	Whitchurch	Crewe		B	D	7.16am	-	2 North	W'church/1	W'church/6	-	-
7.23am	Crewe	Manchester L Rd		B	D	-	7.23am	1 North	-	-		
7.23am	Crewe	Aintree		F	SX	-	7.23am	BHSS North	-	-	21A/—	5B/1297
6.10am	Creswell	Crewe Works		B	D	7.24am	7.29am	2 South			-	-
7.32am	Crewe	Northwich		B	D	-	7.32am		-	-	5A/120	5A/120
5am	Nuneaton TV	Crewe		H	MOQ	7.34am	-	BHSS North			-	-
7.35am	Crewe	Chester		B	D	-	7.35am	2 North	-	-	W'church/1	5A/668
7.36am	Crewe	Northwich		B	D	-	7.36am	9 Bay	-	-		
4.55am	Oxley Sidings	Crewe		H	D	7.38am	-	Gresty Lane			-	-
6.55am	Newcastle Jnt	Crewe South Shed		G	MO	7.38am	-	North Staffs Sdgs			-	-
7.40am	Crewe	Carlisle London Rd		H	SX	-	7.40am	BHSS North	-	-	5B/1034	5B/1293
7.42am	Crewe	Liverpool Lime St		B	D	-	7.42am	8 Bay	-	-	3B/151	5A/593
7.45am	Crewe	Adswood Sidings		K	D	-	7.45am	BHSS North	-	-	5B/1020	5B/1333
7.48am	Crewe	Chester		B	D	-	7.48am	1 North	-	-	7C/2	5A/650
7.25am	Whitchurch	Crewe		G	MO	7.50am	-	Gresty Lane			-	-
7.50am	Crewe	Manchester L Rd		B	D	-	7.50am	1 South	-	-	2A/—	5A/607
12.1am	Willesden	Crewe		H	MO	7.55am	-	BHSS North			-	-
7am	Stafford	Crewe		H	D	8.5am	-	BHSS North			-	-
8.5am	Alsager	Hooton		J	SX	*pass 8.25am*		North Staffs Sdgs				
8.27am	Crewe	Manchester L Rd		E	SX	-	8.27am	BHSS North	-	-		
8.30am	Crewe	Northwich		Min	SX	-	8.30am	BHSS North	-	-		5B/1363
6.30am	Birmingham	Crewe		A	D	8.30am	-	1 North	5A/44	5A/540	-	-
8.20am	Alsager	Crewe South Shed		G	SX	8.35am	-	Gresty Lane			-	-
7.25am	Shrewsbury	Crewe		B	D	8.37am	-	1 North			-	-
8.10am	Stoke	Liverpool Lime St		B	D	8.42am	8.48am	2 North	5A/40	5A/626	5A/40	5A/585
7.30am	Wellington	Crewe		B	D	8.47am	-	3 Bay			-	-
7.10am	Birmingham	Manchester L Rd		A	SX	8.55am	9.2am	2 North				
9am	Crewe	Broxton	41	K	SX	-	9am	BHSS North	-	-		5B/1460
9.10am	Crewe	Liverpool L St		B	D	-	9.10am	1North	-	-	8A/26	5A/582
8.50am	Alsager	Crewe	89	K	D	9.10am	-	North Staffs Sdgs			-	-
9.10am	Crewe	Runcorn		H	SX	-	9.10am	North Staffs Sdgs	-	-	5B/1001	5B/1402
9.13am	Crewe	Manchester L Rd		B	SX	-	9.13am	8 Bay	-	-		
7.15am	Bescot	Grange Junction		J	SX	9.17am	9.25am	BHSS North	5A/22	5B/1197	5A/22	5B/1197
9.20am	Crewe	Holyhead	55	A	D	-	9.20am	7 Bay	-	-	9A/12	5A/656
9.25am	Crewe	Perth	27	A	SX	-	9.25am	2	-	-	66A/2	5A/206
6.40am	Bescot	Adswood Sidings		H	MO	9.30am	10.5am	BHSS North	9A/4	5B/1221	9A/4	5B/1332
7.20am	Derby	Llandudno	351	A	SX	9.32am	9.37am	2				
9.40am	Crewe	Blackpool Central	389	A	MFO	-	9.40am	8 Bay	-	-	5A/45	5A/238
9.40am	Crewe	Waverton	36	K	SX	-	9.40am	BHSS North	-	-	5B/1037	5B/1462
8.30am	Birmingham	Liverpool Lime St	225	A	SX	9.45am	9.52am	2 North				
8.40am	Shrewsbury	Crewe		B	D	9.47am	-	1 North	84G/22	5A/715	-	-
9.27am	Alsager	Garston Speke Sdgs		J	SX	*pass 9.47am*		North Staffs Sdgs				
9.57am	Crewe	Manchester L Rd	227	A	SX	-	9.57am	2 South	-	-		
8.54am	Chatterley Sidings	Crewe	84	H	D	10.2am	-	North Staffs Sdgs			-	-
10am	Basford Hall	Crewe Works	W1	K	D	*pass 10.10am*		BHSS North	5B/1086	5B/2076	5B/1086	5B/2076
9.45am	Stoke	Crewe		B	SX	10.15am	-	5 Bay			-	-
9.45am	Nantwich	Crewe	38	K	D	10.28am	-	BHSS North		5B/1126	-	-
10.29am	Crewe	Healey Mills		H	D	-	10.29am	Gresty Lane	-	-	5B/1003	5B/1334
9.37am	Grange Junction	Crewe North		G	SX	10.35am	-	North Staffs Sdgs			-	-
7.30am	Three Spires Jnt	Aintree		F	MO	10.37am	10.52am	BHSS North				
9.15am	Birmingham	Liverpool Lime St	229	A	D	10.39am	10.45am	2 North	5A/23	5C/84	5A/23	5C/84
10.40am	Crewe	Carlisle		D	SX	-	10.40am	North Staffs Sdgs	-	-	5A/29	11A/101
9.25am	Harlescott Sidings	Neville Hill		H	SX	10.45am	11.15am	Gresty Lane				

Above:
Madeley, 12 March 1955
Rebuilt 'Royal Scot' class No 46144 *Honourable Artillery Company* from Camden 1B shed storms the bank on the Up Fast line with a Blackpool to Euston working.
R.J.Blenkinsop

Time Dep	From	Destination	Rep No	Train Class	Days Run	Crewe Arr	Crewe Dep	Platform or Yard	To Crewe from South Men Diag	To Crewe from South Loco Diag	From Crewe to North Men Diag	From Crewe to North Loco Diag
9.15am	Derby	Crewe	135	A	SX	10.51am	-	5 Bay	9A/14	5A/627	-	-
10.55am	Crewe	Manchester	233	A	SX	-	10.55am	2 South	-	-		
10.55am	Crewe	Chester		B	SX	-	10.55am	1 North	-	-	5A/39	6A/259
3.55am	Willesden	Crewe		F	MO	10.59am	-	BHSS North	5B/1051	2A/648	-	-
6.40am	Euston	Windermere	33	A	D	11.5am	11.14am	2				
9.30am	Sideway	Garston Speke Sdgs		J	SX	11.7am	11.12am	- NSS				
9.45am	Nantwich	Crewe	38	K	D	11.8am	-	BHSS Middle	5B/1126	5B/1126	-	-
8am	Euston	Holyhead	49	A	SX	11.11am	11.21am	1North				
10am	Wellington	Crewe		B	D	11.18am	-	2South			-	-
11.20am	Crewe	Warrington		H	MO	-	11.20am	-	-	-	5A/42	5B/1274
10.35am	Longport Junction	Crewe		G	MO	11.22am	-	North Staffs Sdgs			-	-
8.10am	Euston	Holyhead	37	A	SX	11.25am	11.35am	1				
11.25am	Crewe	Walton Old Junction		H	SX	-	11.25am	BHSS North	-	-		
8.30am	Euston	Liverpool Lime St	39	A	D	11.44am	11.50am	1	1B/6	8A/220	1B/6	8A/220
9.50am	Glebe Colliery	Crewe	50	J	D	11.46am	-	North Staffs Sdgs		5B/1376	-	-
11.40am	Betley Road	Crewe		K	D	11.59am	-	BHSS North	5B/1131	5B/1131	-	-
9.40am	Oxley Sidings	Crewe		H	D	12.3pm	-	Gresty Lane			-	-
12.8pm	Crewe	Blackpool Central	43	A	D	-	12.8pm	8 Bay	-	-	11A/6	28A/75
12.18pm	Crewe	Liverpool Lime St		B	D	-	12.18pm	1 North	-	-	12A/17	5A/592
12.30pm	Crewe	Carlisle	367	C	SX	-	12.30pm	Down Sidings	-	-	12A/18	5A/208
8.55am	Cardiff	Manchester L Rd	241	A	D	12.37pm	12.45pm	1 North	84G/2	84G/73	84G/2	5A/603
11.15am	Birmingham	Glasgow Central	67	A	D	12.40pm	1pm	2	5A/10	5A/549	5A/4	66A/12
10am	Euston	Glasgow Central	63	A	D	*pass 12.55pm*		2 Through	66A/1	12A/62	66A/1	12A/62
11.17am	Derby	Crewe		B	SX	12.57pm	-	5 Bay	84G/2	5A/628	-	-
1pm	Crewe South Shed	Cattle Market		G	MO	-	1pm		-	-	11A/250	5B/1449
1.3pm	Crewe	Manchester L Rd		B	D	-	1.3pm	7 Bay	-	-		
11.25am	Birmingham	Crewe	211	A	SX	1.4pm	-	2 South			-	-
10.8am	Euston	Glasgow Central	57	A	D	1.10pm	1.15pm	2 North	1B/4	1B/200	1B/4	66A/15
1.15pm	Crewe	Chester		B	SX	-	1.15pm	1 North	-	-	7C/7	5A/671

Time Dep	From	Destination	Rep No	Train Class	Days Run	Crewe Arr	Crewe Dep	Platform or Yard	To Crewe from South Men Diag	To Crewe from South Loco Diag	From Crewe to North Men Diag	From Crewe to North Loco Diag
12.55pm	Alsager Junction	Crewe South		G	SX	1.15pm	-	North Staffs Sdgs			-	-
12.5pm	Shrewsbury	Crewe		B	D	1.17pm	-	1 North	5A/44	W'church/6	-	-
10.20am	Euston	Perth	85	A	D	1.22pm	1.33pm	2	1B/1	12A/66	1B/1	12A/66
11.55	Bamfurlong NE	Crewe		F	SX	1.25pm	-	BHSS Middle		5B/1241	-	-
10.30am	Euston	Liverpool Lime St	71	A	D	*pass 1.28pm*		2 Through				
1.30pm	Crewe	Grimesthorpe		F	SX	-	1.30pm	BHSS North	-	-		
1.30pm	Crewe	Mold Junction		H	SX	-	1.30pm	BHSS North	-	-	5B/1052	5B/1466
12.15pm	Wellington	Crewe		B	D	1.36pm	-	3	Wellington	Crewe/1	-	-
12.10pm	Birmingham	Manchester L Rd	221	A	SX	1.36pm	1.43pm	1 North				
10.40am	Normacot	Crewe	46	J	D	1.40pm	-	North Staffs Sdgs			-	-
10.40am	Euston	Carlisle	251	A	D	1.44pm	1.54pm	2	1B/2	5A/319	1B/2	12A/110
12.55pm	Hadnall	Crewe North		G	SX	1.50pm	-	Gresty Lane			-	-
1.50pm	Crewe	Edge Hill		H	SX	-	1.50pm	BHSS North	-	-		
1.55pm	Crewe	Winsford Junction	35	K	D	-	1.55pm	Gresty Lane	-	-	5B/1127	5B/1127
2pm	Crewe	Liverpool Lime St		B	D	-	2pm	8 Bay	-	-	5A/36	8A/267
10.55am	Kingswinford Jnt	Crewe		H	D	2.7pm	-	Gresty Lane			-	-
12.50pm	Stoke	Crewe	89	J	D	2.10pm	-	North Staffs Sdgs			-	-
10.50am	Euston	Blackpool Central	77	A	SX	2.18pm	2.25pm	2	1B/12	1B/116	1B/12	5A/245
11.15am	Euston	Portmadoc	89	A	SX	2.25pm	2.34pm	1	1B/19	8A/217	1B/19	7A/155
2.25pm	Crewe	Bamfurlong		H	D	-	2.25pm	BHSS North	-	-		
2.35pm	Crewe	Sandbach	26	K	SX	-	2.35pm	BHSS North	-	-	5B/1120	5B/1120
12.18pm	Bescot	Crewe		H	MO	2.44am	-	BHSS North	5A/40	3A/185	-	-
11.45am	Euston	Manchester	91	A	SX	2.47pm	2.56pm	2				
11.50am	Euston	Workington	121	A	SX	2.54pm	3.2pm	1	1B/18	5A/327	1B/18	5A/222
12.18pm	Bescot	Crewe		H	D	3.5pm	-	BHSS North	5B/1032	3A/185	-	-
3pm	Crewe	Middlewich	26	K	SX	-	3pm	BHSS North	-	-	5B/1063	5B/1364
1.30pm	Derby	Crewe		B	D	3.12pm	-	5 Bay	5A/97	5A/97	-	-
3.12pm	Crewe	Workington	179	A	SX	-	3.12pm	1	-	-	10B/4	5A/225
1.45pm	Birmingham	Liverpool Lime St	255	A	SX	3.14pm	3.35pm	2 North	8A/15	5A/555	8A/15	5A/581
3.22pm	Crewe	Manchester L Rd	253	A	SX	-	3.22pm	2 South	-	-	12B/—	5A/600
1pm	Oxley Sidings	Crewe		H	D	3.25pm	-	Gresty Lane			-	-
12.30pm	Euston	Liverpool Lime St	83	A	D	*pass 3.28pm*		2 Through	8A/—	1B/142	8A/—	1B/142
2.20pm	Shrewsbury	Crewe		B	D	3.29pm	-	1 North			-	-
3.29pm	Radway Green	Crewe		G	SX	3.32pm	-				-	-
3.35pm	Crewe	Calveley		C	SX	-	3.35pm		-	-	5A/55	5A/909
9.45am	Bournemouth West	Manchester Mayfield	M236	A	SX	3.35pm	3.42pm	2 North				
12.14pm	Broxton	Crewe	41	K	SX	3.45pm	-	Gresty Lane	5B/1056	5B/1460	-	-
3.45pm	Crewe	Neville Hill		D	D	-	3.45pm	Gresty Lane	-	-		
3.48pm	Crewe	Liverpool Lime St	343	A	SX	-	3.48pm	2 South	-	-		8A/217
12.50pm	Heath's Junction	Crewe	93	H	D	3.50pm	-	North Staffs Sdgs			-	-
10.55am	Camden	Crewe		D	SX	3.51pm	-	BHSS North	1A/1	8A/772	-	-
3.55pm	Crewe	Sandbach	21	K	SX	-	3.55pm	BHSS North	-	-		
12pm	Euston	Crewe	95	A	SX	3.59pm	-	1	5A/22	1B/209	-	-
4pm	Basford Hall	Crewe Works		K	D	*pass 4.10pm*		BHSS North	5B/1086	5B/2077	5B/1086	5B/2077
9am	Paignton	Manchester Mayfield	373	A	MFSO	4.12pm	4.20pm	1				
1.15pm	Euston	Glasgow Central	97	A	D	4.17pm	4.24pm	2	1B/3	1B/211	1B/3	5A/141
2pm	Badnall Wharf	Crewe	28	K	SX	4.20pm	-	BHSS North	5B/1110	5B/1110	-	-
11.15am	Swansea High St	Manchester L Rd	265	A	D	4.22pm	4.30pm	1				
4.25pm	Crewe	Bangor	111	A	MFSO	-	4.25pm	7 Bay	-	-	5A/102	5A/102
4.30pm	Crewe	Carlisle Kingmoor		D	D	-	4.30pm	BHSS North	-	-	5B/1030	12A/103
4.32pm	Crewe	Northwich		B	D	-	4.32pm	9 Bay	-	-	5A/121	5A/121
1.30pm	Euston	Blackpool Central	93	A	D	4.33pm	4.40pm	2	28A/—	1B/115	28A/—	1B/115
2.7pm	Bescot	Crewe		H	D	4.45pm	-	BHSS North			-	-
4.47pm	Crewe	Manchester Mayfield		B	D	-	4.47pm	8 Bay	-	-	2A/4	5A/604
8.45pm	Plymouth	Liverpool Lime St	263	A	D	4.50pm	5pm	2 North	5A/1	5A/702	2A/3	5A/579
2.25pm	Nuneaton	Hooton		F	SX	4.51pm	5.25pm	BHSS North	5B/1055	2B/323	5B/1055	6A/270
4.55pm	Crewe	Carriage Works		G	SX	-	4.55pm		-	-		
10.45am	Euston	Crewe	381	C	D	4.58pm	-	1 Through	5A/22	1B/243	-	-
5pm	Crewe	Northwich	27	K	D	-	5pm	BHSS North	-	-		
3.7pm	Derby	Crewe		B	SX	5.2pm	-	5 Bay			-	-
5.3pm	Crewe	Llandudno	125	A	D	-	5.3pm	7 Bay	-	-	7C/12	5A/655
3.55pm	Dudley Port	Crewe	271	C	SX	5.5pm	-		1B/13	1B/218	-	-
5.5pm	Crewe	Liverpool Lime St		B	D	-	5.5pm	8 Bay	-	-	5A/44	5A/598
5.10pm	Crewe	Manchester L Rd	261	A	D	-	5.10pm	2South	-	-	5A/27	9A/608
12.50pm	Aberystwyth	Crewe		B	D	5.12pm	-	2 Bay	W'church/16	W'church/16	-	-
3.50pm	Birmingham	Manchester L Rd	275	A	D	5.13pm	5.20pm	2 North	9A/—	5A/564	9A/—	9A/249
5.17pm	Crewe	Garston Speke Sdgs		H	SX	-	5.17pm	BHSS North	-	-		
5.5pm	Betley Road	Crewe		K	SX	5.27pm	-	BHSS North	5B/1132	5B/1132	-	-
8.45am	Willesden	Crewe		H	SX	5.29pm	-	BHSS North	5B/1054	2A/688	-	-
4.25pm	Shrewsbury	Crewe		B	D	5.32pm	-	1			-	-

Time Dep	From	Destination	Rep No	Train Class	Days Run	Crewe Arr	Crewe Dep	Platform or Yard	To Crewe from South Men Diag	To Crewe from South Loco Diag	From Crewe to North Men Diag	From Crewe to North Loco Diag
2.30pm	Euston	Liverpool Lime St	115	A	D	5.38pm	5.51pm	2		1B/148		1B/148
4.30pm	Leek	Crewe		B	D	5.41pm	-	4 Bay			-	-
5.55pm	Crewe	Northwich		B	D	-	5.55pm	9 Bay	-	-	5A/121	5A/121
6pm	Crewe	Carlisle	397	A	D	-	6pm	8 Bay	-	-	5A/28	12A/83
3.25pm	Grange Jnt Sidings	Crewe	83	K	D	6.5pm	-	North Staffs Sdgs			-	-
6.8pm	Crewe	Chester		B	D	-	6.8pm	7 Bay	-	-		
5.27pm	Stafford	Crewe		B	D	6.8pm	-	1 South	5A/33	5C/104	-	-
6.10pm	Crewe	Manchester L Rd		B	D	-	6.10pm	1 North	-	-	84G/2	5A/601
6.15pm	Crewe	Birkenhead		J	D	-	6.15pm	BHSS North	-	-	5B/1050	6C/373
2.40pm	Camden	Glasgow Buchanan St		C	SX	6.19pm	6.56pm	BHSS North	9A/11	1A/805	12A/300	5B/1233
7.40am	Penzance	Liverpool Lime St	383	A	SX	6.20pm	6.30pm	1 North	9A/10	5A/718		
8.20am	Oxley Sidings	Crewe		K	D	6.24pm	-	Gresty Lane	84B/—	Crewe/13	-	-
5.57pm	Stoke	Crewe		B	SX	6.27pm	-	2			-	-
2.55pm	Camden	Crewe		C	SX	6.28pm	-	BHSS North			-	-
6.35pm	Crewe	Manchester L Rd	437	A	D	-	6.35pm	1 South	-	-		
6.37pm	Crewe	Carlisle	73	C	D	-	6.37pm	Down Sidings	-	-		23C/124
3.15pm	Kingswinford Jnt	Crewe		H	D	6.39pm	-	Gresty Lane			-	-
4.35pm	Harlescott	Crewe		H	D	6.50pm	-	Gresty Lane		5A/709	-	-
6.30pm	Madeley	Crewe	39	K	SX	6.56pm	-	BHSS North	17B/25	5B/1194	-	-
5.8pm	Derby	Crewe		B	D	7.3pm	-	5 Bay	9A/14	5A/623	-	-
5.45pm	Shrewsbury	Crewe		B	D	7.5pm	-	1 South	84G/4	5A/724	-	-
7.10pm	Crewe	Manchester Mayfield		C	SX	-	7.10pm	Down Sidings	-	-		
5.55pm	Wellington	Crewe		B	D	7.18pm	-	2 Bay			-	-
7pm	Alsager	Crewe	89	K	D	7.21pm	-	North Staffs Sdgs			-	-
7.25pm	Crewe	Carlisle		E	SX	-	7.25pm	BHSS North	-	-	12A/321	5B/1245
4.35am	Harlescott Sidings	Crewe		H	SX	7.25pm	-	BHSS North	84G/103	5A/709	-	-
3.58pm	Oxley	Crewe		H	D	7.29pm	-	Gresty Lane	81F/—	Crewe/12		
4.30pm	Euston	Liverpool Lime St	85	A	D	7.32pm	7.37pm	1				
4.40pm	Water Orton	Crewe		E	SX	7.33pm	-	BHSS North	3C/203	3B/326	-	-
6.5pm	Birmingham	Liverpool Lime St	279	A	D	7.40pm	7.48pm	2 North	8A/13	5A/565	8A/13	5A/577
7.50pm	Crewe	Llandudno	197	A	D	-	7.50pm	7 Bay	-	-	7A/1	7A/160
6.20pm	Harlescott Sidings	Crewe		H	TSX	7.52pm	-	Gresty Lane			-	-
7.53pm	Crewe	Manchester L Rd	281	A	FX	-	7.53pm	2 South	-	-	5A/98	5A/98
5.54pm	Derby	Crewe		B	D	7.54pm	-	6 Bay	5A/41	5A/637	-	-
4.55pm	Euston	Heysham	141	A	FSX	7.56pm	8.4pm	2	1B/11	5A/351	1B/11	11A/103
8pm	Crewe	Neville Hill		H	D	-	8pm	Gresty Lane	-	-	25G/301	5B/1353
8.10pm	Crewe	Manchester L Rd		B	D	-	8.10pm	8 Bay	-	-		
5.5pm	Euston	Blackpool Central	159	A	D	8.13pm	8.21pm	2	1B/17	1B/122	1B/17	1B/122
7.55pm	Alsager Junction	Crewe		K	D	8.15pm	-	North Staffs Sdgs			-	-
5.45pm	Oxley Sidings	Crewe		H	D	8.20pm	-	Gresty Lane			-	-
8.27pm	Crewe	Preston	447	A	SX	-	8.27pm	2 South	-	-	5A/43	10A/198
5.20pm	Euston	Holyhead	145	A	D	8.28pm	8.35pm	1	5A/5	5A/268	5A/39	6A/255
8.30pm	Crewe	Northwich		F	D	-	8.30pm	BHSS North	-	-	5B/1053	5B/1363
10.5am	Penzance	Liverpool Lime St	285	A	SX	8.41pm	8.50pm	2 North	8A/5	5A/701	8A/5	8A/276
8.30pm	Alsager	Hooton		J	D	8.52pm	9.3pm	North Staffs Sdgs				
6pm	Euston	Manchester L Rd	139	A	D	*pass 8.55pm*		2 Through	1B/11	1B/176	1B/11	1B/176
9pm	Crewe	Manchester L Rd		B	SX	-	9pm	2	-	-	84G/4	5A/602
9pm	Crewe	Edge Hill		H	FSX	-	9pm	BHSS North	-	-		
6.7pm	Euston	Liverpool Lime St	137	A	D	*pass 9.5pm*		2 Through				
9.5pm	Crewe	Copley Hill		F	D	-	9.5pm	Gresty Lane	-	-		9B/360
9.15pm	Crewe	Carnforth		F	FSX	-	9.15pm	BHSS North	-	-	11A/250	5B/1300
6.20pm	Euston	Preston	131	A	SX	9.16pm	9.27pm	2	1B/12	5A/276	1B/12	5A/223
8.15pm	Stafford	Crewe		H	SX	9.19pm	-	BHSS North	17B/25	5A/382	-	-
8.52pm	Stoke	Crewe	409	B	SX	9.29pm	-	6 Bay	5B/1055	5A/625	-	-
9.35pm	Crewe	Wyre Dock		E	SX	-	9.35pm	BHSS North	-	-	12A/319	5B/1270
8.25pm	Shrewsbury	Crewe		B	D	9.38pm	-	1 South	5B/1035	5C/102	-	-
9.40pm	Crewe	Liverpool Lime St		B	SX	-	9.40pm	8 Bay	-	-	5A/41	5A/597
9.40pm	Crewe	Chester		B	D	-	9.40pm	7 Bay	-	-	7A/11	6A/179
9.22pm	Alsager	Mold Junction		J	SX	*pass 9.44pm*		Station				
9.50pm	Crewe	Manchester L Rd		B	D	-	9.50pm	1 North	-	-		
9.50pm	Crewe	Bamfurlong		H	SX	-	9.50pm	BHSS North	-	-		5B/1279
8.7pm	Stoke	Crewe	41	H	D	9.54pm	-	North Staffs Sdgs			-	-
10pm	Crewe	Manchester L Rd		F	D	-	10pm	Gresty Lane	-	-		9A/254
9.27pm	Whitchurch	Crewe		F	FSX	10.1pm	-	Gresty Lane			-	-
8.50pm	Birmingham	Chester	287	A	D	10.6pm	10.26pm	1 South	3D/—	5A/550	3D/—	5A/652
8.15pm	Derby	Crewe		B	D	10.15pm	-	5 Bay	5A/91	5A/91	-	-
7.20pm	Euston	Inverness	151	A	SX	10.16pm	10.29pm	2	5A/3	1B/230	5A/2	5A/135
7.25pm	Euston	Perth	149	A	FSX	10.23pm	10.36pm	1				
10.25pm	Crewe	Warrington		H	SX	-	10.25pm	BHSS North	-	-	5B/1003	5B/1291
10.30pm	Crewe	Guide Bridge		H	D	-	10.30pm	Gresty Lane	-	-	26A/633	5B/1342

Time Dep	From	Destination	Rep No	Train Class	Days Run	Crewe Arr	Crewe Dep	Platform or Yard	To Crewe from South Men Diag	To Crewe from South Loco Diag	From Crewe to North Men Diag	From Crewe to North Loco Diag
3.30pm	Broad Street	Crewe	17	A	D	10.33pm	-		5A/21	1B/223	-	-
10.35pm	Crewe	Hooton		J	D	-	10.35pm	North Staffs Sdgs	-	-	5B/1041	6C/372
9.25pm	Grange Junction	Crewe	6	H	SX	10.38pm	-	North Staffs Sdgs			-	-
10.40pm	Crewe	Warrington		H	SX	-	10.40pm	BHSS North	-	-		5B/1291
10.40pm	Crewe	Brewery Sidings		H	D	-	10.40pm	Gresty Lane	-	-	26A/624	5B/1328
9.25pm	Wellington	Crewe		B	D	10.42pm	-	2 Bay	Wellington	Crewe/3	-	-
10.27pm	Alsager	Ellesmere Port		J	FX	10.45pm	10.52pm	North Staffs Sdgs				
7.45pm	Curzon Street	Edge Hill		D	SX	10.46pm	11.10pm	BHSS North	8A/33	3B/313	8A/33	5B/1392
7.55pm	Hereford	Crewe	277	A	D	10.50pm	-	1 South		5A/710	-	-
10.50pm	Crewe	Preston		F	D	-	10.50pm	BHSS North	-	-		
7.30pm	Euston	Perth	153	A	FX	10.56pm	11.10pm	3	1B/11	2A/70	5A/1	5A/131
5.15pm	Carmarthen	Crewe	289	C	D	11.3pm	-	1 Through	5A/33	84G/64	-	-
11.5pm	Crewe	Mold Junction		H	FSX	-	11.5pm	BHSS North	-	-		6B/283
10.45pm	Alsager Junction	Speke Sidings		J	D	*pass 11.5pm*		North Staffs Sdgs		5B/1392		5B/1392
7.55pm	Euston	Stranraer Harbour	155	A	SX	11.14pm	11.24pm	2	1B/2	12A/54	1B/2	12A/54
11.15pm	Crewe	Winsford Junction		H	SX	-	11.15pm	BHSS North	-	-	5B/1020	5B/1282
12pm	Penzance	Liverpool	205	A	D	11.21pm	12.30am	2 North	5A/33	5A/712		
6.30pm	Swansea Victoria	York	201	A	D	11.27pm	12.5am	1 North				
10.10pm	Birmingham	Crewe	297	A	D	11.31am	-	1 South	2A/—	5A/561	-	-
11.5pm	Stoke	Crewe		B	D	11.35am	-	5 Bay	84G/5	5A/624	-	-
7.35pm	Camden	Edge Hill		C	SX	11.36pm	12.5am	BHSS North	8A/—	5A/292	8A/—	8A/841
8.10pm	Oxley Sidings	Crewe		H	D	11.40pm	-	Gresty Lane			-	-
8.30pm	Euston	Glasgow Central	157	A	D	11.44pm	12am	2 South	5A/4	5A/284	5A/5	5A/139
8.45pm	Euston	Holyhead	161	A	D	*pass 11.50am*		1 Through	7C/1	7C/32	7C/1	7C/32
8.52pm	Euston	Holyhead	163	A	D	11.58pm	12.11am		5A/12	5A/359		7C/80

Above left:
Madeley Station, 30 June 1951
During the summer period the 'Royal Scot' ran nonstop to Carlisle where a change of train crew was made. Polmadie engines were used throughout at this time. Here No 46220 *Coronation* steams through Madeley station on the descent of Whitmore bank eight miles from Crewe. Notice the tall signals which were visible to crews over the footbridge. Note too the ornate chimneys on the Up side station buildings. A porter stands on the island platform watching the train go by. The well-kept flower beds suggest that perhaps there were not too many trains calling at this time. *Tom Lewis — Manchester Locomotive Society*

Left:
Norton Junction Looking North, June 1957
Class 5 No 45431 on a special working coasts through Norton Bridge on the Up Fast line. The train is composed entirely of Eastern Region stock but details of the working are unknown. Notice the tall signalbox to give visibility over the road bridge. Notice too the three-arm bracket signal on the Down Slow line. The extreme right arm is for the Stoke line. *C. M. and J. M. Bentley Collection*

Down Direction — Tuesdays to Fridays

Note: Italics under departure time denote passing time

Time Dep	From	Destination	Rep No	Train Class	Days Run	Crewe Arr	Crewe Dep	Platform or Yard	To Crewe from South Men Diag	To Crewe from South Loco Diag	From Crewe to North Men Diag	From Crewe to North Loco Diag
8.30pm	Euston	Glasgow Central	157	A	D	11.44pm	12am	2 South	5A/4	5A/277	5A/5	5A/139
6.30pm	Swansea	York	201	A	MX	-	12.5am	1 North				
8.50pm	Burton	Mold Junction		F	MX	12.10am	12.50am	North Staffs Sdgs				
8.35pm	Worcester	Crewe		D	MX	12.12am	-	Gresty Lane			-	-
9.10pm	Euston	Glasgow Central	169	A	D	*pass 12.15am*		2 Through				
12.15am	Crewe	Preston	385	C	MX	-	12.15am	Down Sidings	-	-		
12.25am	Crewe	Birkenhead		H	MX	-	12.25am	BHSS North	-	-		
12pm	Penzance	Liverpool	205	A	MX	-	12.30am	8 Bay			1A/1	5A/590
12.35am	Crewe	Carlisle		F	MX	-	12.35am	Gresty Lane	-	-	5B/1037	5B/1292
12.40am	Crewe	Manchester L Rd	293	A	D	-	12.40am	2	-	-	5A/92	5A/92
8.40pm	Nottingham	Edge Hill		E	MX	12.45am	1.25am	North Staffs Sdgs				
11.30pm	Harlescott Sidings	Brewery Sidings		H	MTX	12.50am	1.20am	Gresty Lane	9A/412	5A/705	9A/412	5B/1348
12.50am	Crewe	Manchester L Rd		E	MX	-	12.50am	Gresty Lane	-	-		
12.50am	Crewe	Glasgow Buch. St	291	A	MSX-Q	-	12.50am	8 Bay	-	-		5A/178
7.35pm	Willesden	Crewe		D	SX	12.53am	-	BHSS North	5B/1051	5B/1135/73	-	-
11.15pm	Birmingham	Glasgow Central	299	A	D	12.53am	1.5am	1	5A/10	3D/149	5A/3	5A/143
1am	Crewe	Edge Hill		E	MX	-	12.55am	Gresty Lane	-	-		
8.40pm	Coventry	Edge Hill		D	SX	1.3am	1.45am	BHSS North	8A/27	2B/334	8A/27	5B/1394
10.5pm	Birmingham C St	Manchester L Rd		E	MX	1.8am	1.12am	BHSS North	9A/21	3B/312	9A/21	9A/640
9.25pm	Euston	Glasgow Central	171	A	D	1.13am	1.25am	2	12A/	5A/283	12A/—	12A/86
10.45pm	Euston	Manchester L Rd	283	A	SX	1.37am	1.43am	1 South				
1.15am	Chatterley Sdgs	Crewe S Shed		G	MSX	1.45am	-	-			-	-
8.50pm	Camden	Carnforth		C	MX	1.45am	1.53am	Station		11A/262	2A/696	11A/262
10.52pm	Euston	Perth	195	A	SX	1.55am	2.5am	2		7C/—	1B/235	12A/—
2.5am	Crewe	Holyhead	1	A	MX	-	2.5am	1 North	-	-		
9pm	Camden	Preston		D	MX	1.53am	2.5am	BHSS North				
11.5pm	Euston	Windermere	193	A	SX	2.8am	2.18am	2	1B/17	5A/293	5A/11	10B/200
2.9am	Crewe	Manchester L Rd	203	C	MX	-	2.9am	1 North		-	-	
2.10am	Crewe	Liverpool Lime St	231	A	MX	-	2.10am	2 South		-	-	
11.50pm	Stoke	Crewe		H	MX	2.10am	-	North Staffs Sdgs			-	-
12.1am	Oxley Sidings	Crewe		F	MX	2.10am	-	Gresty Lane			-	-
10.25pm	Aston	Edge Hill		E	MX	2.11am	2.25am	BHSS North				
12.2am	Birmingham	Carlisle	475	C	MX	2.22am	3.16am	1 South			5A/19	12A/95
2.22am	Crewe	Shrewsbury AF		H	MSX	-	2.22am	BHSS North	-	-		
2.25am	Crewe	Blackpool North	183	A	MX	-	2.25am	2	-	-	5A/33	5A/204
1.40am	Grange Sidings	Birkenhead		J	MSX	2.25am	2.33am	North Staffs Sdgs				

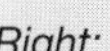

Right:
Crewe, Down Through No 2 Line
Ivatt Class 2MT 2-6-2T No 41229 fitted for pull-push working proceeds towards North Junction with stock that was probably for the Sandbach service. Passenger trains for Northwich were also designated motor trains and usually worked out of No 9 Bay platform. Note the rectangular 'Crewe' enamel sign on the pillar. Crewe station did not have the conventional totem station signs.
Martin Welch

Time Dep	From	Destination	Rep No	Train Class	Days Run	Crewe Arr	Crewe Dep	Platform or Yard	To Crewe from South Men Diag	To Crewe from South Loco Diag	From Crewe to North Men Diag	From Crewe to North Loco Diag
11.14pm	Birmingham C St	Preston		E	MX	2.35am	2.45am	BHSS North	5B/1036	3B/302	5B/1036	5B/1240
9.32pm	Camden	Crewe		D	MSX	2.41am	-	BHSS North	5A/39	5B/1161	-	-
2.42am	Crewe	Manchester L Rd	207	A	D	-	2.42am	8 Bay	-	-	9A/11	5A/621
11.40pm	Euston	Glasgow Central	21	A	SX	*pass 2.50am*		2 Through	1B/1	1B/100	1B/1	1B/100
1.30am	Sideway	Crewe		F	SX	2.57am	-	North Staffs Sdgs	5B/1111	5B/1111	-	-
11.55pm	Birmingham C St	Mold Junction		E	MX	2.59am	3.30am	BHSS North				
10pm	Broad Street	Preston	3	C	SX	3.7am	3.28am	2	5A/24	2B/93	5A/24	5A/221
9.55pm	Willesden Junction	Carlisle		C	MX	3.18am	4.45am	1 North	2A/—	1A/63		
2am	Harlescott Sidings	Edge Hill		H	MX	3.20am	4.30am	Gresty Lane				
12.20am	Euston	Manchester L Rd	9	A	D	*pass 3.25am*		2 Through	9A/	9A/	9A/	9A/
10.50pm	Stourbridge Jnt	Crewe		H	MX	3.29am	-	Gresty Lane	84B/—	Crewe/14	-	-
10pm	Camden	Warrington		D	MX	3.30am	3.35am	BHSS North	8B/1	5A/385	8B/1	8B/
12.30am	Euston	Liverpool Lime St	213	A	D	*pass 3.35am*		2 Through	8A/—	1B/140	8A/—	1B/140
1.47am	Sideway	Crewe		F	MX	3.35am	-	North Staffs Sdgs		5B/1111	-	-
1.15am	Oswestry	Crewe		H	MX	3.39am	-	Gresty Lane			-	-
3.40am	Crewe	Wyre Dock		F	MSX	-	3.40am	BHSS North	-	-	5B/1040	5B/1268
12.45am	Birmingham Cent	Crewe	479	C	MX	3.48am	-	2 South	8A/—	5A/562	-	-
9.10pm	Abergavenny	Crewe		F	MSX	3.50am	-	Gresty Lane			-	-
9.45pm	Worcester	Crewe		F	MX	3.59am	-	Gresty Lane	85A/—	Crewe/15	-	-
2.15am	Bescot	Carlisle Kingmoor		D	MX	4am	4.5am	Station	5A/27	3B/327	5A/27	5B/1296
2pm	Penzance	Crewe	61	C	MX	4.3am	-	1 South			-	-
10.5pm	Willesden	Carlisle		D	MX	4.8am	4.50am	BHSS North	5B/1037	1A/808	12A/320	5B/1277
4.10am	Crewe	Birkenhead		F	MX	-	4.10am	North Staffs Sdgs	-	-	8A/—	5B/1457
12.5am	Cardiff	Liverpool Lime St	215	A	D	4.10am	5.26am	2 South	84G/5	5A/723	84G/5	5A/584
4.20am	Crewe	Copley Hill		H	MX	-	4.20am	Gresty Lane	-	-	5B/1036	5B/1335
10.35pm	Willesden	Adswood Sidings		D	MX	4.25am	4.52am	BHSS North	9A/415	1A/813	9A/415	9A/642
4.45pm	Penzance	Manchester L Rd	217	A	D	4.28am	5.10am	2				
10.30pm	Worcester	Crewe		F	MX	4.35am	-	Gresty Lane			-	-
11.40pm	Monument Lane	Birkenhead		E	MSX	4.54am	4.56am	BHSS North	3D/3	3B/304	3D/3	5B/1465
4.56am	Crewe	Northwich		C	D	-	4.56am	7 Bay	-	-	5B/1062	Middlew/4
12.20am	Camden	Carlisle		D	MX	4.57am	5.15am	BHSS North	1A/1	1A/816		
5am	Crewe	Liverpool Lime St	209	C	MX	-	5am	Down Sidings	-	-	5A/42	5A/583
5am	Crewe	Coal Yard	17	K	MX	-	5am	BHSS North	-	-	5B/1119	5B/1119
12.2am	Euston	Crewe	189	A	D	5.4am	-	3	5A/8	5A/302	-	-
3am	Nuneaton	Crewe		E	MSX	5.10am	-	BHSS Middle	5A/42	2B/326	-	-
5.15am	Crewe	Manchester L Rd	17	C	MX	-	5.15am	1 South	-	-		
5.15am	Crewe	Warrington		D	WFO	-	5.15am	BHSS North	-	-	12A/322	5B/1242
5am	Alsager Junction	Crewe	84	K	D	5.18am	-	North Staffs Sdgs			-	-
3.15am	Bescot	Carlisle London Rd		E	SX	5.22am	5.27am	Station	5B/1038	3B/314	5B/10385B/1295	
5.27am	Crewe	Northwich	27	K	D	-	5.27am	BHSS North	-	-	5B/1017	5B/1368
3.30pm	Nuneaton	Crewe		E	MX	5.25am	-	BHSS North		5A/391(FO)	-	-
5.30am	Crewe	Chester	11	A	MX	-	5.30am	Down Sidings	-	-	6A/	6B/
4am	Oxley Sidings	Neville Hill		D	MSX	5.32am	6.5am	Gresty Lane			5B/1005	5B/1327
5.35am	Crewe	Garston Speke Sdgs		H	MX	-	5.35am	BHSS North	-	-	12A/17	5B/1398
11.20pm	Kirkby	Garston Speke Sdgs		J	MSX	5.35am	6.15am	North Staffs Sdgs				
5.40am	Crewe	Mold Junction		F	MX	-	5.40am	BHSS North	-	-	6B/	6B/
5.45am	Crewe	Morecambe (Prom)	31	C	MX	-	5.45am	Down Sidings	-	-	11A/6	5A/218
5.50am	Crewe	Walton Old Junction		H	MX	-	5.50am	North Staffs Sdgs	-	-	8B/	8B/
4.40am	Harlescott Sidings	Carlisle		E	SX	5.55am	6.30am	Gresty Lane	84G/102	5B/1475	84G/102	5B/1241
6am	Crewe	Warrington		B	D	-	6am	1 North	-	-	10B/20	5A/201
6.7am	Crewe	Walton Old Junction		H	MSX	-	6.7am	BHSS North	-	-	5B/1039	8B/572
1.55am	Kingswinford Jnt	Crewe		H	MX	6.10am	-	Gresty Lane	84B/—	Crewe/16	-	-
6.15am	Crewe	Northwich		B	D	-	6.15am	9 Bay	-	-	5A/120	5A/120
6.15am	Crewe	Edge Hill		H	MX	-	6.15am	BHSS North	-	-	5B/1019	5B/1400
6.38am	Crewe	Longsight		H	MX	-	6.38am	Gresty Lane	-	-	9B/	9B/
3.12am	Rugby	Crewe		H	MX	6.20am	-	BHSS North			-	-
6.20am	Crewe	Sandbach	23	K	D	-	6.20am	BHSS North	-	-	5B/1053	5B/1367
5.20am	Harlescott Sidings	Bamfurlong		H	MSX	6.40am	6.50am	Gresty Lane	5B/1039	10A/196	5B/1039	10A/196
4.30am	Stoke	Crewe		K	MX	6.40am	-	North Staffs Sdgs	5B/1063	5B/1375	-	-
6.45am	Crewe	Manchester L Rd		B	D	-	6.45am	8 Bay	-	-	9A/9	5A/605
2.30am	Northampton	Crewe		H	MSX	6.53am	-	BHSS North			-	-
4.15am	Three Spires Jnt	Middlewich		J	MX	6.59am	7.8am	BHSS North	5B/1054	2B/320	5B/1054	5B/1361
10.25pm	Somers Town	Crewe		E	MX	7.5am	-	BHSS North	2B/116	5B/1192	-	-
4.5am	Washwood Heath	Aintree		F	SX	7.8am	7.23am	BHSS North	21A/—	21A/690	21A/—	5B/1297
9.15pm	Crewe	Neville Hill		F	SX	-	7.15am	Gresty Lane	-	-		5B/1300
6.45am	Whitchurch	Crewe		B	D	7.16am	-	2 North	W'church/1	W'church/6	-	-
7.23am	Crewe	Manchester L Rd		B	D	-	7.23am	1 North	-	-	9A/	9A/
6.10am	Creswell	Crewe Carriage Sdgs		B	D	7.24am	7.29am	2 Sorth	5E/	5E/	5E/	5E/

Time Dep	From	Destination	Rep No	Train Class	Days Run	Crewe Arr	Crewe Dep	Platform or Yard	To Crewe from South Men Diag	To Crewe from South Loco Diag	From Crewe to North Men Diag	From Crewe to North Loco Diag
5am	Bescot	Adswood Sidings		F	MX	7.25am	8.2am	BHSS North	9A/4	5B/1202	9A/4	5B/1347
1.50am	Willesden	Crewe		D	MX	7.25am	-	BHSS North	26A/—	5B/1188	-	-
5.50am	Bushbury	Crewe		H	MX	7.25am	-	BHSS North	9A/4	5B/1202	-	-
2am	Marylebone	Crewe	459	C	MX	7.31am	-	2 Through			-	-
7.35am	Crewe	Chester		B	D	-	7.35am	2 North	-	-	W'church/1	5A/669
2.45am	Northampton	Walton Old Junction		H	MSX	7.35am	8.20am	BHSS North	8B/	8B/	8B/	8B/
7.36am	Crewe	Northwich		B	D	-	7.36am	9 Bay	-	-	5A/120	5A/120
4.55am	Oxley Sidings	Crewe		H	D	7.38am	-	Gresty Lane			-	-
7.40am	Crewe	Carlisle London Rd		H	SX	-	7.40am	BHSS North	-	-	5B/1034	5B/1293
7.42am	Crewe	Liverpool Lime St		B	D	-	7.42am	8 Bay	-	-	3B/151	5A/593
9.45pm	Eastleigh	Crewe		C	MX	7.45am	-	1 Through			-	-
7.45am	Crewe	Adswood Sidings		K	D	-	7.45am	BHSS North	-	-	5B/1020	5B/1333
2.30am	Northampton	Crewe		H	MSX	7.46am	-	BHSS North	1A/525	2A/668	-	-
7.48am	Crewe	Chester		B	D	-	7.48am	1 North	-	-	7C/2	5A/650
7.50am	Crewe	Manchester L Rd		B	D	-	7.50am	1 South	-	-	2A/—	5A/607
6.35am	Harlescott Sidings	Bamfurlong		H	MSX	7.55am	8.35am	Gresty Lane	5B/1032	5B/1478	5B/1032	5B/1294
8am	Crewe	Warrington		H	MSX	-	8am	BHSS North	-	-	5B/1051	5B/1273
7am	Stafford	Crewe		H	D	8.5am	-	BHSS North	17B/25	5B/1196	-	-
3.50am	Northampton	Aintree		F	MSX	8.23am	8.51am	BHSS North	8C/	8C/	8C/	8C/
8.5am	Alsager	Hooton		J	SX	*pass* 8.25am		North Staffs Sdgs	5E/	5E/	5E/	5E/
8.27am	Crewe	Manchester L Rd		E	MX	-	8.27am	Gresty Lane	-	-	9B/	9B/
6.30am	Birmingham	Crewe	219	A	D	8.30am	-	1 North	5A/44	5A/540	-	-
8.30am	Crewe	Northwich		J	SX	-	8.30am	BHSS North	-	-		5B/1363
8.35am	Alsager	Crewe		G	SX	8.35am	-	North Staffs Sdgs	5E/	5E/	-	-
7.25am	Shrewsbury	Crewe		B	D	8.37am	-	1 North	84G/	84G/	-	-
.10am	Stoke	Liverpool Lime St	223	B	D	8.42am	8.48am	2 North	5A/40	5A/626	5A/40	5A/585
7.30am	Wellington	Crewe		B	D	8.47am	-	3 Bay	Wellington	Wellington	-	-
7.10am	Birmingham	Manchester L Rd	249	A	SX	8.55am	9.2am	1 North	9A/	9A/	9A/	9A/
9.10am	Alsager	Crewe	89	K	D	9.10am	-	North Staffs Sdgs	5E/	5E/	-	-
9.10am	Crewe	Liverpool Lime St		B	D	-	9.10am	1 North	-	-	8A/26	5A/582
9.10am	Crewe	Runcorn		H	SX	-	9.10am	North Staffs Sdgs		-	8C/	8C/
9.13am	Crewe	Manchester L Rd		B	SX	-	9.13am	8 Bay	-	-	9A/	9A/
7.15am	Bescot	Guide Bridge		J	SX	9.17am	9.25am	BHSS North	9B/	9B/	9B/	9B/
9.20am	Crewe	Holyhead	55	A	D	-	9.20am	7 Bay	-	-	7C/	6A/
2.40am	Peterborough	Crewe		E	MSX	9.21am	-	BHSS North	2A/515	5B/1175	-	-
9.25am	Crewe	Perth	27	A	SX	-	9.25am	2	-	-	66A/—	5A/206
7.55am	Whitchurch	Crewe		F	WO	9.32am	-	-	5B/1056	5B/1485	-	-
7.20am	Derby	Llandudno	351	A	SX	9.32am	9.37am	2	17A/	17A/	17A/	6A/
9.40am	Crewe	Blackpool North	389	A	MFO	-	9.40am	8 Bay	-	-	5A/45	5A/238
9.40am	Crewe	Waverton	36	K	SX	-	9.40am	BHSS North	-	-	5B/1037	5B/1462
8.30am	Birmingham	Liverpool Lime St	225	A	SX	9.45am	9.52am	2 North	8A/	8A/	8A/	8A/
8.40am	Shrewsbury	Crewe		B	D	9.47am	-	1 North	2B/5	5A/717	-	-
9.27am	Alsager Junction	Garston Speke Sdgs		J	SX	*pass* 9.47am		North Staffs Sdgs	8C/	8C/	8C/	8C/
9.57am	Crewe	Manchester L Rd	227	A	SX	-	9.57am	2 South	-	-	9A/	9A/
8am	Bescot	Crewe		F	MSX	10am	-	BHSS North	5B/1032	5B/1207	-	-
8.54am	Chatterley Sidings	Crewe	84	H	D	10.2am	-	North Staffs Sdgs			-	-
10am	Basford Hall	Crewe Works	W1	K	D	*pass* 10.10am		BHSS North	5B/1086	5B/2076	5B/1086	5B/2076
9.45am	Stoke	Crewe		B	SX	10.15am	-	5 Bay	5D/	5D/	-	-
4.45am	Euston	Crewe	15	C	SX	10.18am	-	1 Through	1B/21	5A/311	-	-
10.29am	Crewe	Healey Mills		H	D	-	10.29am	Gresty Lane	-	-	5B/1003	5B/1343
9.37am	Grange Junction	Crewe North Shed		G		*pass* 10.35am		Station			-	-
9.15am	Birmingham	Liverpool Lime St	229	A	D	10.39am	10.45am	2 North	5A/23	5C/84	5A/23	5C/84
10.40am	Crewe	Carlisle		D	SX	-	10.40am	BHSS North	-	-	12A/	10B/
9.5am	Harlescott Sidings	Neville Hill		H	SX	10.55am	11.15am	Gresty Lane	5B/1001	84G/199	5B/1001	9A/265
9.15am	Derby Midland	Crewe	135	A	SX	10.51am	-	5 Bay	9A/14	5A/627	-	-
10.55am	Crewe	Manchester L Rd	233	A	SX	-	10.55am	2 South	-	-	9A/	9A/
10.55am	Crewe	Chester		B	SX	-	10.55am	1 North	-	-	5A/39	6A/259
6.40am	Euston	Windermere	33	A	D	11.5am	11.14am	2	1B/33	10B/83	1B/33	10B/83
9.30am	Sideway	Garston Speke Sdgs		J	SX	11.7am	11.12am	North Staffs Sdgs	8C/	8C/	8C/	8C/
4.20am	Willesden	Crewe		E	MSX	11.10am	-	BHSS North	5B/1018	2A/695	-	-
8am	Euston	Holyhead	49	A	SX-Q	11.11am	11.21am	1 North	7C/5	7C/45	7C/5	7C/45
10am	Wellington	Crewe		B	D	11.18am	-	2 South	Wellington	Wellington	-	-
9.45am	Nantwich	Crewe	38	K	D	11.8am	-	BHSS Middle	5B/1126	5B/1126	-	-
11.20am	Crewe	Warrington		H	SX	-	11.20am	BHSS Middle	-	-	5A/42	5B/1274
4.40am	Kirkby Sidings	Crewe		J	MSX	11.22am	-	North Staffs Sdgs	5D/	5D/	-	-
6.55am	Chaddesden	Runcorn		J	MSX	11.22am	11.39am	BHSS Middle	17A/317	5E/97	17A/317	5B/1396
8.10am	Euston	Holyhead	37	A	SX	11.25am	11.35am	1	7C/2	7C/35	7C/2	7C/35
11.25am	Crewe	Walton Old Junction		H	SX	-	11.25am	BHSS North	-	-	8B/	8B/
11.37am	Crewe	Mold Junction		J	MSX	-	11.37am	North Staffs Sdgs	-	-	6B/	6A/251
8.30am	Euston	Liverpool Lime St	39	A	D	11.44am	11.50am	1	1B/6	8A/220	1B/6	8A/220

Time Dep	From	Destination	Rep No	Train Class	Days Run	Crewe Arr	Crewe Dep	Platform or Yard	To Crewe from South Men Diag	To Crewe from South Loco Diag	From Crewe to North Men Diag	From Crewe to North Loco Diag
9.50am	Glebe Colliery	Crewe	50	J	D	11.46am	-	North Staffs Sdgs			-	-
8.37am	Euston	Holyhead	489	A	FO-Q	11.51am	11.55am	2	2A/	2A/	2A/	6A/
11.40am	Betley Road	Crewe		K	D	11.59am	-	BHSS North	5B/1131	5B/1131	-	-
12pm	Crewe	Garston Speke Sidings		H	MSX	-	12pm	BHSS North	-	-	8C/4	8C/4
9.40am	Oxley Sidings	Crewe		H	D	12.3pm	-	Gresty Lane			-	-
12.3pm	Crewe	Birkenhead		H	MSX	-	12.3pm	BHSS North	-	-	6C/	6C/
12.8pm	Crewe	Blackpool Central	43	A	D	-	12.8pm	8 Bay	-	-	11A/6	28A/75
9.30am	Bescot	Warrington		F	MSX	12.15pm	12.50pm	BHSS North	3D/205	3B/330	3D/205	5B/1284
12.18pm	Crewe	Liverpool Lime St		B	D	-	12.18pm	1 North	-	-	12A/17	5A/592
12.30pm	Crewe	Carlisle	367	C	SX	-	12.30pm	Down Sidings	-	-	12A/18	5A/208
8.55am	Cardiff	Manchester L Rd	241	A	D	12.37pm	12.45pm	1 North	84G/2	84G/73	84G/2	5A/603
11.15am	Birmingham	Glasgow Central	67	A	D	12.40pm	1pm	2	5A/10	5A/549	5A/4	66A/12
10am	Euston	Glasgow Central	63	A	D	*pass* 12.55pm		2 Through	66A/1	12A/62	66A/1	12A/62
11.17am	Derby Midland	Crewe		B	SX	12.57pm	-	5 Bay	84G/2	5A/628	-	-
1.3pm	Crewe	Manchester L Rd		B	D	-	1.3pm	7 Bay	-	-	9B/	9B/
11.15am	Birmingham	Crewe	211	A	SX	1.4pm	-	2	3D/	3D/	-	-
10.8am	Euston	Glasgow Central	57	A	D	1.10pm	1.20pm	2 North	1B/4	1B/200	1B/4	5A/159
1.15pm	Crewe	Chester		B	SX	-	1.15pm	1 North	-	-	6B/	5A/318
12.55pm	Alsager Junction	Crewe South Shed		G	SX	1.15pm	-	South Shed	5D/	5E/	-	-
12.5pm	Shrewsbury	Crewe		B	D	1.17pm	-	1 North	5A/106	W'church/7	-	-
10.20am	Euston	Perth	65	A	D	1.22pm	1.33pm	2	1B/1	12A/66	1B/1	12A/66
10.30am	Euston	Liverpool Lime St	71	A	D	*pass* 1.28pm		2 Through	8A/	8A/	8A/	8A/
1.30pm	Crewe	Grimesthorpe		F	SX	-	1.30pm	BHSS North	-	-	9B/	9B/
1.30pm	Crewe	Mold Junction		H	SX	-	1.30pm	BHSS North	-	-	6B/	6B/
1.35pm	Crewe	Birkenhead		J	MSX	-	1.35pm	North Staffs Sdgs	-	-	6C/201	5B/1464
12.15pm	Wellington	Crewe		B	D	1.36pm	-	3	Wellington	Crewe/1	-	-
12.10pm	Birmingham	Manchester L Rd	221	A	D	1.36pm	1.43pm	1 North	9A/	9A/	9A/	9A/
10.40am	Normacot	Crewe	48	J	D	1.40pm	-	North Staffs Sdgs	5D/	5D/	-	-
10.40am	Euston	Carlisle	251	A	D	1.44pm	1.54pm	2	1B/2	5A/319/24	1B/2	5A/219

Time Dep	From	Destination	Rep No	Train Class	Days Run	Crewe Arr	Crewe Dep	Platform or Yard	To Crewe from South Men Diag	To Crewe from South Loco Diag	From Crewe to North Men Diag	From Crewe to North Loco Diag
12.25pm	Hadnall	Crewe		G	SX	*pass* 1.45pm		North Shed			-	-
1.50pm	Crewe	Edge Hill		H	SX	-	1.50pm	BHSS North	-	-	8C/	8C/
1.55pm	Crewe	Winsford Junction	35	K	D	-	1.55pm	Gresty Lane	-	-	5B/1127	5B/1127
2pm	Crewe	Liverpool Lime St	79	A	D	-	2pm	8 Bay	-	-	5A/36	8A/267
10.15am	Kingswinford Jnt	Crewe		J	D	2.7pm	-	Gresty Lane			-	-
12.50pm	Stoke	Crewe	89	J	D	2.10pm	-	North Staffs Sdgs	5D/	5E/	-	-
10.50am	Euston	Blackpool Central	77	A	SX	2.18pm	2.25pm	2	1B/12	1B/116	1B/12	1B/116
2.25pm	Crewe	Bamfurlong		H	D	-	2.25pm	BHSS North	-	-	28B/103	5B/1277
11.15am	Euston	Portmadoc	89	A	SX	2.25pm	2.34pm	1	1B/19	8A/234	1B/19	7A/155
2.28pm	Crewe	Manchester L Rd		B	D	-	2.28pm	7 Bay	-	-	9A/	9B/
2.35pm	Crewe	Sandbach	26	K	SX	-	2.35pm	BHSS North	-	-	5B/1120	5B/1120
11.45am	Euston	Manchester L Rd	91	A	SX	2.47pm	2.56pm	2	9A/	9A/	9A/	9A/
11.50am	Euston	Workington	121	A	FO	2.54pm	3.2pm	1	1B/18	1B/241	1B/18	5A/222
3pm	Crewe	Middlewich	26	K	SX	-	3pm	BHSS North	-	-	5B/1063	5B/1364
12.18pm	Bescot	Crewe		H	MSX	3.5pm	-	BHSS Middle	5B/1055	3A/185	-	-
1.30pm	Derby Midland	Crewe		B	D	3.12pm	-	5 Bay	5A/97	5A/97	-	-
3.12pm	Crewe	Workington	179	A	SX	-	3.12pm	1	-	-	10B/4	5A/226
1.45pm	Birmingham	Liverpool L St	255	A	SX	3.14pm	3.35pm	2 North	8A/15	5A/555	8A/15	5A/581
3.22pm	Crewe	Manchester L Rd	253	A	SX	-	3.22pm	2 South	-	-	12B/—	5A/600
1pm	Oxley Sidings	Crewe		H	D	3.25pm	-	Gresty Lane	86G/	86G/	-	-
12.30pm	Euston	Liverpool Lime St	83	A	D	*pass* 3.28pm		2 Through	8A/—	8A/—	8A/—	8A/—
2.20pm	Shrewsbury	Crewe		B	D	3.29pm	-	1 North	86G/	86G/	-	-
10.55am	Camden	Crewe		D	D	3.30pm	-	BHSS North	1A/1	8A/772	-	-
3.23pm	Radway Green	Crewe		G	SX	3.32pm	-	-	5E/	5E/	-	-
9.45am	Bournemouth West	Manchester Mayfield	M236	A	SX	3.35pm	3.42pm	2 North	84G/	9A/	84G/	9A/
3.35pm	Crewe	Calveley		C	SX	-	3.35pm	-	-	-	5A/55	5A/909
12.14pm	Broxton	Crewe	41	K	SX	3.45pm	-	Gresty Lane	5B/1056	5B/1460	-	-
3.45pm	Crewe	Neville Hill		D	D	-	3.45pm	Gresty Lane	-	-	5B/1034	9B/356
3.48pm	Crewe	Liverpool Lime St	343	A	D	-	3.48pm	2 South	-	-	8A/32	8A/231
12.50pm	Heath Junction	Crewe	93	H	D	3.50pm	-	North Staffs Sdgs			-	-

Left:
Crewe South Junction, No Date
'Princess Coronation' Pacific No 46221 *Queen Elizabeth*, a Polmadie 66A engine with Carlisle Upperby men at the controls, pulls away from Crewe with the Up 'Royal Scot' and snakes across to the Up Fast line. The train was not booked to call at Crewe, being timed to pass through the station on the Up Through line at 2.40pm. Coasting into Crewe and heading for Platform 2 is 'Princess Royal' class Pacific No 46209 *Princess Beatrice* with the 11.15am Euston to Portmadoc. This loco was based at Crewe North and would come off at the station, to be replaced by a 'Royal Scot' class loco. *Eric Treacy, Martin Welch*

Above right:
Near Birmingham, 25 April 1955
Crewe North Shed Turn 23 was a two-day diagram booked to Class 6P engines. The first day involved the 11.27pm parcels to Euston, due 4.10am, the engine then going on Camden shed, emerging the same evening to work the 7.5pm to Birmingham New Street, thence light engine to Monument Lane shed. It emerged the second day to work the 2.50am from New Street to Leamington, returning with the 7.55am to New Street, due 8.50am. Engine and stock next worked the 9.15am New Street to Liverpool Lime Street, then worked the 4.17pm passenger back to Crewe, going on North Shed at 5.20pm. It repeated the cycle the same evening. Here North Shed's No 45634 *Trinidad* works the Leamington to New Street part of the diagram. *R. J. Blenkinsop*

Time Dep	From	Destination	Rep No	Train Class	Days Run	Crewe Arr	Crewe Dep	Platform or Yard	To Crewe from South Men Diag	To Crewe from South Loco Diag	From Crewe to North Men Diag	From Crewe to North Loco Diag
10.55am	Camden	Crewe		D	SX	3.51pm	-	BHSS North	1A/1	8A/772	-	-
12pm	Euston	Crewe	95	A	SX	3.59pm	-	1	8A/—	1B/212	-	-
4pm	Basford Hall	Crewe Works	W1	K	D	*pass* 4.10pm		BHSS North	5B/1086	5B/2077	5B/1086	5B/2077
9am	Paignton	Manchester Mayfield	373	A	MFO	4.12pm	4.20pm	1	9A/	84G/	9A/	84G/
1.15pm	Euston	Glasgow Central	97	A	D	4.17pm	4.24pm	2	1B/3	5A/330	1B/3	5A/141mwf
2pm	Badnall Wharf	Crewe	28	K	SX	4.20pm	-	BHSS North	5B/1110	5B/1110	-	-
11.15am	Swansea High St	Manchester L Rd	265	A	D	4.22pm	4.30pm	1	84G/	84G/	84G/	84G/
4.25pm	Crewe	Bangor	111	A	MFSO	-	4.25pm	7 Bay	-	-	6A/	6A/
4.25pm	Crewe	Chester	111	A	TWThO	-	4.25pm	7 Bay	-	-	5A/104	5A/104
4.30pm	Crewe	Carlisle Kingmoor		D	D	-	4.30pm	Gresty Lane	-	-	5B/1030	12A/107
4.33pm	Crewe	Blackpool Central	99	A	FO-Q	-	4.33pm	2 North	-	-	10B/	10B/
1.30pm	Euston	Blackpool Central	93	A	D	4.33pm	4.40pm	2	28A/60	28A/67	28A/60	28A/67
4.34pm	Crewe	Northwich		B	D	-	4.34pm	9 Bay	-	-	5A/121	5A/121
2.7pm	Bescot	Crewe		H	D	4.45pm	-	BHSS North	3E/	3E/	-	-
4.47pm	Crewe	Manchester Mayfield		B	D	-	4.47pm	8 Bay	-	-	2A/4	5A/604
8.45am	Plymouth	Liverpool Lime St	263	A	D	4.50pm	5pm	2 North	5A/1	5A/702	2A/3	5A/579
2.25pm	Nuneaton	Hooton		F	SX	4.51pm	5.25pm	BHSS North	5B/1055	2B/323	5B/1055	6A/270
4.55pm	Crewe	Carriage Sheds		G	SX	-	4.55pm	-	-	-	5E/	5E/
10.45am	Euston	Crewe	381	C	D	4.58pm	-	1 Through	5A/22	2A/103	-	-
5pm	Crewe	Northwich	27	K	D	-	5pm	BHSS North	-	-	M/wich	M/wich
3.7pm	Derby Midland	Crewe		B	SX	5.2pm	-	5 Bay	17A/	17A/	-	-
5.3pm	Crewe	Llandudno	125	A	D	-	5.3pm	7 Bay	-	-	7C/12	5A/655
3.55pm	Dudley Port	Crewe	271	C	SX	5.5pm	-	1 South	1B/13	5A/320	-	-
5.8pm	Crewe	Liverpool Lime St		B	D	-	5.8pm	8 Bay	-	-	5A/44	5A/598
5.10pm	Crewe	Manchester L Rd	261	A	D	-	5.10pm	2 South	-	-	5A/27	9A/246
12.50pm	Aberystwyth	Crewe		B	D	5.12pm	-	2 Bay	W'church/15	W'church/16	-	-
3.50pm	Birmingham	Manchester L Rd	275	A	D	5.13pm	5.20pm	2 North	9A/—	5A/564	9A/—	9A/249
5.17pm	Crewe	Garston Speke Sdgs		H	SX	-	5.17pm	BHSS North	-	-	8C/	8C/
2.22pm	Euston	Liverpool Lime St	113	A	FSO	5.23pm	5.30pm	2	1A/7	1A/73	1A/7	1A/73
5.5pm	Betley Road	Crewe		K	SX	5.27pm	-	BHSS North	5B/1132	5A/1132	-	-
8.45am	Willesden	Crewe		E	SX	5.29pm	-	BHSS North	5B/1054	2A/688	-	-
4.25pm	Shrewsbury	Crewe		B	D	5.32pm	-	1	84G/	84G/	-	-
2.30pm	Euston	Liverpool Lime St	115	A	D	5.38pm	5.51pm	2	8A/—	1B/148	8A/—	1B/148
4.30pm	Leek	Crewe		B	D	5.41pm	-	4 Bay	5D/	5D/	-	-
2.38pm	Euston	Manchester L Rd	177	A	FO	*pass* 5.44pm			1A/10	1A/76	1A/10	1A/76
5.55pm	Crewe	Northwich		B	D	-	5.55pm	9 Bay	-	-	5A/121	5A/121
6pm	Crewe	Carlisle	397	A	D	-	6pm	8 Bay	-	-	5A/28	12A/83
3.25pm	Grange Jnt Sidings	Crewe	83	K	D	6.5pm	-	North Staffs Sdgs	5E/	5E/	-	-
6.8pm	Crewe	Chester		B	D	-	6.8pm	7 Bay	-	-	6A/	6A/
5.27pm	Stafford	Crewe		B	D	6.8pm	-	1 South	5A/33	5C/104	-	-
6.10pm	Crewe	Manchester L Rd		B	D	-	6.10pm	1 North	-	-	84G/2	5A/601
2.40pm	Camden	Glasgow Buchanan St		C	SX	6.14pm	6.19pm	BHSS North	9A/11	1A/805	11A/	10B/
6.15pm	Crewe	Birkenhead		J	D	-	6.15pm	BHSS North	-	-	5B/1050	6C/373
7.40am	Penzance	Liverpool Lime St	383	A	SX	6.20pm	6.30pm	1 North	9A/10	5A/718	9A/10	8A/255
8.20am	Oxley Sidings	Crewe		K	D	6.24pm	-	Gresty Lane	84B/—	Crewe/13	-	-
5.57pm	Stoke	Crewe		B	SX	6.27pm	-	2	5D/	5D/	-	-
2.55pm	Camden	Crewe		C	SX	6.28pm	-	BHSS North	2A/	2B/	-	-
6.35pm	Crewe	Manchester L Rd	437	A	D	-	6.35pm	1 South	-	-	9A/	9A/
6.37pm	Crewe	Carlisle	73	C	D	-	6.37pm	Down Sidings	-	-	12A/	5B/1233
3.15pm	Kingswinford Jnt	Crewe		H	D	6.39pm	-	Gresty Lane			-	-
4.35pm	Harlescott Sidings	Crewe		H	D	6.50pm	-	Gresty Lane	6B/	5A/709	-	-
6.30pm	Madeley	Crewe	39	K	SX	6.56pm	-	BHSS North	17B/25	5B/1194	-	-
6.56pm	Crewe	Carlisle Dentenhome		C	SX	-	6.56pm	BHSS North	-	-	12A/300	5B/1233
5.8pm	Derby Midland	Crewe		B	D	7.3pm	-	5 Bay	9A/14	5A/623	-	-
5.45pm	Shrewsbury	Crewe		B	D	7.5pm	-	1 South	84G/4	5A/714	-	-
4.15pm	Euston	Liverpool Lime St	269	A	FO	7.11pm	7.18pm	2	1B/32	1B/152	1B/32	1B/152
5.55pm	Wellington	Crewe		B	D	7.18pm	-	2 Bay	Wellington	Wellington	-	-
7pm	Alsager	Crewe	89	K	D	7.21pm	-	North Staffs Sdgs	5D/	5E/	-	-
7.25pm	Crewe	Carlisle		E	SX	-	7.25pm	BHSS North	-	-	12A/321	5B/1245
4.35pm	Harlescott Sidings	Crewe		H	SX	7.25pm	-	BHSS Middle	84G/103	5A/709	-	-
3.58pm	Oxley	Crewe		H	D	7.29pm	-	Gresty Lane	81F/—	Crewe/12	-	-
4.30pm	Euston	Liverpool Lime St	85	A	D	7.32pm	7.37pm	1	8A/	8A/	8A/	8A/
4.40pm	Water Orton	Crewe		E	SX	7.33pm	-	BHSS North	3C/203	3B/326	-	-
6.5pm	Birmingham	Liverpool Lime St	279	A	D	7.40pm	7.48pm	2 North	8A/13	5A/565	8A/13	5A/577
6.15pm	Birmingham	Manchester L Rd	281	A	FO	7.46pm	7.53pm	2 South	3D/	3D/	5A/98	5A/98
7.50pm	Crewe	Llandudno	197	A	D	-	7.50pm	7 Bay	-	-	7A/1	7A/160
6.20pm	Harlescott Sidings	Crewe		H	TSX	7.52pm	-	Gresty Lane	2A/9	5A/726	-	-
4.47pm	Euston	Heysham	247	A	FO	7.52pm	7.57pm	2	5A/	1B/247	5A/	11A/106

Time Dep	From	Destination	Rep No	Train Class	Days Run	Crewe Arr	Crewe Dep	Platform or Yard	To Crewe from South Men Diag	To Crewe from South Loco Diag	From Crewe to North Men Diag	From Crewe to North Loco Diag
7.53pm	Crewe	Manchester L Rd	281	A	FX	-	7.53pm	2 South	-	-	9A/	5A/98
5.54pm	Derby Midland	Crewe		B	D	7.54pm	-	6 Bay	5A/41	5A/637	-	-
4.55pm	Euston	Heysham	141	A	FSX	7.56pm	8.4pm	2	1B/11	11A/46	1B/11	11A/46
8pm	Crewe	Neville Hill		H	D	-	8pm	Gresty Lane	-	-	25G/301	5B/1353
8.10pm	Crewe	Manchester L Rd		B	D	-	8.10pm	8 Bay	-	-	9A/	9B/
5.5pm	Euston	Blackpool Central	159	A	D	8.13pm	8.21pm	2	1B/17	1B/122	1B/17	1B/122
7.55pm	Alsager Junction	Crewe		K	D	8.15pm	-	North Staffs Sdgs	5D/	5E/	-	-
5.45pm	Oxley Sidings	Crewe		H	D	8.20pm	-	Gresty Lane	84G/	84G/	-	-
8.27pm	Crewe	Preston	447	A	SX	-	8.27pm	2 South	-	-	5A/43	10A/198
5.20pm	Euston	Holyhead	145	A	D	8.28pm	8.35pm	1	5A/5	5A/251	5A/39	6A/255
8.30pm	Crewe	Northwich		H	D	-	8.30pm	BHSS North	-	-	5B/1053	5B/1363
10.5am	Penzance	Liverpool Lime St	285	A	SX	8.41pm	8.50pm	2 North	8A/5	5A/701	8A/5	8A/276
5.52pm	Euston	Manchester L Rd	139/1	A	FO	*pass* 8.47pm		2 Through	1B/42	9A/217	1B/42	9A/217
8.30pm	Alsager	Hooton		J	D	8.52pm	9.3pm	North Staffs Sdgs	8D/	8D/	8D/	8D/
6pm	Euston	Manchester L Rd	139	A	D	*pass* 8.55pm		2 Through	1B/11	1B/176	1B/11	1B/176
9pm	Crewe	Manchester L Rd	143	A	SX	-	9pm	2	-	-	84G/4	5A/602
9pm	Crewe	Edge Hill		H	D	-	9pm	BHSS North	-	-	8A/	8A/
6.7pm	Euston	Liverpool Lime St	137	A	D	*pass* 9.5pm		2 Through	8A/	8A/212	8A/	8A/212
9.5pm	Crewe	Copley Hill		F	D	-	9.5pm	Gresty Lane	-	-		9B/360
9.15pm	Crewe	Carnforth		F	FSX	-	9.15pm	BHSS North	-	-	11A/250	5B/1300
6.20pm	Euston	Preston	131	A	SX	9.16pm	9.27pm	2	1B/12	10B/97	1B/12	10B/97
8.15pm	Stafford	Crewe		H	SX	9.19pm	-	BHSS North	17B/25	5A/382	-	-
8.52pm	Stoke	Crewe	409	B	SX	9.29pm	-	3	5A/40	5A/625	-	-
9.35pm	Crewe	Wyre Dock		E	SX	-	9.35pm	BHSS North	-	-	12A/319	5B/1270
8.25pm	Shrewsbury	Crewe		B	D	9.38pm	-	1 South	5B/1035	5C/102	-	-
9.40pm	Crewe	Liverpool Lime St		B	SX	-	9.40pm	8 Bay	-	-	5A/41	5A/597
9.40pm	Crewe	Chester		B	D	-	9.40pm	7 Bay	-	-	7A/11	6A/179
9.50pm	Crewe	Manchester L Rd		B	D	-	9.50pm	1 North	-	-	9B/	9B/
9.50pm	Crewe	Bamfurlong		H	SX	-	9.50pm	BHSS North		-	10A/306	5B/1279
8.7pm	Stoke	Crewe	41	H	D	9.54pm	-	North Staffs Sdgs	5D/	5D/	-	-
10pm	Crewe	Manchester L Rd		F	D	-	10pm	Gresty Lane	-	-	9B/	9A/254
10.1pm	Crewe	Bamfurlong		H	SX	-	10.1pm	Gresty Lane	-	-	5B/1032	5B/1247-FO
8.20pm	Birmingham	Chester	287	A	D	10.6pm	10.26pm	1 South	3D/—	5A/550	3D/	6B/
8.15pm	Derby Midland	Crewe		B	D	10.15pm	-	5 Bay	5A/91	5A/91	-	-
7.20pm	Euston	Inverness	151	A	SX	10.16pm	10.29pm	2	5A/3	1B/230	5A/2	5A/135
7.25pm	Euston	Perth	149	A	FSX-Q	10.23pm	10.36pm	1 }	1B/34	1B/249	1B/34	5A/181
7.25pm	Euston	Perth	149	A	FO	10.23pm	10.36pm	1 }				
10.25pm	Crewe	Warrington		H	FSX	-	10.25pm	BHSS North	-	-	5B/1003	5B/1291
10.30pm	Crewe	Guide Bridge		H	D	-	10.30pm	Gresty Lane	-	-	26A/633	5B/1342
3.30pm	Broad Street	Crewe	17	A	D	10.33pm	-		5A/21	1B/223	-	-
10.35pm	Crewe	Hooton		J	D	-	10.35pm	North Staffs Sdgs	-	-	5B/1041	6B/286
9.25pm	Grange Junction	Crewe	6	H	SX	10.38pm	-	North Staffs Sdgs	5D/	5D/	-	-
10.40pm	Crewe	Warrington		H	SX	-	10.40pm	BHSS North	-	-	8D/	5B/1291
10.40pm	Crewe	Brewery Sidings		H	D	-	10.40pm	Gresty Lane	-	-	26A/624	5B/1328
9.25pm	Wellington	Crewe		B	WSO	10.42pm	-	2 Bay	Wellington	Crewe/2	-	-
10.45pm	Crewe	Preston Ribble Sdgs		F	MX	-	10.45pm	BHSS North	-	-	5A/33	5B/1276
10.27pm	Alsager	Ellesmere Port		J	FX	10.45pm	10.52pm	North Staffs Sdgs	8C/	8C/	8C/	8C/
7.45pm	Birmingham C St	Edge Hill		D	SX	10.46pm	11.10pm	BHSS North	8A/33	3B/313	8A/33	5B/1392
10.50pm	Crewe	Perth	307	A	FSX-Q	-	10.50pm	2 }		-	-	
10.50pm	Crewe	Perth	307	A	FO	-	10.50pm	2 }	-	-	5A/60	5BA145
7.55pm	Hereford	Crewe	277	B	D	10.50pm	-	1 South	12A/13	5A/710	-	-
10.50pm	Crewe	Preston		F	D	-	10.50pm	BHSS North	-	-	10B/	10B/
7.30pm	Euston	Perth	153	A	D	10.56pm	11.10pm	3	1B/11	5A/269	5A/1	5A/131
5.15pm	Carmarthen	Crewe	289	C	D	11.3pm	-	1 Through	5A/33	84G/64	-	-
11.5pm	Crewe	Mold Junction		H	FSX	-	11.5pm	BHSS North	-	-	6B/	6B/283
10.45pm	Alsager Junction	Garston Speke Sdgs		J	D	*pass* 11.9pm		Station	8C/	8C/	8C/	8C/
11.15pm	Crewe	Winsford Junction		H	D	-	11.15pm	BHSS North	-	-	5B/1020	5B/1282
7.55pm	Euston	Stranraer Harbour	155	A	SX	11.14pm	11.24pm	2	1B/2	12A/54	1B/2	12A/54
10pm	Birmingham	Holyhead	165	A	FO	11.21pm	11.28pm	1 South	6A/	3D/	6A/	6A/
12pm	Penzance	Liverpool Lime St	205	A	D	11.21pm	12.30am	2 North	5A/33	5A/712	8A/	8A/
7.35pm	Camden	Edge Hill		C	D	11.26pm	12.5am	BHSS North	8A/12	8A/766	8A/12	8A/766
6.30pm	Swansea	York	201	A	D	11.27pm	12.5am	1 North	84G/	84G/	84G/	8A/
10.15pm	Birmingham	Crewe	297	A	D	11.31pm	-	1 South	2A/—	5A/561	-	-
11.5pm	Stoke	Crewe		B	D	11.35pm	-	5 Bay	84G/5	5A/624	-	-
11.36pm	Crewe	Leeds	355	A	FO	-	11.36pm	7 Bay	-	-	9B/	5A/615
7.35pm	Camden	Edge Hill		C	SX	11.36pm	12.5am	BHSS North	8A/	8A/	8A/	8A/
8.10pm	Oxley Sidings	Crewe		H	D	11.40pm	-	Gresty Lane	3D/	5A/722-FO	-	-
8.30pm	Euston	Glasgow Central	157	A	D	11.44pm	12am	2 South	5A/4	5A/277	12A/	11A/
8.45pm	Euston	Holyhead	161	A	D	*pass* 11.50pm		1 Through	7C/1	7C/32	7C/1	7C/32
8.52pm	Euston	Holyhead	163	A	D	11.58pm	12.11am	2	5A/12	5A/359	6A/	6A/

Down Direction — Saturdays Only

Note: Italics under departure time denote passing time

Time Dep	From	Destination	Rep No	Train Class	Crewe Arr	Crewe Dep	Platform or Yard	To Crewe from South		From Crewe to North	
								Men Diag	Loco Diag	Men Diag	Loco Diag
6.30pm	Swansea	York	201			12.1am	1 North	86G/			
7.35pm	Camden	Edge Hill		C	11.26pm	12.5am	BHSS North	8A/12	8A/766	8A/12	8A/766
8.52pm	Euston	Holyhead	163	A	12.2am	12.11am	1 North	7C/1	7C/31	7C/1	7C/31
9.10pm	Euston	Glasgow Central	169	A	*pass 12.10am*		2 Through	12A/	12A/	12A/	12A/
12.15am	Crewe	Preston	385	C	-	12.15am	Down Sidings	-	-		10B/
9.17pm	Euston	Glasgow St Enoch	175	A	*pass 12.23am*		2 Through	12A/	12A/	12A/	12A/
12.25am	Crewe	Birkenhead		H	-	12.25am	BHSS North	-	-	6C/	6C/
10.55pm	Wellington	Crewe			12.26am	-	2 Bay	Wellington	Wellington	-	-
11.5pm	Birmingham	Glasgow Buch St	291	A	12.26am	12.50am	1			5A/22	5A/178
12am	Penzance	Liverpool Lime St	205	A	11.25pm	12.30am	8 Bay	84G/	84G/	1A/1	5A/590
12.35am	Crewe	Bamfurlong Jnt		F	-	12.35am		-	-	5B/1037	5B/1292
12.41am	Crewe	Manchester L Rd	293		-	12.41am	2	-	-	9A/—	9A/307
8.50pm	Stretton Junction	Mold Junction		F	12.10am	12.50am		5D/345	5D/346	5D/345	5B/1468
11.15pm	Birmingham	Glasgow Central	299	A	12.48am	1.5am	1	5A/10	3D/149	5A/3	5A/143
7.35pm	Willesden	Crewe		D	12.53am	-	BHSS North	5B/1051	5B/1135	-	-
9.25pm	Euston	Glasgow Central	171	A	1.3am	1.15am	2	12A/	12A/55	12A/	12A/55
1.5pm	Birmingham C St	Manchester L Rd		E	1.8am	1.12am	BHSS North	9A/21	3B/312	9A/21	9A/640
11.30pm	Harlescott	Brewery Sidings		TF	1.15am	1.20am		25D/124	5A/705	25D/124	5B/1348
1.17am	Crewe	Adswood Sidings		H	-	1.17am	Gresty Lane	-	-		
8.40pm	Nottingham	Edge Hill		E	*pass 1.29am*		2 Through		8A		8A/
10.30pm	Euston	Manchester L Rd	185	C	1.37am	1.43am		9A/—	1B/161	9A/—	1B/161
10.45pm	Euston	Manchester L Rd	283	A	1.37am	1.43am	1 South	7C/			
8.50pm	Camden	Carnforth		D	1.45am	1.53am	2 Through	11A/262	8B/552	11A/262	8B/552
10.50pm	Euston	Perth	195	A	1.55am	2.5am	2	2A/—	1B/235	12A/—	
2.5am	Crewe	Holyhead	1	A	-	2.5am	1 North	-	-	7C/7	7C/40
2.6am	Crewe	Manchester L Rd	203		-	2.9am	1 North	-	-	9A/	9A/
2.10am	Crewe	Liverpool Lime St	231	A	-	2.10am	2 South	-	-	8A/	8A/
11.15pm	Euston	Blackpool North	183	A	2.13am	2.25am	2	2A/		5A/33	5A/204
11.5pm	Euston	Windermere	193	A	2.16am	2.18am	2	1B/17	5A/293	5A/11	10B/200
2.27am	Crewe	Wyre Dock		F	-	2.27am	BHSS	-	-	11A/	
11.25pm	Euston	Holyhead	451	A	2.28am	2.36am		1A/8	1A/70	1A/8	5A/674
12.2am	Birmingham	Carlisle	475		2.22am	3.16am	1 South				
2.30am	Crewe	Preston Ribble S		F	-	2.30am	BHSS	-	-	5B/1039	5B/1267
9.32pm	Camden	Crewe			2.41am	-	BHSS North	5A/39	6A/133	-	-
2.42am	Crewe	Manchester L Rd	207	A	-	2.42am	8 Bay	-	-	9A/11	5A/621
11.40pm	Euston	Glasgow Central	21	A	*pass 2.50am*		2 Through	1B/1	1B/100	1B/1	1B/100
3am	Crewe	Carlisle	35	C	-	3am	Down Sidings	-	-		
1.48am	Stafford	Crewe				2.50am	-	9A/9	84G/57	-	-
6.10pm	Euston	Carlisle	3	C	2.51am	3.2am	2	4B/—	5A/278		
1.30am	Sideway	Crewe		F	2.57am	-	North Staffs Sdgs	5B/1110	5B/1111	-	-
9.45pm	Marylebone	Preston	3	C	3.7am	3.28am	2			5A/24	5A/221
9.55pm	Willesden	Carlisle	167	C	3.18am	4.45am	1 North	2A/—	1A/63		
10pm	Camden	Warrington		D	3.19am	3.35am	BHSS North	8B/1	5A/385	8B/1	8B/567
11.55pm	Curzon Street	Mold Junction		E	3.9am	3.25am	BHSS North				6B/
12.20am	Euston	Manchester L Rd	9	A	*pass 3.25am*		2 Through	1B/42	9A/217	1B/42	9A/217
10.50pm	Stourbridge Jnt	Crewe		TF	3.29am	-	Gresty Lane	82C/—	Crewe/14	-	-
2.30am	Euston	Liverpool Lime St	213	A	*pass 3.35am*		2 Through	8A/—	1B/140	8A/—	1B/140
4.40pm	Penzance	Manchester L Rd	463		3.41am	3.54am	2 North			84G/	
12.45am	Birmingham	Crewe	479	C	3.48am	-	2 South	8A/—	5A/562	-	-
12.40am	Euston	Glasgow Central	311	A	*pass 3.50am*		2 Through	12A/	12A/	12A/	12A/
9.45pm	Worcester	Crewe		F	3.59am	-	Gresty Lane	85A/—	Crewe/15	-	-
12.50am	Euston	Holyhead	481	A	3.56am	4.4am	2	2A/	2A/	2A/	6A/
2.15am	Bescot	Garstang		D	4am	4.5am	2 Through	5A/27	3B/327	5A/27	5B/1296
2pm	Penzance	Crewe	61	C	4.3am	-	1 South		84G/	-	-
1.5pm	Willesden Brent	Crewe		D	4.8am	-	BHSS North	5B/1037	1A/808	-	-
4.10am	Crewe	Birkenhead		F	-	4.10am	North Staffs Sdgs	-	-	6C/201	5B/1458
4.20am	Crewe	Copley Hill		TF	-	4.20am	Gresty Lane	-	-	5B/1036	5B/1335
12.5am	Cardiff	Liverpool Lime St	215		4.10am	5.20am	2 South	84G/5	5A/723	5A/71	5A/599
11.10pm	Monument Lane	Birkenhead		E	4.54am	4.56am	BHSS North			6C/	6C/
10.35pm	Willesden Brent	Adswood		D	4.25am	4.36am	BHSS	9A/415	1A/813	9A/415	9A/642
4.45pm	Penzance	Manchester L Rd	217		4.28am	5.10am	2				9B/
4.56am	Crewe	Northwich			-	4.56am	7 Bay	-	-	5B/1062	M/wich/4
5am	Crewe	Liverpool Lime St	209		-	5am	Down Sidings	-	-	5A/42	5A/583
12.30am	Camden	Crewe		D	4.57am	-	BHSS North	1A/1	1A/816	-	-
12.2am	Euston	Crewe	189	A	5.8am	-	3	1B/22	5A/302	-	-
3am	Nuneaton	Crewe		E	5.10am	-	BHSS North	5A/40	2B/326	-	-
5.15am	Crewe	Manchester L Rd	17		-	5.15am	1 South	-	-	9A/	9A/

Time Dep	From	Destination	Rep No	Train Class	Crewe Arr	Crewe Dep	Platform or Yard	To Crewe from South Men Diag	To Crewe from South Loco Diag	From Crewe to North Men Diag	From Crewe to North Loco Diag
5.15am	Crewe	Bamfurlong		D	-	5.15am	BHSS North	-	-	12A/322	5B/1243
3.15am	Bescot	Carlisle		E	5.22am	5.27am	2 Through				
5.27am	Crewe	Northwich		K	-	5.27am	BHSS	-	-	5B/1017	5B/1368
5.30am	Crewe	Chester	11	A	-	5.30am	Down Sidings	-	-	5A/67	6A/245
5.35am	Crewe BH	Garston Speke Sdgs		TF	-	5.35am	BHSS	-	-	5B/1052	5B/1398
5.45am	Crewe	Morecambe Prom	31		-	5.45am	Down Sidings	-	-		10A/196
2.37am	Rugby	Crewe		TF	5.47am	-	BHSS	2A/9	5A/391	-	-
6am	Crewe	Warrington			-	6am	1 North	-	-	10B/20	5A/201
5.30am	Alsager	Hooton		J	*pass* 6.3am	-		5E/			
1.55am	Kingswinford	Crewe		TF	6.10am	-	Gresty Lane	84B/—	Crewe/16	-	-
6.15am	Crewe	Northwich		B	-	6.15am	9 Bay	-	-	5A/120	5A/120
6.15am	Crewe	Edge Hill		TF	-	6.15am	BHSS	-	-	5B/1019	5B/1400
6.20am	Crewe	Sandbach		Frt	-	6.20am	BHSS North			5B/1053	5B/1367
4.30am	Stoke Yard	Crewe		Min	6.40am	-	North Staffs Sdgs	5B/1063	5B/1375	-	-
4.30am	Stoke Yard	Crewe		(Cpld)	6.40am	-	North Staffs Sdgs	9A/12	5A/631	-	-
6.42am	Crewe	Mold Junction		F	-	6.42am	BHSS	-	-	5B/1037	6B/267
6.45am	Crewe	Manchester L Rd			-	6.45am	8 Bay	-	-	9A/9	5A/605
1.10am	Marylebone	Crewe	237		6.54am	-	1 Through			-	-
10.25pm	Somers Town	Crewe		E	7.5am	-	BHSS North	2B/116	5B/1192	-	-
6.45am	Whitchurch	Crewe		B	7.16am	-	2 North	W'church/8	W'church/11	-	-
7.23am	Crewe	Manchester L Rd			-	7.23am	1 North	-	-	9B/	9A/
1.50am	Willesden	Crewe		E	7.25am	-	BHSS	26A/—	5B/1188	-	-
5.50am	Bushbury	Crewe			7.25am	-	BHSS North	9A/4	5B/1202	-	-
3am	Marylebone	Crewe	459		7.32am	-	2 Through	8A/		-	-
7.35am	Crewe	Northwich			-	7.35am	9 Bay	-	-	5A/120	5A/120
7.35am	Crewe	Chester		B	-	7.35am	2 North	-	-	W'church/8	W'church/11
7.42am	Crewe	Liverpool Lime St			-	7.42am	8 Bay	-	-	2A/8	5A/593
9.45pm	Eastleigh	Crewe			7.45am	-	1 Through			-	-
7.45am	Crewe	Adswood Sidings		Frt	-	7.45am	BHSS	-	-	5B/1020	5B/1333
7.48am	Crewe	Chester			-	7.48am	1 North	-	-	1B/17	5A/651
7.50am	Crewe	Manchester L Rd			-	7.50am	1 South	-	-	2A/—	5A/607
6.20am	Birmingham	Liverpool Lime St	445	A	7.53am	7.58am	2 North	3D/—	3D/150	3D/—	5A/580
8.5am	Alsager	Hooton			*pass* 8.30am				5E/		5E/
6.25am	Birmingham	Blackpool North	323	A	8.1pm	8.6am	2 North	3D/—		3D/—	5A/239
7am	Stafford	Crewe		TF	8.5am	-	BHSS North	17B/25	5B/1176	-	-
6.52am	Walsall	Llandudno	315	A	8.8am	8.15am	2 North	3C/5	3C/86	3C/5	5A/657
7am	Cheadle	Llandudno	239	A	*pass* 8.26am		2 Through				
6.30am	Birmingham	Crewe	219	A	8.28am	-	1 North	5A/44	5A/541	-	-
8.20am	Alsager Jnt	Crewe		TF	8.35am	-	North Staffs Sdgs	5B/1001	6C/371	-	-
7.25am	Shrewsbury	Crewe		A	8.47am	-	1 North		84G/—	-	-
8.10am	Stoke	Liverpool Lime St	223	A	8.42am	8.48am	2 North	5A/40	5A/626	5A/40	5A/586
6.20am	Nottingham	Llandudno	M30	A	8.48am	8.50am	2 Through				6A/—
7.30am	Wellington	Crewe		B	8.49am	-	3 Bay	Wellington	Wellington	-	-
7am	Birmingham	Manchester L Rd	249	A	8.50am	9.13am	1 North	9A/—	9A/—	9A/—	9A/—
6.15am	Coventry	Blackpool North	439	A	8.55am	8.58am	BHSS North	2A/—	2A/212	2A/—	5A/241
8.12am	Stafford	Crewe (Cpld)			8.55am	-		12A/—	5A/508	-	-
9.5am	Crewe	Bangor	307	A	-	9.5am	7 Bay	-	-	9A/12	5A/680
9.10am	Crewe	Liverpool Lime St		B	-	9.10am	8 Bay	-	-	8C/1	5A/582
9.20am	Crewe	Holyhead	55	A	-	9.20am	1 South	-	-	5A/44	6A/246
9.25am	Crewe	Perth	27	A	-	9.25am	2	-	-	66A/2	5A/207
7.15am	Stechford	Llandudno	327	A	9.25am	9.30am	1	3D/8	3D/161	3D/8	5A/682
8.10am	Birmingham	Llandudno	345	A	9.28am	9.40am	BHSS North	3E/7	3E/150	3E/7	5A/684
6.35am	Leamington	Llandudno	333	A	9.34am	9.42am	2	2A/31	2A/210	2A/31	5A/699
6.15am	Harlescott	Crewe Bank	68	K	9.38am	-		5B/1004	84G/182	-	-
9.40am	Crewe	Tattenhall Junction		K	-	9.40am	BHSS North	-	-	6B/—	6B/—
9.40am	Crewe	Blackpool North	389	A	-	9.40am	8 Bay	-	-	28A/64	10B/204
8.20am	Birmingham	Liverpool Lime St	225	A	9.45am	9.56am	2 North	5A/23	3D/162	5A/23	8A/266
8.40am	Shrewsbury	Crewe			9.47am	-	1 North	2B/5	5A/717	-	-
9.12am	Stoke	Blackpool North	351	A	*pass* 9.50am		2 Through				
10.10am	Crewe	Healey Mills		TF	-	10.10am	Gresty Lane	-	-	84G/103	5B/1344
8.38am	Walsall	Blackpool North	257	A	10.5am	10.12am	2	3C/4	3C/89	3C/4	10E/71
9.45am	Stoke	Blackpool North	123	A	10.18am	10.23am	2	5A/36	5A/638	5A/36	5A/242
8.48am	Birmingham	Llandudno	329	A	10.21am	10.23am	BHSS North	2A/35	2A/212	2A/35	5A/688
8.35am	Smethwick	Llandudno	339	A	10.21am	10.23am	BHSS North	3E/10	3E/152	3E/10	5A/672
8.50am	Derby	Llandudno	101	A	10.25am	10.35am	2	17A/—	17A/—	17A/—	5A/686
8.25am	Coventry	Blackpool North	443	A	*pass* 10.30am		2 Through				
9am	Birmingham	Blackpool North	231	A	10.29am	10.31am	BHSS North	3E/8	3E/148	3E/8	5A/237
7.55am	Northampton	Morecambe Euston Rd	373	A	10.37am	10.39am	BHSS	4B/3	4B/44	4B/3	5A/233
9.15am	Birmingham	Liverpool Lime St	229	A	10.39am	10.50am	2 North	3D/10	3D/114	3D/10	5A/587
8.8am	Leicester	Llandudno	M46	A	10.45am	10.47am	BHSS North	2B/—	15C/—	2B/—	5A/685

Time Dep	From	Destination	Rep No	Train Class	Crewe Arr	Crewe Dep	Platform or Yard	To Crewe from South Men Diag	To Crewe from South Loco Diag	From Crewe to North Men Diag	From Crewe to North Loco Diag
9.20am	Birmingham	Manchester L Rd	233	A	10.47am	10.53am	2 South	2A/—	5C/92	2A/—	5A/609
11am	Crewe	Workington	273	A	-	11am	8 Bay	-	-		
11am	Crewe	Llandudno	87	A	-	11am	7 Bay	-	-	7C/2	5A/673
7.42am	Bletchley	Blackpool North	441	A	11.1pm	11.7am	2	4A/—	4A/—	4A/—	5A/240
6.40am	Euston	Windermere	33	A	11.5am	11.14am	1		10B/		10B/
4.20am	Willesden	Crewe		E	11.5am	-	BHSS North	5B/1018	2A/695	-	-
9.45am	Nantwich	Crewe		Frt	11.8am	-	BHSS	5B/1126	5B/1126	-	-
8am	Euston	Holyhead	49	A	11.11am	11.25am	1 North	2A/-	2A/-	5A/8	5A/692
9.15am	Derby	Llandudno	135	A	11.15am	11.16am	2	9A/14	5A/627	9A/14	5A/691
9.20am	Birmingham	Morecambe	295	A	11.21am	11.30am	2				
10am	Wellington	Crewe		B	11.21am	-	2 South	Wellington	Wellington	-	-
11.25am	Crewe	Holyhead	49	A	-	11.25am	1 North	-	-	5A/8	5A/692
8.10am	Euston	Holyhead	37	A	11.25am	11.35am	1	2A/—	2A/—	6A/—	6A/—
7.35am	Cardiff	Blackpool North	449	A	11.32am	11.35am	Gresty Lane	5A/30	84G/74A	5A/30	5A/244
8.30am	Euston	Liverpool Lime St	39	A	11.44am	11.50am	1	1B/6	8A/220	1B/6	8A/220
11.40am	Betley Road	Crewe		Ballast	11.59am	-	BHSS	5B/1131	5B/1131	-	-
12.8pm	Crewe	Blackpool Central	43	A	-	12.8pm	8 Bay	-	-	11A/6	28A/75
12.10pm	Crewe	Manchester L Rd	127		-	12.10pm	7 Bay	-	-	9A/—	9A/—
12.18pm	Crewe	Liverpool Lime St			-	12.18pm	1 North	-	-		8A/287
8.38am	Cardiff	Manchester L Rd	227	A	12.19pm	12.22pm	2		84G/—		84G/—
9.20am	Euston	Llandudno	51	A	12.23pm	12.32pm	1	1B/31	5A/312	1B/31	7A/162
9.35am	Euston	Manchester L Rd	59	A	*pass 12.30pm*		2 Through	9A/—	9A/—	9A/—	9A/—
8.15am	Bristol	Liverpool Lime St	283	A	12.33pm	12/35	1	5A/71	5A/599	5A/71	8A/313
8.55am	Cardiff	Manchester L Rd	241	A	12.37pm	12.45pm	1 North				
12.38pm	Crewe	Sandbach		B	-	12.38pm	9 Bay	-	-	5A/120	5A/122
11.15am	Birmingham	Glasgow Central	67	A	12.40pm	1pm	2	5A/10	5A/549	5A/4	66A/12
10.50am	Derby	Crewe		B	12.45pm	-	5 Bay	5A/33	5A/628	-	-
12.30pm	Whitchurch	Crewe		B	12.50pm	-	1 South	8A/26	5A/711	-	-
10am	Euston	Glasgow Central	63	A	*pass 12.55pm*		2 Through	66A/1	12A/62	66A/1	12A/62
1pm	Crewe	Chester		B	-	1pm	1 North	-	-	5A/39	7A/156
1.1pm	Crewe	Manchester L Rd		B	-	1.1pm	7 Bay	-	-		
11.25am	Birmingham	Glasgow Central	211	A	1.8pm	1.15pm	2			5A/3	12A/108
10.8am	Euston	Glasgow Central	57	A	1.10pm	1.20pm	1	1B/4	1B/200	1B/4	5A/159
12.5pm	Shrewsbury	Crewe			1.17pm	-	1 North	5A/102	5A/107	-	-
12.50pm	Stoke	Crewe			1.21pm	-	5 Bay	5D/—	5D/—	-	-
10.20am	Euston	Perth	65	A	1.22pm	1.33pm	2	1B/1	12A/66	1B/1	12A/66

Time Dep	From	Destination	Rep No	Train Class	Crewe Arr	Crewe Dep	Platform or Yard	To Crewe from South Men Diag	To Crewe from South Loco Diag	From Crewe to North Men Diag	From Crewe to North Loco Diag
10.30am	Euston	Liverpool Lime St	71	A	*pass 1.28pm*		2 Through	8A/—	8A/—	8A/—	8A/—
1.35pm	Crewe	Windermere	317	A	-	1.35pm	8 Bay	-	-	10B/4	28A/72
12.15pm	Wellington	Crewe			1.36pm	-	3	Wellington	Crewe /1	-	-
12.10pm	Birmingham	Manchester L Rd	221	A	1.36pm	1.43pm	1 North	9A/—		9A/—	
1.35pm	Crewe	Birkenhead		J	-	1.30pm	North Staffs Sdgs	-	-	6C/—	6C/—
10.48am	Euston	Blackpool Central	127	A	*pass 1.50pm*		2 Through	28A/60	1B/117	28A/60	1B/117
10.40am	Euston	Carlisle	251	A	1.44pm	1.54pm	2	1B/2	2A/105	1B/2	10B/
1.55pm	Crewe	Winsford Junction		Min	-	1.55pm	Gresty Lane	-	-	5B/1126	5B/1127
1.58pm	Crewe	Llandudno	249	A	-	1.58pm	7 Bay	-	-	1A/1	5A/695
2pm	Crewe	Liverpool Lime St	79		-	2pm	8 Bay	-	-	8A/—	8B/—
11.50am	Bletchley	Blackpool Central	319	A	2.4pm	2.12pm	2	1A/1	9A/259	1A/1	28A/76
1.25pm	Stafford	Crewe				2.11pm	-	8A/32	5A/554	-	-
10.55am	Euston	Blackpool Central	77	A	2.23pm	2.25pm	2	28A/61	1B/237	28A/61	28A/73
2.28pm	Crewe	Manchester L Rd		B	-	2.28pm	1 South	-	-	3D/2	5A/611
12.34pm	Derby	Crewe			2.25pm	-	5 Bay	5A/112	5A/112	-	-
2.33pm	Crewe	Ditton Junction		TF	-	2.33pm	BHSS	-	-	5B/1118	5B/1121
11.15am	Euston	Portmadoc	89	A	2.30pm	2.34pm	1 Through	1B/19	8A/245	1B/19	6A/157
11.22am	Euston	Llandudno	181	A	2.37pm	2.41pm	1 Through	5A/70	5A/322	5A/70	5A/322
2.45pm	Crewe	Llandudno	119	A	-	2.45pm	7 Bay	-	-	5A/28	7A/165
2.50pm	Crewe	Chester			-	2.50pm	1 North	-	-	7C/16	6A/250
11.45am	Euston	Manchester L Rd	91	A	2.51pm	2.56pm	2	9A/	9A/	9A/	9A/
11.52am	Euston	Workington	121	A	*pass 2.56pm*		2 Through		10B/		10B/
3pm	Crewe	Middlewich		K	-	3pm	BHSS North	-	-	5B/1063	5B/1364
10.25am	Swansea	Manchester Mayfield	245	A	3pm	3.9pm	2				
2.10pm	Shrewsbury	Crewe			(Cpld)	3pm	-	28A/59	5A/728	-	-
12.18pm	Bescot	Crewe		F	3pm	-	BHSS	5B/1032	3A/185	-	-
11.58am	Euston	Workington	179	A	3.4pm	3.12pm	1	1B/18	1B/245	1B/18	10B/203
12.5pm	Euston	Liverpool Lime St	83	A	3.5pm	3.10pm	2	4A/	4A/	4A/	8A/
1.30pm	Birmingham	Blackpool North	335	A	3.7pm	3.17pm	1 Through			28A/79	28A/79
1.45pm	Birmingham	Manchester L Rd	253	A	3.16pm	3.20pm	2	8A/15	5A/556	8A/15	5A/610
1.55pm	Birmingham	Crewe	255	A	3.22pm	-	2		5C/	-	-
1.30pm	Derby	Crewe			3.16pm	-	5 Bay	5A/99	5A/99	-	-
3.35pm	Crewe	Liverpool Lime St	255	A	-	3.35pm	2	-	-		8B/
3.35pm	Crewe	Calveley	203	C	-	3.35pm		-	-	5A/55	5A/909
8.10am	Paignton	Manchester Victoria	379	A	*pass 3.42pm*		1 Through		84G/		84G/
11am	Aberystwyth	Manchester L Rd	129	A	3.36pm	3.45pm	1 North	9A/	84G/	9A/	84G/

Left:
Watford Tunnel, 14 April 1952
'Princess Royal' class Pacific No 46207 *Princess Arthur of Connaught* emerges from Watford Tunnel with a Liverpool to Euston express. The locomotive was based at Edge Hill 8A shed and the train was worked by men from the same depot. This was possibly the 10.10am from Lime Street, reporting number 54, which worked throughout without a booked stop. The train was limited load and comprised 15 vehicles, 494 tons, the stock working back with the 6.7pm the same evening. *J. C. Flemons*

Right:
Norton Bridge Looking South, June 1957
No 46161 *King's Own* working the 11.15am Down Euston to Portmadoc, W89, made up of 14 vehicles, 478 tons, steams through the station, past the junction with the line to Stoke-on-Trent. Next stop is Crewe, where the train crew will change but not the locomotive, which will continue to Bangor. The leading six vehicles will be worked through to Pwllheli and Portmadoc, the remaining coaches worked on to Holyhead as empty stock for servicing of the restaurant car.
C. M. and J. M. Bentley Collection

Time Dep	From	Destination	Rep No	Train Class	Crewe Arr	Crewe Dep	Platform or Yard	To Crewe from South		From Crewe to North	
								Men Diag	Loco Diag	Men Diag	Loco Diag
3.45pm	Crewe	Neville Hill		D	-	3.45pm	Gresty Lane	-	-	5B/1034	5B/1341
3.4pm	Stoke	Crewe		C	3.38pm	-	2 Through	5C/	5E/	-	-
3.48pm	Crewe	Birkenhead		H	-	3.48pm	BHSS	-	-	86K/42	5B/1467
9.25am	Bournemouth	Liverpool Lime St	M234	A	3.47pm	3.53pm	2 North	1B/42	8A/233	1B/42	8A/233
4pm	Crewe	Manchester L Rd	349	A	-	4pm	2 South	-	-	9B/	
10.55am	Camden	Crewe		D	3.51pm	-	BHSS North	1A/590	1A/66	-	-
.43pm	Wellington	Crewe			4pm	-	2 Bay	Wellington	Wellington	-	-
3.30pm	Pratt's Sidings	Crewe		ECS	4.2pm	-	2 Through	7A/3	5A/640	-	-
1.5pm	Euston	Glasgow Central	143	A	4.7pm	4.14pm	2	12A/	12A/	12A/	12A/
12.5pm	Euston	Crewe	95	A	4.4pm	-	1 South	5A/22	1B/213	-	-
8.55am	Paignton	Manchester L Rd	373	A	4.12pm	4.20pm	1				
1.15pm	Euston	Glasgow Central	97	A	4.17pm	4.19pm	2	1B/3	5A/330	1B/3	66A/17
4.25pm	Crewe	Bangor	111	A	-	4.25pm	7 Bay	-	-	5A/41	7A/161
4pm	Stoke	Crewe			4.25pm	-	2 Through	5C/	5C/	-	-
4.30pm	Crewe	Carlisle Kingmoor	D	-	4.30pm		BHSS	-	-	5B/1030	12A/103
11.15am	Swansea High St	Manchester L Rd	265	A	4.26pm	4.30pm	1	5A/1	5A/703	2A/—	5A/612
4.32pm	Crewe	Northwich		B	-	4.32pm	9 Bay	-	-	5A/120	5A/122
4.33pm	Crewe	Blackpool Central	93	A	-	4.33pm	2 North	-	-	28A/59	28A/74
1.30pm	Euston	Blackpool Central	99	A	4.33pm	4.35pm	2	1B/12	28A/68	1B/12	28A/68
4.35pm	Crewe	Warrington		TF	-	4.35pm	BHSS	-	-	5B/1034	5B/1283
10.5am	Exeter	Manchester L Rd	433	A	4.36pm	4.37pm	1				
2.25pm	Nuneaton	Hooton		F	4.43pm	5.25pm		5B/1055	2B/323	5B/1055	6A/270
4.47pm	Crewe	Manchester L Rd			-	4.47pm	8 Bay	-	-		
8.45am	Plymouth	Liverpool Lime St	263	A	4.50pm	5pm	2 North	3B/151	84G/76	3B/151	5A/596
10.45am	Euston	Crewe	381	C	4.59pm	-	1 Through	8A/—	5A/325	-	-
5pm	Crewe	Mold Junction	44	F	-	5pm	BHSS	-	-	6B/—	6B/—
5.3pm	Crewe	Llandudno	125	A	-	5.3pm	7 Bay	-	-	7A/2	6A/250
3.17pm	Derby	Crewe			5.5pm	-	5 Bay	17A/	17A/	-	-
5.5pm	Crewe	Liverpool Lime St			-	5.5pm	8 Bay	-	-	5A/97	5A/100
5.10pm	Crewe	Manchester L Rd	261	A	-	5.10pm	2 South	-	-	5A/33	5A/614
5.10pm	Crewe	Carlisle Viaduct Yd		D	-	5.10pm	BHSS	-	-	5B/1040	12A/119
12.50pm	Aberystwyth	Crewe			5.12pm	-	2 Bay	W'church/15	W'church/18	-	
2.7pm	Bescot	Crewe		TF	5.16pm	-	BHSS	5B/1055	3A/191	-	-
3.50pm	Birmingham	Manchester L Rd	275	A	5.13pm	5.24pm	2 North	9A/—	5A/564	9A/—	9A/249
5.5pm	Betley Road	Crewe		Ety	5.27pm	-	BHSS	5B/1131	5B/1132	-	-
2.22pm	Euston	Liverpool Lime St	113	A	5.23pm	5.30pm	2	1A/580	1A/73	1A/580	1A/73
10.40am	Bournemouth	Manchester Victoria	M250	A	5.25pm	5.32pm	1 North	9A/—	9A/—	9A/—	9A/—
4.30pm	Shrewsbury	Crewe			5.37pm	-	1	84G/	84G/	-	-
2.30pm	Euston	Liverpool Lime St	115	A	5.38pm	5.49pm	2	8A/	8A/	8A/	8A/
5.57pm	Crewe	Northwich		B	-	5.57pm	9 Bay	-	-	5A/120	5A/122
6pm	Crewe	Carlisle	397	A	-	6pm	8 Bay	-	-		10B/
3pm	Nuneaton	Crewe		TF	6pm	-	BHSS	5B/1054	5A/386	-	-
8am	Newquay	Manchester L Rd	377	A	6.1pm	6.4pm	2				
5.27pm	Stafford	Crewe		B	6.8pm	-	1 South	1B/13	5A/353	-	-
6.8pm	Crewe	Chester		B	-	6.8pm	7 Bay	-	-	6A/	6A/
6.10pm	Crewe	Manchester L Rd		B	-	6.10pm	1 North	-	-	5A/112	5A/113
6.15pm	Crewe	Birkenhead		J	-	6.15pm	BHSS	-	-		6C/
10.20am	Kingswear	Liverpool Lime St	383	A	6.20pm	6.30pm	1	9A/10	5A/718	9A/10	5A/5761
8.20am	Oxley Sidings	Crewe		Frt	6.24pm	-	Gresty Lane	84B/—	Crewe/13	-	-
6.35pm	Crewe	Manchester L Rd	437	A	-	6.35pm	1 South	-	-		9A/
6.35pm	Crewe	Garston			-	6.35pm		-	-		8C/251
6.37pm	Crewe	Carlisle	73	C	-	6.37pm	Down Sidings	-	-	12A 22pm	5A/172
5.8pm	Derby	Crewe			7.3pm	-	5 Bay	9A/14	5A/623	-	-
7.10pm	Crewe	Manchester Mayfield	259	C	-	7.10pm	Down Sidings	-	-	5A/40	9A/314
5.45pm	Shrewsbury	Crewe			7.11pm	-	1 South		84G/	-	-
4.15pm	Euston	Liverpool Lime St	269	A	7.11pm	7.18pm	2	8A/—	8A/—	8A/—	8A/—
5.55pm	Wellington	Crewe			7.18pm	-	2 Bay	Wellington	Wellington	-	-
4.35pm	Harlescott	Crewe		TF	7.25pm	-	Gresty Lane	84G/103	5A/713	-	-
5pm	Rugby	Crewe		D	7.25pm	-	BHSS North	26A/—	5B/1188	-	-
7.25pm	Crewe	Bamfurlong		E	-	7.25pm	BHSS	-	-	12A/321	5B/1245
3.15pm	Kingswinford	Crewe		T Frt	7.29am	-	Gresty Lane	81F/—	Crewe/12	-	-
4.30pm	Euston	Liverpool Lime St	85	A	7.32pm	7.37pm	1	8A/	8A/	8A/	8A/
6.5pm	Birmingham	Liverpool Lime St	279	A	7.40pm	7.48pm	2 North	8A/13	5A/565	8A/13	8A/259
7.50pm	Crewe	Llandudno	197	A	-	7.50pm	7 Bay	-	-	7A/3	5A/697
6.20pm	Harlescott	Carlisle		TF	7.52pm	7.52pm	Gresty Lane	84G/102	5A/727	84G/102	5B/1278
7.53pm	Crewe	Manchester L Rd	281	A	-	7.53pm	2 South	-	-		
5.54pm	Derby	Crewe			7.54pm	-	6 Bay	5A/93	5A/93	-	-
10.5am	Penzance	Liverpool Lime St	285	A	8.5pm	8.10pm	2				
8.10pm	Crewe	Manchester L Rd			-	8.10pm	8 Bay	-	-	9A/—	5A/613
5.5pm	Euston	Blackpool Central	159	A	8.19pm	8.21pm	1	1B/17	1B/122	1B/17	1B/122
8.27pm	Crewe	Preston	447		-	8.27pm	1 South	-	-	5A/68	10B/205

Right:
Euston, No Date
'Royal Scot' class 4-6-0 No 46146 *The Rifle Brigade* based at Camden 1B shed stands at the head of a train to North Wales. The photographer claimed the working was to Holyhead but it is more likely that this was the 11.15am Euston to Bangor, alias the 'Welshman', which ran under the reporting number W89. Part of the stock worked forward to Pwllheli and Porthmadog. Edge Hill 8A shed men (Turn 217) worked the train from Euston to Crewe where Llandudno Junction men (Turn 101) took over and worked the leg to Bangor. *Eric Treacy*

Time Dep	From	Destination	Rep No	Train Class	Crewe Arr	Crewe Dep	Platform or Yard	To Crewe from South Men Diag	To Crewe from South Loco Diag	From Crewe to North Men Diag	From Crewe to North Loco Diag
8.30pm	Crewe	Northwich		Min	-	8.30pm	BHSS	-	-	5B/1053	5B/1363
5.20pm	Euston	Holyhead	145	A	8.28pm	8.35pm	1	5A/5	5A/251	6A/	6A/
6pm	Euston	Manchester L Rd	139	A	*pass* 8.55pm		2 Through	1B/11	1B/176	1B/11	1B/176
4.50pm	Cardiff	Manchester L Rd	451	A	8.42pm	9pm	1				
12.30pm	Paignton	Manchester L Rd	375	A	8.48pm	9pm	2	9A/7	5A/706	9A/7	9A/252
6.7pm	Euston	Liverpool Lime St	137	A	*pass* 9.5pm		2 Through	8A/—	8A/212	8A/—	8A/212
9.5pm	Crewe	Copley Hill		F	-	9.5pm	Gresty Lane	-	-	5B/1005	5B/1354
8.30pm	Alsager	Mold Junction		J	-	9.9pm	North Staffs Sdgs				
6.30pm	Harlescott	Crewe		H	9.10pm	-	Gresty Lane	5B/1004	84G/195	-	-
9.15pm	Crewe	Preston Ribble Sdgs		E	-	9.15pm	BHSS	-	-	28B/103	5B/1269
6.22pm	Euston	Heysham	443	A	9.18pm	9.26pm	2		11A/		11A/
6.30pm	Euston	Heysham	141	A	9.28pm	9.39pm	2	1B/11	10B/98	1B/11	10B/98
8.25pm	Shrewsbury	Crewe			9.32pm	-	1 South			-	-
9.40pm	Crewe	Chester			-	9.40pm	7 Bay	-	-		
9.40pm	Crewe	Holyhead		H	-	9.40pm	BHSS	-	-		
9.20pm	Stoke	Crewe			9.45pm	-	2 Through			-	-
9.47pm	Crewe	Liverpool Lime St			-	9.47pm	8 Bay	-	-	5B/1052	8A/254
9.50pm	Crewe	Manchester L Rd			-	9.50pm	1 North	-	-		
8.20pm	Birmingham	Chester	287		10.6pm	10.26pm	1 South	3D/5	5A/550	3D/5	5A/652
9.31pm	Stafford	Crewe	287	Cpld	10.6pm	-		3D/13	5A/509	-	-
6.55pm	Hereford	Crewe			10.10pm	-	1 Through			-	-
3.25pm	Willesden	Crewe		E	10.12pm	-	BHSS North	8B/3	5B/1136	-	-
7.15pm	Euston	Lairg	151	A	*pass 10.13pm*		2 Through	7C/2	5A/270	7C/2	5A/270
10.27pm	Crewe	Carnforth			-	10.27pm		-	-		10B/559
8.15pm	Derby	Crewe			10.15pm	-	5 Bay	2A/9	5A/635	-	-
10.30pm	Crewe	Guide Bridge		TF	-	10.30pm	Gresty Lane	-	-	5B/1050	9A/639
10.35pm	Crewe	Mold Junction		J	-	10.35pm	North Staffs Sdgs	-	-	6B/111	6B/282
7.22pm	Euston	Perth	149	A	10.21pm	10.36pm	1				
3.35pm	Broad Street	Crewe	17	A	10.33pm	-		5A/21	1B/224	-	-
9.25pm	Wellington	Crewe			10.42pm	-	2 Bay	Wellington	Crewe/2	-	-
7.25pm	Curzon Street	Edge Hill		E	10.44pm	-	BHSS North	8A/33	3B/306	8A/33	8A/810
10.50pm	Crewe	Perth	307	A	-	10.50pm	8 Bay	-	-		
11pm	Crewe	Preston		F	-	11pm	BHSS	-	-	5B/1003	5B/1276
7.55pm	Hereford	Crewe	277	B	10.50pm	-	1 South	5B/1035	84G/66	-	-
7.30pm	Euston	Perth	153	A	10.56pm	11.10pm	3	9A/—	5A/357	5A/1	5A/132
4.45pm	Swansea Victoria	Crewe	289	C	11.3pm	-	1 Through	2A/3	5A/710	-	-
12pmn	Penzance	Liverpool Lime St	205	A	11.21pm	12.30am	2 North				
6.30pm	Swansea Victoria	York	201		11.27pm	12.1pm	1 North				
10.10pm	Birmingham	Crewe	297	A	11.31pm	-	1 South	8A/—	3D/166	-	-
10.30pm	Stafford	Crewe		TF	11.32pm	-	BHSS	17B/25	5A/557	-	-
11.5pm	Stoke	Crewe			11.35pm	-	5 Bay	84G/5	5A/624	-	-
5.30pm	Willesden	Crewe		E	11.42pm	-	BHSS	1A/525	9B/232	-	-
11.57pm	Crewe	Carlisle Viaduct Yd		E	-	11.57pm	BHSS	-	-	5B/1037	10A/606
8.30pm	Euston	Glasgow Central	157	A	11.44pm	11.58pm	2 South	5A/4	5A/284	5A/5	5A/164
8.45pm	Euston	Holyhead	161	A	*pass* 11.50pm		1 Through	7C	7C	7C	7C

Down Direction — Sundays Only

Note: Italics under departure time denote passing time

Time Dep	From	Destination	Rep No	Train Class	Crewe Arr	Crewe Dep	Platform or Yard	To Crewe from South: Men Diag	To Crewe from South: Loco Diag	From Crewe to North: Men Diag	From Crewe to North: Loco Diag
6.30pm	Swansea	York	201	A	1.27pm	12.5am	1 North			5A/27	5A/622
8.52pm	Euston	Holyhead	163	A	12.2am	12.11am	1	7C/1	7C/32	7C/1	7C/32
9.18pm	Euston	Glasgow Central	169	A	*pass 12.15am*		2 Through	12A/	12A/	12A/	12A/
8.45pm	Tutbury	Crewe	57	H	12.20am	-	North Staffs Sdgs	5C/	5C/	-	-
9.17pm	Euston	Glasgow Central	175 Q	A	*pass 12.23am*		2 Through	12A/	12A/	12A/	12A/
12pm	Penzance	Liverpool L St	205	A	11.21pm	12.30am	8 Bay	5A/43	5A/635	2A/9	5A/591
11.10pm	Bushbury	Adswood Sidings		F	12.40am	12.48am	BHSS North	10C/13	5B/1209	10C/13	9B/365
12.41am	Crewe	Manchester L Rd	293	A	-	12.41am	1 North	-	-	9A/2	9A/239
8.40pm	Nottingham	Edge Hill		E	12.45am	1.28am	North Staffs Sdgs				
11.30pm	Harlescott Sdgs	Brewery Sdgs		H	12.50am	12.58am	Gresty Lane	9A/412	5A/707	9A/412	9A/263
12.55am	Crewe	Carlisle		F	-	12.55am	Gresty Lane	-	-	11A/	10A/661
11.50pm	Harlescott Sdgs	Bamfurlong		H	1.1am	2.45am	Gresty Lane	8B/4	5B/1477	8B/4	10A/650
11.15pm	Birmingham N St	Glasgow Central	299	A	12.48am	1.5am	1	5A/10	3D/149	5A/3	5A/143
8.35pm	Worcester	Crewe		F	1.10am	-	Gresty Lane				
9.25pm	Euston	Glasgow Central	171	A	1.13am	1.25am	2	12A/5	5A/285	12A/5	5A/150
1.25am	Crewe	Manchester L Rd	19	A	-	1.25am	Down Sidings	-	-	8A/—	9A/262
12.35am	Longport Jnt	Crewe		H	1.30am	-	North Staffs Sdgs	86K/42	5B/1378	-	-
10.40pm	Bescot	Carlisle		E	1.30am	1.35am	BHSS North	5B/1038	3B/311	5B/1038	12A/97
1.45am	Crewe	Warrington		H	-	1.45am	BHSS North	-	-	5B/1020	5B/1271
9.25pm	Camden	Carlisle Kingmoor		H	1.53am	2.33am	BHSS North	8B/—	8B/553	5B/1056	10A/149
12.1am	Oxley Sdgs	Crewe		F	2.12am	-	Gresty Lane			-	-
11.15pm	Euston	Blackpool North	183	A	*pass 2.25am*	2	28A/62	1B/130	28A/62	1B/130	28A/62
9.50pm	Northampton	Crewe		H	2.27am	-	BHSS North	2A/515	5A/384	-	-
11.30pm	Euston	Glasgow Central	21	A	*pass 2.35am*		2 Through	1B/1	1B/101	1B/1	1B/101
2.35am	Crewe	Birkenhead		H	-	2.35am	BHSS North	-	-		
10.15pm	Birmingham C St	Birkenhead		H	2.40am	3.40am	BHSS North	3D/3	5B/1201	3D/3	5B/1463
6.10pm	Euston	Crewe	3	C	2.51am	3.2am	2	4B/1	5A/278	10B/	10B/
12.40am	Birmingham N St	Crewe	479	C	3.5am	-	1			-	-
1.40am	Bushbury	Crewe		H	3.11am	-	BHSS North	3D/2	5B/1203	-	-
3.15am	Crewe	Bangor	29	A	-	3.15am	7 Bay	-	-	6A/	6A/
2.35am	Stoke on Trent	Crewe		G	3.15am	-		5A/78	5A/636	-	-
3.15am	Crewe	Mold Junction		H	-	3.15am	BHSS North	-	-	5B/1052	6B/30
10.50pm	Stourbridge Jnt	Crewe		H	3.28am	-	Gresty Lane	82C/—	Crewe14	-	-
3.30am	Crewe	Warrington		H	-	3.30am	BHSS North	-	-	8B/	8B/
12.30am	Euston	Liverpool L St	213	A	3.36am	3.46am	2	8A/	8A/	8A/	8A/
4.40pm	Penzance	Manchester L Rd	329 Q	A	3.41am	3.54am	1	84G/	84G/	84G/	84G/
10.30pm	Willesden Jnt	Crewe	167	C	3.48am	-	1 Through	7C/2	5A/294	-	-
9.45pm	Worcester	Crewe		F	3.59am	-	Gresty Lane	85A/—	Crewe 15	-	-
12.40am	Euston	Manchester L Rd	9	A	4am	4.8am	2	2A/	2A/	5A/11	5A/617
4am	Crewe	Crewe Coal Yard	17	K	-	4am	BHSS North	-	-	5B/1118	5B/1122
2pm	Penzance	Crewe	61	C	4.3am	-	1	9A/4	5A/708	-	-
12.5am	Cardiff	Liverpool L St	215	A	4.10am	5.20am	1 South	9A/4	84G/	8A/	8A/
4.45pm	Penzance	Manchester L Rd	217	A	4.22am	5.15am	2 South	84G/	84G/	84G/	9B/
2.50am	Ellesmere Port	Crewe		TF	4.48am	-	BHSS North	6C/204	5B/1459	-	-
12.5am	Curzon Street	Preston		H	4.50am	5.10am	BHSS North	5A/33	5B/1215	5A/33	5B/1248
9.50pm	Willesden	Crewe		E	4.53am	-	BHSS North	26A/—	5B/1179	-	-
11.55pm	Northampton	Warrington		H	5.3am	5.30am	BHSS North	8B/3	2A/680	8B/3	5B/1290
12.2am	Euston	Crewe	189	A	5.7am	-	2	1B/29	5A/302	-	-
5.10am	Crewe Coal Yard	Crewe		K	5.20am	-	BHSS North	5B/1118	5B/1122	-	-
12.5am	Cardiff	Liverpool L St	215	A	4.10am	5.20am	1 South	84G/5	84G/68	84G/5	5A/588
4am	Oxley Sidings	Crewe		E	5.45am	-	Gresty Lane				
3.25am	Nuneaton	Crewe		F	5.59am	-	BHSS North	8A/27	5B/1184	-	-
1.55am	Kingswinford Jnt	Crewe		H	6.10am	-	Gresty Lane	84B/—	Crewe16	-	-
7.20pm	Penzance	Manchester Vic	467	A	6.13am	6.25am	1	9A/7	9A/279	9A/7	9A/279
6.30am	Crewe	Carlisle	367	C	-	6.30am	Down Sidings	-	-		
6.30am	Crewe	Winsford Jnt	17	K	-	6.30am	BHSS North	-	-	5B/1118	5B/1122
5.20am	Harlescott Sdgs	Hillhouse		H	6.40am	6.55am	Gresty Lane	5B/1033	9B/362	5B/1033	9B/362
6.40am	Crewe	Edge Hill		H	-	6.40am	BHSS North	-	-		
2.25am	Willesden	Crewe		D	6.54am	-	BHSS North	1A/7	2A/56	-	-
6.50am	Stoke on Trent	Crewe		B	7.20am	-	3	5A/78	5A/636	-	-
9.45pm	Stoneham	Crewe		C	7.21am	-	1			-	-
2.15am	Welham	Crewe		H	7.40am	-	BHSS North	2A/9	5B/1178	-	-
7.50am	Crewe	Blackpool North	35	A	-	7.50am	8 Bay	-	-	28A/65	5A/202
9.45pm	Swansea Victoria	Crewe		H	8am	-	Gresty Lane			-	-
8.50am	Crewe	Manchester L Rd		B	-	8.50am	1 North	-	-		
8.55am	Crewe	Harlescott Sdgs		H	-	8.55am	BHSS North	-	-		
9am	Crewe	Middlewich		K	-	9am	BHSS North	-	-	5B/1110	5B/1112

Time Dep	From	Destination	Rep No	Train Class	Crewe Arr	Crewe Dep	Platform or Yard	To Crewe from South Men Diag	To Crewe from South Loco Diag	From Crewe to North Men Diag	From Crewe to North Loco Diag
8.43am	Winsford Jnt	Crewe		K	9.10am	-	BHSS North	5B/1118	5B/1122	-	-
9.20am	Crewe	Chester		B	-	9.20am	1 North	-	-	6B/4	5A/643
7.30am	Oxley Sidings	Crewe		H	9.41am	-	Gresty Lane			-	-
9.20am	Shrewsbury	Crewe		B	10.19am	-	2 Bay			-	-
8.50am	Birmingham N St	Llandudno	231	A	10.27am	10.34am	2 North	3D/7	3D/173	3D/7	5A/698
9.15am	Wellington	Crewe		B	10.33am	-	2 South	Wellington	Crewe/4	-	-
10.35am	Crewe	Carnforth		F	-	10.35am	BHSS North	-	-	5B/1032	5B/1244
9.5am	Birmingham N St	Liverpool L St	229	A	10.37am	10.55am	1 North	9A/8	3D/167	8A/	9A/320
8.25am	Derby	Llandudno	119	A	10.41am	11.10am	2 North	7A/6	17A/264	5A/10	5A/654
10.50am	Crewe	Manchester L Rd	233	A	-	10.50am	1 South	-	-	5A/22	5A/618
6.30am	Euston	Carlisle	363	C	12.18pm	1.7pm	1	5A/19	5A/313	-	-
12.45pm	Crewe	Liverpool L St	369	A	-	12.45pm	Down Sidings	-	-		
11.15am	Birmingham N St	Glasgow Central	219	A	12.47pm	12.54pm	2	3D/	3D/168	5A/4	5A/137
10.50am	Derby	Crewe		B	1pm	-	5 Bay	84G/5	5A/629	-	-
12.10pm	Shrewsbury	Crewe		B	1.15pm	-	1 South			-	-
10am	Euston	Glasgow Central	63	A	1.22pm	1.32pm	2	66A/1	12A/63	66A/1	12A/63
10.10am	Euston	Blackpool Central	65	A	1.36pm	1.45pm	2	28A/60	10B/84	28A/60	10B/84
12pm	Birmingham N St	Blackpool Central	221	A	1.42pm	1.50pm	1 North	5B/1036	10B/209	5B/1036	10B/209
10.20am	Euston	Manchester L Rd	69	A	1.51pm	2pm	2				
10.30am	Euston	Liverpool L St	71	A	2.2pm	2.10pm	1				
12.10pm	B'ham Vauxhall	Crewe North Shed		G	*pass 2.22pm*			8A/—	5A/501	-	-
10.50am	Euston	Carlisle	77	A	2.48pm	2.57pm	2	8A/15	8A/245	8A/15	5A/220
2.55pm	Crewe	Llandudno	41	B	-	2.55pm	7 Bay	-	-	4B/1	5A/664
3.35pm	Crewe	Calveley		C	-	3.35pm	Down Yard	-	-	5A/33	5A/716
1.30pm	Oxley Sidings	Crewe		H	3.41pm	-	Gresty Lane	85A/—	Crewe/17	-	-
4pm	Crewe	Manchester L Rd	371	C	-	4pm	Down Sidings	-	-	3D/5	5A/619
2.10pm	Derby	Crewe		B	4.7pm	-	5 Bay	5A/97	5A/101	-	-
4.30pm	Crewe	Carlisle		D	-	4.30pm	Gresty Lane	-	-		
1.10pm	Euston	Blackpool Central	99	A	4.32pm	4/39	2	1B/12	1B/114	1B/12	1B/114
12.40pm	Cardiff	Manchester L Rd	265	A	4.45pm	5.15pm	1 North	9A/2	9A/332	9A/2	9A/332
1.20pm	Euston	Holyhead	101	A	4.55pm	5.35pm	2	1B/13	9A/215	9A/12	7A/210
5pm	Crewe	Carlisle		E	-	5pm	BHSS North	-	-	12A/23	5B/1301
12.50pm	Bristol	Liverpool L St	263	A	5.5pm	5.25pm	1 South	84G/4	5A/721		
5.30pm	Crewe	Carlisle		D	-	5.30pm	BHSS North	-	-	12A/300	5B/1299
3.55pm	Birmingham N St	Crewe	473	C	5.48pm	-	1	5A/11	5A/502	-	-
2.30pm	Euston	Liverpool L St	115	A	5.56pm	6.6pm	2	8A/—	1B/147	8A/—	1B/147
3.35pm	Euston	Blackpool Central	141	A	*pass 6.50pm*		2 Through	1B/12	28A/68	1B/12	28A/68
6.57pm	Crewe	Llandudno	55	A	-	6.57pm	7 Bay	-	-	7A/6	5A/667
5.55pm	Shrewsbury	Crewe		B	7.3pm	-	1 South	9A/14	9B/73	9A/14	9B/73
5.45pm	Birmingham N St	Liverpool L St	279	A	7.9pm	7.17pm	2 North	9A/—	3D/170	9A/—	5A/589
5.55pm	Birmingham N St	Manchester L Rd	281	A	7.21pm	7.29pm	2 South	9A/3	3D/171	1B/42	9A/207
5.37pm	Derby	Crewe		B	7.30pm	-	5 Bay			-	-
4.5pm	Euston	Blackpool Central	159	A	7.34pm	7.41pm	1	1B/17	1B/121	1B/17	1B/121
7.50pm	Crewe	Preston	361	C	-	7.50pm	Down Sidings	-	-		
7.50pm	Crewe	Carnforth		H	-	7.50pm	Gresty Lane	-	-	11A/1	5B/1272
4.40pm	Euston	Heysham	129	A	7.56pm	8.6pm	2	1B/20	5A/332	1B/20	11A/108
6.35pm	Birmingham N St	Crewe	43	A	8.8pm	-	1 South	9A/8	9A/324	-	-
8.18pm	Crewe	Manchester L Rd		B	-	8.18pm	7 Bay	-	-	9A/9	9A/620
5.20pm	Euston	Liverpool L St	137	A	8.22pm	8.29pm	2				
8.25pm	Crewe	Holyhead	197	A	-	8.25pm	1 North	-	-		
5.25pm	Hillmorton	Adswood Sidings		E	8.29pm	9.15pm	BHSS North	5B/1018	9A/629	5B/1018	9A/629
5.40pm	Euston	Manchester L Rd	139	A	8.36pm	8.42pm	2	1B/11	9A/230	1B/11	9A/230
8.55pm	Crewe	Abergavenny Jnt		E	-	8.55pm	BHSS North	-	-		
6.5pm	Euston	Preston	131	A	9.26pm	9.36pm	2				
3pm	Euston	Crewe	365	C	9.38pm	-	1	9A/—	5A/355	-	-
9.45pm	Crewe	Swansea		H	-	9.45pm	BHSS North	-	-	84G/104	5B/1484
6pm	Cardiff	Crewe	289	A	10.11pm	-	1 North	3B/151	84G/62	-	-
7.20pm	Euston	Inverness	151	A	10.16pm	10.29pm	2	5A/3	1B/230	5A/2	5A/135
10.25pm	Crewe	Adswood Sidings		F	-	10.25pm	Gresty Lane	-	-	5B/1035	5B/1329
5.45pm	Euston	Crewe	177	C	10.27pm	-	1	8A/—	1A/61	-	-
8.40pm	Derby	Crewe		B	10.30pm	-	5 Bay	84G/5	5A/630	-	-
5.40pm	Bristol	Crewe	301	A	10.50pm	-	1 South	5A/33	5A/716	-	-
7.30pm	Euston	Perth	153	A	10.56pm	11.15pm	3	8A/—	5A/271	5A/1	5A/130
7.55pm	Euston	Stranraer Harbour	155	A	11.7pm	11.20pm	2	1B/2	12A/54	1B/2	12A/54
11.15pm	Crewe	Neville Hill		H	-	11.15pm	Gresty Lane	-	-	84G/103	5B/1346
10.10pm	Birmingham N St	Crewe	297	A	11.29pm	-	2 Bay	5B/1050	5A/504	-	-
11.5pm	Stoke on Trent	Crewe		B	11.35pm	-	5 Bay			-	-
8.30pm	Euston	Glasgow Central	157	A	11/44	12am	2	5A/4	5A/279	5A/5	5A/139
8.45pm	Euston	Holyhead	161	A	*pass 11.51pm*		1	7C/	7C/	7C/	7C/
8.52pm	Euston	Holyhead	163	A	12am	12.11am	2				

Above:
Carlisle Kingmoor, No Date
Jubilee No 45553 *Canada*, a Manchester Longsight 9A shed engine, heads north passing Kingmoor shed. This could have been the 9.30am Manchester Victoria to Glasgow Central, reporting number C384. An unidentified Class 5 working a Class D freight plods south under clear signals. The signalpost is a Caledonian Railway standard design. *Eric Treacy*

Below:
Shap, No Date
The 'Patriot' class 4-6-0s attached to Carlisle and Crewe North were frequently diagrammed to work Class C fully fitted trains and were ideally suited to this kind of work. Here Carlisle Upperby 12B shed 'Patriot' No 45507 *Royal Tank Corps* works the 12.33pm Saturdays Excepted Garston to Carlisle Viaduct Yard, banked by an unidentified Tebay 11D Shed Fowler 2-6-4T. Class C trains were designated as 'Parcels, Fish, Fruit, Horse, Livestock, Meat, Milk, Pigeon or Perishable train composed entirely of vehicles conforming to coaching stock requirements'. *Derek Cross*

Up Direction — Monday Only

Commence 18 June 1951

Note: Italics under departure time denote passing time

Time Dep	From	Destination	Rep No	Train Class	Days Run	Crewe Arr	Crewe Dep	Platform or Yard	To Crewe from North Loco Diag	To Crewe from North Men Diag	From Crewe to South Loco Diag	From Crewe to South Men Diag
9.35pm	Blackpool Central	Euston	326	A	D	11.57pm	12.25am	5				
11.30pm	Manchester L Rd	Crewe	308	A	MO	12.9am	-	4			-	-
6.25pm	Glasgow Central	Euston	148	A	MO	12.25am	1237	4	5A/5	66A/15	5A/4	5A/266
11.35pm	Liverpool Lime St	Euston	140	A	MO	12.31am	12.51am	6				
12.40am	Crewe	Sudbury Junction		F	MO	-	12.40am	BHSS Middle	-	-	1A/7	5B/1177
7.55pm	Holyhead	Birmingham	170	A	D	11.30pm	12.45am	3			5A/44	5A/540
5.45pm	Glasgow Central	Euston	146	A	MO	12.48am	1.10am	5	5A/2	66A/10	1B/13	5A/274
11.55pm	Manchester L Rd	Crewe	150	A	MO	12.54am	-	4 North			-	-
11.45pm	Liverpool Lime St	Crewe	158	A	MO	12.54am	-	4			-	-
1am	Crewe	Leicester		E	MO	-	1am	BHSS Middle	-	-	5B/1054	5B/1192
9.50pm	York	Swansea	C487	A	MO	1.7am	2.15am	3			84G/1	5A/715
12.10am	Liverpool Lime St	Euston	152	A	D	1.13am	1.22am	5				
5.30am	Carlisle	Crewe		H	D	1.20am	-	BHSS Middle		5B/1275	-	-
1.25am	Crewe	Cardiff	176	A	D	-	1.25am	4	-	-		
12.35am	Manchester L Rd	Penzance	262	A	D	1.25am	2am	6			-	-
6.5pm	Carlisle	Crewe		H	MO	1.32am	-	Gresty Lane			-	-
12.33am	Warrington	Coventry		F	D	1.37am	1.42am	BHSS South			5B/1055	5B/1185
1.40am	Crewe	Nuneaton		H	SX	-	1.40am	BHSS South	-	-		
1.45am	Crewe	Bushbury		E	MO	-	1.45am	BHSS South	-	-	84G/102	5B/1217
10.45pm	Carnforth	Crewe		H	MO	2.25am	-	BHSS Middle	12A/331	5B/1299	-	-
1am	Mold Junction	Bushbury		H	D	2.30am	2.50am	BHSS Middle	5B/1055	6B/265	5B/1055	5B/1211
10.15pm	Carlisle	Broad Street	156	C	MO	2.32am	3am	5			1B/17	5A/286
1.35am	Warrington	Nuneaton		F	MO	2.36am	3.10am	BHSS Middle	8A/27	8B/570	8A/27	5B/1187
2.50am	Crewe	Stoke		B	D	-	2.50am	5 Bay	-	-		
12.55am	Holyhead	Euston	198	A	SX	3.5am	3.15am	3				
1.10am	Holyhead	Euston	4	A	SX	3.20am	3.30am	3				
9.25pm	Glasgow Central	Euston	10	A	D	3.22am	3.37am	4	12A/—	1B/102	12A/—	1B/102
2.50am	Manchester L Rd	Crewe	184	A	D	3.33am	-	5			-	-
1.57am	Edge Hill	Curzon St		F	MO	3.26am	3.37am	BHSS South	5A/40	8A/840	5A/40	5B/1221
8.25pm	Perth	Euston	12	A	D	3.40am	4am	4	5A/1	5A/134	5A/3	5A/281
10.10pm	Glasgow Central	Euston	6	A	D		*pass 3.50am*	Up Through				
2.50am	Mold Junction	Rugby		E	D	3.53am	4.8am	BHSS South	2A/515	6B/266	2A/515	5B/1159
4.2am	Crewe	Shrewsbury		H	MO	-	4.2am	Gresty Lane	-	-	5B/1001	84G/194
4.10am	Crewe	Stoke		A	D	-	4.10am	5	-	-	5A/40	5A/626
4.10am	Crewe	Whitchurch		F	MO	-	4.10am	BHSS Middle	-	-	5B/1055	5A/660
8.55pm	Perth	Euston	14	A	MO	4.10am	4.27am	4	1A/11	12A/102	1B/11	5A/290
10.25pm	Glasgow Central	Euston	224	A	D		*pass 4.20am*	Up Through	1A/3	12A/56	1A/3	12A/56
3am	Hooton	Newcastle Junction		F	MO	4.20am	4.32am	North Staffs Sdgs	86K/42	6C/368	86K/42	5B/1378
3am	Bamfurlong	Bushbury		E	MO	4.38am	4.45am	6	5B/1032	10A/654	5B/1032	5B/1200
4.50am	Crewe	Worcester		H	D	-	4.50am	Gresty Lane	-	-		84B/—
11.15pm	Glasgow Central	Birmingham	18	A	D	5am	5.14am	5	66A/2	12/81	5A/10	5A/549
5am	Crewe	Willesden HL		E	SX	-	5am	BHSS Middle	-	-	5B/1037	5B/1166
5.5am	Crewe	Stafford		H	MO	-	5.5am	BHSS Middle	-	-	1A/590	5B/1197
5.7am	Crewe	Derby		B	SX	-	5.7am	6 Bay	-	-	9A/14	5A/627
5.20am	Crewe	Newcastle Junction	3	H	D	-	5.20am	North Staffs Sdgs	-	-		
9.10pm	Carlisle	Crewe		H	MO	5.25am	-	BHSS Middle			-	-
12.40am	Copley Hill	Crewe		H	MO	5.35am	-	BHSS Middle	25G/301	5B/1331	-	-
5.40am	Crewe	Birmingham	200	A	D	-	5.40am	4 Bay	-	-	2A/—	5A/541
3.40am	Heaton Norris Jnt	Shrewsbury Coleham		H	MO	5.45am	6.29am	Gresty Lane		5B/1329		
4.15am	Speke Sidings	Crewe		H	MO	5.45am	-	BHSS Middle	6C/201	5B/1393	-	-
3.25am	Birkenhead Docks	Grange Junction		J	SX	5.47am	5.55am	North Staffs Sdgs				
4.15am	Garston	Crewe		H	MO	5.47am	-	BHSS	6C/201	5B/1393	-	-
5.50am	Crewe	Betley Road		K	D	-	5.50am	BHSS Middle	-	-	5B/1131	5B/1131
3.40am	Heaton Norris	Shrewsbury Coleham		H	MO	5.50am	6.29am	Gresty Lane	5B/1035	5B/1329	5B/1035	84G/193
2.30am	Bescot	Warrington		H	MO	5.57am	6.50am	BHSS North				5B/1298
6.5am	Crewe	Sudbury Jnt		H	MO	-	6.5am	BHSS Middle	-	-	5B/1018	5B/1164
6.5am	Crewe	Wellington		B	D	-	6.5am	3 Bay	-	-	Well	Crewe/1
1.30am	Copley Hill	Bushbury		H	MO	6.7am	7am	BHSS Middle				
6.10am	Crewe	Whitchurch		G	SX	-	6.10am	Station	-	-		
4.15am	Stott Lane Sidings	Bushbury		H	D-Q	6.10am	6.15am	Up Through	10C/13	10C/535	10C/13	3A/192
6.25am	Crewe	Longport Junction	84	K	D	-	6.25am	North Staffs Sdgs	-	-		
5.40am	Longsight	Crewe		C	D	6.35am	-	Up Through			-	-
6.35am	Crewe	Nantwich	38	K	D	-	6.35am	BHSS North	-	-	5B/1126	5B/1126
3.55am	Mold Junction	Crewe		H	MO	6.39am	-	BHSS Middle	5B/1053	5B/1461	-	-
6.45am	Crewe	Derby		B	D	-	6.45am	5 Bay	-	-	84G/2	5A/628
6.50am	Crewe	Birmingham		B	D	-	6.50am	5	-	-	5A/33	5A/553

Time Dep	From	Destination	Rep No	Train Class	Days Run	Crewe Arr	Crewe Dep	Platform or Yard	To Crewe from North Loco Diag	To Crewe from North Men Diag	From Crewe to South Loco Diag	From Crewe to South Men Diag
6.55am	Crewe	Oxley Sidings		H	D	-	6.55am	Gresty Lane	-	-		84B/—
3.22am	Carnforth	Bushbury		H	SX	6.55am	7.55am	BHSS Middle	5B/1032	5B/1239	5B/1032	5B/1213
5am	Birkenhead	Longport Junction		F	MO	7am	7.10am	North Staffs Sdgs	25D/124	6C/369	25D/124	5B/1376
7.5am	Crewe	Wellington		K	D	-	7.5am	Gresty Lane	-	-	84B/—	Crewe/10
5.50am	Manchester L Rd	Crewe		B	D	7.8am	-	6			-	-
5am	Stott Lane Sidings	Crewe		H	D	7.10am	-	BHSS Middle	5B/1005	10C/534	-	-
5am	Warrington	Crewe		H	MO	7.16am	-	North Staffs Sdgs	11A/250	5B/1280	-	-
6.36am	Chester	Crewe		B	D	7.19am	-	4	5A/39	6A/259	-	-
6.50am	Northwich	Crewe		B	D	7.25am	-	10 Bay	5A/120	5A/120	-	-
7.32am	Crewe	Shrewsbury		B	D	-	7.32am	5	-	-	84G/	84G/63
5.30am	Preston	Crewe		B	D	7.33am	-	5	10B/4	5A/209	-	-
2.55am	Crofton West	Crewe		J	MO	7.37am	-	BHSS Middle	5B/1033	5B/1345	-	-
7.30am	Crewe Works	Basford Hall		K	D	*pass 7.40am*		BHSS Middle	5B/1086	5B/2076	5B/1086	5B/2076
7.45am	Crewe	Bescot		H	D	-	7.45am	BHSS Middle	-	-	5B/1050	5B/1218
7.50am	Crewe	Euston	24	A	D	-	7.50am	3	-	-	5A/5	5A/299
8.3am	Crewe	Whitchurch		G	D	-	8.3am	North Shed	-	-		
8.10am	Crewe	Derby		B	D	-	8.10am	6 Bay	-	-	5A/97	5A/97
8.10am	Crewe	Peterborough		E	D	-	8.10am	BHSS Middle	-	-	5B/1038	5B/1172
8.2am	Carriage Works	Crewe		G	SX	8.11am	-	Gresty Lane			-	-
8.15am	Crewe	Whitemoor Sidings		E	D	-	8.15am	BHSS Middle	-	-		5B/1172
3.10am	Carlisle	Crewe		D	D	8.20am	-	Gresty Lane	5B/1038	5B/1246	-	-
7.15am	Manchester L Rd	Crewe		B	D	8.28am	-	4			-	-
6.30am	Heysham	Euston	32	A	D	8.31am	8.42am	5	1B/20	11A/104	1B/20	5A/305
8.37am	Crewe	Shrewsbury		B	D	-	8.37am	4 Bay	-	-		
6.30am	Morecambe	Crewe	272	A	D	8.44am	-	5		5A/205	-	-
6.30am	Llandudno	Euston	302	A	D	8.45am	9am	3	4B/1	6A/247	4B/1	5A/303
9am	Crewe	Whitchurch		K	SX	-	9am	BHSS Middle	-	-	5B/1056	5B/1460
8.5am	Manchester L Rd	Crewe	30	A	D	8.55am	-	4 North			-	-
8.33am	Northwich	Crewe		B	D	9am	-	5	5A/120	5A/120	-	-
8am	Liverpool Lime St	Birmingham	34	A	D	9.2am	9.10am	4	8A/15	8A/266	8A/15	5A/555
6.35am	Bamfurlong	Crewe		H	SX	9.5am	-	Gresty Lane	1A/525	5B/1239	-	-
9.8am	Crewe	Derby		A	D	-	9.8am	5 Bay	-	-		
8.20am	Liverpool Lime St	Euston	36	A	D	9.10am	9.18am	3				
9.15am	Crewe	Badnall Wharf	28	K	SX	-	9.15am	BHSS Middle	-	-	5B/1110	5B/1110
3.45am	Crofton West Jnt	Crewe		J	MO	9.25am	-	BHSS Middle			-	-
9.30am	Crewe	Wellington		B	D	-	9.30am	3 Bay	-	-		
9.45am	Crewe	Oxley Sidings		H	D	-	9.45am	Gresty Lane	-	-		
8.50am	Runcorn	Crewe South Shed		G	MO	9.50am	-	South Shed			-	-
8.42am	Manchester L Rd	Crewe		B	D	9.54am	-	5			-	-
7.25am	Heysham	Crewe	26	A	D	9.55am	-	4	11A/6	28A/75	-	-
9.55am	Crewe	Oxley		K	D	-	9.55am	Gresty Lane	-	-		84B/—
9.15am	Manchester L Rd	Plymouth	212	A	D	*pass 10.3am*		Up Through		5A/605		5A/605
9.5am	Liverpool Lime St	Plymouth	208	A	SX	10.4am	10.20am	4	84G/5	5A/594	5A/1	5A/702
8am	Blackpool Central	Euston	296	A	SX	10.9am	10.18am	3	1B/12	1B/118	1B/12	1B/118
9.25am	Manchester L Rd	Swansea High St	210	A	D	10.14am	10.30am	5			9A/10	5A/718
8.56am	Northwich	Crewe	25	K	D	10.16am	-	BHSS Middle		5B/1368	-	-
9.45am	Manchester L Rd	Euston	58	A	D	*pass 10.27am*		Up Through	9A/—	1B/167/72	9A/—	1B/167/72
7.30am	Holyhead	Euston	48	A	D	10.28am	10.35am	3				
10.30am	Crewe	Stoke	89	H	D	-	10.30am	North Staffs Sdgs	-	-		
4.5am	Carlisle	Sudbury Junction		D	SX	10.43am	10.50am	BHSS South			5B/1051	5B/1160
10.10am	Liverpool Lime St	Euston	54	A	D	*pass 10.55am*		Up Through				
10.10am	Manchester L Rd	Birmingham	214	A	SX	10.57am	11.12am	4 South				
11am	Crewe	Oxley Sidings		H	SX	-	11am	Gresty Lane	-	-	85A/—	Crewe/11
10.15am	Liverpool Lime St	Crewe	62	A	SX	11.1am	-	4 North	9A/—	8A/310	-	-
9.10am	Llandudno	Euston	56	A	SX	11.06am	11.28am	3	1B/19	7A/155	1B/19	5A/308
9.40am	Heaton Norris	Bushbury		H	SX	11.7am	11.15am	BHSS South	5B/1018	9B/356	5B/1018	5B/1208
10.25am	Manchester L Rd	Bournemouth	220	A	SX	11.8am	11.20am	5			9A/—	5A/564
11.15am	Crewe South Shed	Crewe NSS		J	D	-	11.15am	South Shed	-	-		
11.20am	Crewe	Derby		B	D	-	11.20am	6 Bay	-	-	9A/14	5A/623
10am	Runcorn	Wichnor		J	MO	11.24am	11.38am	BHSS South	5B/1040	5B/1395	5B/1040	5B/1212
9.35am	Northwich	Crewe		K	D	11.25am	-	BHSS Middle	5B/1017	5B/1368	-	-
11.30am	Crewe	Etruria Junction	84	K	D	-	11.30am	North Staffs Sdgs	-	-		
6.5am	Carlisle	Crewe	274	B	D	11.40am	-	5	12A/13	5A/200	-	-
11.40am	Crewe Coal Yard	Crewe	17	K	SX	11.50am	-	BHSS Middle	5B/1118	5B/1118	-	-
11.10am	Liverpool Lime St	Euston	112	A	D	11.56am	12.2pm	4				
12pm	Crewe	Oxley Sidings		H	D	-	12pm	Gresty Lane	-	-	84B/—	Crewe/12
12.1pm	Crewe	Shrewsbury		B	D	-	12.1pm	4 Bay	-	-		
10.50am	Runcorn	Alsager Junction		F	SX	*pass 12.1pm*		North Staffs Sdgs				
10.20am	Mold Junction	Crewe		H	MO	12.8pm	-	North Staffs Sdgs	5B/1041	5A/668	-	-
12.10pm	Crewe	Shrewsbury		B	D	-	12.10pm		-	-	5A/33	5A/709
10am	Blackpool Central	Euston	330	A	SX	12.10pm	12.18pm	4	1B/17	1B/123	1B/17	1B/123

Time Dep	From	Destination	Rep No	Train Class	Days Run	Crewe Arr	Crewe Dep	Platform or Yard	To Crewe from North Loco Diag	To Crewe from North Men Diag	From Crewe to South Loco Diag	From Crewe to South Men Diag
8.25am	Holyhead	Crewe	72	A	SX	12.13pm	-	3	7C/12	5A/656	-	-
11.10am	Manchester L Rd	Crewe		B	D	12.20pm	-	6			-	-
11.36am	Garston Dam Bdge	Crewe		D	SX	12.43pm	-	North Staffs Sdgs			-	-
10.55am	Edge Hill	Crewe		H	SX	12.44pm	-	North Staffs Sdgs			-	-
11.55am	Manchester L Rd	Plymouth	228	A	D	12.45pm	1.10pm	4				
11.17am	Jubilee Sidings	Crewe		J	SX	12.45pm	-	BHSS Middle	26A/633	5B/1327	-	-
8.20am	Carlisle	Euston	74	A	D	12.51pm	1pm	3	1B/1	12A/91	1B/1	5A/323
12.39pm	Rookery Bridge	Crewe	23	G	SX	12.54pm	-	North Staffs Sdgs	5B/1053	5B/1367	-	-
12.56pm	Crewe	Wellington		B	D	-	12.56pm	3 Bay	-	-		
11.40am	Liverpool Lime St	Rugby Midland	84	A	D	12.59pm	1.8pm	5	8A/13	8A/267	8A/13	5A/565
1.5pm	Crewe	Betley Road		K	SX	-	1.5pm	BHSS Middle	-	-	5B/1132	5B/1132
1.15pm	Crewe	Pratt Sidings	50	J	D	-	1.15pm	North Staffs Sdgs	-	-		
5.30am	Carlisle	Crewe		H	SX	1.20pm	-	BHSS Middle	12A/332	5B/1275	-	-
11.55am	Bamfurlong	Crewe		F	SX	1.25pm	-	BHSS Middle	10A/306	5B/1241	-	-
1.30pm	Crewe	Oxley Sidings		F	D	-	1.30pm	Gresty Lane	-	-		84B/—
1.35pm	Crewe	Derby		B	D	-	1.35pm	6 Bay	-	-	5A/41	5A/637
11.50am	Edge Hill	Shrewsbury		F	SX	1.42pm	1.47pm	Gresty Lane		5A/582		
5.15am	Carlisle	Bushbury		E	D	1.40pm	1.50pm	BHSS South				
12.10pm	Edge Hill	Bushbury		F	SX	1.50pm	2pm	BHSS Middle	3B/151	5A/593	3B/151	5B/1210
1.45pm	Crewe Works	Basford Hall		K	D	-	1.55pm	BHSS Middle	5B/1086	5B/2077	5B/1086	5B/2077
1.55pm	Crewe	Willesden Junction	232	C	FSX	-	1.55pm		-	-	2A/—	5A/394
7.50am	Holyhead	Crewe	76	C	SX	1.58pm	-	5	9A/12	5A/650	-	-
12.40pm	Garston Dam Bdge	Crewe		D	SX	2pm	-	BHSS Middle			-	-
6.50am	Carlisle	Crewe		H	SX	2.10pm	-	Gresty Lane	12A/23	5B/1293	-	-
10.50am	Windermere	Euston	86	A	SX	2.15pm	2.23pm	4	1B/12	10B/81	1B/12	10B/81
9.30am	Neville Hill	Bushbury		H	MO	2.21pm	2.55pm	BHSS South	25G/337	5B/1352	25G/337	5B/1214
2.20pm	Crewe	Chaddesden		H	D	-	2.25pm	North Staffs Sdgs	-	-		16A/626
1.18pm	Manchester L Rd	Crewe		B	D	2.28pm	-	4			-	-
12.50pm	Mold Junction	Alsager Junction		F	SX	-	2.38pm	North Staffs Sdgs				
1pm	Edge Hill	Crewe		H	SX	2.44pm	-	Gresty Lane			-	-
2pm	Liverpool Lime St	Euston	92	A	D	*pass 2.45pm*		Up Through				
12.35pm	Ellesmere Port	Egginton Junction		F	MWFO	2.47pm	2.52pm	North Staffs Sdgs				
1.30pm	Edge Hill	Willesden HL		D	SX	2.50pm	2.50pm	Station		5A/585		
9.30am	Glasgow Central	Birmingham	98	A	D	2.55pm	3.15pm	4	5A/4	5A/138	5A/10	5A/550
1.10pm	Mold Junction	Crewe		F	SX	2.57pm	-	BHSS Middle			-	-
1.25pm	Runcorn	Alsager Junction		F	SX	3.3pm	3.8pm	North Staffs Sdgs	5B/1019	8C/247	5B/1019	8C/247
3.5pm	Crewe	Whitchurch		G	SX	-	3.5pm	Gresty Lane	-	-		
10am	Glasgow Central	Euston	96	A	D	*pass 3.8pm*		Up Through	66A/1	12A/60	66A/1	12A/60
11am	Portmadoc	Euston	100	A	SX	3.15pm	3.25pm	3	1B/17	5A/318	1B/17	5A/318
3.26pm	Crewe	Stoke	48	K	SX	-	3.26pm	North Staffs Sdgs	-	-		
3.28pm	Crewe	Shrewsbury		B	D	-	3.28pm	4 Bay	-	-	84G/22	5A/724
8.26am	Heaton Norris	Crewe		K	D	3.30pm	-	BHSS Middle	5B/1020	5B/1333	-	-
2pm	Edge Hill	Nuneaton		F	SX	3.32pm	3.40pm	BHSS South	5A/40	5A/585	5A/40	5B/1186

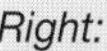

Right:
Heaton Norris, 1951
Horwich 'Crab' 2-6-0 No 42828 draws past No 1 signalbox with a Manchester London Road train. Perhaps the fireman is having trouble, hence the black smoke. The length of train would suggest that the 'Crab' has been pressed into service at short notice, deputising for another loco, since the train is a Class A working.
N. W. F. Dyckhoff

Time Dep	From	Destination	Rep No	Train Class	Days Run	Crewe Arr	Crewe Dep	Platform or Yard	To Crewe from North Loco Diag	To Crewe from North Men Diag	From Crewe to South Loco Diag	From Crewe to South Men Diag
10.6am	Glasgow Central	Euston	106	A	D	3.32pm	3.49pm	4	1B/4	12A/98	1B/4	1B/236
1.25pm	Holyhead	Euston	88	A	SX	3.33pm	3.41pm	3				
2.10pm	Garston Dam Bdge	Crewe		D	SX	3.35pm	-	BHSS Middle			-	-
3.40pm	Crewe	Alsager Junction	89	J	D	-	3.40pm	North Staffs Sdgs	-	-		
1.40pm	Llandudno	Derby	124	A	D	3.51pm	4.2pm	6			5A/91	5A/91
3.5pm	Manchester L Rd	Birmingham	236	A	D	3.54pm	4.7pm	5	2A/—	5A/607	2A/—	5A/561
3pm	Liverpool Lime St	Cardiff	234	A	SX	3.55pm	4.9pm	3				
3.55pm	Crewe	Oxley Sidings		H	SX	-	3.55pm	Gresty Lane	-	-		84B/—
3.57pm	Crewe	Birmingham	186	A	SX	-	3.57pm	4 North	-	-		
8.55am	Perth	Euston	110	A	MFSO	4.6pm	4.15pm	4	1B/1	12A/65	1B/1	12A/65
10.50am	Workington	Euston	254	A	MFO	4.18pm	4.26pm	4				
4.18pm	Crewe	Bushbury		H	SX	-	4.18pm	BHSS Middle	-	-	5B/1004	5B/1206
4.20pm	Crewe	Leek		B	D	-	4.20pm	6 Bay	-	-		
2.54pm	Garston Dam Bdge.	Crewe		D	SX	4.20pm	-	BHSS Middle			-	-
8.35am	Carlisle	Crewe	356	C	SX	4.28pm	-	Up Through	5A/19	10A/151	-	-
4.30pm	Crewe	Radway Green	93	G	D	-	4.30pm	North Staffs Sdgs	-	-		
4.20pm	Manchester M'field	Crewe		B	D	4.39pm	-	6			-	-
2.25pm	Waverton	Crewe	36	K	SX	4.41pm	-	BHSS Middle	5B/1037	5B/1462	-	-
2.40pm	Llandudno	Crewe	140	A	D	4.50pm	-	3	7A/1	7A/160	-	-
1.30pm	Barrow	Crewe	266	A	FX	4.51pm	-	5	5A/11	11B/108	-	-
3.15pm	Edge Hill	Bushbury		H	SX	4.53pm	4.55pm	BHSS South				
4.10pm	Liverpool Lime St	Euston	114	A	D	4.56pm	5.2pm	4				
4.50pm	Calveley	Crewe	132	C	SX	5.6pm	-	-	5A/55	5A/909	-	-
10.50am	Copley Hill	Crewe		H	SX	5.8am	-	Gresty Lane	5B/1034	9B/360	-	-
5.10pm	Crewe	Stafford via Stoke		B	D	-	5.10pm	6 Bay	-	-	84G/5	5A/624
5.10pm	Crewe	Wellington		B	D	-	5.10pm	3 Bay	-	-	Well	Crewe/3
2.50pm	Wyre Dock	Broad Street		C	SX	5.10pm	5.40pm	Up Through	5A/33	5A/206	1A/1	1A/62
5.15pm	Crewe	Willesden HL		E	SX	-	5.15pm	BHSS Middle	-	-	1A/525	5B/1173
4.35pm	Manchester L Rd	Birmingham	238	A	D	5.17pm	5.30pm	4 South				
4.17pm	Liverpool Lime St	Crewe	162	A	D	5.20pm	-	4 North	5A/23	8A/255	-	-
3.5pm	Speke Junction	Alsager Junction		F	SX	5.20pm	5.30pm	North Staffs Sdgs				
5.22pm	Crewe	Madeley	39	J	SX	-	5.22pm	BHSS Middle	-	-	17B/25	5B/1194
5.25pm	Crewe	Shrewsbury		B	D	-	5.25pm	4 Bay	-	-	8A/5	5A/701
3.50pm	Garston Dam Bdge	Crewe		D	SX	5.30pm	-	BHSS Middle			-	-
5.35pm	Crewe	Oxley Sidings		H	SX	-	5.35pm	Gresty Lane	-	-		84B/—
2.20pm	Port Sunlight	Crewe		H	SX	5.38pm	-	North Staffs Sdgs	5B/1004	6C/364	-	-
5.15pm	Northwich	Crewe		B	SX	5.42pm	-	3	5A/121	5A/121	-	-
4.28pm	Manchester L Rd	Crewe		B	D	5.52pm	-	5			-	-
5.10pm	Chester	Crewe		B	D	5.54pm	-	3	5A/39	6A/255	-	-
5.55pm	Crewe	Stafford		B	D	-	5.55pm	6 Bay	-	-	2A/—	5A/382
5.52pm	Carriage Works	Stoke		B	SX	6pm	6.5pm	6	5B/1055	5A/625	5B/1055	5A/625
5.20pm	Warrington	Crewe		B	D	6.04pm	-	5	5B/1039	5A/208	-	-
6.10pm	Crewe	Shrewsbury		B	D	-	6.10pm	4 Bay	-	-	12A/13	5A/710
5.25pm	Liverpool Lime St	Euston	122	A	D	6.10pm	6.15pm	4	1B/6	1B/141	1B/6	1B/141
5.11pm	Manchester L Rd	Crewe		B	D	6.18pm	-	6	84G/2	5A/603	-	-
2.40pm	Holyhead	Birmingham	278	A	SX	6.25pm	7.10pm	3				
5.05pm	Garston Dam Bdge	Crewe		D	SX	6.30pm	-	BHSS Middle			-	-
5.50pm	Manchester L Rd	Euston	130	A	D	6.33pm	6.38pm	4	9A/—	1B/187	9A/—	1B/187
6.35pm	Crewe	Derby	B	D		6.35pm	-	5 Bay	-	-		
6.35pm	Crewe	Rugby		H	D	-	6.35pm	BHSS Middle	-	-	2A/8	5B/1174
6.40pm	Crewe	Shrewsbury	312	C	SX	-	6.40pm	Up Sidings	-	-	5A/33	5A/712
4.20pm	Edge Hill	Crewe		H	SX	6.50pm	-	North Staffs Sdgs	12A/17	5A/592	-	-
1.30pm	Glasgow Central	Euston	126	A	SX	6.55pm	7.3pm	4	1B/2	66A/12	1B/2	5A/329
5.40pm	Liverpool Lime St	Crewe		B	D	7.5pm	-	5			-	-
6pm	Manchester L Rd	Crewe		B	SX	7.9pm	-	6			-	-
6.50pm	Northwich	Crewe		B	SX	7.16pm	-	10 Bay	5A/121	5A/121	-	-
7.25pm	Crewe	Alsager Junction	83	K	D	-	7.25pm	North Staffs Sdgs	-	-		
7.25pm	Crewe	Rugby		H	D	-	7.25pm	BHSS Middle	-	-	5B/1017	2B/323
5.40pm	Dundas Sidings	Normacot Junction		F	D	7.28pm	7.40pm	North Staffs Sdgs	5B/1052	5A/671	5B/1052	5E/98
5.5pm	Blackpool Central	Euston	136	A	D	7.30pm	7.39pm	4	28A/1	28A/66	28A/1	28A/66
6.25pm	Manchester M'field	Crewe		B	D	7.40pm	-	6	12B/—	5A/600	-	-
7.50pm	Crewe	Wellington		B	FX	-	7.50pm	3 Bay	-	-	Whit/16	Whit/16
7.10pm	Sandbach	Crewe	21	K	SX	7.50pm	-	BHSS Middle	5B/1119	5B/1119	-	-
7.55pm	Crewe	Longport Junction	89	K	D	-	7.55pm	North Staffs Sdgs	-	-		
7.10pm	Manchester L Rd	Cardiff	246	A	D	7.58pm	8.33pm	5		9A/11	9A/254	
7.20pm	Chester	Crewe		B	D	8pm	-	3	7A/11	6A/179	-	-
7.5pm	Liverpool Lime St	Birmingham	250	A	SX	8pm	8.17pm	4	8A/—	8A/276	8A/—	5A/562
6.40pm	Folly Lane	Crewe		F	SX	8pm	-	BHSS Middle	5B/1001	8D/237	-	-
8.5pm	Crewe	Oxley Sidings		H	D	-	8.5pm	Gresty Lane	-	-	84F/—	Crewe/14
6.25pm	Edge Hill	Crewe		F	D	8.10pm	-	Gresty Lane	8A/15	5A/581	-	-

Right:
Clifton & Lowther, 1950
Clifton & Lowther station, located between Shap and Penrith, was closed to passengers on 4 July 1938 and lost its freight services on 1 June 1951. 'Patriot' Class 4-6-0 No 45537 *Private E. Sykes, VC* from Preston 10B shed storms north through the site of the station with a Class B local passenger train. This was possibly the 12.50pm Saturdays Only Oxenholme to Carlisle. *E. D. Bruton*

									To Crewe from North		From Crewe to South	
Time Dep	**From**	**Destination**	**Rep No**	**Train Class**	**Days Run**	**Crewe Arr**	**Crewe Dep**	**Platform or Yard**	**Loco Diag**	**Men Diag**	**Loco Diag**	**Men Diag**
8.16pm	Crewe	Shrewsbury		B	SX	-	8.16pm		-	-	9A/412	5A/705
6.15pm	Llandudno	Derby	80	A	SX	8.16pm	8.20pm	6		5D/101		5D/101
8.20pm	Crewe	Bristol	248	A	D	-	8.20pm	5	-	-		
7pm	Garston Dam Bdge	Crewe		D	SX	8.20pm	-	BHSS Middle			-	-
7.57pm	Winsford Junction	Crewe	35	K	SX	8.31pm	-	BHSS Middle	5B/1127	5B/1127	-	-
8pm	Middlewich	Crewe	26	K	SX	8.34pm	-	BHSS Middle	5B/1063	5B/1364	-	-
7.20pm	Liverpool Lime St	Crewe		B	D	8.41pm	-	5	8A/27	5A/579	-	-
6.3pm	Ellesmere Port	Etruria Junction		F	D	-	8.45pm	North Staffs Sdgs				
8.50pm	Crewe	Wellington		B	D	-	8.50pm	2 Bay	-	-		
8.50pm	Crewe	Euston	306	C	D	-	8.50pm	Up Through	-	-	5A/24	5A/385
7.32pm	Garston Dam Bdge	Willesden HL		D	SX	*pass 8.53pm*		BHSS South				
8.55pm	Crewe	Newcastle Junction		H	SX	-	8.55pm	North Staffs Sdgs	-	-	5B/1111	5B/1111
4.42pm	Carlisle	Willesden HL		C	SX	8.59pm	9.20pm	4	5B/1037	10A/104	5B/1033	5B/1161
9.18pm	Crewe	Shrewsbury		B	D	-	9.18pm	5	-	-	5B/1032	5A/723
7.15pm	Birkenhead	Birmingham C St		E	SX	9.20pm	9.58pm	BHSS Middle	3D/3	6B/283	3D/3	3B/326
9.25pm	Crewe	Newcastle Junction		H	D	-	9.25pm	North Staffs Sdgs	-	-		5B/1111
8.15pm	Manchester L Rd	Crewe		B	D	9.26pm	-	6			-	-
7.45pm	Ravenshead	Willesden HL		E	SX	9.28pm	9.48pm	BHSS South	8B/3	10E/317	8B/3	1A/817
9.35pm	Crewe	Birmingham	90	C	D	-	9.35pm	Up Sidings	-	-		
9.35pm	Crewe	Worcester		F	D	-	9.35pm	Gresty Lane	-	-		84B/—
8.30pm	Edge Hill	Camden		D	SX	*pass 9.39pm*		Up Through				
7pm	Wyre Dock	Broad Street		C	SX	9.32pm	10pm	4	5B/1039	10A/197	9A/11	5B/1134
9.42pm	Crewe	Abergavenny		E	FSX	-	9.42pm	BHSS Middle	-	-	86K/42	5B/1476
7.38pm	Wyre Dock	Crewe		C	SX	9.50pm	-	5			-	-
9.55pm	Crewe	Stoke		B	D	-	9.55pm	5 Bay	-	-		
8.50pm	Manchester L Rd	Oxley Sidings		D	SX	9.55pm	10.24pm	Gresty Lane	2A/4	5A/604	2A/4	Crewe/16
9.10pm	Warrington	Camden		D	SX	*pass 10.3pm*		Up Through				
6.40pm	Blackpool	Crewe		D	SX	10.7pm	-	BHSS Middle	5B/1036	10B/560	-	-
8.20pm	Llandudno	Crewe	406	A	SX	10.18pm	-	5			-	-
8.50pm	Edge Hill	Birmingham C St		E	SX	10.18pm	10.23pm	BHSS South	3D/2	8A/841	3D/2	5B/1205
12.35pm	Perth	Willesden Junction	38	A	MO	10.23pm	10.30pm	Up Through	8A/32	5A/151	5A/22	5A/391
8.15pm	Northwich	Crewe	27	K	D	10.32pm	-	BHSS Middle			-	-
9.50pm	Liverpool Lime St	Euston	304	A	SX	10.44pm	10.49pm	3				
9.37pm	Manchester L Rd	Crewe		B	D	10.46pm	-	4			-	-
8.30pm	Blackpool North	Crewe	418	A	MFO	10.50pm	-	5	28A/64	5A/225	-	-
9.45pm	Warrington	Crewe		H	SX	10.52pm	-	North Staffs Sdgs	5A/42	8B/76	-	-
9.5pm	Edge Hill	Crewe		E	SX	10.55pm	-	Gresty Lane			-	-
10.55pm	Crewe	Stoke	41	H	SX	-	10.55pm	North Staffs Sdgs	-	-		
10.58pm	Crewe	Swansea		F	FSX	-	10.58pm	BHSS Middle	-	-	84G/104	5B/1475
8.30pm	Kendal	Euston	400	A	SX	11.1pm	11.27pm	4			5A/23	5A/250
11.5pm	Crewe	Burton		H	SX	-	11.5pm	BHSS Middle	-	-		
9.30pm	Manchester	Shrewsbury		F	SX	11.8pm	12.58am	Gresty Lane	84G/2	5A/601	84G/2	84G/64
10.10pm	Liverpool Lime St	Crewe	142	A	D	11.25pm	-	5	5A/44	5A/598	-	-
10.27pm	Manchester L Rd	Crewe	144	A	D	11.29pm	-	6			-	-
7.35pm	Holyhead	Birmingham	170	A	D	11.35pm	12.45am	3		5A/102	6A/13	
10.33pm	Manchester L Rd	Euston	138	A	SX	*pass 11.36pm*		Up Through	9A/—	1B/162	9A/—	1B/162
12.10pm	Aberdeen	Broad Street	392	C	FSX	11.40pm	11.52pm	Up Through			5A/21	1B/201
9.50pm	Edge Hill	Northampton		E	SX	11.48pm	12.40am	BHSS Middle				
11.18pm	Chester	Camden		D	SX	11.59pm	12.28am	BHSS Middle	5A/39	6A/132	5A/39	6A/132
10.15pm	Edge Hill	Northampton		E	SX	12.1am	1am	North Staffs Sdgs				
8.30pm	Windermere	Euston	370	A	D	12.3am	12.25am	3				

Up Direction — Tuesdays to Fridays

Commence 18 June 1951

Note: Italics under departure time denote passing time

Time Dep	From	Destination	Rep No	Train Class	Days Run	Crewe Arr	Crewe Dep	Platform or Yard	To Crewe from North Loco Diag	To Crewe from North Men Diag	From Crewe to South Loco Diag	From Crewe to South Men Diag
7.35pm	Holyhead	Birmingham	170	A	D	11.35pm	12.45am	3		5A/104	5A/44	5A/540
9.50pm	Edge Hill	Northampton		E	MX	11.48pm	12.40am	BHSS Middle	2A/3	8A/814	2A/3	5B/1188
10.15pm	Edge Hill	Nottingham		E	SX	12.1am	1am	North Staffs Sdgs	8A/505	8A/818	8A/505	5A/631
8.30pm	Windermere	Euston	370	A	MX	12.3am	12.25am	5	1B/18	10B/96	1B/18	10B/96
12.5am	Crewe	Birmingham	342	C	MX	-	12.5am	6	-	-		
10.8pm	Manchester L Rd	Birmingham C St		E	SX	12.7am	12.14am	BHSS South	9A/21	9A/640	9A/21	3B/313
11.30pm	Manchester L Rd	Crewe	308	A	D	12.9am	-	4	5A/98	5A/98	-	-
6.25pm	Glasgow Central	Euston	148	A	D	12.25am	12.37am	4	5A/5	66A/15	5A/4	5A/266
5.15pm	Carlisle	Crewe		D	SX	12.35am	-	North Staffs Sdgs	12A/17	5B/1245	-	-
5.40pm	Glasgow Central	Euston	146	A	MX	12.41am	1.10am	5	5A/3	5A/140	1B/13	5A/274
11.45pm	Northwich	Crewe		J	D	12.42am	-	BHSS Middle	5B/1053	5B/1363	-	-
10.55pm	Edge Hill D S	Crewe		H	MSX	12.44am	-	North Staffs Sdgs	3B/151	5A/593	-	-
11.40pm	Chester	Crewe		H	MX	12.45am	-	BHSS Middle	9A/400	5A/655	-	-
11.45pm	Liverpool Lime St	Crewe	158	A	MX	12.46am	-	4 South			-	-
11.55pm	Manchester L Rd	Crewe	150	A	MX	12.50am	-	4 North			-	-
1am	Crewe	Leicester		E	MX	-	1am	BHSS Middle	-	-	5A/1054	5B/1192
1.4am	Crewe	Hockley		F	MX	-	1.4am	Gresty Lane	-	-		
1.6am	Crewe	Leicester		E	MX	-	1.6am	BHSS Middle	-	-		
9.50pm	York	Swansea	C487	A	SX	1.7am	2.15am	3				
10.55pm	Birkenhead	Crewe		H	MSX	1.8am	-	North Staffs Sdgs	5B/1041	5A/669	-	-
12.10am	Liverpool Lime St	Euston	152	A	D	1.13am	1.22am	5				
1.25am	Crewe	Cardiff	176	A	D	-	1.25am	4	-	-		
12.35am	Manchester L Rd	Penzance	262	A	D	1.25am	2am	6				
12.12am	Warrington	Nuneaton		F	MX	1.26am	1.30am	BHSS South	3D/205	8B/572	3D/205	5B/1202
1.30am	Crewe	Newcastle Junction	6	H	MX	-	1.30am	North Staffs Sdgs	-	-		
10.30pm	Birkenhead Docks	Grange Junction		J	MX	1.30am	2.18am	North Staffs Sdgs				
2.50pm	Carlisle	Crewe		F	MX	1.34am	-	Gresty Lane	12A/321	5B/1270	-	-
12.33am	Warrington	Nuneaton		F	MX	1.37am	1.42am	BHSS South	8A/27	8B/567	8A/27	5B/1175
6.30pm	Holyhead	Crewe	160	C	MX	1.37am	-	4	8C/1	6A/245	-	-
1.42am	Crewe	Coventry		F	MX	-	1.42am	BHSS South	-	-	5B/1055	5B/1185
1.40am	Crewe	Nuneaton		H	SX	-	1.40am	BHSS South	-	-		
7.20pm	Law Junction	Birmingham	362	C	MX	1.42am	2.30am	5			5A/22	5A/559
2.50pm	Carlisle	Crewe		H	MX	1.50am	-	North Staffs Sdgs		5B/1270	-	-
1.50am	Crewe	Stafford		H	MX	-	1.50am	BHSS Middle	-	-		5B/1196
1.10am	Liverpool Lime St	Crewe	182	C	MX	2.1am	-	4		8A/257	-	-
2.10am	Crewe	Stafford		H	MX	-	2.10am	BHSS Middle	-	-	17B/25	5B/1196
12.40am	Edge Hill	Stoke		F	MSX	2.21am	2.26am	Station	5A/36	5A/577	5A/36	5B/1381
2.22am	Crewe	Shrewsbury		H	MSX	-	2.22am	BHSS Middle	-	-	5B/1001	5B/1478
1am	Mold Junction	Bushbury		H	D	2.30am	2.55am	BHSS Middle	5B/1055	6B/265	5B/1055	5B/1207
11.25pm	Burn Naze	Willesden HL		F	TThO	2.36am	2.50am	BHSS South			5B/1031	5B/1167
2am	Stockport	Bristol	8	C	MX	2.45am	4.3am	6	84G/4	5A/602	84G/4	5A/717
2.50am	Crewe	Stoke		B	D	-	2.50am	5 Bay	-	-	5B/1063	5B/1375
1.10am	Edge Hill	Crewe		F	MX	2.50am	-	Gresty Lane		5A/577	-	-
2.50am	Crewe	Rugby		F	TThO	-	2.50am	BHSS South	-	-		5B/1167
3am	Crewe	Shrewsbury		C	MX	-	3am	5	-	-		
12.55am	Holyhead	Euston	198	A	SX	3.5am	3.15am	3				
1.40am	Edge Hill	Birmingham C St		F	MX	3.15am	3.37am	BHSS South	8A/33	8A/275	8A/33	3B/312
1.10am	Holyhead	Euston	4	A	SX	3.20am	3.30am	3				
1.50am	Heaton Norris	Shrewsbury		H	MX	3.20am	4.25am	Gresty Lane				
9.25pm	Glasgow Central	Euston	10	A	D	3.22am	3.37am	4	12A/—	1B/102	12A/—	1B/102
2am	Speke Sidings	Crewe		H	MX	3.30am	-	BHSS Middle	5A/41	5A/597	-	-
2.50am	Manchester L Rd	Crewe	184	A	D	3.33am	-	5			-	-
3.35am	Crewe	Oxley Sidings		H	MX	-	3.35am	Gresty Lane	-	-		
8.25pm	Perth	Euston	12	A	D	3.40am	4am	4	5A/2	5A/136	1B/11	5A/281
3.40am	Crewe	Stoke		H	MX	-	3.40am	North Staffs Sdgs	-	-		
3.44am	Crewe	Birmingham	180	A	MX	-	3.44am	3 Bay	-	-		
10.10pm	Glasgow Central	Euston	6	A	D	*pass 3.50am*		Up Through				
7.40pm	Carlisle	Rugby	380	C	MX	3.53am	5.50am	6				
2.50am	Mold Junction	Rugby		E	D	3.53am	4.8am	BHSS South	2A/515	6B/266	2A/515	5B/1159
4.5am	Crewe	Whitchurch		F	MX	-	4.5am	BHSS Middle	-	-	5B/1035	84G/57
4.10am	Crewe	Stoke		A	D	-	4.10am	5	-	-	5A/40	5A/626
4.45pm	Inverness	Euston	14	A	TO	4.10am	4.27am	4	5A/	12A/105	5A/	1B/210
10.55pm	Neville Hill	Aston		H	MX	4.16am	4.30am	BHSS South	5A/27	5B/1342	5A/27	3B/302
10.25pm	Glasgow Central	Euston	224	A	D	*pass 4.20am*		Up Through	1B/3	12A/56	1B/3	12A/56
12.40am	Birkenhead	Beeston		F	MSX	*pass 4.20am*						
2.30am	Chester	Alsager Junction		F	MSX	*pass 4.35am*		North Staffs Sdgs				

Time Dep	From	Destination	Rep No	Train Class	Days Run	Crewe Arr	Crewe Dep	Platform or Yard	To Crewe from North Loco Diag	To Crewe from North Men Diag	From Crewe to South Loco Diag	From Crewe to South Men Diag
9.5pm	Carlisle	Crewe		F	MX	4.40am	-	BHSS Middle	12A/319	5B/1279	-	-
4.50am	Crewe	Worcester		H	D	-	4.50am	Gresty Lane	-	-		84B/—
10pm	Stranraer	Euston	68	A	MX	4.42am	4.52am	3	1B/2	12A/82	1B/2	1B/214
5.35pm	Inverness	Euston	16	A	MX	4.52am	5.6am	4	5A/1	5A/133	5A/5	5A/291
5am	Crewe	Willesden HL		E	SX	-	5am	BHSS South	-	-	5B/1037	1A806
11.15pm	Glasgow Central	Birmingham	18	A	D	5am	5.14am	5	66A/2	5A/144	5A/10	5A/549
5am	Crewe	Willesden HL		E	SX	-	5am	BHSS Middle	-	-		5B/1166
2.40am	Newton Heath	Crewe S Shed		G	MSX	5.8am	-				-	-
5.7am	Crewe	Derby		B	SX	-	5.7am	6 Bay	-	-	9A/14	5A/627
4.23pm	Perth	Maiden Lane		D	WThFO	5.17am	5.55am	BHSS South			2A/—	2B/93
5.20am	Crewe	Newcastle Junction	3	H	D	-	5.20am	North Staffs Sdgs	-	-		
3.40am	Heaton Norris	Crewe		H	MX	5.25am	-	North Staffs Sdgs			-	-
3.30am	Ellesmere Port	Crewe		H	MX	5.30am	-	North Staffs Sdgs			-	-
3.30am	Edge Hill	Alsager Junction		F	MX	5.31am	5.36am	Station				
5.35am	Crewe	Whitchurch		B	MX	-	5.35am	6 bay	-	-		
5.40am	Crewe	Birmingham	200	A	D	-	5.40am	4 bay	-	-		
11.50pm	Carnforth	Crewe		H	MX	5.45am	-	BHSS Middle	11A/250	5B/1292	-	-
3.25am	Birkenhead Docks	Grange Junction		J	SX	5.47am	5.55am	North Staffs Sdgs				
5.50am	Crewe	Betley Road		K	D	-	5.50am	BHSS Middle	-	-	5B/1131	5B/1131
4.15am	Heaton Norris Jnt	Crewe		H	MX	6am	-	Gresty Lane	5A/92	5A/92	-	-
6.5am	Crewe	Wellington		B	D	-	6.5am	3 Bay	-	-	Wellington	Crewe/1
5am	Warrington	Crewe		H	MX	6.5am	-	BHSS Middle	5B/1003	5B/1291	-	-
6.10am	Crewe	Whitchurch		G	SX	-	6.10am	Station	-	-		
4.10am	Birkenhead Docks	Grange Junction		J	MSX	*pass 6.10am*		North Staffs Sdgs				
4.15am	Stott Lane Sidings	Bushbury		H	D	6.10am	6.15am	Station	10C/13	10C/535	10C/13	3B/304

Below:
Carlisle Upperby Yard, No Date
A clean Class 5 4-6-0 No 45386 pulls out of Upperby yard with an unidentified freight working, heading south. Fellow classmate No 45259 stands on one of the shed roads awaiting its next turn of duty. Stacks of sleepers in the yard suggest that some spot sleepering or relaying of sections of track is imminent. A solitary six-wheel stores van stands in the middle distance awaiting removal to return to Crewe. *Eric Treacy*

Time Dep	From	Destination	Rep No	Train Class	Days Run	Crewe Arr	Crewe Dep	Platform or Yard	To Crewe from North Loco Diag	To Crewe from North Men Diag	From Crewe to South Loco Diag	From Crewe to South Men Diag
4.20am	Edge Hill	Crewe		H	MX	6.18am	-	BHSS Middle	8A/33	5B/1392	-	-
6.25am	Crewe	Longport Junction	84	K	D	-	6.25am	North Staffs Sdgs	-	-		
4.30am	Stanlow & Thornton	Lawley St		F	WO	6.25am	6.30am	BHSS South	6C/205A	6C/365	6C/205A	5B/1204
5.40am	Longsight	Crewe		C	D-Q	6.35am	-	Up Through			-	-
6.35am	Crewe	Sudbury Junction		H	MX	-	6.35am	BHSS Middle	-	-	5B/1018	5B/1165
6.35am	Crewe	Nantwich	38	K	D	-	6.35am	BHSS North	-	-	5B/1126	5B/1126
11.55pm	Copley Hill	Shrewsbury		H	MX	6.35am	7.50am	Gresty Lane				
5.15am	Edge Hill	Sudbury Junction		E	MX	6.40am	6.53am	Station	1A/1	5A/590	1A/1	5B/1169
6.45am	Crewe	Derby		B	D	-	6.45am	5 Bay	-	-	84G/2	5A/628
1.30am	Copley Hill	Crewe		H	MX	6.50am	-	BHSS Middle	25G/301	5B/1348	-	-
6.50am	Crewe	Birmingham		B	D	-	6.50am	5	-	-	5A/33	5A/553
6.55am	Crewe	Oxley Sidings		H	D	-	6.55am	Gresty Lane	-	-		84B/—
3.22am	Carnforth	Bushbury		H	SX	6.55am	7.55am	BHSS Middle	5B/1032	10A/642	5B/1032	3B/314
4.55am	Ellesmere Port	Crewe		H	MX	6.57am	-	BHSS Middle	5B/1050	6C/392	-	-
5.15am	Hooton	Alsager Junction		J	MX	7am	7.10am	North Staffs Sdgs	5B/1001	6C/371	5B/1001	6C/371
7.5am	Crewe	Hollinswood		K	D	-	7.5am	Gresty Lane	-	-	84B/—	Crewe/10
10.35pm	Somers Town	Crewe		E	MX	7.6am	-	BHSS North		5B/1192	-	-
5.50am	Manchester L Rd	Crewe		B	D	7.8am	-	6			-	-
5am	Stott Lane Sidings	Crewe		H	D	7.10am	-	BHSS Middle	5B/1005	10C/534	-	-
6.36am	Chester	Crewe		B	D	7.19am	-	4			-	-
7.23am	Crewe	Aintree		F	D	-	7.23am	BH	-	-		5B/1297
6.50am	Northwich	Crewe		B	D	7.25am	-	10 Bay	5A/120	5A/120	-	-
7.32am	Crewe	Shrewsbury		B	D	-	7.32am	5	-	-		
5.30am	Preston	Crewe		B	D	7.33am	-	5			-	-
7.30am	Crewe Works	Basford Hall		K	D	*pass 7.40am*		BHSS North	5B/1086	5B/2076	5B/1086	5B/2076
12.1am	Glasgow Central	Euston	372	C	MX	7.43am	7.55am	6	5B/1034	5A/204	5A/22	5A/383
7.45am	Crewe	Bescot		H	D	-	7.45am	BHSS Middle	-	-	3C/203	3B/327
7.50am	Crewe	Euston	24	A	D	-	7.50am	3	-	-	5A/3	5A/299
4.28am	Carlisle	Crewe	390	C	MX	7.55am	-	6	5A/28	5A/160	-	-
8.3am	Crewe	Whitchurch		G	D	-	8.3am	North Shed	-	-		
8.10am	Crewe	Derby		B	D	-	8.10am	6 Bay	-	-	5A/97	5A/97
8.10am	Crewe	Peterboro'		E	D	-	8.10am	BHSS Middle	-	-	5B/1038	5B/1172
6.5am	Mold Junction	Crewe		H	MX	8.10am	-	BHSS Middle			-	-
8.2am	Carriage Works	Crewe		G	SX	8.11am	-	Down HL			-	-
8.15am	Crewe	Whitemoor Sidings		E	D	-	8.15am	BHSS Middle	-	-		5B/1172
3.10am	Carlisle	Crewe		D	D	8.20am	-	Gresty Lane	5B/1038	5B/1296	-	-
7.15am	Manchester L Rd	Crewe		B	D	8.28am	-	4			-	-
6.30am	Heysham	Euston	32	A	D	8.31am	8.42am	5	1B/11	11A/100	1B/11	1B/219/31
8.37am	Crewe	Shrewsbury		B	D	-	8.37am	4 Bay	-	-	5A/106	W'church/6
6.30am	Morecambe	Crewe	272	A	D	8.44am	-	5			-	-
6.30am	Llandudno	Euston	302	A	D	8.45am	9am	3	7C/7	6A/248	1B/22	1B/244
3.35am	Crofton Hall	Crewe		J	MX	8.50am	-	BHSS Middle	5B/1003	5B/1335	-	-
8.5am	Manchester L Rd	Crewe	30	A	D	8.55am	-	4 North			-	-
8.33am	Northwich	Crewe		B	D	9am	-	5	5A/120	5A/120	-	-
9am	Crewe	Whitchurch		K	SX	-	9am	BHSS Middle	-	-	5B/1056	5B/1360
8am	Liverpool Lime St	Birmingham	34	A	D	9.2am	9.10am	4	8A/15	8A/266	8A/15	5A/555
4.15am	Carnforth	Crewe		H	SX	9.5am	-	Gresty Lane	5B/1030	5B/1277	-	-
9.8am	Crewe	Derby		A	D	-	9.8am	5 Bay	-	-		
8.20am	Liverpool Lime St	Euston	36	A	D	9.10am	9.18am	3	8A/—	1B/144/9	8A/—	1B/144/9
9.15am	Crewe	Badnall Wharf	28	K	SX	-	9.15am	BHSS Middle	-	-	5B/1110	5B/1110
9.30am	Crewe	Wellington		B	D	-	9.30am	3 Bay	-	-		
9.37am	Crewe	Derby		C	MX-Q	-	9.37am	Up Sidings	-	-		
9.45am	Crewe	Oxley Sidings		H	D	-	9.45am	Gresty Lane	-	-		
8.42am	Manchester L Rd	Crewe		B	D	9.54am	-	5			-	-
7.25am	Heysham	Crewe	26	A	D	9.55am	-	4	11A/6	28A/75	-	-
9.55am	Crewe	Oxley			D	-	9.55am	Gresty Lane	-	-		84B/—
8.20am	Edge Hill	Nuneaton		F	MSX	10am	10.5am	BHSS South	5A/42	5A/583	5A/42	5B/1189
9.15am	Manchester L Rd	Plymouth	212	A	D	*pass 10.3am*		Up Through		5A/605		5A/605
9.6am	Liverpool Lime St	Plymouth	208	A	SX	10.4am	10.20am	4			5A/1	5A/702
8am	Blackpool Central	Euston	296	A	SX	10.9am	10.18am	3	1B/12	1B/118	1B/12	1B/118
9.25am	Manchester L Rd	Swansea High St	210	A	D	10.14am	10.30am	5	9A/10	5A/621	9A/10	5A/718
8.56am	Northwich	Crewe	25	K	D	10.16am	-	BHSS Middle		5B/1368	-	-
9.45am	Manchester L Rd	Euston	58	A	D	*pass 10.27am*		Up Through	9A/—	1B/167	9A/—	1B/167
7.30am	Holyhead	Euston	48	A	D	10.28am	10.35am	3	7C/—	6A/251	7C/—	1B/226/32
10.30am	Crewe	Stoke	89	H	D	-	10.30am	North Staffs Sdgs	-	-		
4.5am	Carlisle	Sudbury Junction		D	SX	10.43am	10.50am	BHSS South			5B/1051	5B/1160
9.20am	Edge Hill	Crewe		E	MSX	10.45am	-	Gresty Lane	84G/5	5A/584	-	-
10.10am	Liverpool Lime St	Euston	54	A	D	*pass 10.55am*		Up Through				
10.10am	Manchester L Rd	Birmingham	214	A	SX	10.57am	11.12am	4 South				
11am	Crewe	Oxley Sidings		H	SX	-	11am	Gresty Lane	-	-	85A/—	Crewe/11

Time Dep	From	Destination	Rep No	Train Class	Days Run	Crewe Arr	Crewe Dep	Platform or Yard	To Crewe from North Loco Diag	To Crewe from North Men Diag	From Crewe to South Loco Diag	From Crewe to South Men Diag
10.15am	Liverpool Lime St	Crewe	62	A	SX	11.1am	-	4 North	9A/—	8A/310	-	-
9.10am	Llandudno	Euston	56	A	SX	11.6am	11.28am	3	1B/19	7A/155	1B/19	5A/308-WF
9.40am	Heaton Norris	Bushbury		H	SX	11.7am	11.15am	BHSS South	9B/101	9B/356	9B/101	5B/1208
10.25am	Manchester L Rd	Bournemouth	220	A	SX	11.8am	11.20am	5			9A/—	5A/564
11.15am	Crewe South Shed	Crewe NSS		J	D	-	11.15am	South Shed	-	-		
11.20am	Crewe	Derby		B	D	-	11.20am	6 Bay	-	-	9A/14	5A/623
9.35am	Northwich	Crewe		K	D	11.25am	-	BHSS South	5B/1017	5B/1368	-	-
11.30am	Crewe	Etruria Junction	84	K	D	-	11.30am	North Staffs Sdgs	-	-		
6.5am	Carlisle	Crewe	274	B	D	11.40am	-	5	12A/13	5A/201	-	-
10.25am	Mold Junction	Crewe		H	MSX	11.45am	-	North Staffs Sdgs			-	-
10.50am	Runcorn	Alsager Junction		F	SX	11.49am	11.56am	Station				
11.40am	Crewe Coal Yard	Crewe	17	K	SX	11.50am	-	BHSS Middle	5B/1119	5B/1119	-	-
11.10am	Liverpool Lime St	Euston	112	A	D	11.56am	12.2pm	4	8A/—	1B/150	8A/—	1B/150
1pm	Crewe	Oxley Sidings		H	D	-	1pm	Gresty Lane	-	-	84B/—	Crewe/12
12.1pm	Crewe	Shrewsbury		B	D	-	12.1pm	4 Bay	-	-		
10.50am	Runcorn	Alsager Junction		F	SX	-	12.1pm	North Staffs Sdgs				
10am	Blackpool Central	Euston	330	A	SX	12.10pm	12.18pm	3	1B/17	1B/123	1B/17	1B/123
12.10pm	Crewe	Shrewsbury		B	D	-	12.10pm		-	-	5A/33	5A/709
8.25am	Holyhead	Crewe	72	A	SX	12.13pm	-	6	7C/12	7C/40	-	-
11.10am	Manchester L Rd	Crewe		B	D	12.20pm	-	6			-	-
11.36am	Garston Dam Bdge	Crewe		D	SX	12.43pm	-	North Staffs Sdgs			-	-
10.55am	Edge Hill	Crewe		H	SX	12.44pm	-	North Staffs Sdgs		5A/593	-	-
11.55am	Manchester L Rd	Plymouth	228	A	D	12.45pm	1.10pm	4				
11.26am	Jubilee Sidings	Crewe		J	SX	12.45pm	-	BHSS Middle	26A/633	5B/1327	-	-
8.20am	Carlisle	Euston	74	A	D	12.51pm	1pm	3	1B/1	12A/91	1B/1	5A/309/23
12.39pm	Rookery Bridge	Crewe	23	G	SX	12.54pm	-	North Staffs Sdgs	5B/1053	5B/1367	-	-
12.56pm	Crewe	Wellington		B	D	-	12.56pm	3 Bay	-	-		
11.40am	Liverpool Lime St	Rugby Midland	84	A	D	12.59pm	1.8pm	5	8A/13	8A/267	8A/13	5A/565
1.5pm	Crewe	Betley Road		K	SX	-	1.5pm	BHSS Middle	-	-	5B/1132	5B/1132
10.56am	Birkenhead	Crewe		H	D	1.8pm	-	North Staffs Sdgs	5B/1041	5A/669	-	-
1.15pm	Crewe	Pratt Sidings	50	J	D	-	1.15pm	North Staffs Sdgs	-	-		
5.30am	Carlisle	Crewe		H	SX	1.20pm	-	BHSS Middle	12A/322	5B/1295	-	-
11.55am	Bamfurlong	Crewe		F	SX	1.25pm	-	BHSS Middle	6C/203	5B/1241	-	-
1.30pm	Crewe	Oxley Sidings		F	D	-	1.30pm	Gresty Lane	-	-		84B/—
1.35pm	Crewe	Derby		B	D	-	1.35pm	6 Bay	-	-	5A/41	5A/637
11.50am	Edge Hill	Shrewsbury		F	SX	1.42pm	1.47pm	Gresty Lane	8A/26	5A/582	8A/26	84G/184
5.15am	Carlisle	Bushbury		E	D	1.40pm	1.50pm	BHSS South	84G/102	5B/1293	84G/102	5B/1216
12.10pm	Edge Hill	Bushbury		F	SX	1.50pm	2pm	BHSS Middle	3B/151	5A/593	3B/151	3B/330
1.55pm	Crewe	Willesden Junction	232	C	SX	-	1.55pm		-	-	2A/—	5A/394
1.45pm	Crewe Works	Basford Hall		K	D	*pass 1.55pm*		BHSS North	5B/1086	5B/2077	5B/1086	5B/2077
7.50am	Holyhead	Crewe	76	C	SX	1.58pm	-	5	9A/12	5A/650	-	-
12.55pm	Warrington	Crewe		H	MSX	2pm	-	Gresty Lane	5B/1051	5B/1273	-	-
12.40pm	Garston Dam Bdge	Crewe		D	SX	2pm	-	BHSS Middle			-	-
6.50am	Carlisle	Crewe		H	SX	2.10pm	-	Gresty Lane	12A/23	5B/1293+4	-	-
2.13pm	Crewe	Chaddesden			MSX	-	2.13pm		-	-		16A/626
10.50am	Windermere	Euston	86	A	SX	2.15pm	2.23pm	3	1B/12	10B/81	1B/12	10B/81
9.30am	Neville Hill	Bushbury		H	SX	2.21pm	2.55pm	BHSS South	25G/337	5B/1352	25G/337	5B/1214
2.20pm	Crewe	Chaddesden		H	D	-	2.25pm	North Staffs Sdgs	-	-		
1.18pm	Manchester L Rd	Crewe		B	D	2.28pm	-	4			-	-
1.15pm	Edge Hill	Willesden		D	FSO	2.32pm	2.46pm	Station	12A/320	8A/774	12A/320	5B/1176
2.35pm	Crewe	Pontypool Road	190	C	MSX	-	2.35pm	Up Sidings	-	-	2B/5	5A/714
12.50pm	Mold Junction	Alsager Junction		F	SX	*pass 2.38pm*		North Staffs Sdgs				
1pm	Edge Hill	Crewe		H	SX	2.44pm	-	Gresty Lane			-	-
2pm	Liverpool Lime St	Euston	92	A	D	-	2.45pm	Up Through				
12.35pm	Ellesmere Port	Egginton Junction		F	TWThO	2.47pm	2.52pm	North Staffs Sdgs				5B/1380
1.30pm	Edge Hill	Willesden HL		D	SX	2.50pm	2.50pm	Station		5A/585		
12.25pm	Stanlow & Thornton	Egginton Junction		F	TWThO	2.52pm	2.55pm	North Staffs Sdgs	6C/205	6C/366	6C/205	5B/1380
9.30am	Glasgow Central	Birmingham	98	A	D	2.55pm	3.15pm	4	5A/4	12A/94	5A/10	5A/550
1.10pm	Mold Junction	Crewe		F	SX	2.57pm	-	BHSS Middle			-	-
1.29pm	Heaton Norris	Crewe		H	MSX	3.1pm	-	Gresty Lane	5B/1033	5B/1347	-	-
1.25pm	Runcorn	Alsager Junction		F	SX	3.3pm	3.8pm	North Staffs Sdgs	5B/1019	5D/485	5B/1019	5D/485
3.5pm	Crewe	Whitchurch		G	SX	-	3.5pm	Gresty Lane	-	-		
10am	Glasgow Central	Euston	96	A	D	*pass 3.8pm*		Up Through	66A/1	12A/60	66A/1	12A/60
11am	Porthmadoc	Euston	100	A	SX	3.15pm	3.25pm	3	1B/17	5A/318	1B/17	5A/318
3.15pm	Crewe	Wellington		B	WSO	-	3.15pm	3 Bay	-	-	Wellington	Crewe/2
3.26pm	Crewe	Stoke	48	K	SX	-	3.26pm	North Staffs Sdgs	-	-		
3.28pm	Crewe	Shrewsbury		B	D	-	3.28pm	4 Bay	-	-	2A/9	5A/726
8.26am	Heaton Norris	Crewe		K	D	3.30pm	-	BHSS Middle	5B/1020	5B/1333	-	-
10.6am	Glasgow Central	Euston	106	A	D	3.32pm	3.49pm	4	1B/4	12A/98	1B/4	1B/236
1.25pm	Holyhead	Euston	88	A	SX	3.33pm	3.41pm	3				

Time Dep	From	Destination	Rep No	Train Class	Days Run	Crewe Arr	Crewe Dep	Platform or Yard	To Crewe from North Loco Diag	To Crewe from North Men Diag	From Crewe to South Loco Diag	From Crewe to South Men Diag
2.10pm	Garston Dam Bdge	Crewe		D	SX	3.35pm	-	BHSS Middle			-	-
3.40pm	Crewe	Alsager Junction	89	J	D	-	3.40pm	North Staffs Sdgs	-	-		
2.10pm	Edge Hill	Nuneaton		E	SX	3.40pm	3.45pm	BHSS South	5A/40	5A/385	5A/40	5B/1186
12.14pm	Broxton	Crewe		K	SX	3.45pm	-	Gresty Lane	5B/1056	5B/1460	-	-
1.40pm	Llandudno	Derby	124	A	D	3.51pm	4.2pm	6			5A/91	5A/91
3.5pm	Manchester L Rd	Birmingham	236	A	D	3.54pm	4.7pm	5	2A/—	5A/607	2A/—	5A/561
3pm	Liverpool Lime St	Cardiff	234	A	SX	3.55pm	4.9pm	3	2A/—	3E/108		
3.55pm	Crewe	Oxley Sidings		H	SX	-	3.55pm	Gresty Lane	-	-		84B/—
3.57pm	Crewe	Birmingham	186	A	SX	-	3.57pm	4 North	-	-		
8.55am	Perth	Euston	110	A	FSO	4.6pm	4.15pm	4	1B/1	12A/65	1B/1	12A/65
3.15pm	Manchester L Rd	Plymouth	240	A	FS	4.10pm	4.20pm	5	9A/37	9A/315	9A/37	5A/722-FO
10.50am	Workington	Euston	254	A	FO	4.18pm	4.26pm	4				
8.55am	Perth	Euston	110	A	TWThO	4.18pm	4.26pm	4				
4.18pm	Crewe	Bushbury		H	SX	-	4.18pm	BHSS Middle	-	-	5B/1004	5B/1206
4.20pm	Crewe	Leek		B	D	-	4.20pm	6 Bay	-	-		
2.54pm	Garston Dam Bdge	Crewe		D	SX	4.20pm	-	BHSS Middle			-	-
8.35am	Carlisle	Crewe	356	C	SX	4.28pm	-	Up Through	5A/19	11A/57	-	-
4.30pm	Crewe	Radway Green	93	G	D	-	4.30pm	North Staffs Sdgs	-	-		
3.20pm	Manchester M'field	Crewe		B	D	4.39pm	-	6			-	-
2.25pm	Waverton	Crewe	36	K	SX	4.41pm	-	BHSS Middle	5B/1037	5B/1462	-	-
2.40pm	Llandudno	Crewe	140	A	D	4.50pm	-	3	7A/1	7A/160	-	-
1.30pm	Barrow	Crewe	266	A	FX	4.51pm	-	5	5A/11	11A/98	-	-
1.30pm	Barrow	Euston	266	A	FO	4.51pm	5pm	5			1B/31	5A/352
3.15pm	Edge Hill	Bushbury		H	SX	4.53pm	4.55pm	BHSS South				
4.10pm	Liverpool Lime St	Euston	114	A	FX	4.56pm	5.2pm	4				
4.10pm	Liverpool Lime St	Euston	114	A	FO	4.56pm	5.8pm	4				
4.50pm	Calveley	Crewe	132	C	SX	5.6pm	-		5A/55	5A/909	-	-
10.50am	Copley Hill	Crewe		H	SX	5.8pm	-	Gresty Lane	5B/1034	9B/360	-	-
5.10pm	Crewe	Stafford via Stoke		B	D	-	5.10pm	6 Bay	-	-	84G/5	5A/624
5.10pm	Crewe	Wellington		B	WSX	-	5.10pm	3 Bay	-	-	Wellington	Crewe/3
2.50pm	Wyre Dock	Broad Street		C	SX	5.10pm	5.40pm	Up Through	5A/33	5A/206	1A/1	1A/64
5.15pm	Crewe	Willesden HL		E	SX	-	5.15pm	BHSS Middle	-	-	1A/814	5B/1173
4.35pm	Manchester L Rd	Birmingham	238	A	D	5.17pm	5.30pm	4 South				
4.17pm	Liverpool Lime St	Crewe	162	A	D	5.20pm	-	4 North	5A/23	8A/255	-	-
3.5pm	Speke Junction	Alsager Junction		F	SX	5.20pm	5.30pm	North Staffs Sdgs				
5.22pm	Crewe	Madeley	39	J	SX	-	5.22pm	BHSS Middle	-	-	17B/25	5B/1194
5.25pm	Crewe	Shrewsbury		B	D	-	5.25pm	4 Bay	-	-	8A/5	5A/701
3.50pm	Garston Dam Bdge	Crewe		D	SX	5.30pm	-	BHSS Middle			-	-
5.35pm	Crewe	Oxley Sidings		H	SX	-	5.35pm	Gresty Lane	-	-		84B/—
2.20pm	Port Sunlight	Crewe		H	SX	5.38pm	-	North Staffs Sdgs	5B/1004	6C/364	-	-
5.15pm	Northwich	Crewe		B	SX	5.42pm	-	3	5A/121	5A/121	-	-
4.28pm	Manchester L Rd	Crewe		B	D	5.52pm	-	5			-	-
5.10pm	Chester	Crewe		B	D	5.54pm	-	3	5A/39	6A/255	-	-
5.55pm	Crewe	Stafford		B	D	-	5.55pm	6 Bay	-	-	2A/—	5A/382
5.52pm	Carriage Works	Stoke		B	SX	6pm	6.5pm	6	5A/40	5A/625	5A/40	5A/625
5.20pm	Warrington	Crewe		B	D	6.4pm	-	5	5B/1039	5A/208	-	-
6.10pm	Crewe	Shrewsbury		B	D	-	6.10pm	4 Bay	-	-	12A/13	5A/710
5.25pm	Liverpool Lime St	Euston	122	A	D	6.10pm	6.15pm	4	1B/6	1B/141	1B/6	1B/141
5.11pm	Manchester L Rd	Crewe		B	D	6.18pm	-	6	84G/2	5A/603	-	-
2.40pm	Holyhead	Birmingham	278	A	SX	6.25pm	7.10pm	3				
5.5pm	Garston Dam Bdge	Crewe		D	SX	6.30pm	-	BHSS Middle			-	-
5.50pm	Manchester L Rd	Euston	130	A	D	6.33pm	6.38pm	4				
6.35pm	Crewe	Derby		B	D	-	6.35pm	5 Bay	-	-		
6.35pm	Crewe	Rugby		H	D	-	6.35pm	BHSS Middle	-	-	2A/8	5B/1174
6.40pm	Crewe	Shrewsbury	312	C	SX	-	6.40pm	Up Sidings	-	-	5A/33	5A/712
3.20pm	Holyhead	Crewe	284	C	TThO	6.46pm	-				-	-
4.20pm	Edge Hill	Crewe		H	SX	6.50pm	-	North Staffs Sdgs	12A/17	5A/592	-	-
6.50pm	Crewe	Whitchurch		F	WO	-	6.50pm	Gresty Lane	-	-	5B/1056	5B/1485
1.30pm	Glasgow Central	Euston	126	A	SX	6.55pm	7.03pm	4	1B/2	5A/142	1B/2	5A/329
5.40pm	Liverpool Lime St	Crewe		B	D	7.5pm	-	5			-	-
6pm	Manchester L Rd	Crewe		B	SX	7.9pm	-	6			-	-
6.50pm	Northwich	Crewe		B	SX	7.16pm	-	10 Bay	5A/121	5A/121	-	-
7.25pm	Crewe	Alsager Junction	83	K	D	-	7.25pm	North Staffs Sdgs	-	-		
7.25pm	Crewe	Rugby		H	D	-	7.25pm	BHSS Middle	-	-	5B/1017	2B/323
5.40pm	Dundas Sidings	Normacot Junction		F	D	7.28pm	7.40pm	North Staffs Sdgs	5B/1052	5B/1464	5B/1052	5E/98
5.5pm	Blackpool Central	Euston	136	A	D	7.30pm	7.39pm	4	28A/1	28A/66	28A/1	28A/66
6.25pm	Manchester M'field	Crewe		B	D	7.40pm	-	6	12B/—	5A/600	-	-
3.50pm	Carlisle	Broad Street		C	TWThO	7.45pm	8pm	Up Through				
7.50pm	Crewe	Whitchurch		B	SX	-	7.50pm		-	-	W'church/16	W'chrch/16
7.50pm	Crewe	Wellington		B	FX	-	7.50pm	3 Bay	-	-		

Time Dep	From	Destination	Rep No	Train Class	Days Run	Crewe Arr	Crewe Dep	Platform or Yard	To Crewe from North Loco Diag	To Crewe from North Men Diag	From Crewe to South Loco Diag	From Crewe to South Men Diag
7.52pm	Crewe	Wellington		B	FO	-	7.52pm	3 Bay	-	-		
7.10pm	Sandbach	Crewe	21	K	SX	7.50pm	-	BHSS Middle	5B/1120	5B/1120	-	-
7.55pm	Crewe	Longport Junction	89	K	D	-	7.55pm	North Staffs Sdgs	-	-		
7.10pm	Manchester L Rd	Cardiff	246	A	D	7.58pm	8.33pm	5				
7.20pm	Chester	Crewe		B	D	8pm	-	3	7A/11	6A/179	-	-
7.5pm	Liverpool Lime St	Birmingham	250	A	SX	8pm	8.17pm	4	8A/—	8A/276	8A/—	5A/562
6.40pm	Folly Lane	Crewe		F	SX	8pm	-	BHSS Middle			-	-
8.5pm	Crewe	Oxley Sidings		H	D	-	8.5pm	Gresty Lane	-	-	84F/—	Crewe/14
5.30pm	Carnforth	Willesden		C	MX	8.9pm	8.30pm	Station	11A/262	11A/90	11A/262	11A/90
6.25pm	Edge Hill	Crewe		F	D	8.10pm	-	GrestyLane		5A/581	-	-
8.16pm	Crewe	Shrewsbury		B	SX	-	8.16pm		-	-	5B/1039	5A/709
6.15pm	Llandudno	Derby	80	A	SX	8.16pm	8.20pm	6		5D/101		5D/101
8.20pm	Crewe	Bristol	248	A	D	-	8.20pm	5	-	-		5A/705
7pm	Garston Dam Bdge	Crewe		D	SX	8.20pm	-	BHSS Middle			-	-
6.25pm	Edge Hill DS	Crewe		F	SX	8.28pm	-	Gresty Lane	8A/15	5A/581	-	-
7.57pm	Winsford Junction	Crewe	35	K	SX	8.31pm	-	BHSS Middle	5B/1127	5B/1127	-	-
8pm	Middlewich	Crewe	26	K	SX	8.34pm	-	BHSS Middle	5B/1063	5B/1364	-	-
8.35pm	Crewe	Abergavenny		E	FO	-	8.35pm	BHSS Middle	-	-	86K/42	5B/1479
7.20pm	Liverpool Lime St	Crewe		B	D	8.41pm	-	5	8A/27	5A/578/9	-	-
6.3pm	Ellesmere Port	Etruria Junction		F	D	*pass 8.45pm*		North Staffs Sdgs				
8.50pm	Crewe	Wellington		B	D	-	8.50pm	2 Bay	-	-		
8.50pm	Crewe	Euston	306	C	D	-	8.50pm	Up Through	-	-	5A/24	5A/385
8.55pm	Crewe	Newcastle Junction		H	SX	-	8.55pm	North Staffs Sdgs	-	-	5B/1111	5B/1111
7.32pm	Garston Dam Bdge	Willesden HL		D	SX	*pass 8.53pm*		BHSS South				
4.42pm	Carlisle	Willesden HL		C	SX	8.59pm	9.20pm	4	5B/1037	5B/1234	5B/1033	1A/809
9.18pm	Crewe	Shrewsbury		B	D	-	9.18pm	5	-	-	5B/1032	5A/723
7.15pm	Birkenhead	Birmingham C St		E	SX	9.20pm	9.58pm	BHSS Middle	3D/3	6B/283	3D/3	3B/326
9.25pm	Crewe	Newcastle Junction		H	D	-	9.25pm	North Staffs Sdgs	-	-		5B/1111
8.15pm	Manchester L Rd	Crewe		B	D	9.26pm	-	6			-	-
7.45pm	Ravenshead	Willesden HL		E	SX	9.28pm	9.48pm	BHSS South	8B/3	10E/317	8B/3	1A/817
7pm	Wyre Dock	Broad Street		C	SX	9.32pm	10pm	4	5B/1039	10A/197	9A/11	5B/1134
9.35pm	Crewe	Birmingham	90	C	D	-	9.35pm	Up Sidings	-	-		
9.35pm	Crewe	Worcester		F	D	-	9.35pm	Gresty Lane	-	-	84B/102	84B/—
9.42pm	Crewe	Abergavenny		E	FSX	-	9.42pm	BHSS Middle	-	-	86K/42	5B/1476
8.30pm	Edge Hill	Camden		D	SX	-	9.39pm	Up Through	8A/12	8A/765	8A/12	8A/765
7.38pm	Wyre Dock	Crewe		C	SX	9.50pm	-	5			-	-
9.55pm	Crewe	Stoke		B	D	-	9.55pm	5 Bay	-	-		
8.50pm	Manchester L Rd	Oxley Sidings		D	SX	9.55pm	10.24pm	Gresty Lane	2A/4	5A/604	2A/4	Crewe/16
9.10pm	Warrington	Camden		D	SX	*pass 10.3pm*		Up Through	8B/1	8B/551	8B/1	8B/551
6.40pm	Blackpool	Crewe		D	SX	10.7pm	-	BHSS Middle	5B/1036	10B/560	-	-
9.25pm	Manchester L Rd	Penzance	252	A	FO	*pass 10.17pm*		Up Through				
8.20pm	Llandudno	Crewe	406	A	SX	10.18pm	-	5			-	-
8.50pm	Edge Hill	Birmingham C St		E	SX	10.18pm	10.23pm	BHSS South				5B/1205
12.25pm	Perth	Willesden Jnt	38	A	MFO	10.23pm	10.30pm	Up Through	8A/32		5A/22	5A/391-FO
8.15pm	Northwich	Crewe	27	K	D	10.32pm	-	BHSS Middle			-	-
9.10pm	Manchester Victoria	Paignton	C478	A	FO	*pass 10.34pm*		Up Through				
9.5pm	Edge Hill	Crewe		E	SX	10.36pm	-	Gresty Lane			-	-
9.50pm	Liverpool Lime St	Euston	304	A	SX	10.44pm	10.49pm	3				
9.37pm	Manchester L Rd	Crewe		B	D	10.46pm	-	4			-	-
8.30pm	Blackpool North	Crewe	418	A	FO	10.50pm	-	5	28A/64	5A/227	-	-
10.50pm	Crewe	Burton			MSX	-	10.50pm		-	-		5C/102
9.45pm	Warrington	Crewe		H	SX	10.52pm	-	North Staffs Sdgs	5A/42	8B/76	-	-
9.5pm	Edge Hill	Crewe		E	SX	10.55pm	-	Gresty Lane			-	-
10.55pm	Crewe	Stoke	41	H	SX	-	10.55pm	North Staffs Sdgs	-	-		
10.58pm	Crewe	Swansea		F	FSX	-	10.58pm	BHSS Middle	-	-	84G/104	5B/1475
8.30pm	Kendal	Euston	400	A	SX	11.1pm	11.27pm	4			5A/23	5A/250
11.5pm	Crewe	Burton		H	SX	-	11.5pm	BHSS Middle	-	-		
9.30pm	Manchester	Shrewsbury		F	SX	11.8pm	12.58am	Gresty Lane	84G/2	5A/601		
10.10pm	Liverpool Lime St	Crewe	142	A	D	11.25pm	-	5	5A/44	5A/598	-	-
10.27pm	Manchester L Rd	Crewe	144	A	D	11.29pm	-	6			-	-
5.30pm	Glasgow St Enoch	Plymouth	154	A	FO	11.30pm	11.44pm	4			5A/30	5A/732
7.35pm	Holyhead	Birmingham	170	A	D	11.35pm	12.45am	3			5A/44	5A/540
10.33pm	Manchester L Rd	Euston	138	A	SX	*pass 11.36pm*		Up Through	9A/—	1B/162	9A/—	1B/162
9.25pm	Blackpool Central	Euston	326	A	FO	11.40pm	11.50pm	5	28A/61	28A/79	28A/61	5A/337
12.10pm	Aberdeen	Broad Street	392	C	FSX	11.40pm	11.52pm	Up Through			5A/21	1B/201
9.50pm	Edge Hill	Northampton		E	SX	11.48pm	12.40am	BHSS Middle				
10.35pm	Manchester Victoria	Paignton	258	A	FO	*pass 11.51pm*		Up Through				
11.18pm	Chester	Camden		D	SX	11.59pm	12.28am	BHSS Middle	5A/39	6A/132	5A/39	6A/132
11.15pm	Manchester L Rd	Penzance	292	A	FO	*pass 12am*		Up Through				
10.15pm	Edge Hill	Northampton		E	SX	12.1am	1am	North Staffs Sdgs				
8.30pm	Windermere	Euston	370	A	D	12.3am	12.25am	5				

Up Direction - Saturdays Only

Note: Italics under departure time denote passing time

Time Dep	From	Destination	Rep No	Train Class	Crewe Arr	Crewe Dep	Platform or Yard	To Crewe from North Men Diag	To Crewe from North Loco Diag	From Crewe to South Men Diag	From Crewe to South Loco Diag
11.18pm	Chester	Camden		D	11.59pm	12.28am		5A/39	5A/676	5A/39	5B/1180
7.35pm	Holyhead	Birmingham	170		11.35pm	12.45am	3			5A/44	5A/541
9.50pm	Edge Hill	Northampton		E	11.48pm	12.40am	BHSS Middle	2A/3	8A/814	2A/3	5B/1188
8.30pm	Windermere	Euston	370	A	12.3am	12.25am	5	1B/18	10B/96	1B/18	10B/96
12.5am	Crewe	Birmingham	342	C	-	12.5am	6	-	-		
11.30pm	Manchester L Rd	Crewe	308	A	12.9am	-	4			-	-
6.35pm	Glasgow	Euston	148	A	12.25am	12.37am	4	5A/5	5A/179	5A/4	5A/266
11.15pm	Manchester Victoria	Paignton	268	A	*pass 12.27am*		Up Through				
11.35pm	Liverpool Lime St	Penzance	168	A	12.31am	12.48am	6	3B/151	5A/579	3B/151	84G/79
11.45pm	Liverpool Lime St	Crewe	158	A	12.40am	-	4 South			-	-
5.40pm	Glasgow	Euston	146	A	12.41am	1.10am	5	5A/3	5A/140	1B/13	5A/274
11.43pm	Northwich	Crewe			12.42am	-	BHSS Middle	5B/1053	5B/1363	-	-
11.40pm	Chester	Crewe		H	12.45am	-	BHSS Middle	9A/350	6A/	-	-
10.8pm	Manchester L Rd	Birmingham C St		E	12.45am	12.51am	BHSS South	9A/21	9A/640	9A/21	3B/313
11.55pm	Manchester L Rd	Crewe	150	A	12.50am	-	4 North			-	-
10.20pm	Leeds	Crewe	C486	A	12.57am	-	3	25G/	5A/615	-	-
1am	Crewe	Leicester		E	-	1am	BHSS Middle	-	-	5B/1054	5B/1192
1.4am	Crewe	Hockley		F	-	1.4am	Gresty Lane	-	-		84B/
9.50pm	York	Swansea	C487	A	1.7am	2.15am	3	9A/—	9A/—	86G/—	
12.10am	Liverpool Lime St	Euston	152	A	1.13am	1.22am	5	8A/	8A/	8A/	8A/
12.12am	Warrington	Bushbury			1.15am	1.30am	BHSS South	3D/205	8B/572	3D/205	5B/1202
1.25am	Crewe	Cardiff	176	A	-	1.25am	4	-	-		
12.35am	Manchester L Rd	Penzance	262	A	1.25am	2am	6	9A/8	9A/240	9A/8	9A/240
12.33am	Warrington	Nuneaton		F	1.26am	1.30am	BHSS South	8A/27	8B/567	8A/27	5B/1175
1.30am	Crewe	Newcastle Junction	6	H	-	1.30am	North Staffs Sdgs	-	-		
10.30pm	Birkenhead	Grange Junction		J	1.30am	2.18am	North Staffs Sdgs				
6.30am	Holyhead	Crewe	160	C	1.37am	-	4			-	-
12.53am	Warrington	Birmingham C St		F	1.37am	1.42am	BHSS South			5B/1055	5B/1185
2.50pm	Carlisle	Crewe		H	1.39am	-	North Staffs Sdgs	12A/321	5B/1270	-	-
1.40am	Crewe	Nuneaton		H	-	1.40am	BHSS Middle	-	-		
7.20pm	Law Junction	Broad Street	362	C	1.42am	2.15am	5			5A/21	1B/202
9.30pm	Carlisle	Birmingham (Fish)	440	C	1.47am	2.45am		12A/	12A/104	12A/	5A/508
1.50am	Crewe	Stafford		H	-	1.50am	BHSS Middle	-	-		
1.10am	Liverpool Lime St	Crewe	182	C	2.1am	-	4	2A/	8A/257	-	-
2.10am	Crewe BH	Stafford			-	2.10am	BHSS	-	-	17B/25	5B/1196

Left:
Manchester London Road, No Date
In 1953 two BR Standard Class 7MT members of the 'Britannia' class, Nos 70043/4, emerged from Crewe Works equipped with Westinghouse air pumps which necessitated the omission of their smoke deflectors. Nominally the engines were destined for the Eastern Region but were temporarily assigned to the London Midland Region, and to Manchester Longsight 9A Shed for testing and evaluation. Here No 70044 runs into Manchester London Road with a West of England working. On the extreme right can be seen the overhead catenary for the MSJ&A electrified tracks. Note too the flat roof over the signalbox, perhaps a wartime safety measure against air raid attacks. *Kenneth Field*

Time Dep	From	Destination	Rep No	Train Class	Crewe Arr	Crewe Dep	Platform or Yard	To Crewe from North Men Diag	To Crewe from North Loco Diag	From Crewe to South Men Diag	From Crewe to South Loco Diag
12.40am	Edge Hill	Stoke		E	2.21am	2.26am	Station	5A/36	5A/577	5A/36	5A/638
1am	Mold Junction	Bushbury		H	2.30am	2.50am	BHSS Middle	5B/1055	6B/265	5B/1055	5B/1207
11.25pm	Burn Naze	Badnall Wharf		F	2.36am	3.7am	BHSS South				
12.5am	Birkenhead	Beeston		F	2.43am	3.18am	North Staffs Sdgs				
2am	Stockport	Bristol	8	C	2.45am	4.3am	6	84G/4	5A/602	84G/4	5A/717
1.10am	Edge Hill	Crewe		F	2.50am	-	Gresty Lane			-	-
2.50am	Crewe	Stoke		B	-	2.50am	5 Bay	-	-	5B/1063	5B/1375
9pm	Glasgow	Euston	120	A	*pass 2.57am*		Up Through	1B/1	1B/103	1B/1	1B/103
3am	Crewe	Shrewsbury		C	-	3am	5	-	-		
12.55am	Holyhead	Euston	198	A	3.5am	3.15am	3	7C/1	7C/30	7C/1	7C/30
2am	Chester	Alsager		F	*pass 3.8am*						
1.10am	Holyhead	Euston	332	A	3.20am	3.30am	3		7C/5	5A/675	
3.35am	Crewe	Oxley Sidings		H	-	3.35am	Gresty Lane	-	-		
1.40am	Edge Hill	Birmingham C St		F	3.15am	3.25am	BHSS South	8A/33	8A/275	8A/33	3B/312
1.50am	Heaton Norris	Shrewsbury		H	3.20am	4.25am	Gresty Lane				
9.25pm	Glasgow	Euston	10	A	3.22am	3.37am	4	12A/	12A/116	12A/	1B/240
2am	Garston	Crewe		H	3.30am	-	BHSS Middle	5A/41	5A/597	-	-
2.50am	Manchester L Rd	Crewe	184	A	3.33am	-	5			-	-
3.40am	Crewe	Stoke		H	-	3.40am	North Staffs Sdgs	-	-		
8.15pm	Perth	Euston	12	A	3.40am	4am	4	5A/2	5A/136	1B/7	5A/281
3.44am	Crewe	Birmingham	180	A	-	3.44am	3 Bay	-	-	9A/	3D/151
10.10pm	Glasgow Central	Euston	6	A	*pass 3.50am*		Up Through	12A/	12A/	12A/	12A/
7.40pm	Carlisle	Rugby	380	C	3.53am	5.50am				2A/	2B/93
2.50am	Mold Junction	Rugby		E	3.53am	4.5am	BHSS Middle				
1.45am	Holyhead	Euston	4	A	4.1am	4.11am	3				
4.5am	Crewe	Whitchurch		F	-	4.5am	BH	-	-	5B/1035	84G/57
4.10am	Crewe	Stoke		A	-	4.10am	5	-	-	5A/40	5A/626
4.45pm	Inverness	Euston	14	A	4.10am	4.27am		12A/	12A/120	12A/	1A/69
11.5pm	Neville Hill	Aston			4.16am	4.45am	BHSS South	5A/27	5B/1342	5A/27	3B/302
10.25pm	Glasgow	Euston	224	A	*pass 4.20am*		Up Through	1B/3	12A/56	1B/3	12A/56
10pm	Stranraer	Euston	68	A	4.42am	4.52am	3	1B/2	12A/82	1B/2	1B/214
4.50am	Crewe	Worcester		H	-	4.50am	Gresty Lane	-	-		84B/
5.15pm	Inverness	Euston	16	A	4.52am	5.6am	4	5A/1	5A/133	5A/5	5A/291
11.15pm	Glasgow Central	Birmingham	18	A	5am	5.14am	5	66A/6	5A/144	5A/10	5A/549
5.10am	Crewe	Derby		B	-	5.10am	6 Bay		-	-9A/14	5A/627
12.29am	Carstairs	Birmingham	42	A	5.14am	5.30am	4	12A/	12B/118	12A/	5A/512
5.20am	Crewe	Newcastle Junction	3	H	-	5.20am	North Staffs Sdgs	-	-		
3.40am	Heaton Norris	Crewe		H	5.25am	-	BHSS Middle	9A/366	9A/641	-	-
3.20am	Ellesmere Port	Crewe		H	5.30am	-	Station			-	-
5.35am	Crewe	Whitchurch		C	-	5.35am	6 Bay	-	-	Wellington	
3.30am	Speke Sidings	Alsager Junction		F	*pass 5.40am*		North Staffs Sdgs				
5.40am	Crewe	Birmingham	200	A	-	5.40am	4 Bay	-	-	5A/33	3E/109
5.50am	Crewe	Betley Road		K	-	5.50am	BHSS Middle	-	-	5B/1131	5B/1131
11.50pm	Carnforth	Crewe		H	5.45am	-	BHSS Middle			-	-
4.55am	Ellesmere Port	Crewe			5.57am	-	BHSS	5B/1050	6C/392	-	-
6.5am	Crewe	Wellington		B	-	6.5am	3 Bay	-	-	Wellington	Crewe/1
5am	Warrington	Crewe		H	6.5am	-	BHSS Middle			-	-
4.15am	Stott Lane	Bushbury		H	6.10am	6.15am	Up Through	10C/13	10C/535	10C/13	5B/1222
4.20am	Edge Hill	Crewe		H	6.25am	-	BHSS Middle			-	-
6.25am	Crewe	Longport Junction		K	-	6.25am	North Staffs Sdgs	-	-		
5.40am	Longsight	Crewe ECS		C	6.35am	-	Up Through			-	-
6.35am	Crewe	Sudbury Junction		H	-	6.35am	BHSS Middle	-	-	5B/1018	5B/1165
11.55pm	Copley Hill	Shrewsbury		H	6.35am	7.50am	Gresty Lane				
5.10am	Mold Junction	Crewe		H	6.31am	-	North Staffs Sdgs	5D/345	5B/1468	-	-
5.15am	Edge Hill	Sudbury Junction		E	6.40am	6.53am	Up Through	1A/1	5A/590	1A/1	1A/807
6.45am	Crewe	Derby		B	-	6.45am	5 Bay	-	-	5A/33	5A/628
1.30am	Copley Hill	Crewe		H	6.50am	-	BHSS Middle	25G/301	5B/1348	-	-
6.50am	Crewe	Birmingham		B	-	6.50am	5	-	-	8A/32	5A/554
6.55am	Crewe	Oxley			-	6.55am	Gresty Lane	-	-		84B/
5.40am	Hooton	Beeston		F	7am	7.10am	North Staffs Sdgs	5B/1001	6C/371	5B/1001	6C/371
7.5am	Crewe	Hollinswood		K	-	7.5am	Gresty Lane			84B/	Crewe/10
5.50am	Manchester L Rd	Crewe		B	7.8am	-	6			-	-
5am	Stott Lane	Crewe		H	7.10am	-	BHSS Middle	5B/1005	10C/534	-	-
6.36am	Chester	Crewe		B	7.19am	-	4			-	-
6.59am	Northwich	Crewe		B	7.25am	-	10 Bay	5A/120	5A/120	-	-
7.32am	Crewe	Shrewsbury		B	-	7.32am	5	-	-		
5.30am	Preston	Crewe		B	7.33am	-	5			-	-
12.1am	Glasgow Central	Willesden Junction	372	C	7.43am	7.55am	6	5B/1034	5A/204	5A/19	5A.383
7.45am	Crewe	Bescot		H	-	7.45am	BHSS Middle	-	-	3C/203	3B/327
7.50am	Crewe	Euston	24	A	-	7.50am	3	-	-	5A/61	1B/242

Time Dep	From	Destination	Rep No	Train Class	Crewe Arr	Crewe Dep	Platform or Yard	To Crewe from North Men Diag	To Crewe from North Loco Diag	From Crewe to South Men Diag	From Crewe to South Loco Diag
4.28am	Carlisle	Crewe Fish	390	C	7.55am	-	6	5A/28	5A/160	-	-
8.10am	Crewe	Derby		B	-	8.10am	6 Bay	-	-	5A/112	5A/112
6.5am	Mold Junction	Crewe		H	8.10am	-	BHSS Middle	5B/1055	6B/269	-	-
8.15am	Crewe	Whitemoor Sidings		E	-	8.15am	BHSS.	-	-	5B/1038	5B/1172
3.10am	Carlisle	Crewe		D	8.20am	-	Gresty Lane	5B/1038	5B/1296	-	-
7.15am	Manchester L Rd	Crewe		B	8.28am	-	4			-	-
6.30am	Heysham	Euston	32	A	8.31am	8.42am	5	1B/11	11A/100	1B/11	1B/219
8.37am	Crewe	Shrewsbury		B	-	8.37am	4 Bay	-	-	5A/107	5A/107
6.30am	Morecambe	Crewe	272	A	8.44am	-	5	5A/24	5A/221	-	-
6.30am	Llandudno	Euston	302	A	8.45am	9am	3	7C/7	6A/249	7C/7	5A/300
3.35am	Crofton Hall	Crewe		J	8.50am	-	BHSS Middle	5B/1003	5B/1335	-	-
8.5am	Manchester L Rd	Crewe	30	A	8.55am	-	4 North			-	-
8.33am	Northwich	Crewe		B	9am	-	5	5A/120	5A/120	-	-
8am	Liverpool Lime St	Coventry	34	A	9.2am	9.10am	4	8A/15	8A/266	8A/15	5A/556
8.10am	Manchester L Rd	Penzance	204	A	9.6am	9.15am	5				
9.8am	Crewe	Derby		A	-	9.8am	5 Bay	-	-	5A/99	5A/99
8.20am	Liverpool Lime St	Euston	36	A	9.10am	9.18am	3	8A/		8A/	
9.30am	Crewe	Wellington		B	-	9.30am	3 Bay	-	-		
8.50am	Liverpool Lime St	Penzance	446	A	*pass 9.36am*		Up Through	5A/71	5A/599	5A/71	5A/599
9.37am	Crewe	Derby ECS		C	-	9.37am	Up Sidings	-	-		
9.45am	Crewe	Oxley Sidings		H	-	9.45am	Gresty Lane	-	-	84B/	
8.20am	Preston	Bristol	306	A	9.48am	10am	3			5A/69	5A/729
8.42am	Manchester L Rd	Crewe		B	9.54am	-	5	9A/14	9A/247	-	-
7.25am	Heysham	Crewe	26	A	9.55am	-	4	11A/6	28A/75	-	-
9.15am	Manchester L Rd	Paignton	212	A	10.5am	10.7am	Up Through	9A/9	5A/605	9A/9	5A/719
8am	Blackpool Central	Euston	296	A	10.6am	10.15am	3	1B/12	1B/118	1B/12	1B/118
9.25am	Manchester L Rd	Swansea High St	210	A	10.14am	10.30am	5	9A/10	5A/621	9A/10	5A/718
9.15am	Liverpool Lime St	Plymouth	208	A	10.16am	10.40am	4			5A/1	5A/703
8.56am	Northwich	Crewe	25	K	10.16am	-	BHSS Middle	-	-		
9.45am	Manchester L Rd	Euston	58	A	*pass 10.27am*		Up Through	9A/	1B/167	9A/	1B/167
7.30am	Holyhead	Euston	48	A	10.28am	10.35am	3	7C/2	6A/250	7C/2	1B/232
10.30am	Crewe	Stoke	89	H	-	10.30am	North Staffs Sdgs	-	-		
9.20am	Rhyl	Birmingham N St	244	A	*pass 10.33am*		via Basford Hall	5A/66	3C/87	5A/66	3C/87
9.55am	Liverpool Lime St	Euston	222	A	*pass 10.45am*		Up Through	1A/7	1A/74	1A/7	1A/74
8.55am	Llandudno	Euston	66	A	10.50am	10.55am	3	5B/1031	7A/162	5B/1031	1B/248
10.10am	Liverpool Lime St	Euston	54	A	*pass 10.55am*		Up Through	8A/	1B/145	8A/	1B/145
10.10am	Manchester L Rd	Birmingham N St	214	A	10.57am	11.4am	4 South	1B/42	3D/159	1B/42	3D/159
11am	Crewe	Oxley Sidings			-	11am	Gresty Lane	-	-	85A/	Crewe/11
10.15am	Liverpool Lime St	Birmingham N St	62	A	11.1am	11.12am	4 North	9A/	8A/313	9A/	5A/564
9.5am	Llandudno	Euston	56	A	11.6am	11.28am	3	1B/19	7A/156	1B/19	5A/386
9.15am	Blackpool North	Cardiff	404	A	*pass 11.10am*		Up Through	28A/59	28A/72	28A/59	5A/728
10.30am	Liverpool Lime St	Walsall	242	A	11.15am	11.30am	4 South	5A/42	5A/583	5A/42	3C/86
11.20am	Crewe	Derby		B	-	11.20am	6 Bay	-	-	9A/14	5A/623
11.20am	Crewe	Whitchurch ECS		C	-	11.20am	Down Sidings	-	-	8A/26	5A/711
11.20am	Crewe Coal yard	Crewe	17	K	-	11.20am	BHSS Middle	5B/1119	5B/1119	-	-
10.38am	Manchester L Rd	Bournemouth	196	A	11.21am	11.33am	4 North	9A/20	9A/318		
9.35am	Northwich	Crewe			11.25am	-	5	5B/1017	5B/1368	-	-
11.30am	Crewe	Etruria	84	K	-	11.30am	North Staffs Sdgs	-	-		
9.25am	Llandudno	Coventry	226	A	*pass 11.33am*		via Basford Hall	2A/6	5A/677	2A/6	5A/677
6.5am	Carlisle	Crewe	274	B	11.40am	-	5	12A/13	5A/201	-	-
10.50am	Manchester L Rd	Aberystwyth	304	A	11.49am	11.57am	3				
11.10am	Liverpool Lime St	Euston	112	A	11.56am	12.2pm	4	8A/	1B/153	8A/	1B/153
12pm	Crewe	Oxley Sidings		H	-	12pm	Gresty Lane	-	-	84B/	Crewe/12
9.45am	Blackpool Central	Euston	330	A	12.1pm	12.9pm	3	1B/17	1B/124	1B/17	1B/124
10.15am	Llandudno	Derby	72	A	12.4pm	12.12pm	6	7A/6	7A/166	7A/6	5A/639
9.55am	Blackpool Central	Bletchley	324	A	12.9pm	12.14pm	4	2A/	28A/73	2A/	4A/95
9.55am	Llandudno	Leicester	218	A	*pass 12.10pm*		via Basford Hall		2B/102		2B/102
12.10pm	Crewe	Shrewsbury		B	-	12.10pm	4 Bay	-	-	9A/	5A/713
6.35am	Workington	Euston	70	A	12.17pm	12.25pm	4	1B/33	10B/203	1B/33	1B/250
11.10am	Manchester L Rd	Crewe		B	12.20pm	-	6			-	-
12.20pm	Crewe	Derby		B	-	12.20pm	5 Bay	-	-		
8.5am	Carlisle	Birmingham New St	456	A	12.23pm	12.32pm	3	1B/34	5A/175		
12.28pm	Crewe	Stafford		B	-	12.28pm	3 Bay	-	-	8A/13	5C/92
11.5am	Rhyl	Stoke	108	A	12.33pm	12.40pm	5	7A/2	6A/250	7A/2	6A/250
8.50am	Penychain	Stoke	164	A	12.43pm	12.55pm	6	7A/3	7A/161	7A/3	5A/640
12pm	Sandbach	Crewe	23	K	12.45pm	-	BHSS Middle	5B/1053	5B/1367	-	-
8.20am	Carlisle	Euston	74	A	12.51pm	1pm	3	5A/27	12A/91	5A/29	1B/227
11.55am	Manchester L Rd	Plymouth	228	A	12.55pm	1.10pm	4				
12.56pm	Crewe	Wellington		B	-	12.56pm	3 Bay	-	-		
11.40am	Liverpool Lime St	Rugby	84	A	12.59pm	1.11pm	5	8A/13	5A/593	8A/13	5A/565

Time Dep	From	Destination	Rep No	Train Class	Crewe Arr	Crewe Dep	Platform or Yard	To Crewe from North Men Diag	To Crewe from North Loco Diag	From Crewe to South Men Diag	From Crewe to South Loco Diag
12pm	Manchester L Rd	Cardiff	314	A	1.5pm	1.15pm	3				
10.55am	Blackpool North	Crewe	384	A	1.9pm	-	6	28A/79	28A/79	-	-
12.27pm	Chester	Crewe		A	1.13pm	-	10 Bay			-	-
1.15pm	Crewe	Pratts Sidings	50	J	-	1.15pm	North Staffs Sdg	-	-		
1.30pm	Crewe	Oxley Sidings		F	-	1.30pm	Gresty Lane	-	-		84B/-
11.30am	Blackpool	Stechford	412	A	1.32pm	1.37pm	BHSS South	5A/45	10A/202	5A/45	3C/89
1.35pm	Crewe	Derby		B	-	1.35pm	6 Bay	-	-	5A/93	5A/93
9.55am	Porthmadoc	Euston	100	A	*pass 1.43pm*		Up Through	1B/21	2A/201	1B/21	2A/201
11.45am	Blackpool North	Coventry		A	1.44pm	1.52pm	BHSS South	28A/65	28A/77	28A/65	5A/388
10.50am	Windermere	Euston	86	A	1.53pm	2.2pm	4	1B/12	10B/82	1B/12	10B/82
7.50am	Holyhead	Crewe Pcls	76	C	1.58pm	-	5			-	-
12.15pm	Blackpool Central	Euston	396	A	2pm	2.10pm	3	28A/63	28A/74	28A/63	1B/252
1.45pm	Northwich	Crewe Motor		B	2.11pm	-	10 Bay	5A/122	5A/122	-	-
1.5pm	Liverpool Lime St	Crewe	192	A	2.15pm	-	6	5A/23	5A/582	-	-
6.50am	Carlisle	Crewe		H	2.20pm	-	North Staffs Sdg			-	-
12.15pm	Blackpool North	Birmingham New St	264	A	2.24pm	2.27pm	3	3D/13	5A/239	3D/13	5A/509
2.25pm	Crewe	Chaddesden		H	-	2.25pm	North Staffs Sdgs	-	-		16A/626
1.18pm	Manchester L Rd	Crewe		B	2.28pm	-	4	9A/23	9A/261	-	-
12.20pm	Llandudno	Euston	496	A	2.32pm	2.36pm	BHSS South	1B/32	5A/651	1B/32	1B/254
2.37pm	Crewe	Pontypool Rd Pcls	190	C	-	2.37pm	Up Sidings	-	-	2B/5	5A/725
2.2pm	Chester	Crewe		B	2.43pm	-	3			-	-
2pm	Liverpool Lime St	Euston	92	A	*pass 2.45pm*		Up Through	8A/	8A/	8A/	8A/
12.55pm	Llandudno	Nottingham	290	A	2.50pm	2.58pm	6			3C/5	5A/657
1.15pm	Edge Hill	Willesden		D	2.40pm	2.46pm	Station	12A/320	5A/585	12A/320	5B/1176
9.30am	Glasgow	Birmingham New St	98	A	2.55pm	3.15pm	4	5A/4	66A/	5A/10	5A/550
1.25pm	Heaton Norris	Crewe		J	3.1pm	-	BHSS Middle	5B/1001	9B/279	-	-
10am	Glasgow Central	Euston	96	A	*pass 3.8pm*		Up Through	66A/1	12A/60	66A/1	12A/60
1pm	Edge Hill	Crewe		H	3/13	-	BHSS Middle			-	-
3.15pm	Crewe	Wellington		B	-	3.15pm	3 Bay	-	-	Wellington	Crewe/2
10.12am	Edinburgh	Birmingham New St	156	A	3.20pm	3.28pm	5	5A/19	12A/124	3D/	3D/157
1.5pm	Llandudno	Euston	270	A	3.21pm	3.31pm	3	9A/12	5A/680	9A/12	5A/310
3.28pm	Crewe	Shrewsbury		B	-	3.28pm	4 Bay	-	-	2A/9	5A/727
8.26am	Heaton Norris	Crewe		K	3.30pm	-	BHSS Middle	5B/1020	5B/1333	-	-
1.20pm	Llandudno	Derby	116	A	3.32pm	3.40pm	6				
10.6am	Glasgow Central	Euston	106	A	3.32pm	3.49pm	4	1B/4	5A/182	1B/4	1B/236
3.40pm	Crewe	Alsager Junction	89	J	-	3.40pm	North Staffs Sdgs	-	-		
1.55pm	Blackpool North	Stoke	388	A	3.40pm	3.48pm	5	2A/	5A/241	2A/	5A/641
1.40pm	Llandudno	Derby	124	A	3.51pm	4.2pm	6				
3.5pm	Manchester L Rd	Birmingham New St	236	A	3.54pm	4.7pm	5	2A/4	5A/607	2A/4	5A/908
3.55pm	Crewe	Oxley Sidings		H	-	3.55pm	Gresty Lane	-	-		84B/-
3pm	Liverpool Lime St	Cardiff	234	A	3.55pm	4.9pm	3				
4pm	Crewe	Madeley	39	J	-	4pm	BHSS Middle	-	-		
2.50pm	Rhyl	Birmingham New St	468	A	*pass 4.6pm*		BHSS South	3D/8	5A/682	3D/8	5A/514
4.2am	Crewe	Derby			-	4.2pm		-	-	5A/43	5A/635
3.15pm	Manchester L Rd	Plymouth	240	A	4.10pm	4.20pm	5	9A/7	9A/314	9A/7	5A/706
8.55am	Perth	Euston	110	A	4.6pm	4.15pm	4	1B/	12A/122	1B/	1A/65
1.55pm	Holyhead	Euston	310	A	4.18pm	4.26pm		1B/20	7C/82	1B/20	1A/72
4.20pm	Crewe	Leek		B	-	4.20pm	6 Bay	-	-	5D/34	5D/34
10.50am	Workington	Euston	254	A	4.24pm	4.34pm	4	10B/		10B/	
2.25pm	Llandudno	Birmingham New St	282	A	4.28pm	4.37pm	Up Through	3D/7	5A/684	3D/7	3D/158
4.30pm	Crewe	Radway Green	93	G	-	4.30pm	North Staffs Sdgs	-	-		
3.20pm	Manchester M'field	Crewe		B	4.39pm	-	6	9A/420	9A/252	-	-
4.40pm	Crewe	Stoke	48	H	-	4.40pm	North Staffs Sdgs	-	-		
2.30pm	Holyhead	Birmingham New St	492	A	4.50pm	4.58pm		1B/20	5A/673	1B/20	3D/157
1.30pm	Barrow	Crewe	266	A	4.51pm	-	5	5A/11	5A/207	-	-
4.10pm	Liverpool Lime St	Euston	114	A	4.56pm	5.2pm	4	8A/	8A/	8A/	8A/
2.50pm	Llandudno	Birmingham	140	A	5.3pm	5.11pm	3	2A/35	5A/688	2A/35	5A/510
2.25pm	Edge Hill	Longport Junction		F	5.8pm	5.15pm	North Staffs Sdgs	6C/201	8C/251	6C/201	5B/1377
5.10pm	Crewe	Wellington		B	-	5.10pm	3 Bay	-	-		
5.10pm	Crewe	Stafford (via Stoke)		B	-	5.10pm	6 Bay	-	-	84G/5	5A/624
5.15pm	Crewe	Willesden HLS		E	-	5.15pm	BH	-	-	2B/116	1A/814
3.5pm	Holyhead	Euston	88	A	5.17pm	5.27pm		7C/1	5A/692	7C/1	5A/354
4.35pm	Manchester L Rd	Birmingham	238	A	5.17pm	5.30pm	4 South				
4.17pm	Liverpool Lime St	Crewe	162	A	5.20pm	-	4 North	3D/10	5A/587	-	-
5.25pm	Crewe	Shrewsbury		B	-	5.25pm	4 Bay	-	-	1B/22	5A/701
5.13pm	Calveley	Crewe Milk	132	C	5.27pm	-	Up Sidings	5A/55	5A/909	-	-
3.40pm	Blackpool North	Birmingham	268	A	5.30pm	5.39pm	5	3E/8	5A/237	3E/8	3D/160
5.35pm	Crewe	Oxley Sidings		H	-	5.35pm	Gresty Lane	-	-		84B/-
5.38pm	Northwich	Crewe		B	5.38pm	-	3	5A/122	5A/122	-	-
5.40pm	Crewe	Willesden HL		E	-	5.40pm	BHSS South	-	-		

Time Dep	From	Destination	Rep No	Train Class	Crewe Arr	Crewe Dep	Platform or Yard	To Crewe from North Men Diag	Loco Diag	From Crewe to South Men Diag	Loco Diag
11.59pm	Carnforth	Crewe			5.45pm	-	BH	11A/250	5B/1292	-	-
4.28pm	Manchester M'field	Crewe		B	5.52pm	-	5			-	-
5.10pm	Chester	Crewe		B	5.54pm	-	3			-	-
5.55pm	Crewe	Stafford		B	-	5.55pm		-	-		
6.1pm	Crewe	Bushbury			-	6.1pm	BH	-	-	5B/1004	5B/1209
5.20pm	Warrington	Crewe		B	6.4pm	-	5	5B/1086	8B/108	-	-
6.5pm	Crewe	Stoke		B	-	6.5pm	5 Bay	-	-		
6.5pm	Crewe	Willesden Jnt	232	C	-	6.5pm		-	-	2A/	5A/395
6.10pm	Crewe	Shrewsbury		B	-	6.10pm	4 Bay	-	-	12A/13	5A/710
5.25pm	Liverpool Lime St	Euston	122	A	6.10pm	6.15pm	4	1B/6	1B/141	1B/6	1B/141
6.10pm	Crewe	Banbury		H	-	6.10pm	BHSS South	-	-		
5.11pm	Manchester L Rd	Crewe		B	6.18pm	-	6			-	-
4.40pm	Manchester Exch	Crewe ECS		C	6.20pm	-	Up Through	-	-		
4pm	Bangor	Birmingham N St	278	A	6.33pm	7.10pm	3	5A/67	6A/206	9A/101	5A/557
5.50pm	Manchester L Rd	Euston	130	A	6.33pm	6.38pm	4	9A/	1B/187	9A/	1B/187
6.30am	Crewe	Salop Coleham		F	-	6.30am	Gresty Lane	-	-	5B/1001	5B/1477
4.40pm	Edge Hill	Shrewsbury		F	6.35pm	7.20pm	Gresty Lane	8A/26	5A/711	8A/26	84G/58
6.35pm	Crewe	Nuneaton		H	-	6.35pm	BHSS South	-	-	2A/8	5B/1174
6.35pm	Crewe	Derby		B	-	6.35pm	5 Bay	-	-		
4.43pm	Speke Sidings	Longport Junction		F	-	6.55pm	Station				
1.30pm	Glasgow Central	Euston	126	A	6.55pm	7.3pm	4	1B/2	5A/142	1B/2	5A/329
5.40pm	Liverpool Lime St	Crewe		B	7.5pm	-	5			-	-
4.45pm	Mold Junction	Crewe		H	7.8pm	-	North Staffs Sdgs	6B/111	6B/282	-	-
12.14pm	Perth	Crewe	44	A	7.14pm	-	4	5A/22	5A/186	-	-
2.5pm	Copley Hill	Crewe		H	7.24pm	-	Gresty Lane	5B/1034	5B/1341	-	-
7.25pm	Crewe	Alsager Junction	83	K	-	7.25pm	North Staffs Sdgs	-	-		
7.25pm	Crewe	Rugby		H	-	7.25pm	BHSS Middle	-	-	5B/1017	2B/323
6.50pm	Northwich	Crewe Motor		B	7.26pm	-	3	5A/122	5A/122	-	-
5.40pm	Dundas Sidings	Normacot Junction		F	7.28pm	8.30pm	North Staffs Sdgs	5B/1037	5B/1456	5B/1037	5B/1456
5.5pm	Blackpool Central	Euston	136	A	7.30pm	7.39pm	4	28A/60	28A/66	28A/60	28A/66
5.15pm	Llandudno	Stoke	430	A	7.41pm	7.45pm	5	9A/14	5A/691	9A/14	5A/641
4.30pm	Heysham	Crewe Pcls	356	C	7.40pm	-	Up Through	4B/3	1A/109	9A/	
6.25pm	Manchester M'field	Crewe		B	7.40pm	-	6	9A/420	9B/76	-	-
7.50pm	Crewe	Whitchurch		B	-	7.50pm	3 Bay	-	-	W'chrch/15	W'church/18
7.55pm	Crewe	Longport Junction	89	K	-	7.55pm	North Staffs Sdgs	-	-		
7.10pm	Manchester L Rd	Cardiff	246	A	7.58pm	8.33pm	5				
7.20pm	Chester	Crewe		B	8pm	-	3			-	-
7.5pm	Liverpool Lime St	Birmingham	250	A	8pm	8.17pm	4				
7.32pm	Winsford Junction	Crewe	35	K	8.2pm	-	BHSS Middle	5B/1127	5B/1127	-	-
8.5pm	Crewe	Stourbridge		H	-	8.5pm	Gresty Lane	-	-	84F/	Crewe/14
5.30pm	Carnforth	Willesden HLS		C	8.9pm	8.30pm	Up Through	11A/262	11A/90	11A/262	11A/90
6.5pm	Blackpool North	Stoke	276	A	8.10pm	8.18pm	6				
6.25pm	Edge Hill	Crewe		F	8.10pm	-	North Staffs Sdgs			-	-
6.15pm	Llandudno	Derby	80	A	8.17pm	8.20pm	6				
8.20pm	Crewe	Bristol	248	A	-	8.20pm	5	-	-	84G/2	5A/707
6.3pm	Wyre Dock	Broad Street		C	8.21pm	8.21pm	4	5B/1039	10B/559	9A/420	1A/810
6.15pm	Longsight	Bushbury		F	8.31pm	8.50pm	BHSS South	3D/2	5A/611	3D/2	5B/1203
6.15pm	Bamfurlong	Crewe		F	8.40pm	-	BHSS Middle			-	-
6.25pm	Edge Hill	Crewe		F	8.41pm	-	Gresty Lane	8A/33	5B/1448	-	-
7.20pm	Liverpool Lime St	Crewe		B	8.41pm	-	5	8A/32	8A/254	-	-
6.3pm	Ellesmere Port	Etruria Junction		F	*pass 8.21pm*		North Staffs Sdgs				
8.50pm	Crewe	Wellington		B	-	8.50pm	2 Bay	-	-		
8.50pm	Crewe	Euston Pcls	306	C	-	8.50pm	Up Through	-	-	5A/24	5A/384
7.40pm	Middlewich	Crewe	24	K	8.56pm	-	BHSS Middle	5B/1063	5B/1364	-	-
7.38pm	Edge Hill	Rugby		F	9.11pm	9.14pm	BHSS South				
9.18pm	Crewe	Shrewsbury		B	-	9.18pm	5	-	-		84G/75
8.10pm	Edge Hill	Birmingham C St		E	*pass 9.24pm*		Up Through	3D/1	3D/379	3D/1	3D/379
9.25pm	Crewe	Newcastle Junction		H	-	9.25pm	North Staffs Sdgs	-	-	6C/201	5B/1377
8.15pm	Manchester L Rd	Crewe		B	9.26pm	-	6	8A/15	5A/610	-	-
7.45pm	Ravenhead	Willesden HL		E	9.28pm	9.58pm	BHSS South	8B/1	8B/78	8B/1	1A/818
6.45pm	Wyre Dock	Crewe		C	9.30pm	-	Up Through	5B/1032	10A/644	-	-
7.15pm	Birkenhead	Birmingham C St		H	9.30pm	10.5pm	BHSS Middle	3D/3	6C/370	3D/3	5B/1201
9.35pm	Crewe	Worcester			-	9.35pm	Gresty Lane	-	-		84B/
9.35pm	Crewe	Birmingham Pcls	90	C	-	9.35pm	Up Sidings	-	-	3D/10	5A/552
4.34pm	Carlisle	Crewe		D	9.40pm	-	BHSS Middle	12A/17	5B/1235	-	-
9.22pm	Alderley Edge	Crewe LE		G	9.54pm	-	South Shed	5A/113	5A/113	-	-
9.55pm	Crewe	Stoke		B	-	9.55pm	5 Bay	-	-		

Time Dep	From	Destination	Rep No	Train Class	Crewe Arr	Crewe Dep	Platform or Yard	To Crewe from North Men Diag	To Crewe from North Loco Diag	From Crewe to South Men Diag	From Crewe to South Loco Diag
8.50pm	Edge Hill	Camden		D	9.56pm	9.58pm	Up Through	8A/12	8A/773	8A/12	1A/803
8.30pm	Edge Hill	Nottingham		E	10.7pm	10.35pm	North Staffs Sdgs	8A/12	8A/765	8A/12	8A/765
8.30pm	Manchester L Rd	Oxley Sidings		E	10.10pm	10.35pm	Gresty Lane	2A/4	5A/612	2A/4	Crewe/16
8.50pm	Bamfurlong	Sudbury Junction		D	10.15pm	10.35pm	BHSS South			5B/1051	5B/1179
8.15pm	Northwich	Crewe	27	K	10.32pm	-	BHSS Middle			-	-
9.5pm	Edge Hill	Shrewsbury		E	10.36pm	10.55pm	Gresty Lane	3B/151	5A/596	3B/151	84G/195
10.40pm	Crewe	Nuneaton		H	-	10.40pm	BHSS Middle	-	-	5B/1018	5B/1191
9.37pm	Manchester L Rd	Crewe		B	10.46pm	-	4	5A/33	5A/614	-	-
9.20pm	Speke Sidings	Nuneaton		F	10.52pm	11pm	BHSS South	8A/508	8A/809	8A/508	5B/1184
10.20pm	Chester	Crewe		B	10.59pm	-	4			-	-
6.3pm	Copley Hill	Crewe		J	11.7pm	-	Gresty Lane			-	-
11.30pm	Crewe	Pratts Sidings	41	H	-	11.30pm	North Staffs Sdgs	-	-		
6.35pm	Neville Hill	Aston		E	11.20pm	11.28pm	BHSS South	3D/200	9B/365	3D/200	3B/306
11.20pm	Crewe	Burton		H	-	11.20pm	BHSS Middle	-	-		5C/104
10.10pm	Liverpool Lime St	Crewe	142	A	11.25pm	-	5	5A/99	5A/100	-	-
5.25pm	Carlisle	Crewe		D	11.25pm	-	Gresty Lane	5B/1037	5B/1245	-	-
10.37pm	Manchester L Rd	Crewe	144	A	11.29pm	-	6	9A/8	9A/262	-	-
7.35pm	Holyhead	Birmingham	170	A	11.35pm	-	3				
5pm	Low Gill	Crewe		H	11.37pm	-	Gresty Lane			-	-
8.21pm	Lancaster	Bushbury		E	11.40pm	12am	BHSS South				
10.45pm	Warrington	Birmingham C St		F	11.52pm	12.23am	BHSS South	5B/1034	5B/1283	5B/1034	5B/1215
11.18pm	Chester	Camden		D	11.59pm	1am	BHSS Middle			5A/39	5B/1180

Below:
Dillicar, No Date
'Princess Royal' Pacific No 46209 *Princess Beatrice* picking up water on the Up 'Mid-Day Scot' floods the leading coach as the tank overflows. The locomotive is at the end of the troughs, so possibly the scoop has jammed in the down position, not an unknown experience! Pity anyone looking out of a window at the time. *Eric Treacy*

Up Direction - Sundays Only

NOTE: Italics under departure time denote passing time

Time Dep	From	Destination	Rep No	Train Class	Crewe Arr	Crewe Dep	Platform or Yard	To Crewe from North Loco Diag	To Crewe from North Men Diag	From Crewe to South Loco Diag	From Crewe to South Men Diag
10.45pm	Warrington	Birmingham C St		F	11.52pm	12.23am	BHSS Middle	5B/1034	5B/1283	5B/1034	5B/1215
7.35pm	Holyhead	Birmingham N St	170	A	11.35pm	12.45am	3			9A/8	3E/107
8.30pm	Windermere	Euston	37	A	12.3am	12.25am	5				
12.5am	Crewe	Birmingham N St	342	C	-	12.5am	6	-	-	4A/5	5C/
11.30pm	Manchester L Rd	Crewe	308	A	12.9pm		Up Through	9A/9	9A.263	-	-
10.45pm	Mold Junction	Crewe		E	12.18am	-	BHSS South	6B/4	5B/1469	-	-
6.25pm	Glasgow Central	Euston	148	A	12.25am	12.37am	4	5A/5	5A/179	5A/4	5A/267
8.50pm	Lancaster	Bushbury		E	12.29am	12.50am	BHSS South	84G/102	5B/1278	84G/102	5B/1220
12.30am	Crewe	Whitchurch		F	-	12.30am	BHSS North	-	-	W'church/1	W'church/4
11.55pm	Manchester L Rd	Crewe	150	A	12.41am	-	6	9A/—	5A/613	-	-
5.40pm	Glasgow Central	Euston	146	A	12.41am	1.10am	5	5A/3	5A/140	1B/13	5A/275
11.40pm	Chester	Crewe		H	12.45am	-	BHSS South	3D/5	5A/652	-	-
11.45pm	Liverpool Lime St	Crewe	158	A	12.46am	-	4	9A/10	5A/576	-	-
11.45pm	Northwich	Crewe		K	12.59am	-	BHSS Middle	5B/1053	5B/1363	-	-
1.4am	Crewe	Hockley		F	-	1.4am	Gresty Lane	-	-		
9.50pm	York	Shrewsbury	C487	A	1.7am	2.15am	3	9A/7	9A/279	-	-
12.10am	Liverpool Lime St	Euston	152	A	1.13am	1.22am	5				
1.25am	Crewe	Cardiff	174	A	-	1.25am	4	-	-	9A/—	84G/65
1.30am	Crewe	Newcastle Jnt		F	-	1.30am	North Staffs Sdgs	-	-		
6.30pm	Holyhead	Crewe	160	C	1.37am	-	4	5A/28	5A/697	-	-
2.50pm	Carlisle	Crewe		H	1.38am	-	North Staffs Sdgs			-	-
1.40am	Crewe	Plymouth	174/2	A	-	1.40am	6	-	-	84G/5	84G/66
7.20pm	Law Junction	Broad Street	362	C	1.42am	2.15am	5			8A/—	1B/203
1.45am	Crewe	Stoke on Trent		B	-	1.45am	5 Bay	-	-	5A/78	5A/636
10.10pm	Leeds City South	Crewe	C478	C	2.6pm	-	6	9A/3	5A/616	-	-
2.10am	Crewe	Stoke Yard	57	H	-	2.10am	North Staffs Sdgs	-	-		
12.52am	Edge Hill	Stoke Yard		F	2.25am	2.30am	North Staffs Sdgs	1B/42	8A/837		
10.30pm	Carnforth	Crewe		H	2.35am	-	BHSS Middle			-	-
1.42am	Chester	Alsager Junction		F	*pass 2.41am*	-				-	-
1.10am	Holyhead	Euston	332	A	3.20am	3.30am	3			-	-
1.35am	Speke Sidings	Trentham		H	3.25am	3.42am	North Staffs Sdgs	-	-		
9.25pm	Glasgow Central	Euston	10	A	3.22am	3.37am	4	12A/—	1B/102	12A/—	1B/102
1.40am	Heaton Norris	Crewe		H	3.30am	-	BHSS Middle				
2.50am	Manchester L Rd	Crewe	184	A	3.33am	-	5				
3.35am	Crewe	Oxley Sidings		H	-	3.35am	Gresty Lane				
8.15pm	Perth	Euston	12	A	3.40am	4am	4	5A/2	5A/136	12A/—	5A/282
9.5pm	Carlisle	Crewe		E	3.40am	-	BHSS Middle			-	-
3.44am	Crewe	Birmingham N St	180	A	-	3.44am	3 Bay	-	-	9A/	3D/151
10.10pm	Glasgow Central	Euston	6	A	*pass 3.52am*		Up Through				
4am	Crewe	Crewe Coal Yard		K	-	4am	BHSS North	-	-	5B/1118	5B/1122
1.45am	Holyhead	Euston	4	A	4.1am	4.11am	3				
4.10am	Crewe	Stoke on Trent		A	-	4.10am	5	-	-	5A/78	5A/636
4.45pm	Inverness	Euston	14	A	4.12am	4.27am	4	5A/60	5A/146	1B/34	1B/238
2.40am	Speke Sidings	Crewe		H	4.20am	-	North Staffs Sdgs	5B/1019	8C/248	-	-
10.20pm	Glasgow Central	Euston	224	A	*pass 4.20am*		Up Through	1B/3	12A/56	1B/3	12A/56
10pm	Stranraer Harbour	Euston	68	A	4.42am	4.52am	3	1B/2	12A/82	1B/2	1B/214
2.55am	Ellesmere Port	Crewe		H	4.48am	-	BHSS Middle			-	-
4.50am	Crewe	Oxley Sidings		H	-	4.50am	Gresty Lane	-	-		
5.15pm	Inverness	Euston	16	A	4.52am	5.6pm	4	5A/1	5A/133	5A/3	5A/298
11.15pm	Glasgow Central	Birmingham N St	18	A	5am	5.14am	3	66A/2	5A/144	9A/3	3D/165
5.10am	Crewe Coal Yard	Crewe	17	G	5.20am	-	BHSS Middle	5B/1118	5B/1122	-	-
3.10am	Edge Hill	Crewe		H	5.30am	-	Gresty Lane			-	-
4.25am	Warrington	Crewe		H	5.35am	-	BHSS Middle	5B/1020	5B/1271	-	-
12.30am	Carnforth	Crewe		H	5.56am	-	North Staffs Sdgs			-	-
3.45am	Holyhead	Euston	52	A	5.58am	6.8am	4	1A/8	5A/683	1A/8	1B/246
6am	Crewe	Willesden Jnt	314	C	-	6am		-	-	5A/	1A/67
6am	Crewe	Oxley Sidings		H	-	6am	Gresty Lane	-	-		
6.18am	Crewe	Birmingham N St	200	A	-	6.18am	4 Bay	-	-		
6.30am	Crewe	Winsford Jnt		K	-	6.30am	BHSS North	-	-	5B/1118	5B/1122
5am	Edge Hill	Crewe		H	6.38am	-	BHSS Middle	5A/43	5A/591	-	-
6.40am	Crewe	Wellington		B	-	6.40am	3 Bay	-	-	Wellington	Crewe/4
6.50am	Crewe	Derby		B	-	6.50am	6 Bay	-	-	84G/5	5A/629
6.55am	Crewe	Oxley Sidings		H	-	6.55am	Gresty Lane	-	-		
7.55pm	Aberdeen	Crewe	390	C	7.59am	-	5	8A/6	5A/161	-	-
6.15am	Heysham	Euston	26	A	8.25am	8.35am	4	1B/43	11A/107	1B/43	5A/297
8.30am	Crewe	Oxley Sidings		H	-	8.30am	Gresty Lane	-	-		
4.30am	Crofton South Jnt	Crewe		J	8.38am	-	BHSS Middle	84G/103	5B/1336	-	-

Time Dep	From	Destination	Rep No	Train Class	Crewe Arr	Crewe Dep	Platform or Yard	To Crewe from North Loco Diag	To Crewe from North Men Diag	From Crewe to South Loco Diag	From Crewe to South Men Diag
8.55am	Crewe	Birmingham N St	318	C	-	8.55am	5 Bay	-	-	4A/5	3D/153
8.55am	Crewe	Harlescott Sidings		H	-	8.55am	BHSS	-	-	5B/1032	84G/68
2.35am	Carlisle	Crewe		E	9am	-	Gresty Lane	5B/1030	10A/643	-	-
8.43am	Winsford Jn	Crewe	17	G	9.10am	-	BHSS Middle	5B/1118	5B/1122	-	-
7am	Heysham	Euston	32	A	9.10am	9.12am	3	1B/11	11A/102	1B/11	1B/228
8.10am	Liverpool Lime St	Birmingham N St	34	A	9.22am	9.31am	4	8A/—	8A/278	8A/—	5A/501
8.30am	Liverpool Lime St	Euston	66	A	9.30am	9.41am	3	1A/580	1A/75	1A/580	1A/75
9.30am	Crewe	Oxley Sidings		H	-	9.30am	Gresty Lane	-	-	85A/—	Crewe17
9.35am	Crewe	Derby		B	-	9.35am	6 Bay	-	-	5A/97	5A/101
8.42am	Manchester L Rd	Crewe		B	9.53am	-	5	5A/11	5A/617	-	-
10am	Crewe	Newport Mon	204	C	-	10am	6	-	-		
7.45am	Blackpool Central	Euston	296	A	10.8am	10.16am	4	1B/17	1B/119	1B/17	1B/119
9.45am	Liverpool Lime St	Euston	36	A	*pass 10.34am*		Up Through				
8.10am	Bangor	Birmingham N St	74	A	10.38am	11.20am	3	7B/	7B/	5A/11	5A/502
9.20am	Wigan NW	Crewe		B	10.49am	-	6				
10.5am	Manchester L Rd	Euston	218	A	*pass 10.51am*		Up Through	9A/14	1B/174	9A/14	1B/174
10.10am	Liverpool Lime St	Euston	54	A	10.59am	11.5am	4	8A/—	1B/151	8A/—	1B/151
10.15am	Manchester L Rd	Euston	220	A	11.3am	11.13am	5	5B/1033	1A/79	5B/1033	1A/79
11.30am	Crewe	Oxley Sidings		H	-	11.30am	Gresty Lane	-	-		
10.40am	Liverpool Lime St	Plymouth	208	A	11.40am	12.20pm	3	84G/5	5A/588	84G/5	5A/721
10.50am	Manchester L Rd	Cardiff	38	A	11.46am	12.10pm	4	84G/4	9A/322	84G/4	5A/721
11.50am	Crewe	Oxley Sidings		H	-	11.50am	Gresty Lane	-	-		
11.45am	Chester	Crewe		B	12.24pm	-	4	1B/17	5A/653	-	-
12.35pm	Crewe	Shrewsbury		B	-	12.35pm	4 Bay	-	-		
12.50pm	Crewe	Euston	84	A	-	12.50pm	3	-	-	5A/22	5A/317
7.5am	Carlisle	Crewe		TF	1.44pm	-	Gresty Lane	5B/1040	5B/1244	-	-
10.30am	Heysham	Euston	40	C	1.50pm	3.20pm	5	11A/1	5A/202	9A/—	5A/500
12.5pm	Llandudno	Euston	164	A	2pm	2.10pm	4	1B/31	7A/210	1B/31	5A/326
1.30pm	Middlewich	Crewe		K	2.4pm	-	BHSS Middle	5B/1110	5B/1112	-	-
12.10pm	Blackpool North	Euston	386	A	2.22pm	2.30pm	5	28A/62	1B/125	28A/62	1B/125
2.30pm	Crewe	Derby		B	-	2.30pm	5 Bay	-	-	17A/23	17A/256
8.20am	Workington	Euston	86	A	2.38pm	2.47pm	4				
1.52pm	Manchester L Rd	Euston	8	A	*pass 2.40pm*		Up Through	1B/11	1B/189	1B/11	1B/189
2.5pm	Manchester L Rd	Euston	94	A	2.58pm	3.5pm	5				
2.10pm	Liverpool L St	Euston	92	A	2.59pm	3.12pm	4				
2.30pm	Manchester L Rd	Birmingham N St	90	A	3.17pm	3.30pm	5	5A/22	5A/618	5A/22	3D/168
9.30am	Glasgow C	Birmingham N St	98	A	3.34pm	3.53pm	4	5A/4	5A/173	3D/	3D/173
10am	Glasgow C	Euston	96	A	*pass 3.46pm*		Up Through	66A/1	12A/61	66A/1	12A/61
2pm	Llandudno	Birmingham N St	166	A	3.56pm	4.5pm	5	3D/7	5A/698	3D/7	5A/507
3.15pm	Manchester L Rd	Bristol	240	A	4.2pm	4.15pm	3				
10.15am	Glasgow C	Euston	136	A	4.17pm	4.28pm	4	5A/3	12A/64	5A/22	12A/64
2.50pm	Blackpool Central	Euston	392	A	4.40pm	4.47pm	4	3C/4	10A/203	3C/4	5A/511
1.30pm	Mirfield	Crewe		H Q	4.45pm	-	BHSS Middle			-	-
4.5pm	Manchester L Rd	Crewe	118	A	4.51pm	-	5	9A/8	9A/324	-	-
4.10pm	Liverpool Lime St	Euston	114	A	4.55pm	5.5pm	4				
1.20pm	Holyhead	Euston	50	A	5pm	5.12pm	3				
1.35pm	Barrow	Euston	254	A Q	5.3pm	5.20pm	5				
2.45pm	Blackpool C	Euston	360	A	5.14pm	5.28pm	4	1A/1	28A/70	1A/1	28A/70
5.5pm	Calveley	Crewe	132	C	5.22pm	-		5A/33	5A/716	-	-
4.23pm	Edge Hill	Sudbury Jnt		D	*pass 5.33pm*		Up Through				
5.35pm	Crewe	Derby		B	-	5.35pm	5 Bay	-	-	84G/5	5A/630
5.45pm	Crewe	Willesden		E	-	5.45pm	BHSS Middle	-	-	5B/1054	5B/1168
4.5pm	Llandudno	Birmingham N St	102	A	6.14pm	6.42pm	3	5A/10	5A/694	5A/10	5A/503
5.30pm	Manchester L Rd	Euston	130	A	6.14pm	6.22pm	5	9A/3	9A.222	9A/3	9A/222
5.25pm	Liverpool Lime St	Euston	122	A	6.22pm	6.32pm	4				
6.45pm	Crewe	Shrewsbury		B	-	6.45pm	6	-	-	5A/33	5A/716
2.50pm	Carlisle	Euston	284	C	6.50pm	8.35pm	Up Through	5A/27	5A/165	9A/—	5A/350
6.20pm	Manchester L Rd	Crewe		B	7.38pm	-	6	9A/22	9A/325	-	-
3.50pm	Carlisle	Broad Street		C Q	7.39pm	7.55pm	Up Through				
7.5pm	Manchester L Rd	Birmingham N St	248	A	7.54pm	8.5pm	5	3D/5	5A/619	3D/5	3D/170
5.35pm	Llandudno	Crewe		A	7.56pm	-	3			-	-
7.5pm	Liverpool Lime St	Birmingham N St	250	A	8.10pm	8.25pm	4	8A/	8A/	8A/	3D/167
8.20pm	Crewe	Rugby		H	-	8.20pm	BHSS Middle	-	-	2A/	2A/678
8.35pm	Crewe	Wellington		B	-	8.35pm	2 Bay	-	-	Wellington	Crew/5
5.30pm	Holyhead	Crewe	316	C	8.46pm	-		7C/11	5A/667	-	-
8.50pm	Crewe	Derby		B	-	8.50pm	5 Bay	-	-		
7.50pm	Manchester L Rd	Crewe		C	8.53pm	-	Up Sidings	9A/7	9A/327	-	-
9.15pm	Crewe	Shrewsbury		B	-	9.15pm	4 Bay	-	-		
9.30pm	Chester	Crewe	100	A	10.3pm	-	4	5A/41	5A/664	-	-
6.5pm	Carlisle	Crewe		D	10.46pm	-	Gresty Lane	5B/1056	5B/1301	-	-

Time Dep	From	Destination	Rep No	Train Class	Crewe Arr	Crewe Dep	Platform or Yard	To Crewe from North Loco Diag	To Crewe from North Men Diag	From Crewe to South Loco Diag	From Crewe to South Men Diag
11.15pm	Crewe	Birmingham N St	324	C	-	11.15pm	Up Sidings	-	-	3D/1	3D/168
11.15pm	Crewe	Bushbury		F	-	11.15pm	BHSS Middle	-	-	8A/33	5B/1219
10.10pm	Liverpool Lime St	Crewe	142	A	11.25pm	-	5	5A/44	5A/589	-	-
10.25pm	Manchester L Rd	Crewe	144	A	11.29pm	-	6			-	-
7.55pm	Holyhead	Birmingham N St	170	A	11.30pm		3	6A/41	7A/157		
9.40pm	Blackpool Central	Birmingham N St	328	A	11.46pm	11.56pm	4	5B/1036	28A/184	5B/1036	28A/184
9.55pm	Blackpool Central	Euston	326	A	11.57pm	12.25am	5	1B/12	1B/131	1B/12	1B/131

Below:
Carlisle, November 1959
No 46256 *Sir William A. Stanier FRS* was shedded briefly at Crewe North, from 7 to 21 November 1959 and then from 24 September 1960 until it was withdrawn in the week commencing 3 October 1964. By the time this photograph was taken the loco had lost its steam generator and reverted to oil lamps for headcode display, although there are three larger brackets mounted on the buffer beam. What a waste that this superb engine was scrapped to satisfy the accountants who decreed that steam was inefficient. *Author's collection*

Front cover, main image:
Crewe North End
'Royal Scot' class 4-6-0 No 46125 *3rd Carabinier* of North Shed (5A) awaits the green whilst standing at Platform 1N, northward bound on the Down Slow West Coast main line, signified by the illuminated 'S' alongside the multi-aspect signal. This might be the 6.40am Euston to Windermere working, one of only a few trains that worked into and out of Platform 1 during the morning. The pressure gauge and lifting safety valves show that there is no shortage of steam, whilst the coal in the tender is somewhat depleted. *Martin Welch*

Front cover, upper inset:
Crewe Station Platform 2 1957
'Duchess' class Pacific No 46224 *Princess Alexandra* stands at Platform 2 with the northbound 'Caledonian' working. *Ron White collection*

Front cover, lower inset:
Longsight, June 1957
'Patriot' class 4-6-0 No 45519 *Lady Godiva* roars through Longsight with an Up express passing under a superb LNWR gantry. *W. Oliver - Colour Rail (BRM 1002)*

Back cover, upper:
Crewe North End
A glorious array of motive power stands at the north end of the station. In the foreground standing at Platform 1 is 'Jubilee' class 4-6-0 No 45670 *Howard of Effingham* sporting Class 1 lamps. In No 8 Bay is BR Standard Class 4 No 75054, whilst alongside in No 7 Bay is Class 5 4-6-0 No 44761. Stanier 'Princess Royal' class Pacific No 46211 *Queen Maud* stands off No 2 Platform, exhaust injector blowing back whilst driver and fireman survey the scene, oblivious to the wastage. Behind the screen is a DMU, without warning panels. This view was taken from the footbridge that spanned all the tracks and was a popular haunt of loco spotters. *Martin Welch*

Back cover, lower:
Crewe North Junction, 23 June 1951
Class 2P 4-4-0 No 40528 pulls out of the sidings at the North Junction with Class C train which was probably the 2.37pm Parcels to Pontypool Road, reporting number W190. This was a Nuneaton 2B engine, and why an engine from this class was working this duty is unclear. A study of the Working Time Tables and programme of special trains for the period does not throw any light on what might be an unusual engine working. *Tom Lewis — Manchester Locomotive Society*

CREWE
W239